East Sails West

East Sails West

The Voyage of the *Keying*, 1846–1855

Stephen Davies

香港大學出版社
HONG KONG UNIVERSITY PRESS

Hong Kong University Press
The University of Hong Kong
Pokfulam Road
Hong Kong
www.hkupress.org

ISBN 978-988-8208-20-3 (*Hardback*)

British Library Cataloguing-in-Publication Data
A catalogue record for this book is available from the British Library.

10 9 8 7 6 5 4 3 2

Printed and bound by Liang Yu Printing Factory Ltd. in Hong Kong, China

A ship is worse than a jail. There is, in a jail, better air, better company, better conveniency of every kind; and a ship has the additional disadvantage of being in danger. When men come to like a sea-life, they are not fit to live on land.

—James Boswell, *Life of Johnson*

On the land a worm; on the sea a dragon.

—traditional saying of the sea people (水上人, *shuǐshàng rén*)

In memoriam
Geoffrey Bonsall

For
Elaine—best mate
and
Catalina—co-skipper of a happy, cross-cultural ship

Contents

List of Illustrations

Diagrams

Maps

Tables

Plates

Preface

Between 1846 and 1848, one of the most extraordinary voyages ever undertaken created a record that has never been broken. The Chinese junk *Keying* became the first—and only—Chinese junk to sail on its own bottom from China via the Cape of Good Hope into the North Atlantic. In the process, it also became the first ever Chinese-built vessel to visit both Britain and the east coast of the United States.

That is not widely known. This book explains why that might be so.

The project was put together by a group of Hong Kong investors, some of whom became founders of major Hong Kong institutions. It was carried out by a mixed crew comprising a minority of British officers and sailors, and a majority of Cantonese sailors under their Cantonese sailing master. And along for the ride went a few passengers, including some of the investors, a possible mandarin of the fifth rank,[1] a painter and perhaps even a tailor, a props manager and a troupe of celebrated jugglers.[2] Thanks to problems both with the weather and the junk's performance, the voyage had to divert to the east coast of the United States, where it stopped in both New York and Boston before, following a serial break-up in the ship's crew, it finally reached London.

This is the only verified voyage of a junk into the Atlantic Ocean and on to America and Europe. Its object was not science or exploration—those twin poles of non-commercial and non-belligerent nineteenth-century seafaring—but was typical Hong Kong: a business proposition aiming to make money by entertaining visitors with exhibits of the crew members in live tableaux on deck and displaying a rather eccentric collection of Chinese objects in the accommodation below. A theme park before its day.

The voyage was a success, in that the junk completed it. But very slow progress, the detour to America and crewing problems, which resulted in a court case in New York, took their toll. A voyage expected to take four to six months took fifteen. Once in London, what today we'd probably call an over-extended business plan saw the project go steadily downhill. So the story is also about the aftermath of the voyage, from 1848 to 1855. At the end of a long drawn out dénouement, the few remaining crew dispersed to disappear from the historical record, while the junk, more or less ignored, came to an ignominious end on the mudflats of the River Mersey at Birkenhead, opposite Liverpool.

The *Keying*'s story thus has two major foci, both blurred almost beyond recognition by the passage of time, thanks to ways of being and seeing in the long nineteenth century, both in the Western world and in China, that have condemned the episode to near oblivion.

First, we have a unique and unprecedented voyage by a Chinese junk, conducted as an unintended experiment in cross-cultural co-operation—in the way of Sino-Western relations of the period, the result was as ships passing in the night. As a result, it left little other than an almost accidental record.

Second, we have the junk in which the voyage was undertaken: the only full-sized, working representative of traditional Chinese naval architecture, as far as we know unaffected by any Western influence, to have arrived in Europe as the building wave of Victorian scientific interest in everything was cresting. Yet it was, from a scientific and ethnological perspective, utterly ignored.

Trying to understand why we have very little of the detail of the first, save what can be quarried from newspapers, magazines, a report of court proceedings, some letters and a couple of publicity pamphlets, and why we know almost nothing clear or certain about the second, save what can be inferred from a dubious pictorial record and some casual and not very well-informed descriptions, is what the two parts of this book are about.

In Part I, we attempt to reconstruct what happened on this remarkable and obviously historically and nautically important voyage, as eloquent with regard to its missed cultural connections and voyaging problems as in its actual achievements.

In Part II, we attempt to understand better the ship in which the voyage was undertaken and the missed opportunities it represented for a fuller and better understanding in the West of the unique qualities of Chinese naval architecture.

In both parts, we attempt to understand why the event made so little lasting 'splash'—as far as we can tell, not even an evanescent ripple in China—and why, in the century and a half that has followed, there has been little significant scholarly or popular interest—in the East as in the West—in either the voyage or the ship.

As an exercise in comparative maritime social history and comparative naval architecture, the object in the pages that follow is to dredge some clogged channels and buoy a fairway through a neglected passage that links two of the most important traditions of going down to the sea in ships and doing business in great waters—traditions normally treated as two separate worlds each to be viewed in its own exclusive terms. It is in its status as such a bridge—albeit unintended as such and something of a failure—that the *Keying*'s historical importance lies.

Today, people in the Atlantic-Mediterranean world and its offshoots in Australasia are often and rightly much excited by re-enactment voyages, either in replica or equivalent vessels that trace again courses that their forefathers—or someone's forefathers—travelled as they pushed out the sea boundaries of the world.[3] These initiatives have started to spread beyond the world of Western maritime historians and archaeologists, as the recent voyages of the *Princess Cocachin* (2008–09), the *Taiping Gongzhu* (2008–09), the *Ngandahig* (2009) and the *Jewel of Muscat* (2010–11) attest, but as yet the main foci seem to be mainly Western, or Western-inspired.

These replicas, restorations and re-enactments elicit major sponsorship from corporations and governments. They attract TV companies. They spawn best-selling books. And because the stories are important and inspiring, exciting, even gripping, and always instructive, they appeal to a wide audience.

But even in the West, this widespread enthusiasm is a recent development. It gained a full head of steam only in the 1970s. That was a time of affluence, of the peaking of Western expansionism and economic dominance, and above all of the popularization, thanks to today's mass media, of a particular way of seeing the maritime world. That way of seeing was and is characterized by an attendant interest in the growth and flourishing of maritime history that is arguably and certainly in origin unique to Western cultures.[4]

Before the Western world's late twentieth-century enthusiasm for an increasingly more generously conceived, though still very Western-orientated world of maritime exploration, discovery and diasporas, the approach was very different. There was the Western maritime world, which could be and largely was understood as *the* maritime world. And there were the also-rans that had been left behind by progress, largely, as the story went, through their own civilizational ineptitude.

That is a crude and necessarily incomplete adumbration, but for most Western people in the nineteenth century, even for the more thoughtful observers, only Westerners explored and discovered. Only they had invented the ships, the technologies, the instruments and the systems that made discovery and exploration possible. Everyone else was stuck up a backwater going nowhere, unable and unwilling to find their way out of the maritime (and often more general) cultural impasse down which they had benightedly sailed long before.

And of nowhere had that come to be seen as more true than of China.

Because of such attitudes, the 1846–48 voyage of the junk *Keying* has been almost entirely neglected since the ship and its crew left the new port of the City of Victoria, Hong Kong, on 6 December 1846. No story has been written. No replica has been researched and built. No corporation has seen in the saga a vector for publicity, for the gaining of social responsibility brownie points and for the chance of some earnings through spin-offs. No TV or film company has been provoked to a froth of excitement by the prospect of a gripping docu-drama series and lucrative tie-ins. No government has seen an opportunity for burnishing national maritime credentials and wagging the national flag in distant places.

Yet the potential for all these ingredients are there in the story that follows. Another aim of the story is thus to bring closer to the light why, in the last century and a half, the eyes that could have seen this potential richness have neither seen nor wanted to see. The half-world of Western imperialism's many awkward, often not entirely successful (because usually mutually racist), working compromises—the world most Western and Chinese workaday people inhabited most of the time during that awkward epoch—is one most people would rather bury than learn from.[5] We're better than that today . . . or we like to flatter ourselves we are.

Today, we may live in more enlightened times, so here's hoping that this story of the Chinese junk *Keying*, of captains Charles Kellett and So Yin Sang Hsi, of mates Mr. G. Burton and Mr. Edward Revett, of *toumou* and *hoke* Hia Siang, Sim Agu, Ung Ti, Ling Chensi, Kho Sing Thiam, Lia Lai, Lei Na Kung, Khor Per Le, Lip Hap, Chin Ten Yeng, Tam Sam Seng, Ung Tian Yong, Chein A Tai, Yer A Chin, Lim A Lee, Go Bun Hap, Che Va A Sa, Chi Va A Chan, Lim Tai Chong, Tan A Lak, Chia A Soey, Ong A Hiong, Chien A Te, Kho Te Sun, Ung A Cong and Sio A Chiok, of 'mandarin' He Sing and ship's artist Sam Shing and perhaps two dozen other nameless European and Chinese sailors, will at last begin to attract the attention it has long deserved.

A few early readers of the manuscript commented that it was rather 'nautical' and that perhaps I should either change the specialist terms to something more familiar to a landlubber or provide a glossary. My own thought, following the lead of that titan of the maritime world—whom we shall meet again in these pages—Richard Henry Dana, is that technical terms are not usually that much of an obstacle to understanding. As Dana put it:[6]

> There may be in some parts a good deal that is unintelligible to the general reader; but I have found from my own experience, and from what I have heard from others, that plain matters of fact in relation to customs and habits of life new to us, and descriptions of life under new aspects, act upon the inexperienced through the imagination, so that we are hardly aware of our want of technical knowledge. Thousands read the escape of the American frigate through the British channel, and the chase and wreck of the Bristol trader in the *Red Rover*, and follow the minute nautical manoeuvres with breathless interest, who do not know the name of a rope in the ship; and perhaps with none the less admiration and enthusiasm for their want of acquaintance with the professional detail.

Stephen Davies
Hong Kong, 2013

Acknowledgements

This book started life as a result of three quite unrelated stimuli. All three resulted from the creation by the nascent Hong Kong Maritime Museum's curatorial team, under the supervision of Mr. K. L. Tam and with the advice of the late Geoffrey Bonsall, my acquaintance and colleague of many years, of the *Keying* model in the museum's displays.

The first stimulus came when Mr. Y. K. Chan, a member of the museum's board of directors, drew my attention to a fairly critical Wikipedia entry on the museum's model. Reading its strictures, which came down to saying that the model did not look sufficiently like the floating banana in the best known images, forced me to think about why it did not, why it should not, and in general about what the *Keying* must really have been like. In effect, the book started as Part II.

A few months later, in a quite unrelated way, I got an enquiry from New Zealand asking what the Hong Kong Maritime Museum (HKMM) knew about the *Keying* and its voyage. The answer was 'Not a lot'. But the enquirer turned out to be Susan Simmons, the great-great-granddaughter of Charles Kellett, the *Keying*'s Western captain, who had amassed an amazing archive of press clippings and genealogical material which, in an act of amazing generosity, she made copies of and sent to the HKMM. In them, I realized I had the detail that would enable me to get a far clearer picture of the voyage, not only as a navigational accomplishment but also as an exercise in the vexed business of nineteenth-century cross-cultural co-operation—or its absence. To Susan, I owe the most profound thanks. Without her work over the years—supported by a family of equally interested Charles Kellett descendants—this book would have been nigh impossible.

In responding to these first two stimuli, I began reading and came across the third stimulus, John Rogers Haddad's fascinating and illuminating *The Romance of China*, which had some very hard things indeed to say about Charles Kellett, when it described the *Keying*'s stay in New York and the court case that took place. Hard things that I already knew, from Susan Simmons, had been very difficult for Charles Kellett's descendants to read and to accept.

I am a sailor and grew up in a sailor's world. It seemed to me then, and seems to me now, seven years and many thousand words later, that Charles Kellett's story needed better contextualization; needed to be seen from the sea, as I have put it, in the context of what would have been perfectly ordinary nineteenth-century sea-going, however that may outrage our more enlightened, early twenty-first-century sensibilities habitually blind, as they too often are, to anachronism.

To be sure, the *Keying*'s Chinese crew were probably not treated as today we would expect any crew to be treated anywhere. To be sure, it is to the credit of Samuel Wells Williams, Lin King-chew, W. Daniel Lord and Samuel Betts, the New York magistrate, that they helped twenty-six people from far away, who were in need of help. But we need also to understand the other side of the story; how ships were run in the mid-nineteenth century, and not expect Charles Kellett, his mate and his co-captain to conduct themselves in a manner that could not be required of mid-nineteenth-century mariners, either British or Chinese. We needed to see the twenty-six disaffected Cantonese crewmen rather more in the round, as denizens of a nineteenth-century, post-Opium War, Chinese waterfront. As canny enough men, who were alive to the rough-and-tumble of a contact zone and not raw bumpkins, gulls to any unscrupulous Western or Chinese chancer.

To achieve this, it would be necessary to share that troubled and troubling voyage from Hong Kong. To understand in its appropriate context what this young and obviously capable skipper had achieved. To understand the inescapable tensions and flat misunderstandings that inevitably resulted from trying to run a Chinese ship with a majority Chinese crew in 'shipshape and Bristol fashion'. And thereby to enable myself and my readers to get a handle on why everything fell apart in the way that it did, without going down the ever-tempting route of easy, moralistic outrage.

So Part II led into Chapter 6 . . . And to try to stitch the two together in a way that was not too glaringly inchoate, the rest of the book followed.

I am deeply grateful to two incisive anonymous readers for Hong Kong University Press, who astutely identified weaknesses, especially the poor structure that resulted from putting the ship before the people; Part II before Part I. I am equally grateful to the press's commissioning editor, Christopher Munn, for his comments and for his belief in the book's value. I also owe a debt of real thanks to the press's editors, especially Jessica Wang, whose care and interest have made all the difference. Good editors always improve any text. Both Vicki Low and Jessica tightened, polished and eliminated a superfluity of waffle.

I owe an obvious debt of gratitude to the Hong Kong Maritime Museum, its board of directors and its staff, especially Catalina Chor, who have put up with me maundering on for hours about the story. To Anthony Hardy, the Chairman of the Board, always interested, always with a thoughtful idea and always a strong supporter of my research work, I owe more than I can say. To Cat, Moody Tang, Phoebe Tong and Jamie Mak I am grateful for their patient help with my fumbling efforts with the Chinese language.

I am obviously grateful to the many scholars of China, Hong Kong and the maritime world on whose work I have depended. I am especially grateful to Paul van Dyke, who from his deserved eminence has always encouraged my more tarry-handed approach to maritime history and told me about the *Account*, which would otherwise probably have escaped the net. I owe much thanks as well to my friend and maritime-replica-doyen Nicholas Burningham, from whose wide-ranging knowledge and seamanship I have learned greatly. I hope I have managed to acknowledge all the main sources I have used and from whom I have learned vastly. Evidently, however, the reading of fifty years in the field of maritime history and the maritime world in general means that many who have formed my understanding, almost without my knowing it, do not appear in the bibliography. This is a blanket thanks to a world that several lifetimes of reading would never allow one honestly to say one had mastered.

I must thank Paola Calanca and Pierre-Yves Manguin of the *École française de l'Extrême Orient* for getting me to write an article about this exercise in joint crewing for the proceedings of a conference they co-organized in Beijing in 2009, which has informed much of Chapters 2 and 6. And I must thank the director and staff at the China Maritime Museum, Shanghai, who asked me to present a paper at their first ever International Academic Symposium in July 2010, held at the same time as the opening of this impressive new contribution to Shanghai's— and China's—maritime culture, which contributed greatly to Chapters 11 and 12. They were also kind enough to invite me back to give a talk in May 2013, which led to the appendix as a way of supplementing elements of the discussion in Part II and in the conclusion. On both occasions I owed a special debt to Ms. Zhao Li, without whose help my contributions would have been much diminished. The same debt is owed to Catalina and Phoebe at HKMM, who turned frenetically full English PowerPoints into polished Chinese. Acute questions from Zhao Li, Cat and Phoebe always helped me greatly to clarify my ideas.

I am grateful to Emma Lefley and Julie Cochrane, the Picture Librarians of the Greenwich National Maritime Museum and to Cynthia CM Woo, Assistant Curator (Registration) at the Hong Kong Museum of Art, for their help with images. Thanks too to Patrick Conner of the Martyn Gregory Gallery in London, who showed the way to the second Chinese image of the *Keying* by the Chinese artist.

After she had read the manuscript and helped improve its flow and intelligibility, Suzan Walker gamely volunteered to produce the index. Friends don't come better.

I owe the biggest debt to my mate—in all three senses of that term—Elaine Morgan. With her over fifteen years I put in the fifty thousand miles of seagoing in a small sailing yacht in many of the waters where the *Keying* sailed that helped me recreate the 'view from the sea' so essential to understanding the *Keying*'s voyage. Elaine has lived with the manuscript as long as I have. She has put up with my rabbiting on and on about the *Keying*. And she has not minded too much as days of our 2012 holiday at our other home in France disappeared with me tapping away, *la taupe dans sa taupinière*, revising the manuscript, too often leaving her and my sister-in-law, Elaine's equally forbearing sister Jill Sellars, to enjoy the beauties of the Roussillon without me.

All books are joint efforts. This is no exception. But as usual, whatever the contributions of others, and they have been many and most gratefully received, the errors are all mine.

Stephen Davies

Introduction: Views from Different Seas

Because of its record-making and very singular voyage, the sailing junk[1] *Keying* is an interesting and apposite synecdoche for early—and enduring—British colonial Hong Kong. To understand the successes and failures of the *Keying*, to understand its missed opportunities and achievements born of lucky breaks, to understand its radically separate microcosms that had to pull together or drown together, to grasp the *Keying*'s erratic course towards an overambitious destination, with its drawn-out and sorry dénouement, to see that the knowledge and work of the largely anonymous many were the indispensable foundation for the small achievements of the marginally recorded but more fortunate few is to begin to have a sense of Hong Kong's peculiar identity and the main tropes of its story.

Why is a relatively unknown, mid-nineteenth-century, late Qing dynasty (1644–1912) Chinese vessel, which made a voyage that was a nine-day wonder in contemporary eyes, of true historical importance? What makes it more than a mere footnote for the enthusiastic maritime antiquarian of the Chinese and colonial maritime past? Above all, what makes it more than an interesting *aperçu* on a small place that thought it beat, and even continues to think it beats, a big drum in the rhythm of the histories of China, Britain and the larger world?

Looking at the Hong Kong Waterfront

To get a grip on the answers to these questions, it is necessary to elaborate a little on context. There is nowhere better to start than with a mental image of Hong Kong harbour in the last quarter of 1846, with our eyes focused on the roadstead immediately off the shores of the still new City of Victoria, seeing things through the eyes of the Western inhabitants of this rough diamond of a China-coast débutante. What we are looking at are ships. And what we are seeing is a dramatic contrast.

This is before the days of photography, so our reconstruction must rely on the work of Murdoch Bruce, Overseer of Roads and Superintendent of Convict Labour, whose images of Hong Kong in 1846 are well known.[2] We can supplement the images with what documentary evidence there is about the harbour traffic that fell within the purview of the Harbour Master, Lieutenant William Pedder, late of the Royal Navy.[3]

Happily, one of Bruce's images was made looking westwards from Murray's Battery; another westwards from the Chief Justice's house, which we know was atop the more westerly of two low ridges pushing out from where Kennedy Road now meets Queen's Road East; a third filling the gap in between by viewing the waterfront of the Spring Gardens, today a busy street in Wanchai; and a fourth looking northwest from Causeway Bay towards Jardine Matheson's East Point complex.[4] So the whole harbour is quite well covered. With our eyes wholly biased by our Western maritime tradition, what do we see?

Traditional Chinese Sail

Concentrated towards the western end of the new settlement, already sprawling the three miles along the shoreline from present-day Sheung Wan to Causeway Bay, is a busy, jumbled congeries of traditional Chinese vessels, both small and large. There are many rowing sampans and small, single-masted sailing sampans. These are scattered along the western shore, become less frequent as we pass the embryo naval dockyard, and thicken up again along the Wanchai waterfront to Causeway Bay. Further out from the shore of Sheung Wan, already the focus of the new city's growing Chinese population, are a score or so two- and three-masted junks. None of the latter is very large because the terms of the Supplementary Treaty of the Bogue,[5] signed at Humen just three years previously by Sir Henry Pottinger, then Governor of Hong Kong, and the Imperial Commissioner, Qiying, meant that Hong Kong was effectively excluded from the flourishing Chinese coastal and *nanyang* trades.[6] So, of the large 35- to 55-metre-long A- and B-class junks of China's sea trade, there are few, if any.

All the Chinese vessels we can see are very workaday. Their joinery is rough, often with the external planking of unfaired timber, as if someone had just split a few trees and nailed things together. The masts, with their 'bat-wing', single sails made of woven bamboo or tattered, tanbark canvas, are not straight. They are made from single tree trunks that, like most, have a twist here and a turn there. Nor are the masts parallel with each other. The foremast seems to lean drunkenly forward, the mainmast varies between a slight forward lean and upright. And the mizzen, where it exists, is peculiarly set off to one side and is very small. The look of the hull is weird—at the front there is no wave-cleaving, raked bow but instead a flat plate sometimes tapering trapezoidally towards the waterline with, in the larger junks, two soaring 'wings' on each side of the top joined by a horizontal windlass, from which two ropes disappear down below the hull. The stern is unaccountably higher than the bow, so the whole vessel looks as if it is trimmed bow down.

The rigging—what there is of it—is not all a-tanto with the standing rigging Stockholm-tarred and with the falls of halyards and sheets neatly coiled down and hung on ordered ranks of belaying pins on neat pinrails round the mast partners. There are no trimly white-painted topmasts. There is no obvious coppering, but instead a coating of ashy-grey *chunam*. The running rigging and the anchor cables—and those curious lines disappearing over the bow and into the water below the hull—come to pretty rough-looking horizontal windlasses working in simple plain bearings. The hulls lack gingerbread and fine joinery on the Chinese equivalents of the trailboards, cap rails and taffrail. The paintwork, where there is any, is brightly coloured, and the transoms are decorated with an amazing swirl of curlicues and flourishes with, here and there on the larger examples, some enormous bird.[7] It all looks simultaneously exotic, crude and archaic.[8]

When junks up hook to sail away, there is a cacophonous outburst. Gongs thrum. Drums beat. Firecrackers explode in a rattle of smoke, flashes and sounds. There is a tumult of voices and a rush and flurry of movement every which way. Everything seems almost random and as if there is no system; no one in charge of each evolution to ensure it is carried out in regimented sequence at an appropriate word of command or shrill of a bosun's call.

And then there is the contrast.

The Ships from the West

Dominating the harbour are the ships of the Royal Navy. In August 1846, the strength of the China Squadron of the East Indies Station was much reduced from the immediate aftermath of the First Opium War. Its main task had become suppressing piracy.[9] But even so, at any one time there would have been a representative sample of the ships that had gained Britain not only dominance of the world's seas, but dominance of the coast of China. The largest ship would have been HMS *Agincourt*, the flagship of Rear-Admiral Thomas John Cochrane, Commander-in-Chief of the squadron. She was a third-rate ship of the line launched in 1817, armed with 74 guns and crewed by 442 officers and men, 53 boys and 125 marines. Her skipper was Captain Henry William Bruce, who, in the manner of the mid-nineteenth-century Royal Navy, was Admiral Cochrane's brother-in-law. Although only a third-rate, she packed a massive punch.[10] For those in Hong Kong who could recall the naval fights of the recent war, the *Agincourt* alone seems to have been able to fire, in a single broadside, a far heavier weight of metal than the entire fleet of junks that constituted the naval defences of Canton (Guangzhou) in 1840.[11]

Her construction was a masterpiece of wooden shipbuilding at the apex of its development in the West. It was massive. It was hugely strong, to take the smashing recoil of her armament or the crashing impact of an enemy ship's response. It was, above all, breath-takingly complex, involving tens of thousands of specialized fastenings and thousands of uniquely shaped pieces of timber, many selected from 'natural crooks', or curves and shapes that had grown with a particular radius or shape.[12] Her rigging was a maze of complexity, each of the three made masts[13] with their topmasts and topgallant masts held up by some eighteen backstays, four forestays and ten shrouds; each of the eleven squaresails managed by up to nineteen different control lines; and each of the four or five fore-and-aft sails by four.

Different Ships, Different Long Splices

Supporting the flagship were frigates, like the 46-gun HMS *Daedelus*, and sloops like the 26-gun HMS *Iris* and the 18-gun HMS *Columbine*. Each was a similarly complex structure; even these smaller vessels were heavily armed by comparison to even the best-armed equivalent Chinese naval ship or pirate junk. All were operated with almost machine-like precision, by well-drilled crews ordered in strict hierarchy, whether making their way across the oceans or engaged in battle. Bosuns' calls shrilled. Hands leapt into the rigging. Gun crews five to seven strong clustered around their weapons, each man with a specific, regimented task in the orchestrated, eight-stage exercise of firing the gun, all done to the word of command of each gun captain as the cannons crashed every minute and a half or so.[14] Watches rotated to the stroke of the ship's bell. Each man of the new watch relieved his opposite number of the old. Ritual handover exchanges were passed between watch officers—'Course west by a quarter south running free, all plain sail set, wind North East blowing a fresh gale, no ships in sight. Your watch, Mr Jolyon.'

A precise chain of command ran from the lowest ship's boy to the commander-in-chief. Complex visual signalling using code flags and detailed code books ensured intentions were understood, instructions conveyed and intelligence passed. The ships could sustain themselves in full fighting trim on a three-month voyage from Europe to Asia, and in principle—and usually in practice—could engage in battle at the end of it as well as they could a day out from their port of departure. Indeed, with a settled, fully integrated crew, arguably better. They would have completed the voyage in fair wind or foul, the Royal Navy's routines having been honed by the years of blockading during the French Wars in which many of the senior officers of the 1840s had begun their service.[15] Routines that had since been maintained in providing the worldwide reach of the still growing British empire held together by the sea lanes the ships patrolled.

Of course all that was true, though in significantly different ways, for the Chinese maritime world too, though the ships were far less complex and required, to sail, much less by way of ordered orchestration and routine. There was a similar, though perhaps less codified and ramified, organizational hierarchy. Ships were similarly operated, though as much by effective customary practices as by tabulated, organized systems. There were, quite evidently, signalling systems by which commanders controlled the ships of their squadrons and fleets.[16] But all this was little understood by Westerners; had understanding been better, the difference in orders of magnitude on almost any chosen measure might perhaps have stood out even more plainly.

Steaming to the Future

But the Westerners' eyes on this still half-started, modern waterfront—as much matshed (rush mats covering a bamboo frame) and mudflat as buildings and sea-walls—would necessarily also have been drawn to novelty. To a pregnant, inno-vative and still bizarre military sign of the future: the Royal Navy and East India Company Indian Navy's steam-paddle ships. The *Nemesis*, which had dominated the naval fighting during the First Opium War, was still on station along with others, though there would seldom have been more than one or two in Hong Kong at once. The revolutionary *Nemesis* was iron-hulled. The rest, like the *Pluto*, *Vixen*, *Phlegethon* and *Spiteful*, were wooden. They only mounted six guns, but these included two pivoting thirty-two pounders, allowing firing over com-prehensive arcs, as well as four or so more conventional, broadside-mounted, smaller-calibre weapons. The paddle boxes and coal bunkers got in the way of the array of larger broadside-mounted guns characteristic of sailing warships of the day. But this still-radical solution was pointing forward to the turret-mounted guns of the future. Despite the paucity of guns, however, the ships' ability to manoeuvre independently of the wind made them deadly not only in themselves, but also because they could tow the larger, massively armed vessels like the *Agincourt* to where they could wreak their havoc, as Britain's navy had proved, in the ascent of the Yangzi to Nanjing that had ended the First Opium War. These odd, thrashing, smoking, puffing vessels were ships that were utterly changing the face of naval warfare, especially in Asia. They would soon change the face of merchant shipping, too.[17]

The Coming Apogee of Square Rig

Finally, it is highly probable that our observant Westerner, looking out at the harbour and having dismissed the specimens of China's long and fascinating naval architectural tradition as archaic relics of no account, would have known about ships and the sea. Few in Hong Kong in 1846 would not have had a pro-longed and intimate acquaintance with both, merely in order to have reached Hong Kong in the first place. Many would have been directly involved in the shipping world, especially in the nefarious bedrock of early Hong Kong's sea trade—opium. The language that Admiral Smyth's *The Sailor's Word-book* would begin to tabulate in 1858, over some 15,000 terms in its 744 pages, would have been familiar to them. So, having assessed the Royal Navy's protective 'wooden walls'—their eyes passing over the out-of-commission, mastless 'hulks' used as floating warehouses for opium waiting to be smuggled into China, or the hulked warship serving as a hospital ship, with its trim awnings covering the entirety of its deck,[18]—they would have focused on the ships used to do the smuggling: the opium clippers.

Despite their scabrous and blatantly illegal trade, these were revolutionary ships, representing the beginning of the last hurrah of Western sail. Small, heavily rigged for maximum power, sleek in shape, these vessels could outrun and out beat[19] almost anything on the water. Pioneered by the American Baltimore schooner *Dhaulle* of 1825 and the famous—or perhaps infamous—*Red Rover* of 1829, itself based on the lines of a French-designed, American-built privateer, the whole object of the vessels was to overcome the main limitation on seaborne trading since time immemorial: the monsoons.[20] For a millennium and more, Asia's sea traders had set out from China, with their cargoes of ceramics, ironware, tea, herbs and countless other goods, on the wings of the winter, northeast monsoon. Once at their destinations, they would trade their outward cargo and amass their backhaul cargo—tin, rice, spices, tropical woods, trepang and other foodstuffs—while waiting for the change of monsoon in the spring, and then set sail for home.

The opium clippers broke that mould. Of course, it had been broken long before when the occasional ship toughed it out. We know, for example, that a Dutch despatch ship made Java against the monsoon to summon help when Zheng Chenggong was besieging Fort Zeelandia in Tainan, Taiwan, in 1661.[21] But it was hard, unrelenting work, and wrought expensive havoc on the vessels that tried it. They got to their destination, if they did, with ripped sails, damaged rigging, broken spars and sprung masts and planks. Or they went the very long way round, south of the Equator and up east of the Philippines, almost doubling the length of their voyage.[22] Only dire necessity would induce anyone to try either. That is, until the fabulous profits of smuggled opium beckoned. Well-armed, heavily canvassed, run like warships by well-paid, hard-driving, crack skippers, with crews of seasoned and skilled seamen, the opium clippers were well suited to their wicked trade. No other vessels could begin to match them, unless there was no wind . . . and then those guns would come into play.

But, if you forget the malignity of the opium trade for a moment, as our typical Western observer on the 1846 Hong Kong waterfront very easily could, the clippers were beautiful. A clean sheer, running from a sharply raked bow and preceded by a long, stabbing finger of bowsprit and jib-boom. A low freeboard and a narrow beam for the vessel's length, suggesting fast, clean lines below the water, developed from ever-refined half-models with the help, increasingly, of drafted plans by better and better informed naval architects. Raked, sky-reaching masts interstitched with a thicket of finest-quality running and standing rigging, crossed by yards with sails neatly furled and stopped in gaskets along them. Here was the epitome of speed and grace under sail. The cynosure of anyone with an eye to see what a masterpiece of naval architecture should look like.

Why the *Keying* Looked So Different: Naval Architectures Poles Apart . . .

Our observer, as a nautical insider, will also have been aware that this was an age of increasingly scientific naval architecture. In just a few years, the first systematic treatise in English would be published[23]—in London, of course—confirming that what could be seen in the new Port of Victoria in the harbour of Hong Kong was the product, not of some vernacular shipwright reproducing the patterns—and the errors—of aeons, but of the subtle theories of science. Fincham's history was itself a development of a textbook he had written a generation earlier, for the use of the young naval officers at the Royal Navy's new naval academy in Portsmouth, for whom an understanding of the technicalities of the ships they would work and later command was increasingly being considered essential.[24] That too would have been an apparent contrast of which our observer would have been aware.

And then again, there were those junks and sampans. To our Westerner's eyes, there was no competition. These were mere relics of the past; at best curiosities for the antiquarian, at worst complete irrelevancies. And yet, had he looked more closely—and with that relative novelty, a keen and thoughtful naval architect's eye, especially the eye of a Western naval architect at the cutting edge, like I. K.

Brunel, who was among the first to bring engineering principles to the construction of the newfangled iron hulls—he might have been surprised. For there was much in the structure of a typical junk that solved the basic problems of how to design a strong, seaworthy ship that was economical to build and economical to operate, in ways that might be seen to 'anticipate' what Western naval architects would develop, as the nineteenth century gave way to the twentieth.

If you are familiar with the broad development of comparative Chinese and Western naval architectures and of their more broadly defined maritime social histories—specifically in relation to the social role of the sea, to the history of navigation and to the evolution of ship organization—you can ignore the next few pages. But if these are for you, as for most, esoteric subjects, then what follows is important. For what these deeper and wider issues betoken is the importance of the *Keying* and its voyage, not just as a cypher for the microcosm of colonial Hong Kong, but as a cypher for the vast seascape of the vexed relationship between China and the Western world, the heavy swell from which is still being felt today.

The fascinating feature of Chinese naval architecture—what sets it so distinctly apart and, as instantiated in the *Keying*, should have been of enormous interest to the naval architects and budding marine ethnologists of late 1840s and early 1850s New York, Boston, London and Liverpool—is that Chinese ship construction seems to have used a unique blend of both Western approaches to building ships: the 'skin-first' and 'frame-first' techniques.[25] That no such thought crossed the minds of those directly or peripherally involved in the *Keying* story, despite the intellectual context of mid-nineteenth-century Europe being such as to lead one to expect exactly the contrary, is what this book sets out to understand.

At the level of high theory, of course, family resemblances can always be found between Chinese watercraft and their Western cognates. The laws of physics inevitably constrain the solutions to how we move about on the water to a fundamentally similar set. But as is manifestly evident from the reports of early European witnesses, what had emerged over the course of the first few thousand years of maritime development in China had its roots so 'buried' that what Western sailors saw did not easily 'map onto' the shapes, structures and rigs familiar to them. And that puzzlement evidently endured into the nineteenth century, as the observation from the best known version of the *Keying*'s visitor's guide, of which there are two or three,[26] plainly states:

> It is a most singular circumstance, and which requires actual inspection to convince of the reality of it, that there is neither in the building nor in the rigging and fitting up of a Chinese junk, one single thing which is similar to what we see on board a European vessel.
>
> Every thing is different; the mode of construction, the absence of keel, bowsprit and shrouds; the materials employed, the mast, the sail, the yard, the rudder, the compass, the anchor, all are dissimilar. The native crew are not more unlike the sailors of Europe, than the vessel in which they sail is unlike the ships of other countries. Both the one and the other are men, and the respective vessels are meant to pass over the sea; this is all they have in common, here all similitude begins and ends.[27]

It is this 'cross-mappable only at the level of high theory' aspect that explains much about our ignorance of the structural detail of the Chinese ship *Keying*. Had contemporaries in New York, Boston, London or Liverpool been more curious about why the *Keying* looked so different, why there is 'neither in the building nor in the rigging . . . one single thing which is similar', and sought to investigate the reasons and causes for this by close interrogation of its form and structure, this book would be unnecessary. On the other hand, that they were not in the slightest interested, other than as in a travelling freak show, is why the story of the *Keying* is important and has provoked what follows.

It was in the fifteenth century that differences of great importance emerged in local naval architectural practices. For around that time, development in Europe began to accelerate in response to unique social, economic and military pressures. In short order, European naval architecture 'took off', and over a period of about three centuries followed a trajectory that placed European ships and seafarers in a position of absolute maritime supremacy over any non-European maritime civilization.

In the simplest terms, the 'take off' entailed two things. First, by the early sixteenth century, the basic design envelope[28] of sea-going ships was swiftly zeroing in on one fundamental system of construction[29] that proved to have a property of practical scalability that up until that time was extremely rare, if, indeed, it can be seriously identified anywhere.[30] This was related to a larger set of social changes vis-à-vis the sea and ships to which we shall revert below. Second, a consequence of these changes was that European naval architecture became increasingly theorized. The result was a more and more sophisticated exploration of the extent to which the emergent basic design envelope was not only scalable, but also adaptable. That in turn allowed the development of specialist designs, nowhere more distinct and historically important than in the late sixteenth- and early seventeenth-century emergence of the all-gun warship—the man-of-war—with its revolutionary implications for the prosecution of overseas commerce and interstate relations.

Why this should have occurred in Europe is complex; a largely coincidental conjunction of many different forces. Some were geographical, for example Europe's convoluted shape, with its many 'narrow seas', the available timber types, their main growing areas and rates of depletion, and the sources of other vital materiel like pitch, flax, hemp, iron, and so on, for ships' furniture and fittings. Some were, broadly understood, economic, for example typical trading routes, cargoes, methods of financing voyages and the structures of labour markets. Some were regulatory or legal, for example the development of tonnage rules for taxation purposes, the ubiquity of cross-border trade and the development of common frameworks for contracts and dispute resolution. Some were demographic, for example the critical Portuguese turn seawards into the Atlantic when too many people were trying to eke subsistence from too little land. Some were intellectual—the turn to empirical science that has been so widely studied but is still hard fully to explain.[31] Some—most significantly—were political. Here, especially, figures the seemingly unending rivalry between the numerous emergent European nation-states and the resultant regular warfare that, because of Europe's geographical shape, often entailed the employment of maritime forces in either aggression or defence. And, finally, there was also the perennially troubled, mainly maritime interface between Christian Europe and an expansionist Islam.

Meanwhile, in broadly unified and generally well-governed dynastic China, nothing similar occurred. Other than in the interregnum periods every few centuries, a single governmental system imposed widespread order, within which an intricate and mostly self-sustaining economic system could and did develop.[32] When things fell apart, the focus of problem-solving was for the most part resolutely terrestrial. The sea was the periphery. Through the long periods of a settled state had developed a vernacular naval architecture to suit the economic purposes of this complex but interlinked world.[33] The hull form and rig that had evolved by the Song dynasty (960–1279) from Han riverine craft and Yue kingdom coasting vessels to bear early traders carrying cargo in their own bottoms, as the nautical phrase has it, from China to Korea, Japan and Southeast Asia, was admirably adapted to its monsoon-season sailing rhythms and its growing nexus of ports of call on mainly northeast-to-southwest routes between 40°N and 10°S. But such change as then took place in the near millennium between the eleventh and nineteenth centuries was narrowly incremental. For various reasons and causes, there was no impetus that would drive radical change, even had the design envelope been more hospitable to change than we shall hypothesize that it was. For the design envelope of the ramified family of vessels that had emerged would prove to have certain intrinsic properties quite different from the dominant design in the West, which had emerged far more slowly in response to different imperatives.

The largest Chinese ships of the mid-nineteenth century had developed incrementally from vessels from a millennium before; they would have been familiar in almost all respects to a seafarer of that earlier epoch. If we ignore the highly contentious, indeed technically extremely dubious, claims of the Zheng He treasure-ship boosters,[34] it will have moved from being 20–30 metres in length to 60–70 metres, and from 100 or so tons burthen to at most 1,500 tons burthen.[35] The unstayed, multi-single-tree-masted[36] rigs barely changed, though over a 900-year period the sails passed from conjoined panels of a sandwich of woven rattan or bamboo and leaves, through panels of tightly woven rattan or bamboo, to battened, complete sails of a hemp- and flax-based canvas. And their steering systems, based on a stern-hung rudder developed from a vertically mounted, centreline steering oar controlled by crew working gun or luff tackles,[37] changed only in respect of refinements to the rudder blade and the development of a bow-mounted bowsing tackle[38] to try to overcome the system's inherent weaknesses when running down sea in a blow.

The single-tree masts, most commonly two to three in number, though instances of six have been recorded, carried the brilliantly conceived sail—in Western terms a fully battened, balanced, standing lug rig—that by the Song dynasty had evolved into a uniquely efficient and potentially labour-saving solution to getting power from the wind. But here too development stopped, save for minor, incremental improvements. As with the steering system, mechanical inefficiencies from crude materials and working gear meant large demands for the brute force of many hands.[39] Almost all crew, indeed most of the maritime world of China, were products of a domain below the bottom of the Chinese social hierarchy; most of the ordinary deckhands were mere muscle power and never called on to exercise significant maritime skills.

The absence of state involvement, the very different manner of capital formation, ships that were cheap to build and economical to operate, systemic illiteracy and a seemingly inexhaustible pool of cheap labour meant there were few, if any, significant competitive or cultural pressures encouraging shipbuilders to improve hull and rig designs, or shipowners to seek them. Indeed, the pressures were quite in the opposite direction, since the socio-economic result of the socio-cultural nexus was arguably the most naked competitive market ever seen in shipping. The structure and rig of the junk were thus, technically, subtle vernacular solutions to producing an easily built hull from the minimum quantity of low-cost materials with minimum high-skill shipwright input, to be operated by dirt-cheap labour. A wide-open market ensured that it paid no one to introduce radical innovations. Of course, this did not exclude innovation—bright and thoughtful minds are what they are and, as Joseph Needham and his collaborators' monumental study shows,[40] China had as many of those as the Western world—but it did make it spasmodic and unlikely to produce runaway or wholesale change. Additionally, the indifference of the Chinese government and elite towards matters maritime, swinging occasionally into outright hostility, created a climate in which, even were there to have been potential gains from innovation considered purely from a business point of view, the risks of a sudden policy change meant it was unlikely to have been worth trying.

China's maritime story was thus just as much a product of the interplay of complex forces as in Europe. Over the first few centuries, Chinese naval architecture, shipping organization and fluctuating maritime policy, in the context of the Asian maritime world, worked in ways distinctly to China's advantage. Thus by the beginning of the fifteenth century, the largest products of China's shipwrights would seem to have been larger than anything produced in the Western world; the average trading vessel was probably bigger than the average Western equivalent.[41] Their multi-masted rigs drove them efficiently on trading voyages that ranged more widely than the relatively 'short-seas' world of the contemporary northwestern Europe and the Mediterranean. Their compartmented hulls enabled carriage of separated consignments, while at the same time reducing catastrophic flooding and the fell effects of unrestricted free surface of what water did flood the hull as the result of holing.

But it can be argued that outwith some truly major technical changes, for any glimmerings of which there is no obvious historical evidence, the naval architecture that had evolved in China by the Ming dynasty (1368–1644) may have faced some intrinsic limitations in its basic design envelope. In effect, the design and performance envelopes of the Chinese junk hull and rig had nearly identical boundaries, such that if there were demands for enhanced performance as a result of competitive or other pressures, there may not have been any margin to spare without radical changes in materials and fastening technologies. By contrast, the scalability and adaptability of the Western design envelope created larger margins outside the initial performance envelope that could accommodate increased performance demands. Simply put, among several design constraints built into the Chinese design envelope, two were arguably the most important. Given the system of transverse solid framing, it was difficult to increase internal capacity by adding depth to the hull. Given the rig, it was difficult to add more driving power—in the form of increased sail area—to propel a larger, heavier hull. The system that had evolved in the West, on the other hand, allowed the ready development of multiple continuous decks in the hull. In the rig, by the addition of topmasts and topgallant masts with further staying, more sail area could be added to drive the larger hulls.

... To an Unsympathetic Eye

It follows that the *Keying* presented a unique and intriguing opportunity for analysing and cataloguing these naval architectural differences. Had that happened, Victorian naval architects might have been surprised. For it was in the 1840s, as iron-(and later steel-)built ships began their rapid replacement of wooden build, that Western naval architecture faced a problem with which it was to wrestle for half a century and more. The matter can be simply put. Was the best way to build a metal ship to act as if metal and rivets were architecturally indistinguishable from wood, bolts and nails and thus continue to use the 'frame first' construction method that had dominated—and got ever more complex as ship sizes increased—since the late sixteenth century? Was the wooden world's system of transverse framing at close intervals the most suitable to iron and steel?

In 1835, just over a decade before the arrival of the *Keying* in London, the young British naval architect John Scott Russell had built an iron ship using a revolutionary new system:

> I had to do it entirely out of my own head, and after my own fashion. I gave it a longitudinal central bulkhead, and four transverse ones, connected with a few longitudinal bars. It had absolutely no frame. My second was for a purpose which rendered a longitudinal bulkhead inconvenient, and I employed more numerous bulkheads, longitudinal stays and no frames, and my third the same.

But the young shupbuilder's innovative approach—which incidentally created more usable cargo space below—did not catch on. Scott Russell is clear as to why: 'The practical difficulty of continuing to build vessels on this system consisted not only in the prejudices of owners, but later in the Regulations of Lloyd's.' And he goes on to attribute the continuation of the older system to the weight of established practice: 'Out of these ruts it is hard to rise.'[42]

Scott Russell read that revolutionary paper in 1862, a generation after he had built his first longitudinally framed ship and four years after the most revolutionary example of the technique had been launched: I. K. Brunel's *Great Eastern*. The *Leviathan*, as it was first named, was a ship pregnant with the promise of the new. Yet coincidentally for this story, it too ended its life as did the *Keying*. As a failed visitor attraction at Rock Ferry on the south bank of the River Mersey opposite Liverpool, then broken up on the mudflats there in 1889–90, almost exactly as the *Keying* had met her end thirty-four years before.

The longitudinal system was not to be widely adopted until 1908, when Joseph Isherwood designed the *Paul Paix* on the lines of the system of longitudinal framing he had patented in 1906. Despite Scott Russell's pioneering work, the longitudinal system is today still often known as the Isherwood system.[43]

If we stop for a moment to consider how Scott Russell described his system, we can see how a closer look at the construction of the *Keying*, when it arrived in Britain, might have opened minds. For Scott Russell's main principles were two.

One was that the 'skin of the ship (is) the most important in point of its func-
tions in giving strength and durability to a ship'. The other is to have 'as many
transverse water-tight iron bulkheads as the practical use of the ship will admit'.
He then places between each of these complete bulkheads 'partial bulkheads, or
the outer rim of a complete bulkhead'. And the longitudinal strength is provided
by stringers that run from bow to stern on the inside of the skin plating, one to
each row of plating along its centreline. In modern terms, what Scott Russell was
advising was to build a ship as if it were a composite, multi-cellular box girder.

Translate that to wood and you get not a bad description of the construction
of a Chinese junk along traditional lines. It too was very like a composite, multi-
cellular box girder. It had Scott Russell's structural skin, achieved by edge-joining
every plank to its neighbour by nails. It had his multiple transverse bulkheads. It
had a version of his partial bulkheads. And in the massive wales that ran down
the outside of the hull planking, the shelf that ran beneath the deck on the inside
of the top of the hull planking and in the keel plank, it had his longitudinals.

Scott Russell and I. K. Brunel were both in London during the *Keying*'s stay.
Scott Russell had moved to London in 1844 and opened his Napier Yard at
Millwall, just around the corner of the Isle of Dogs from Blackwall, where the
Keying spent most of its London stay. He was elected a fellow of the Royal Society
in 1849 and was the organizer of the Royal Commission for the Exhibition of
1851, at which the mandarin He Sing was to star. That was also the body that sub-
sequently decided to spend the profits on creating the centre of education and
information in Kensington, popularly known as Albertopolis, which included
Imperial College, the Natural History Museum, the Science Museum and the
Victoria and Albert Museum, among others.

Meanwhile, Brunel lived in Westminster. In the early 1850s, following the
success of the *Great Britain*, launched in 1843, he was already at work planning
the *Great Eastern*. Had he and Scott Russell visited the *Keying*, would they have
seen what was there? Or would they merely have had their prejudices confirmed
like Charles Dickens:[44]

> Nothing is left but China. How the flowery region ever came into this lati-
> tude and longitude is the first thing one asks, and it is certainly not the least
> of the marvel. As Aladdin's palace was transported hither and thither by the
> rubbing of a lamp, so the crew of Chinamen aboard the *Keying* devoutly

believed that their good ship would turn up quite safe at the desired port if they only tied red rags enough upon the mast, rudder, and cable. Somehow they did not succeed. Perhaps they ran short of rag; at any rate they had not enough on board to keep them above water; and to the bottom they would have undoubtedly gone if it had not been for the skill and coolness of half-a-dozen English sailors, who brought them over the ocean in safety. Well, if there be any one thing in the world that this extraordinary craft is not at all like, that thing is a ship of any kind. So narrow, so long, so grotesque, so low in the middle, so high at each end, like a china pen-tray; with no rigging, with nowhere to go aloft; with mats for sails, great warped cigars for masts, dragons and sea-monsters disporting themselves from stem to stern, and on the stern a gigantic cock of impossible aspect, defying the world (as well he may) to produce his equal—it would look more at home on the top of a public building, or at the top of a mountain, or in an avenue of trees, or down in a mine, than afloat on the water. As for the Chinese lounging on the deck, the most extravagant imagination would never dare to suppose them to be mariners. Imagine a ship's crew without a profile amongst them, in gauze pinafores and plaited hair, wearing stiff clogs a quarter of a foot thick in the sole, and lying at night in little scented boxes, like back-gammon or chess pieces, or mother-of-pearl counters! But, by Jove! even this is nothing to your surprise when you get down into the cabin. There you get into a torture of perplexity; as, what became of all those lanterns hanging to the roof, when the junk was out at sea; whether they dangled there, banging and beating against each other, like so many jester's baubles; whether the idol Chin Tee, of the eighteen arms, enshrined in a celestial Punch's show, in the place of honour, ever tumbled out in heavy weather; whether the incense and the joss-stick still burnt before her, with a faint perfume and a little thread of smoke, while the mighty waves were roaring all around? Whether that preposterous tissue-paper umbrella in the corner was always spread, as being a convenient maritime instrument for walking about the decks with in a storm? Whether all the cool and shiny little chairs and tables were continually sliding about and bruising each other, and if not, why not? Whether anybody on the voyage ever read those two books printed in characters like bird-cages and fly-traps? Whether the mandarin passenger, He Sing, who had never been ten miles from home in his life before, lying sick on a bamboo couch in a private china closet of his own (where he is now perpetually writing autographs for inquisitive barbar-ians), ever began to doubt the potency of the Goddess of the Sea, whose counterfeit presentiment, like a flowery monthly nurse, occupies the sailor's joss-house in the second gallery? Whether it is possible that the second mandarin, or the artist of the ship, Sam Shing, Esquire, R.A. of Canton, can ever go ashore without a walking-staff in cinnamon, agreeably to the usage

of their likenesses in British tea-shops? Above all, whether the hoarse old
ocean could ever have been seriously in earnest with this floating toy-shop;
or had merely played with it in lightness of spirit roughly, but meaning no
harm?—as the bull did with another kind of china-shop on St. Patrick's-day
in the morning.

The *Keying* is therefore intriguing because, despite the existence of contemporary documentation, remarkably little is known in detail about what kind of a
vessel it was, exactly who all of the crew were and most of the human detail of
how its unprecedented voyage unfolded. Almost nothing is known about what
happened to it and its crew when the voyage ended, and nothing at all, bar a few
isolated reports, about the fate of its majority Chinese crew. There are no known
remaining log books or diaries, though one can hope that the serendipitous
ejectamenta maris of attics and auction rooms may one day reveal a happy sur-
vival. The documentation there is—newspaper reports, a publicity pamphlet or
two, some letters and diary entries, a court record, one public letter and what can
be culled from various archive and narrative sources—tends towards generalities
rather than specifics and in any case gives the impression of the ship's voyage as a
'nine days wonder' rather than something of any historical importance. There are
more holes in the record than there are records proper.

The junk is, accordingly, revealing precisely because of that remarkable
paucity of evidence. In European terms the *Keying*'s voyage took place during
the sea change in the human, natural, and (above all) observational sciences that
was surging towards the full flood it reached in the last half of the nineteenth
century. Central to this trend was the idea of careful, neutral, quantified measurement and description of the world around us, whether natural or of human
artifice. Nothing demonstrated this idea in principle so fully, and yet in practice
so partially, as the Great Universal Exhibition of 1851 in London, in which Scott
Russell was so closely involved, and which was held at the very time that a sample
of the vernacular genius of a different technological tradition was lying in the
River Thames, open to public view.

Here was an opportunity for close study of a ship—and its crew—from an
utterly different maritime and naval architectural tradition. To the observant
and charitable eye—evidently none too common in Victorian Britain—here
were solutions to the problems of building a strong, seaworthy sailing ship,

economical and quick of construction, and, as we should put it today, user-friendly. Yet this opportunity was refused in a manner that, given what we know naval architects like Scott Russell were thinking about and working on, is close to purblind. In finding answers to why this should be so, we can see the social limitations of the supposedly 'objective' and 'universal' science and scholarship of the Victorian imperialist era in Britain, particularly where the more lowly and artisanal pursuits like shipbuilding, seamanship and maritime commercial practice were concerned. For another element in this story has to do with its main protagonists. Given the attitudes of the day, hardening in their racial prejudices as the century wore on, the Chinese crew would have been marginalized—or at best patronized—by mainstream British Victorian culture anyway. But what about its European officers?

Seafarers on the Make

For Victorian Britain, the sea may have become mainstream for the admirals and victors, for the explorers and discoverers—the latter whether successful and alive or, in that favoured Victorian icon, failing and heroically dead—and for the maritime merchant princes. An ordinary Joe of the maritime world—a merchant marine officer with no family connection, serving in the rag, tag and bobtail of the merchant service—might attract enough attention and strike lucky or, more likely, never rise from decent, or as often rather downmarket, waterfront riff-raff, obscurity. Joseph Conrad's brilliant novels of this world fully catch the flavour, in Tom Lingard and his mate Shaw, in 'Lord' Jim, even in Marlow, and we know Conrad painted from life.[45]

Charles Kellett and his officers were trying to catch their moment and strike lucky. Perhaps on that memorable day in May 1848, when Queen Victoria and her entourage came aboard and Captain Kellett showed them round, it felt like the moment had come. It had not. It never did. In its inception, in its execution and in its fading away, the *Keying* pressed none of the right Victorian buttons. Not quite the right chaps. Not quite on message. Not quite the right timing.

And yet. What is important is precisely this mid-nineteenth-century world of mutual blindness. For it was Charles Kellett, his partners, his officers and his European sailors, and So Yin Sang Hsi and his fellow Chinese crewmen who are actually what the story of Britain in China is all about. Their attitudes and understandings, prejudices and closures of mind, shouts, gestures, shoves and kicks, mute, stony-faced and no doubt resentful and bitter acceptance were what made the patchwork sails of the hybrid rigs that powered the single hull of nineteenth-century Sino-British—even Sino-Western—relations.

So the *Keying*'s voyage is instructive in maritime historical terms. In the passages from Hong Kong to Europe in 1846–48, we have the only certain voyage of a vessel from the Chinese naval architectural tradition that reached Europe from China via the Cape of Good Hope. Thanks to what documentation there is, it has been possible in this book to reconstruct the voyage such that we have one of the only clear, if limited, accounts of a long ocean voyage by a Chinese, junk-rigged vessel traversing a wide band of latitude, on all points of sail, in a full range of wind and sea conditions. From this, it has been possible to reach some broad conclusions about the performance envelope of a junk-rigged vessel vis-à-vis the performance of contemporary Western vessels sailing the same route. The results should not surprise any thoughtful and thorough student of marine ethnography or comparative naval architecture.

Another item of instruction concerns the crewing of the *Keying* and the light this casts on the great differences in organizational, regulatory and operational practices of nineteenth-century Chinese and Western ships. For this was a Chinese ship officered by both European and Chinese personnel, and crewed by a combination of European and Chinese seamen, in ways that could not avoid combining, willy-nilly, both Western and Chinese modes of shipboard organization and operation. As an experiment, it was something of a crewing failure, whatever its success as purely and simply a navigational feat. In its failures, however, there is much of interest to be gleaned.

The World of the Sailing Junk

All of this is of interest for the simple reason that, until the advent of the twentieth century, to Western scholars and mariners the detailed world of the Chinese junk was little known, whether in terms of how one was built and how it was rigged, or how it was crewed and sailed.

There is still scant material in English translation; some warranted supposition that primary sources in Chinese are by no means numerous; and much reasonable doubt that secondary sources, where they exist, rest firmly on a suitable wealth of detailed primary evidence as to what was the case. There is little in the Chinese tradition, for example, that would equate to the Western world's vast accumulation of logs and voyage diaries or shipyard and dockyard documents and plans. Nor are there the equivalents of the voluminous studies of ship organization and crewing that have appeared over the last century or so, distilled from Western records from the sixteenth century onwards,[46] whether considering Western mariners themselves or those from other cultures that sailed as Western ships' crew, like lascars.[47]

Where knowledge of pre-twentieth-century Chinese craft is concerned, bar the work of François-Edmond Pâris in the 1830s, most of which was primarily a matter of careful sketches rather than sets of lines, there were and are few images of junks, whether from Western or Chinese sources, that are faithful representations in scale and detail of these unique craft. What images we have are artists' renderings, some good, some bad, but few to be relied upon for a precise sense of China's intriguing and unique technical responses to the challenge of moving people and goods by water and of fighting afloat.

Among Chinese renderings, despite a far older written and pictorial tradition, there are almost no accurate, precisely scaled depictions of sea-going craft. What exist are mostly graphical notes intended to indicate a broad general structure, mostly devoid of any sense of true perspective or scale and containing only such detail as served the immediate, usually decorative or expository rather than technical, purpose. Only in the Qing dynasty does anything more carefully depicted occur—by which time much would have changed—and even then, with one noted Japanese exception,[48] the sort of specificity one can find in the West in contemporary line drawings and models, leave alone actual draughts and tables of offsets, is wholly lacking.

Where Western images of Chinese craft are concerned, the earliest of which date only from the fifteenth century, the first examples are the merest hints of a craft different from anything in the Western tradition. Different in shape and possibly rig, to be sure, but not otherwise observed in detail. One does need to note, however, that at this date Western representations of Western ships were far from trustworthy depictions. By the seventeenth century, more detail does begin to appear for both Western and Eastern craft; such images are often helpful in terms of broad proportion and other very general detail. Few if any, however, may be relied on for technical conclusions, especially with respect to the details of construction, fittings or rig. With the exception of one fairly detailed dissection by Pâris of a Qing naval inshore patrol craft, it was not until the work of Worcester in the twentieth century—by which time inevitable changes distinguished the vessels he researched from their forerunners in the Ming and early Qing dynasties and before—that detailed drawings were available.[49]

Although there are some technical details available today from what, to most Western students, were previously unknown Chinese sources, even these bear little or no resemblance to the technical treatises, timber and fastenings lists, lines drawings, tables of offsets, detailed builders' models, early encyclopedia articles and other materials from which we know in extraordinary detail the construction of Western craft, especially warships, from the late sixteenth century onwards.[50] And none of the more detailed Chinese sources seems to go back beyond the later Ming dynasty. Before that date, such detail as there is in works like the Song-dynasty *Wujing Zongyao* (武經總要, Collection of the most important military techniques, 1044) is a matter of general description rather than of detailed specification.[51]

Similar comparisons may be made between what has been discovered by maritime archaeologists in China, where the maritime side of the science is still young,[52] and maritime archaeology in the Western world. The number of completed wreck excavations in Chinese waters is remarkably small; while a good number of examples go back to before the common era, with some, including one of the world's oldest extant vessels, to the Neolithic, these are small craft like dugouts. From the secondary literature, it would seem that almost none are sea-going ships. Of the latter, very few excavated examples go back beyond the Song dynasty—two Tang dynasty (618–907) examples, neither sea-going nor large, are cited by McGrail[53]—but those seem the only well-known ones to date. This is in marked contrast to what has been discovered of pre-steam vessels, especially medieval and earlier ship construction and proportions, from archaeological work in Europe. In Steffy's important work, for example, the earliest fully reconstructed example discussed is the royal ship of Cheops of 2650 BCE; from the same millennium and territory come the details of the Saqqara shipwrights at work in the tomb of the courtier Ti. Bronze Age sea-going vessels of the twelfth or thirteenth centuries BCE are known from the eastern Mediterranean and northern Europe, as are several vessels from the middle and end of the first millennium BCE and the early centuries of the modern era.[54]

In contrast to the plethora of Western examples, what we actually know in detail about the ships built by traditional Chinese shipwrights before, say, the mid-nineteenth century (and even that may be setting the date too far in the past), especially in terms of regional variations and with respect to changes through time, is small. What we actually know about their performance envelope is not great and has to be inferred from secondary and tertiary sources almost devoid of specific detail, since the practice of keeping detailed logbooks of voyages—given the systemic illiteracy of many in China's water world[55]—never seems to have existed until the transformations in China's maritime world towards the end of the nineteenth century.

Seeing the *Keying*

The curious state of partial knowledge that has resulted has in its turn stood in the way of any accurate grasp of the shape, rig and construction of the *Keying*, as well as more or less ensuring that the extant depictions as much deceive as enlighten. It has also stood in the way not so much of the theoretical investigation of junk rig performance, which has been the subject of careful research using replicas and models, but of understanding how the rig worked in practice. Here the *Keying* is a vessel of singular significance.

Much the same deficiency exists, though perhaps to a lesser extent, in our knowledge of how Chinese ships were operated. Such evidence as there is appears in few sources, though its importance for understanding the great differences between the practices of the eighteenth- and nineteenth-century Western sea world and those which prevailed in China until the late nineteenth century, and possibly later still, is impossible to underestimate, especially when it comes to understanding the troubled voyage of the *Keying*.

As a final point in introducing the story of the *Keying*, the view of events that you will read is 'the view from the sea'. The maritime world is not the world of the landsman—the lubber, as sailors dismissively say. In unravelling the story of the *Keying*, in reconstructing as best we can its voyage and onboard life, and in interpreting such documentary evidence as there is, we shall therefore be approaching matters from an unfamiliar direction, one necessarily dependent on its own specialist vocabulary and ways of seeing. This will apply in three ways.

First, we shall come at the evidence respecting the ship, its crew and the voyage from the point of view of someone versed in the maritime world and the conduct of a voyage. What might look like a clear statement of fact from the point of view of someone unfamiliar with the arcana of ships and the sea is often a startling alarm call to someone with more intimate knowledge. By way of illustration, and to choose a highly general example, one often reads of the vital contribution made by the ship's compass to both Chinese and Western voyaging in the fifteenth through eighteenth centuries. Yet once one knows the history of the compass and is aware of the enormous technical and theoretical hurdles that had to be leapt before truly accurate, stable and reliable magnetic steering compasses were a fixture on ships at sea—towards the end of the nineteenth century, shortly before the invention of the gyro-compass made magnetic compasses all but obsolete—it is immediately evident that any narrative about fifteenth-century voyaging that attributes accurate navigation to a ship's compass rests on a failure to understand how medieval ships actually did maintain direction.[56]

In respect of the relationships between the ship's European and Chinese crew members, my focus will be less on the contrasts in everyday habits and mores that were such a distinct feature of the nineteenth century in the treaty ports, and more on the specific contrasts in shipboard organization and operation. Accordingly, running at the back of much of the discussion will be the vast contrasts that, despite the common endeavour of voyaging blue water, divided the world of the Western ship from that of the junk. There was the already large, and in the 1840s and '50s, rapidly increasing gulf between the regulatory environments in which Western shipping operated in terms of certification, ship-flagging, registration, surveying and measurement, safety equipment, and so on, and the less formal world of the junk trade. There was also the significant difference in complexity between the two types of vessel, and the starkly different approaches to order, hierarchy, organization and discipline that resulted, above all in the comparative status of ships' officers vis-à-vis the rank and file and what might be expected in terms of deference and obedience.

Finally, if more nebulously, there will be an understanding of the contrasts in senses of self and of roles as between representatives of an increasingly hegemonic, proud and successful Britannia, for whom a life at sea was potentially a path to wealth and social advancement, and a group of people treated, although no longer officially, as 'mean people', for whom life at sea promised little save continuing as they were and avoiding starvation or worse, and who in addition had volunteered not only to work for the *fan kwae*[57] but to quit their native shores, without official permission, for foreign and barbarous parts.

Part I

The Voyage of the *Keying*

Chapter 1
Origins, Purchase and Commissioning

The Junk and the Project

The *Keying* was a large, sea-going junk, somewhere between fifty and possibly one hundred years old, that was illegally purchased in China in 1846 and smuggled out to Hong Kong. There the ship was prepared for its voyage. Its crew was completed. It gained the valediction of Hong Kong's official good and great. It set out and, eventually, after much vicissitude, completed its intended voyage. It failed to achieve the business success intended, at least for more than a few years. It was sold and its crew dispersed. Towed to Liverpool for a forlorn and failed last hurrah, it fades from the record in circumstances still far from clear.

That is a bald narrative; for the last nearly 170 years its terse summary represents almost all there was thought worth knowing. As we shall see, however, there was far more to it that, teased out of the traces that remain, tells us not only about the *Keying*, but about the world in which her drama played out.

The enterprise was undertaken by a group of Hong Kong investors. Their object was to sail the vessel on its own bottom from Hong Kong to London, where it would be put on public display and, presumably, earn the investors a handsome return. For excise and possibly other regulatory reasons, the ship sailed without a cargo,[1] but was equipped instead with a small 'collection' of Chinese artefacts that would be displayed on the ship upon arrival, while the Chinese crew doubled as performers and musicians. The voyage of the *Keying* was therefore a promotional trip. It was possibly intended to cash in on enthusiasm in London for 'things Chinese', fomented by Nathan Dunn's Chinese Museum, featuring 'Ten thousand Chinese things'[2] that had been all the rage just two years previously. However, the promoters of the *Keying's* voyage would appear to have intended a very different 'spin' on things Chinese to the respectful and admiring tone of Dunn's exhibition.[3]

Dunn's museum had been moved to London in 1842, and was on display in a specially built enclosure, 225 feet long and 50 feet wide at St. George's Place, Hyde Park Corner, for two years thereafter. The wonderfully titled catalogue by William Langdon, *Ten Thousand Things Relating to China and the Chinese: An Epitome of the Genius, Government, History, Literature, Agriculture, Arts, Trade, Manners, Customs, and Social Life of the People of the Celestial Empire, Together with a Synopsis of the Chinese Collection,*[4] gives an insight into the show the *Keying's* promoters could hardly be supposed to have hoped they could surpass. One can only surmise the intention was to ride on Dunn's coat-tails while conveying a rather different message.

Nathan Dunn, a Quaker from Philadelphia who had spent thirteen years in Canton (Guangzhou) as a trader, had strong views on the opium trade and opposed the war fought by the British in furtherance of it in 1839–42.[5] Certainly, the catalogue's preface by Langdon, despite its evangelical zeal for the Christianization of China, makes a very strong case for the reader—and the visitor to the collection—to learn the correct lesson: that of a great and admirable civilization much of profit can be learned. There was a clear message that the more benighted contemporary portrayals of China in the popular media, emphasizing a backward and stagnant condition, gave a greatly distorted view. Langdon does not hide from the contrasts between the fast industrializing Western world and the pre-industrial world of China, but the lesson he draws is not to China's discredit, as was so much contemporary writing in service of justifying the Opium War. More to the point, the catalogue ends, in its final essay, 'Foreign Intercourse with China',[6] with a ringing denunciation of the opium trade:

> The Chinese have been, repeatedly, denounced in terms savouring little of Christian forbearance and charity. In their business transactions, they have been presented to our imagination as a nation of cheats; in their bearing towards foreigners, as scornful and repulsive to the last degree of supercilious self-complacency; and in their own social relations, as bereft of every noble sentiment and generous sympathy. . . . If European and American traders may justly blame the illiberality of the Chinese, these have certainly just ground of complaint against them in the illegal practices to which their

cupidity tempts them. Fifteen to twenty millions worth of opium has been for years, in defiance of the laws and known wishes of the government annually been emptied upon the shores of China by Christian merchants![7]

In short, Dunn's exhibition was intended to showcase the glories of Chinese civilization (albeit glories that were going through a bad patch) and, in so doing, to cast a distinctly unfavourable light on the motivation of the recently ended war.

A review of the 'ten thousand things' on display reveals a brilliant if rather inchoate exhibition. From the very outset, as the visitor entered through a doorway modelled on a Chinese summer house in Nathan Dunn's collection, he or she was immersed in a scene unrelievedly Chinese and covering, as best it could, the panoply of Chinese civilization: gods, officials, priests, literary gentlemen, ladies of rank, actors, tradesmen of every description, means of transport, domestic architecture, furnishings and *objets d'art*, rites, rituals, more tradesmen and scenes from everyday life, books and horticulture, riverine, canal and sea-going shipping, the system of government and aspects of the flora and fauna. The 1,341 displays, if they did not exactly amount to ten thousand objects, quite certainly came very close.

It is against this 'pro-China', backdrop that we must place the *Keying* and its travelling exhibition. For what Charles Kellett and his partners put together pales in comparison to Dunn's large, comprehensive and culturally better informed exhibition. The juxtaposition of philistine trivialization against a connoisseur's conspectus in their respective treatments of Chinese culture was devastating. In one edition of the *Description*, the *Keying*'s sparse catalogue lists just 114 separate entries.[8] The whole could not have run to more than 200 items. They were grossly unrepresentative of any single aspect of Chinese life, leave alone the vast conspectus of different ways of life, occupations, ranks, roles, classes, conditions and subcultures that constituted 'things Chinese'. The most elaborate single display, with a dozen individual objects, was a tray 'containing all the necessary apparatus for smoking opium';[9] it and it alone is accompanied by a full caption piously describing the 'pernicious effects' of the opium habit, as if this were a uniquely Chinese vice.[10] Nothing was displayed in a context that might have helped explain it—the exhibition was just a gallimaufry of curiosities.

In like manner, the narrative part of the booklet the *Keying*'s captain, Charles Kellett, either wrote or had written for him has one major and very marked difference from its equivalent in *Ten Thousand Things*. *Ten Thousand Things* is about Chinese culture and the objects in the exhibition. Insofar as Chinese culture is mentioned in the *Description*, it is mentioned belittlingly and disparagingly. The focus instead is the *Keying*. The ship is the prime object in the collection; in demonstrating the peculiarities of Chinese naval architecture, as interpreted by Captain Kellett and his partners, it serves as a commentary on the backward culture that gave the maritime world so awkward an exotic.

There is therefore good reason to see in the *Keying* and its collection an almost contrary semiosis to that of *Ten Thousand Things*. Where Nathan Dunn's exhibition treats Chinese civilization and its achievements with respect, even a certain awe, the *Keying* and its collection seem almost deliberately intended to denigrate and belittle.

Perhaps despite themselves, the Hong Kong investors in the venture— Captain C. A. Kellett, Mr. G. Burton (Mate), Mr. Edward Revett (Second Mate), Mr. T. A. Lane, Mr. Douglas Lapraik and an unknown number of unnamed others—were not merely 'cashing in' on the thirst for 'Chinese things' created by Nathan Dunn's exhibition, but, as beneficiaries of both the opium war and the opium trade, 'redressing' what some might have held to be an imbalance in public perception. China and Chinese things were not so much as objects of sympathy as of derision; the recent war was not so much a disgrace, as the naysayers would have it, but a *mission civilisatrice*.

The ship accordingly carried a small cargo of idiosyncratically—and probably utterly ignorantly—chosen Chinese artefacts intended to be displayed aboard to paying visitors. The Hong Kong investors in the project arranged for the purchase of the ship and the stock of goods, as well as the recruitment of the crew. One investor, Douglas Lapraik, deeply involved in the opium trade throughout his nearly thirty years in Hong Kong, would become eminent among early European businessmen in Hong Kong, founder of the Douglas Steam Ship Company (which traded well into the twentieth century) as well as a co-founder of the Hongkong and Shanghai Banking Corporation,[11] the Hong Kong and Whampoa Dock Co. and the Hong Kong Chamber of Commerce. Whether he was as astute at this stage in his career as he later proved to be is a different question. As a business venture, the voyage of the *Keying*, as we shall see, was far from an unalloyed success.

The Investors

All of the investors and actors, the five whose names we know and the four or more others who may or may not have existed, were European denizens of early Hong Kong, of the inhabitants of which almost no one has a polite word to say. *Ruffians* and *adventurers* were the politest terms. The most scathing implied that many had escaped Botany Bay only by luck or cunning.

These are harsh judgements. Hong Kong was a frontier; frontiers attract the young, restless and aspiring—people who in settled, stratified societies may find their avenues of advance blocked or restricted and who have nothing to lose by cutting out for less trammelled lands. There was an inevitable roughness to life, a choice of harsh, quick solutions, especially where, as was the case on the China coast, the reach of the law was short and the attitudes of many Europeans towards Chinese people brutally condescending. It is in that light we should consider our 'investors' in the *Keying* and what they may have thought were their goals.[12]

Let us start with Charles Kellett. He was born in the sea and naval port of Plymouth in 1818. He was just twenty-eight when the *Keying* set sail. He had gone to sea in 1833 or 34, when he was between fifteen and sixteen years old. That was quite late for a young boy seaman, most of whom usually went to sea when they were twelve to fourteen, so argues that he came from a middle class family who could afford to keep him in school.[13] He had probably arrived in Hong Kong as part of the crew of an opium clipper or, perhaps, of an Indiaman or Royal Naval vessel that had arrived in Chinese waters to prosecute the First Opium War. What his qualifications were as a ship's master at that date we do not know. They cannot have been paper qualifications, which were only just beginning to come into existence.[14] Whatever they were, they were sufficient for him to be trusted by his fellow investors with the tough and challenging task of getting a Chinese sailing junk that may have been a century old from Hong Kong to London.

Douglas Lapraik was born in 1818, so he was the same age as his chosen ship's captain.[15] He had settled in the Pearl River Delta in Macao in 1839, seeking avenues that were perhaps closed to him in his native Scotland. He had originally landed in Hong Kong 'in somewhat straitened circumstances' and had crossed to Macao to apprentice himself to a watch and clockmaker, Leonard Just.

Leonard Just is recorded as having been in business as a watchmaker for the Chinese market in London as early as 1790. He had arrived in Canton in 1826 to set up there and was joined by his son Leonard Junior in 1829; some time in the early 1830s, Just & Son moved to Macao. They appear to have been a reasonably successful business. There is a record in November 1830 of L. Just & Son 'having four excellent chronometers for sale', and in 1837 of the firm as being 'watch and chronometer makers'. From 1842 until 1844, the young 24-year-old Douglas Lapraik was Leonard Just Sr.'s apprentice, at which point an announcement by Leonard Just Jr. told of part of the company moving to Hong Kong under Lapraik's supervision and opening at No. 1 D'Aguilar Street.[16]

What happened next is utterly obscure. All we know is that by 1850 Just and Lapraik had either split up, with Lapraik starting his own watch and clockmaking business, or Lapraik had taken over the Just business. Certainly, by 1859, one of Just's sons was working for Lapraik as a clerk.[17] It follows that at the time of the *Keying* venture, Douglas Lapraik, aged twenty-eight, was at the very outset of an independent life as a businessman. Eventually, his watch and clockmakers and silversmith company was bought out by one of his employees, George Falconer.[18] In 1846, Douglas Lapraik was still new in Hong Kong and cannot be said to have made his way. With a fortune yet to make and an eye for the main chance like most in Hong Kong at the time, Douglas Lapraik was not in the same league as Nathan Dunn by a very long way.

Thomas Ash Lane's birth year is unknown, though he was baptized in 1825.[19] By 1850, he and Ninian Crawford had set up a sea-biscuit emporium in a matshed; this became what is now the Harrods of Hong Kong, Lane Crawford. Lane had started life as a government clerk, although his family was engaged in business in Canton, Macao and Hong Kong well before the middle of the nineteenth century. At this stage, according to the contemporary *Hongkong Almanac and Directory*, he was part of Lane, Rowland & Co., ship chandlers of Queen's Road, the other named member being Thomas H. Rowland.[20] Evidently, Lane came from a background where seed money for a project might have been forthcoming. It is unlikely, if he was still making his way and to establish a relatively modest ship-provadoring operation in 1850, that he was more than thirty. His baptismal date suggests his mid-twenties. We do know that in 1846 Lane set off on a 'sourcing' journey that lasted until 1849.[21] Since these dates coincide precisely with the *Keying*'s voyage, it is a racing certainty that Lane was one of the investors who set off with the ship when it left Hong Kong.

Of G. Burton we know less than nothing. If he was first mate of the *Keying*, he is likely to have been a professional seaman like Charles Kellett.[22] They had probably served together, which is also a feasible explanation for the choice of the second mate, Edward Revett.[23] The only trace of a G. Burton on a British-flagged vessel is when a person of that name was skipper in 1895 of the brig *Magic* out of London, flag signal WBJH, owned by E. J. Billingham.[24] Whether this is our G. Burton we cannot know, although by 1895 someone old enough to have been a first mate in 1846 would have been at least 75 and possibly pushing 80—this was, in fact, not uncommon for skippers of small craft in European waters who were down on their luck. Retirement pensions are a feature of the twentieth century. If this is our man—and it is of note that only two G. Burtons appear in either the *American Lloyd's Register* or the *Record of American and Foreign Shipping* as captains in the period 1850–1900—he had clearly not prospered greatly. Either way, G. Burton and Edward Revett were likely to have been young men on the make on the waterfront in 1846 Hong Kong, and probably in their mid- to late twenties or at most early thirties.

In short, of those Europeans connected with the *Keying* of whom we know anything at all, there are three common features. None was very old, the late twenties being the probable average. None was highly educated. None could be said to have come from the privileged stratum of British or Anglo-Indian society. All were probably adventurers out for the main chance and not necessarily particularly scrupulous as to how they seized it. That does not suggest they were not in principle law-abiding, god-fearing, upwardly aspiring young men, anxious to achieve wealth and respectability in the burgeoning Victorian middle classes. It does suggest that they had not yet reached that status and that, in coming to Hong Kong to make their way, they were not inclined to entirely orthodox avenues of advancement.

When we therefore consider the *Keying*'s voyage and its cargo of 'Chinese things', we do have some reason to suppose that, far from being a high-minded endeavour on par with Nathan Dunn and William Langdon's opulent offerings, it was touched with the spirit of the music hall in its perennial appeal to populist sentiments. That is not to say unequivocally that the investors in the *Keying* were embarking on some sort of vindication of British conduct in China and the acquisition of Hong Kong—still in 1846 by no means a settled deal.[25] It is to imply that such sentiments were probably not far beneath the surface. Nathan Dunn, after a successful career in China amassing his fortune and imbibing deeply of Chinese civilization and culture, was a rich man, at least in principle; he could perhaps afford a certain high-minded and quixotic tilt at the rapidly turning windmill of popular attitudes to China.[26] Five young men on the make—in China for less than a decade during a period of intense turmoil, who had arrived in the young colony when its existence was precarious and when it was a haven for more than its fair share of reprobates, all equally anxious to use the system for their personal advantage and holding less than adulatory views of Chinese people and culture—would very probably have had different goals and beliefs.[27]

A Chinese or British Ship?

One minor, but telling, detail that suggests quite strongly that a subtext to the voyage was vindication of contemporary Western—especially British—conduct in China can be seen in the chosen ensigns flown aft in port. Nautical flag etiquette was still in flux in the mid-nineteenth century, although in this as in many other aspects of the maritime world, rules, regulations and conventions were ever more firmly established and applied, with the process getting its first definitive legal form with the Merchant Shipping Act, 1854. By 1846, it would have been normal and expected practice for a British vessel, when in port or transiting other states' territorial waters, to wear a national ensign either aft on the ensign staff or, in the case of a sailing ship, at the peak of the aftermost mast or gaff. The *Description* and many newspaper reports described the *Keying* as a British ship. Had that been so, then strictly the red ensign should have been worn aft. In no depiction is this so. Instead, we are told that the junk had five ensign staffs along its taffrail, on which were hoisted the 'flags of the treaty ports'.

As corroboration that some sort of new Western presence in China was perhaps being signalled, Nathaniel Currier's engraving of the *Keying* in New York may be compared with the well-known engraving of the 'The Chinese Junk Keying' in the offing of Gravesend on her arrival in Britain.[28] In the first, the American flag is flown, correctly in terms of nautical etiquette, as a courtesy flag from the foremast head. In the second, either the red ensign is correctly flown, or a Union flag is incorrectly flown.[29] To the nautical eye, this speaks volumes: the *Keying* was arriving as a ship of the treaty ports—its 'home ports', as indicated by its ensigns—and London, like New York, was a 'foreign' port whose merchant ensign should thus be flown as a courtesy flag. If anything, that small fact alone affirms that the *Keying* was not considered by its captain a British ship.

Indeed, Currier's careful drawing, backed up by the Rock Brothers and Payne engraving, suggests that the *Keying* may have been sailed as a Chinese vessel. For in both images, the flag worn at the mizzen mast—one customary Western position for a national ensign—is a plain, yellow flag. In 1846, there was no such thing as a Chinese national merchant ensign. China had yet to conform to the Western manner of these matters; there was no conception of a national merchant fleet. The most likely explanation is that a plain yellow flag epitomized China. Support for this theory can also be had from the main mast. Both images have a standard masthead flag flown, as with the ensign at the mizzen, askew on a short staff in the Chinese manner. In Western etiquette, this would be the vessel's house flag, showing the person or company that owned it or, sometimes, its name. The *Keying*'s flag has an indecipherable symbol in the centre and, down one side, a string of what are obviously intended as four Chinese characters. Since these were drawn by someone who knew no Chinese, the result is unreadable. A later nineteenth-century merchant flag carried a four-character inscription down one edge, *Tiānshàng Shèngmǔ* (天上聖母, heavenly goddess of the sea), though whether this is what *Keying*'s house flag showed is mere guesswork. In addition to the masthead flag, there is also a long, red, two-tailed pennant flying from the mainmast weathervane. Finally, in the bow, where in a Western vessel a jack would be worn, the *Keying* has a Chinese flag, blue with green side bars, also with indecipherable characters.

In short, the images show the *Keying* was being signalled as a Chinese vessel through the use of Chinese-like flags, but worn in the established Western manner of jack, courtesy flag, house flag, and national ensign.

Reverting to the five flags on the taffrail, the obvious point is that the treaty ports were an exaction by force by the British from the Chinese government. Using these flags—or at least telling people that that is what the five flags were—thus represented a form of Western triumphalism. Doubly so, in fact, since it seems unlikely that, formally, there were any such flags unless they had been devised by their new residents to represent the foreign enclaves there. Flying from the taffrail, successively from port to starboard, are a blue pennant with a narrow green border, a white pennant with a red or pink border, a red pennant with a white border, a yellow pennant with a blue border, and a green pennant with a yellow border. No such flags appear in any standard vexillogical reference book.[30] Indeed, there are no references to civic or municipal flags in imperial China; the structures of government and society make any such entities unlikely.

Whatever was flown from the five staffs on the *Keying*'s taffrail do not seem to be anything traditionally or officially Chinese but, more probably, something devised by the investors in the project to represent the five treaty ports opened to foreign commerce by the First Opium War; namely, Canton, Amoy (Xiamen), Foochow (Fuzhou), Ningpo (Ningbo) and Shanghai. The designs bear a passing resemblance, in concept if not in detail, to four of the Eight Banners of the ruling Manchus in Qing China, categorized in terms of a dominant colour and its surrounding border; for example, the 'Bordered Blue Banner'.[31] Given the general level of knowledge of China and Chinese culture the *Keying* enterprise reveals, these supposed treaty port flags were more likely an exercise of the triumphalist imagination than demonstration of well-founded fact.

The Cost of the Project

The ship itself was bought in Canton—quite illegally, since foreigners were not allowed to buy Chinese vessels—and smuggled to Hong Kong, apparently with some of the European crew in disguise. At least, that is one story. There is another version in which British entrepreneurship comes second to American feistiness. In this second account,[32] the *Keying* was originally bought by an American, whose name is not known, who in 1845 or 1846 had either paid for it to be built in a Chinese shipyard—which may account for some of the many subsequent questioning comments on its general conformity to traditional hull types—or bought it from an existing owner. He then is held to have sold it for $75,000 to Charles Kellett in the latter year. If that is true, then much of what follows with respect to the *Keying* story in respect of its financial difficulties could be explained, since $75,000 for a secondhand Chinese junk between fifty and one hundred years old would have been a phenomenal sum; recovering that money through the project, given all the inevitable costs, would have been near impossible.

Interesting though the story is, it lacks credibility precisely because of the price cited, since none of the investors can be thought to have been wholly unacquainted with the shipping market either in the Pearl River Delta or in general. What we do know of costs in the general period makes the tale improbable. For example, almost twenty years later in 1861, Warren Delano, Jr., spent US$45,000[33] on the secondhand, 456-tonne steamer *Surprise*; in 1877, the Shanghai Steam Navigation Co., through its managing agents Russell & Co., bought the steamer *Moyune* for 74,500 Haekwan taels.[34] In somewhat different waters in the 1830s, a state-of-the-art, brand-new transatlantic packet built at a New York yard cost only between $40,000 and $50,000.[35] So anyone in 1845 who paid $75,000 for an old junk had been seen coming. To suppose Douglas Lapraik, even if he was yet to develop the full panoply of business skills of later years, would have been green enough to countenance spending that sort of money on an antique junk beggars belief.

The only trace of this tale so far located, outside of J. R. Haddad's reference is a story run early in 1847 in the British *Northern Star and National Trades Journal*, repeating undated news from a story in the *New York Express*:[36]

> An enterprising Yankee at Canton has recently built a Chinese junk of 300 tons fitted and rigged entirely after the Chinese mode; which he intends taking to New York, loading her with every species of China knicknacs [*sic*], curiosities, etc. to be sold on board after arrival off that city. He takes also a Chinese crew, a theatrical and juggling company, males and females, and everything curious, illustrative of the manners and customs of the Celestials. The junk will have canvass [*sic*] sails and a Christian rudder to make her suitable for the long voyage, but upon arrival at the Narrows, everything will be replaced by Chinese articles, clumsy rudder and all, and the junk anchor off the city in her entire oriental costume and build, where she will remain as a show-shop, sale room and mountebank exhibition. It is expected she will make the passage in five months. The cost of the whole affair will be about 30,000 dollars, and the 'cute' proprietor will undoubtedly realize a large fortune.

This is certainly a more understandable price, but none of the other elements— above all, the size of the vessel—seems to fit. So whether this was just garbled news about the actual *Keying* story making its slow way back to America, or there were two such projects, one of which never got off the ground, we shall probably never know. Most probably, a project of this general sort may have been bruited about in Canton and Hong Kong for a number of years by more than one individual or syndicate; some sort of distillate of it may have percolated back once the *Keying* project itself got underway. The money cited in this version of the story goes even further towards suggesting that either the British investors were unbelievably green or the suggestion that they parted with $75,000 is false.

A third story, starkly at odds with the central tenets of the other two, appeared as a news story from a Hong Kong-based correspondent in the *Hampshire Telegraph and Sussex Chronicle*, published in Portsmouth, on 13 February 1847.[37] The two key differences are with respect to the cost of the junk and her age. The 'letter' from 'A correspondent, dating Hong Kong, Nov. 28, 1846' states that the junk cost Captain Kellett and partners, 'all known to me', the sum of 'nineteen thousand dollars (each 4s 2d English)'. This sum is repeated, though possibly from the same source, in a brief comment in the *Liverpool Mercury* 'Multum in Parvo' column on 26 February 1847[38] as well as in the *Manchester Times and Gazette* of the same day.[39] This could be reconciled with the alternative versions of events by supposing either that the anonymous American investor had been seen coming by an astute Canton shipowner and, having lost his shirt, was then desperate enough to have the junk taken off his hands for a pittance—for the difference between $19,000 and $75,000 is huge—or alternatively, if the $30,000 price was correct, that a distressed American progenitor was forced into a heavily discounted sale.

The sum of $19,000 is also more credible, one which makes the project look not merely feasible but very likely, if all went as imagined, to prove quite profitable. The second story helps us see how this might be so by describing the cost of the whole potential exercise—junk, Western sails and rudder, full cargo of knickknacks, curios and all—at $30,000. As we shall see at the end of this tale, however, the question of the original purchase price is unlikely ever to be solved.

Kellett himself lends credence to the high price, in that he is reported in the *Account* as saying, or perhaps writing:

> She was purchased by her present owners, at an enormous expense, almost the price of a first class American packet, after she had returned from Cochin China, to which she had carried some Mandarins of high rank. She possesses the combined qualities of a Trader and a vessel of War.[40]

It strains credulity to believe that anyone from downy, money-obsessed, sea trade- and shipping-orientated Hong Kong in 1846 would have paid the price of a new American packet for a very old junk. This has all the air of a story devised for publication, not least to justify the relatively high price being asked for admission on board when the ship reached New York.

The only other stories about price write of 'not less than 30,000 dollars, which (a select number of residents of Hong Kong) have raised by shares, expecting to make a very good thing of the venture'.[41] While considerably more than $19,000, this is well within Captain Kellett's comparison with a US-built packet, while also fitting with the *New York Tribune* story. Both are a far cry from $75,000. This last version is also compatible with a chance of success and with what we know of ship prices in mid-nineteenth-century China. In any case, there is a feasible explanation that would make both $19,000 and $30,000 true. For the first could have been the cost of the junk and the second the gross cost of the entire enterprise[42]—the purchase price of the junk, the fitting-out work needed to prepare it for the voyage, the cost of stores and provisions for the anticipated length of the voyage, and, if they were paid, which the court case in New York found to its satisfaction that they had not been, the advances in wages for the crew.

The second signal difference is, however, irreconcilable with any other story, not least the version in the *Description*. This is the claim that the junk was 'nearly new' and 'recently built'. Obviously, the correspondent could have been wholly mistaken; given that no other source suggests the junk was anything other than venerable, this is probably the correct interpretation. Despite those three stories, little is known of the ship's provenance before it passed into Western ownership. Despite the claim of comparative youth, every other source reputed the *Keying* to be up to a century old. It would seem to have been at the very least half a century old, since the *Description*[43] speaks of one of the crew as having served on her for that period. However, since the only evidence we have of the vessel's antiquity is hearsay, with one countervailing voice, nothing certain can be concluded.

We do not know when exactly the ship was bought, whether in terms of the beginning of negotiations, which are likely to have been protracted, or when or how the deal was sealed. It is occasionally implied that the *Keying* was a British ship, though it seems impossible she was registered as such, with Hong Kong as her home port; the matter of the ensigns and courtesy flags makes it unlikely.[44]

There is, in any case, a great deal of cloudiness about what might be meant by any claim of ship registration at this period, since it was nowhere a formal requirement in the way that it is today. So the absence of the ship in *Lloyd's Register* would not at that date have been unusual, since changes to shipping law did not make registration compulsory until long after the *Keying* had come to the end of her days. In Hong Kong, there was no formal system of registration until 1855, when an ordinance was passed for registering the young colony's own ships, with the infamous lorcha *Arrow*, proximate trigger of the disgracefully contrived and opportunist, if very ill-timed, Second Opium War (1856–60) being the twenty-seventh vessel registered.[45] A greater likelihood is that, once she had passed out of Chinese hands and into British Hong Kong ownership, she became in formal official eyes merely one of the many Hong Kong junks that worked the junk trade, albeit one owned by British residents.

Again, the *Account* does not help a great deal, since its version of events elides as much as it specifies:

> This vessel was not obtained from the Chinese owners without stratagem and the aid of the more intelligent. A very large sum was given for her, and when a suspicion began to be excited that she was going to Europe, she was charged 185 taels while at anchor, within shot of the Bogue forts although she had obtained her clearance or chop at Canton for 83, with permission to sail in ballast. It is believed that there is some edict against the sale of Chinese vessels to foreigners; no doubt arising from the fear, that their model may be adopted, to the injury of the Celestial Empire! It is certainly very singular, that no junk ever before was purchased by foreigners for exhibition.[46]

It is impossible that there could have been a legal Chinese bill of sale, for the obvious reason that junks could not be bought. Kellett's description above raises the intriguing possibility, even a fighting certainty, that the *Keying* was bought through a Chinese intermediary or 'front' who ensured the vessel was able to leave Whampoa (Huangpu) and make her way to Hong Kong. The same person would have had a presence in Hong Kong, so that, once the *Keying* reached Hong Kong, he could have completed with clear title to the ship a proper bill of sale with the investors.

Many of the influential compradors of Western business houses over the following century were by 1846 both active and well-connected in both Canton and Hong Kong with Chinese and foreign concerns, so such an arrangement is highly probable. If there had been such Chinese involvement in the acquisition of the ship, the name of the intermediary appears nowhere in the records that remain. That said, whether any such legal niceties attended the buying and selling of local craft in Hong Kong seems moot; it is as likely that the paperwork was non-existent. An intriguing possibility, though it is the merest speculation resting only on a hint, is that the 'mandarin' Hesing could have been the intermediary. As we reach the end of the *Keying*'s story, we shall consider this further.

When we come to consider the end of the *Keying*'s life and the fate of her British master, it is of much relevance that these were still days when the formal system of national merchant fleets, national flags and a national register of ships, all resting on a panoply of legal provisions and regulations with respect to build, equipment, crewing and crew certification lay in the immediate future. In a sense, the *Keying* and its voyage were possible because the law was still loose enough to allow the ship to be equipped and sailed without satisfying the increasing web of regulations that a generation or so later would have stood firmly in the way not just of the voyage, but of signing aboard the formally unqualified Western master and officers, and drawing up the unofficially sanctioned articles, which the crew signed, that were the focus of dispute in New York.

The Crew, Whampoa and Hong Kong

Whenever and however the deal was done, we know the junk left Whampoa on 19 October 1846. She would have already had signed aboard the twenty-six Chinese crew members who hailed from Whampoa and who were to return thither from New York. They were probably part of the deal, since their New York claim dates their involvement to September. The New York court record, however, leaves it open that the purchase of the ship and the recruitment of the crew were separate exercises, and that the crew were not at that point told the truth about the voyage that was planned. As we shall see, there is a fine quibble here about what may be formally written in what crewmen sign (known as the ship's articles and often prudently short of fine detail, the paths of sailing ships being subject as they are to the vagaries of wind, season and the market) and what may more largely be bruited about on the waterfront and during recruitment. There is also the claim, noted above, that the *Keying's* departure from Whampoa was in a swirl of rumour about an intended European destination. The state of the crew's knowledge of what voyage the *Keying* was bound upon is a subject to which we shall return.

One story has it that, before the *Keying* left Whampoa she was also joined by the European members of the crew. If this was the case, given that we are dealing with a genuine attempt to break the law, it was a high-risk strategy, since it would surely have been close to impossible to achieve entire secrecy—waterfronts attract many pairs of interested eyes. So bringing a dozen or so strapping 'round-eye' mariners aboard would likely have been a dead giveaway. Despite this, the story has it that the European members of the crew were disguised, so that to Chinese official eyes all that was before them was a vessel in the Canton junk trade, going about its lawful occasions.[47] Since, as we have noted from the *Account,* another version has it that the junk's European destination was already part of waterfront scuttlebutt, the likelihood is that everyone knew perfectly well what was going on, the appropriate bribes had been paid and the disguises were a pantomime to save face and conform to protocol. As with so much about the *Keying,* what is true and what smokescreen is hard to decide. Again, in this part of the tale we pick up resonances that, when we come to the court case in New York, will help us navigate our way through its eddies and overfalls.

The point here is simple. The Chinese crew must have been a bunch of raw simpletons not to have picked up the 'vibes' about this most peculiar junk. As Paul van Dyke argues persuasively,[48] Canton was a generally very efficiently run port, even if the common European and American canards suggested the opposite. Of course, it had its peculiarities; in the aftermath of the First Opium War, we can assume that not all would have been working as efficiently as might have been the case before hostilities broke out. But it is stretching the imagination a great deal to suppose that a large, B-class junk in working condition, formally registered with the Canton authorities, which by report had just returned from an official or quasi-official voyage to Cochinchina (the southern part of present-day Vietnam),[49] can have been sold to Westerners—through no matter how many intermediaries—and then sailed away with a part-European crew without Qing officialdom being any the wiser. One has to recall that, on van Dyke's figures, there will only have been perhaps twenty-five to thirty-five or so such vessels working out of the port in any one year.[50] They were not, as a river sampan might have been, invisible. It would thus be a fair inference that the sale was known about and connived at through the usual medium—hefty bribes paid to the appropriate people. Not only to the port authorities, who had to provide the appropriate documentation for the junk to set sail, but to the congeries of officials at various checkpoints on the passage down river, as the quotation from the *Account* above makes elliptically clear.

So, with all the potential pitfalls having been dealt with in the way of an illegally acquired, illegally crewed vessel, heading illegally into foreign owner-ship and control, we can assume that the voyage down the Pearl River via the Bogue Forts, restored to their defensive glory after the grave aggressions of five years previously, will have taken the usual two days working the tides. A reason-able inference will thus be that the ship arrived in Hong Kong on or around 21 October—Trafalgar Day, a pretty conceit if anyone thought about it, which in early colonial Hong Kong is possible—to begin the long process of preparing for the voyage.

Getting Ready

To a sailor, the preparations for a voyage are like getting ready for a journey and packing are to the present-day traveller. What papers we get, what inoculations and vaccinations we seek, what lotions and potions we buy, and what clothes and other accoutrements we pack are all entirely dependent on where we are going, why and for how long. To a sailor of any nationality, in the weeks before a voyage commences, how the ship is prepared, what stores are taken aboard, what cargo is or is not stowed aboard and how and where it is stowed are all equally charged with meaning. As the crew go about their preparations, so they evaluate and chat; tally this bale of cargo against what they've heard about the coming voyage; cast an eye over that quantity of rice being stowed in the galley store and relate it to how long they signed on for.

Unpack someone's suitcase and you can probably work out roughly where they are going, for how long and pretty much why. So the preparations for the *Keying*'s voyage, even though we know little for certain and must assume that what was necessary for any voyage would also have been necessary for the *Keying*, will assist us later in evaluating the New York court case and the appar-ently definitive clash of two maritime cultures.

A vital step once the ship was securely berthed in Hong Kong was to complete the crew. Charles Kellett and his partners would have found European seamen to supplement the European officers and, presumably, protect them if necessary.[51] And their Chinese captain, So Yin Sang Hsi, assuming he was already aboard, would have found the balance of the Chinese crew, which, as we shall see, was a difficult task given the normal system of crew recruitment on Chinese vessels.

The ship needed provisions for a voyage of several months. How many months is not certain. We know from the later New York court record that the crew was signed aboard for eight months, but it is unlikely that the ship will have provisioned in everything for the whole voyage. Perhaps staples like rice and the standard European dry and salted ships' stores were taken aboard in quantities to last eight months. Other provisions would have been stocked aboard sufficient only for the longest expected passage time to the next possible provisioning point. If that is assumed to be the Sunda Straits area, it would have been a matter of two weeks plus a 'fudge factor' of another two or three—say, a total of six weeks—to ensure the ship could cope with emergencies. If it was Cape Town or St. Helena, stores for three or more months would be necessary; tongues would certainly have wagged. However the calculation was worked, the provisioning of the ship created problems once the ship was into the Atlantic, because the voyage progressed much more slowly than one imagines Captain Kellett planned for.

Had we more detail on this score, we might have a further clue as to exactly how transparent Charles Kellett had been with his crew about the intended voyage. Since their claim in New York was that they had been deceived about the duration and destination—a claim we should view with some suspicion—were we to know exactly what scale of stores were loaded, we should have a further means of evaluating the crew's claims to have been duped. Captain Kellett, for example, must have known that he did not intend to stop before, at earliest, Cape Town, and that on any reckoning was three or more months distant.

Depending on the general condition of the junk—it is unlikely the ship was refitted upon returning from Vietnam, before its sale—and given the marathon voyage ahead, there would have been the need to make any repairs necessary, overhaul all the running rigging and otherwise check that everything aboard was not only in working order but in a condition sufficient to serve for thousands of miles. That would have required Charles Kellett and his partners to source, order, pay for and stow away a vast range of spares—blocks and tackles, bamboo sail materials, bamboo cable and manila cordage, nails, the makings of *chunam*,[52] wooden planks, spare spars, probably a spare rudder (which most Chinese junks carried) and much else beside. Again, as experienced seamen the crew would have known perfectly well what scale of furniture and fittings suited a junk bound on a short-seas voyage to Southeast Asia (what they claimed they had been told); unless somehow the crew were isolated from the events of this busy period—a laughable supposition—in the preparations lay a mountain of implicit information. If we had full details, we should have a better clue as to the credibility of the crew's New York testimony, but even as it stands, to think they had been duped is to know nothing about the way of a ship.

We do know from a later report that the blocks used in the steering gear were not traditional Chinese examples, which were not very efficient, but the best patent blocks,[53] presumably from a Hong Kong chandlery or shipyard. Since the ship would be navigated by Europeans, there will also have been a need to provide the ship with navigational instruments—compass, charts, sextant, tables and other navigational books and instruments, not least given Douglas Lapraik's business, one to three chronometers—which would not have been aboard already, because they had no place in vernacular Chinese navigation. These were more clues as to the probability that the *Keying* was not bound on any normal voyage.

There is also a suggestion both in a newspaper story and in one of the later images of the *Keying* that preparations may have involved some changes of the sort that would have been another alert for the crew. The story is the one from the *New York Express* we have already considered and relegated to a case of muddled intelligence. In it was claimed,[54]

> The junk will have canvass [*sic*] sails and a Christian rudder to make her suitable for the long voyage, but upon arrival at the Narrows, everything will be replaced by Chinese articles, clumsy rudder and all ...

This then takes us to the two images of the *Keying*, which analysis suggests were painted by the same hand (see Plates 5 and 6). That hand, though not a marine artist, was almost certainly aboard the ship and possibly Sam Shing—the ship's artist. When we compare the Chinese artist's image with all the Western images in one way or another (see Appendix), one thing stands out: the *Keying* is fitted with shrouds to the masts and a triatic stay joining the caps of the foremast and mainmast.

Detail is of course lacking, but the presence of these distinctly non-Chinese devices is plain.[55] They are made down to iron eye-bolts fastened in some manner outboard of the bulwarks. The main- and the foremasts both have two shrouds on each side. The mizzen is hard to interpret since the artist suggests two shrouds on the weather side behind the sail, but shows nothing on the lee side. This may either mean the mizzen had what is called a burton, a moveable shroud that is set up only to weather, no shrouds, or both that simply got missed out by an artist who was not a seaman. Whatever there actually was and whatever the fine detail of how it was set up, there is an undeniable suggestion that the *Keying*'s rigging was adapted by Charles Kellett and his officers to conform more with Western practices with their higher stress rigs.

Whether the small, square main topsail, shown by the Chinese artist is another Kellett adaptation is moot. Such topsails are shown on junks in eighteenth-century Chinese sources, so even if they owe their inspiration to cross-influence from Western rig, one may already have been part of the *Keying*'s inventory. Interestingly, this main topsail appears only in the most direct copy of the Chinese paintings by a Western artist (see Plate 9). In all other images of the junk under sail it is not present.

This connects back to the *New York Express* writer's suggestion that all adaptations 'to make her suitable' were to be removed upon arrival at the destination so that, again, the *Keying* became an authentic Chinese ship. In the majority of the images, not only does the topsail not appear, all the shrouds and the triatic stay disappear too. And to add a last small piece of evidence—perhaps an artist's mistake, or perhaps not—it is interesting to compare the rudders in all paintings with the rudder in the image in the *Description*. All the images bar the *Description*'s show the classic, Cantonese fenestrated rudder. Yet the *Description* shows a solid, unfenestrated blade (see Plate 12). Was this the 'unclumsy' rudder Charles Kellett had kept aboard for the transatlantic crossing that the artist— probably Birket Foster—still saw in place when the *Keying* reached Gravesend?

Whatever was actually done, the evidence at least suggests that when the *Keying* was in Hong Kong changes were made to her rig, possibly to her sail plan, and perhaps to her rudder that seasoned Chinese seaman could not possibly have missed. Would these really be the sort of preparations the strange *fan kwae* would make to take the *Keying* on a voyage exactly the same as she had been built to make?

Of course, it may be said from the crew's side that all the extensive preparation that one might say to a seafarer "this is for a long voyage" failed to do so because so much of the equipment was of and for foreigners, and who could know what the fancies of foreign devils might betoken? Possibly. But then we must consider the preparation of the junk itself.

If it had not been done in Canton as a condition of sale, before it left Hong Kong the ship would have been careened and given a new coat of *chunam* to protect the hull against marine borers. We know Chinese vessels, much like Western vessels, were regularly treated to cope with fouling in two ways. For periodic maintenance, the ship was breamed—that is, hauled over to one side (careened), with fires lit beneath it to kill the accumulation of marine growth, burn off some of it and enable the rest to be scraped clean, before the other side was treated in the same way. About once a year, after breaming, the whole bottom would be prepared and a new coat of *chunam* applied: it is this more complete exercise that was likely part of Charles Kellett's commissioning list.

Finally, of course, there was also the cargo. Or, rather, the absence of anything like a regular cargo. Instead, what was loaded aboard would have been a few crates of seemingly randomly-chosen Chinese objects to be used as exhibits in Europe. As all this was going on, the officers and crew will have been busy checking all the items over; verifying the labelling; taking an inventory of the boxes, crates and bales; sending them down to the holds and arranging their secure stowage. Here, again, it beggars the imagination to believe that such an eccentric cargo, the only one loaded aboard, would not have raised questions about the nature and purpose of the voyage, at least among the sharper crew members, who, if the *Account* is to be believed, will already have been alerted by Canton waterfront scuttlebutt. It would have taken a deaf, dumb and blind crewman not to have had a clue that the *Keying* was not destined for a quick jaunt down to Batavia (present-day Jakarta) or Singapore for a cargo of sugar or opium.

We can assume that, by the time all the preparations had been made, the *Keying* may have loaded aboard equipment and stores of perhaps 50 tonnes, at the very outside 100 tonnes.[56] Given her size, and as explained more fully in Part

II, she can have loaded at most perhaps one-quarter of her cargo capacity. The great unknown is whether Charles Kellett and his partners decided that, before they loaded all their stores, they should first load additional ballast.

Junks did use ballast, though it is not clear how often or in what circumstances—it is a matter on which Worcester, our leading Western authority, is completely silent. From what we know, ballast sometimes appears to have been a permanent property to ensure sufficient stability when the ship was riding light. Chinese build was remarkably light and economical, so a 'light ship', as ships without a cargo are called, would have ridden very high in the water. For the most part, however, it seems that ballast, if needed, was created through the choice of cargo—stones for temples, cargoes of porcelain, lead ingots and other heavy goods stowed low. There is little or no evidence to show that, when a ship was about to make a passage in ballast, additional ballast was loaded or if so how much. In Hans van Tilburg's otherwise very comprehensive work, there is no mention of ballast nor, in the most useful glossary, is there a term given.[57] The pictorial evidence of the *Keying* suggests that the ship rode light throughout its voyage, so if additional ballast was loaded in Whampoa or Hong Kong, it would not appear to have been sufficient to bring the ship closer to its normal working waterline.

So, as the day for departure drew close, we have a Chinese junk, bought by Westerners, smuggled out of China, almost certainly with the connivance of the authorities and very probably with the intermediation of a Chinese businessman with connections in both Whampoa and Hong Kong. It has been extensively and relatively expensively—compared to a standard trading junk, wildly and profligately—prepared for a voyage that, from the quantity of stores, is clearly not going to be a matter of a week or two. A coterie of foreign officers has taken charge, supported by a dozen or so Western sailors, much as if this were a country trader bound at least as far abroad as Mauritius, India or Australia. And to cap it all, no cargo is loaded save for a motley collection of Chinese artefacts, including weaponry.

Given the world of the waterfront, the scuttlebutt in the bars and brothels, in the godowns, on the wharves and in shipping offices will have been intense. It is impossible to conclude that, in all this, not a word was said in Chinese on Hong Kong's busy waterfront about the intended wowing of the London crowds. After

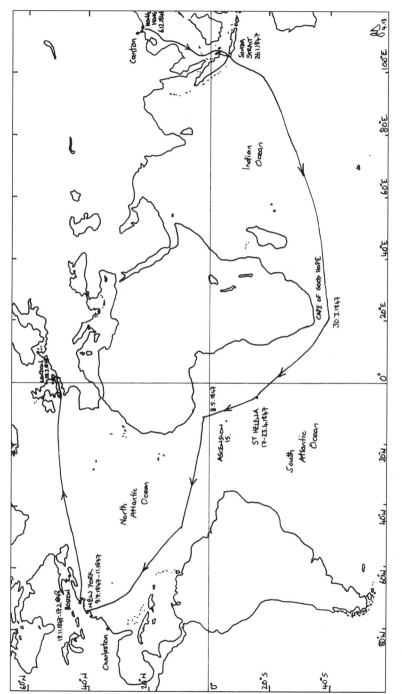

Map 1 The Voyage and Its Legs

all, though obviously we must allow for journalistic licence, when the *Keying* had first arrived in the recently established colony:[58]

> on her destination becoming known, an immense excitement was created in the colony, and all classes flocked on board or to the shore to obtain a view of the first Junk which ever attempted a voyage to Great Britain, comprehending a circuit of nearly one-half of the globe.

Had that not been enough to alert the *Keying*'s crew while the ship was still in port, when the time came to depart, she was 'escorted out of the harbour by a numerous assemblage of boats and small vessels'. Hardly run-of-the-mill experiences of a workaday *nanyang* trade junk, off for a cargo of opium and sugar and away for a month or three.

Chapter 2
The Ship's Name

Before we consider the name by which the junk has passed into record, it is worth pausing to ponder life before the ship became the *Keying*. We know that almost all Chinese trading junks had names.[1] These were usually redolent of the hopes and expectations of the owners in a world governed by forces no one could control. They were auspicious names inviting the gods to bring the ship safe home to her haven laden with a rich cargo, borne on the back of fair winds; names intended to protect the ship from the cruel implacability of the sea when the weather turned rough or when it was voyaging in uncertain waters about which knowledge was slight.

So before she was acquired by Charles Kellett and his fellow investors, the ship will have had a name; it is characteristic of this entire tale that no mention was made of it. We know both from the *Account* and the *Description*, as well as from an illustration in the latter, that in standard fashion the whole stern of the ship was elaborately painted with the traditional auspicious symbols. We also know from China-trade paintings that part of this decorative paintwork usually included the ship's name, and sometimes also other auspicious phrases. It therefore follows that, when she was bought, either the name was painted out and a new name painted in, or the old name was painted out and no name substituted—which from the only illustration we have seems most likely—or that the old name remained because no one bar the Chinese crew had a clue that it was a name because they could not read it.

In the image of the transom in the *Description* no Chinese characters appear. This is very unusual, for otherwise the imagery shown is consistent with how we know junk sterns to have been decorated. Once we look closer, we can see that the pattern drawn is not quite convincing as a faithful reproduction of the look of an actual junk stern. The transom and its decoration are overly two-dimensional. This is clearly one type of traditional Guangdong junk stern so what would normally have been present could be expected to be evident, but, as we only have Western images of it, we have no means of knowing whether what we see is indeed what was there, or the best a Western jobbing artist could make of what he saw.

So we cannot decide whether the picture shows no Chinese characters because there were none, or whether it shows no Chinese characters because the jobbing artist employed to do the work could not 'see' them, seeing instead only swirly-twirly decorative flourishes.

This is yet another moment in the preparations for departure—redecorating the very important and auspicious transom—which the Chinese crewmen could not and *would* not have ignored. A Western sailor may not have been all that concerned about how and where the ship's name was painted. He would have wanted things to be 'tickety-boo', as the naval phrase has it, so that his was a smart ship and an object of pride. But if someone did not do a proper job with the paintwork, no sailor would have concluded that the ship might be cursed.

Given the very important role of the gods in Chinese maritime, as in everyday life, and the need to properly acknowledge their roles, to invoke their aid, and to appease any possible anger, the business of the *Keying's* transom and name would have been of lively interest to the Chinese crew. Even the *Description* acknowledges this when, in relation to some damage to an image of a goddess in the saloon, it reports:

> The great Joss, or image of a deity, which is in the saloon, and which we shall describe hereafter, lost some of its gilding from accident; this (the painter) was requested to repair, but positively refused to do, alleging as a reason, that he was not of a sufficiently high rank to venture to touch what to him, in his unhappy ignorance, is accounted so holy a thing.

It will have been important that things were done properly—for example, a change of name would very likely have required an appropriate ritual, especially when it came to painting out the old and painting in the new. Whether any such consideration was given to the sensibilities of the Chinese crew we do not know. If it was not, then perhaps therein may have lain the first seeds of dissension that in the end would rip the crew apart in New York.

That the crew would indeed have cared about the highly auspicious painting on the transom may be concluded from the *Description*'s account of the main shipboard shrine, which every junk had and most Chinese fishing vessels still have, dismissive though its tone may be:

> In front (of the rudder head) is a piece of wood, on which is inscribed, "May the waters of the sea never wash over this junk." The native sailors thought much of this as a charm, and nailed two pieces of red rag to it. At the back (of the second poop deck) is the sailors' Joss-house, containing the deity of the sea, with her two attendants, each with a red scarf.[2] Near the principal goddess is a piece of wood from the first timber of the "Keying," that was laid; this was taken to one of their principal temples and there consecrated, and then brought on board, and placed as symbolic of the whole vessel being under the protection of that deity . . . A lighted lamp is also placed, which was kept burning the whole of the voyage, as, if it had gone out, it would have been considered an omen of bad luck.

Given the tenor of normal Western attitudes to Chinese beliefs at the time, it is quite likely that the crew's opinion as to the name change might not have been sought. There is nothing in the narratives of the *Keying*, certainly nothing in the *Account* or the *Description*, that suggests anything other than an amused conde-scension at the bizarre superstitions of the benighted heathen. The tone of the *Account* speaks volumes:

> The Captain (remonstrated) with them on the folly of their idolatrous customs, such as burning paper, beating gongs, &c. in honour of their gods, or deceased relatives. The tying of red rags on the rudder, cable, mast and principal parts of the vessel, was one of their frequent employments, as they considered them a safe guard against danger. . . . at the commencement (of the voyage), it was absolutely necessary for Capt. Kellett to furnish provisions, tinfoil, silvered paper, and josh [*sic*] sticks to a large amount, before the Chinese would sign the articles.
>
> One of their most revered objects was the Mariner's Compass, before this they would place tea, sweet cake and pork, in order to keep it true and faithful.[3]

So the crew's thoughts about changing the name, or how this should best be done, especially with respect to altering the display on the ship's transom, is not likely to have given pause for thought. As it might be put today, renaming the ship was a rebranding exercise to reposition it for a new market.

The name change itself is curious, because in Western maritime lore changing the name of a ship was and is thought by many sailors to be unlucky—though not by many shipowners, for whom pride of ownership, and a tendency to suppose their opinions are like the voice of God, usually outweigh any other consideration. In this case, the choice of name would seem to have been dictated more by the 'mission' of the junk—to reinforce, perhaps, a particular set of views about China, the Opium War and the conduct of the British traders—than to connect with the maritime world of China.

Indeed, as a name, *Keying* is very much in the British, not the Chinese, tradition. For a British ship, as we can see from the East India Company's Indiamen and the country traders down the years—*Marquis of Ely, Charles Grant, Earl Balcarres, Lord Amherst, Rustomjee Cowasjee* and many, many more—it is often owners, patrons and potentates who are honoured. Or the vessel's hoped-for qualities are signalled—*Sylph, Red Rover, Falcon*. Or places ancestral, venturesome or commercial—*Buckinghamshire, Samarang*—are marked. The name of the junk *Keying* was of the first kind, in that it invoked a kind of patron.

Keying (耆英, or *Qiying*, in the modern pinyin spelling) was the Sinified personal name of the Manchu dignitary, Ciyeng, a descendant of Babutai, the ninth son of Nurhaci, the Taizu emperor and first ruler of the Qing dynasty.[4] Qiying was a member of the imperial Aisin-Gioro house or clan and belonged to the Plain Blue Banner, the second-most junior of the eight banners, the administrative and military divisions to which all Manchus belonged. The characters of Qiying's name mean 'brave (stout-hearted) senior (elderly) man' and, at a considerable stretch of the imagination, could be construed as having been chosen as a name for the ship simply for their lexical meaning. However, that the ship was named after Qiying is not in doubt, for the *Description* says as much, as does a report in the *Belfast News-Letter* of 26 May 1848, which reads, 'The *Keying* is so named out of compliment to the Chinese Commissioner at Canton.'[5]

This brings us immediately, if a trifle in advance of events, to another typical aspect of the *Keying*'s story. When the ship eventually got to London, a publicity booklet was produced to help guide visitors around the ship and to provide a souvenir of their visit. The London booklet, the *Description* (unlike that for New York, the *Account*) had the name of the ship written in Chinese on the cover; a line in Chinese also reproduced on the Rock Brothers & Payne print, which is one of the best known images of the junk. However, the characters used for the ship's name were not the correct ones for the commissioner's Chinese name. The characters used on the title page, 其衣, in spoken Cantonese sound like '*Kei Yi*', perhaps an attempt to convey the sound of the commissioner's name. They mean, if anything, 'his/her/its clothes'. The imperial commissioner's actual name was 耆英—in Hong Kong/Guangzhou Cantonese *Gei Ying*—so the weird rendering of the ship's name begs a few questions about the source's knowledge of the Chinese language. The next four characters on the title page, 喊挨炯知—in Cantonese (roughly!), *Wei Ai Gwing Zi*—make little sense to a modern Chinese reader. It is possible that in some dialect or sub-dialect they may sound like the English word 'description'. They may possibly be a semi-literate translator's attempt to say something like 'Greetings (here is something) ordered clear(ly) (for you to) know (about) the *Keying*', though that would be torturing the Chinese characters to render a meaning—any meaning!—rather than the nonsense they convey to any normal Chinese reader. Perhaps as indicative is the point that the Chinese reads from left to right, against the most usual convention in the mid-nineteenth century.[6] In short, the Chinese was for show. No one involved in the project felt it necessary to make sure that what was written was correct. After all, as the *Account* had it:

> The language of the Chinese has been a great puzzle to Europeans . . . It has no resemblance whatever to any other language, living or dead; the written character is just now as distinct from any alphabetical arrangement as it was thousands of years ago. The foundation of the language is purely hiero-glyphical and symbolical.[7]

Fairbank indicates that Qiying was a well-connected, rich and experienced Manchu bureaucrat.[8] However, he had had a chequered career, as had his father before him; the cause of his fall(s) is reported to have been corruption. These peccadilloes aside, he was obviously able and, despite the occasional fall from grace, had risen again.

When the cessation of hostilities brought about by the Convention of Chuenbi had fallen apart in 1842, the newly arrived Sir Henry Pottinger, Hong Kong's first official governor, resumed fighting, moving the scene of battle northwards first to Shanghai, then on up the Yangzi, intending to cut the Grand Canal at Zhenjiang, threaten Nanjing and force the Qing government back to the negotiating table.

Despite stout resistance by Manchu troops, Zhenjiang was taken, with Nanjing in imminent danger of bombardment. The result on 29 August 1842 was the Treaty of Nanjing, agreed between Sir Henry Pottinger, General Sir Hugh Gough and Vice-Admiral William Parker for the British, and for China, imperial commissioners Yilibu and Qiying; China's main and extremely adept negotiator had been Qiying.

The treaty was in fact a masterpiece of ambiguity. As worded, it enabled the Chinese authorities to believe that an age-old Qing system had merely been extended to more ports than one. Foreigners in Chinese ports would continue to be expected to look after themselves within a thicket of restrictions largely at the discretion of Qing officials. In that respect, it could be thought that nothing had changed. The establishment of Hong Kong could be glossed as being merely a clone, on the other side of the Pearl River estuary, of the concession already made to the Portuguese centuries previously. At the same time, however, this subtle treaty allowed the British—and other foreigners with trading interests in China—to believe they had brought the Qing into the new, increasingly free trade-based, international commercial world, which, perhaps with a bit more pushing and shoving, the Chinese would conform to more fully in time. In Robert Bickers's masterly phrasing, 'The Qing saw restrictions modified, access still controlled and commerce still regulated; the British saw China opened and trade freed.'[9]

But that is to look at Qiying from today's perspective. The choice of his name for the junk—which could be read by optimistic China-coast Britons as symbolising a hope-for improvement, indeed radical transformation, in post-war Sino-British relations—is the very high esteem he was held in by the British side.

Qiying's subtle and skilled diplomacy in helping bring the First Opium War to an end had led many to conclude that the British—and in a sense Westerners in general—had a friend in the commissioner. In short, that the commissioner shared in some way the received British view of matters,[10] which held that opening China up to Western trade and overthrowing the hated Canton system would be to the universal benefit of all (but let us not mention opium). For example, Sir Henry Pottinger and Qiying seemed—at least to Pottinger—to have developed a genuine respect and liking for each other, exchanging warm personal communications, portraits of their wives and, in the case of Pottinger's son Frederick, an offer for adoption and a suggestion that the boy be renamed Frederick Keying Pottinger.[11]

All this came about when Qiying visited Hong Kong in June 1843 to seal the treaty arrangements that would bring a fraught period of hostilities to a final end the following October:

> Afterwards a dinner was given by the Governor. Fifty people were present and ended by most of the Celestials getting drunk, Keying amongst their number, who sung a Chinese love-ditty . . . The Celestials were delighted with their entertainment. Keying said he should like to see Sir Henry Pottinger's legs under his table at Pekin . . .[12]

Just like us in short, chaps ready for a boozy evening round the dinner table and some high jinks while the port decanter was doing its rounds.

His visit was a huge success, was attended with much celebration and banqueting and, upon departure, quite unprecedented displays of emotion and warmth—fierce embraces and parting tears no less. Much the same is true of Qiying's subsequent visit to the new British colony in autumn 1845, early in the governorship of Sir John Davis, who appears to have been less susceptible to Qiying's advances than Sir Henry.

But despite Sir John's comparative *froideur*, Qiying's final visit to Hong Kong appears to have been carried off with as much éclat as his first. The general flavour of his reputation is extremely well shown in the contemporary diary kept by Edward Cree, a surgeon in the Royal Navy serving in the steam-paddle sloop HMS *Vixen*, which had brought Qiying to Hong Kong from Whampoa. The diary is illustrated *inter alia* by a sketch of Qiying embracing the diminutive British admiral, Sir Thomas Cochrane, in farewell:[13] a charming, though perhaps slightly misleading, vignette of a supposed entente cordiale, brought about by a man who understood which way the tides of history were flowing, but which was probably nothing of the sort.

Fairbank not surprisingly makes the point that 'the foreign community's regard for Ch'i-ying as their patron made him a temporary vogue. A few months later the "spacious and commodious premises" of a new British hotel on Queen's Road were christened "Keying House." In December of 1846 the famous Chinese junk *Keying* . . . sailed for England'.[14] And so the *Keying* takes her place as part of the new Hong Kong's happy conviction that right was on the British side, that China had recognized its own backwardness and the tutelary status that this implied, and that Qiying himself was the symbol of this new dawn. What better name to give the junk that was to be the embodied emissary of these new understandings on the River Thames at London?

Of course, this may offer another reason why the Chinese crew's views on the change of name might not have been sought. For while Qiying's standing was high in British eyes, his reputation among the average Cantonese denizens of waterfront and street was less secure. Bringing a destructive war to an end was undoubtedly in the average Cantonese person's interest. Doing so in a manner which seemed to cede to the British all that they demanded was less popular, especially among the rank and file of the inhabitants of Canton (Guangzhou) and its surrounding villages, for whom a visceral hatred of the British had taken root in the aftermath of the First Opium War.[15] This popular attitude would serve as a reason for the Chinese authorities' refusal to open Canton to Westerners, in accordance with the provisions of the Treaty of Nanjing, until the issue was finally forced by the Second Opium War. It must be admitted, however, that whether any sense of this different view of the commissioner had penetrated the aura of self-satisfaction of Hong Kong's British community is moot.

Given what happened in the course of the junk's voyage and its final fate, the symbolic choice of name was in most respects more apt than may first have been intended. Not only had Qiying fallen from favour by 1848 and in 1850 been demoted to a fifth-rank mandarin. Not did he finally fail to corral the rambunctious foreigners and as a result have to take his own life. But Qiying's actual feelings towards the British were perhaps less warm than his outer behaviour had suggested when Charles Kellett and his fellow investors concluded that the commissioner was their sort of man.

This became apparent in 1858, after the outbreak of the Second Opium War, in the early negotiations for ending which Qiying had been called out of retirement. In the storming of Canton in 1857, documents had been seized from the *yamen* of the governor-general, Ye Mingchen (葉名琛); among these papers was a memorial, written by Qiying thirteen years previously. In it, he explicitly described what had appeared to men like Pottinger as gestures of genuine friendship as instead deliberate ruses to pacify otherwise unruly and unregenerate barbarians: 'with this type of people from outside the bounds of civilization

. . . if we adhered to the proper forms in official documents and let them be weighed according to the status of superior and inferior . . . truly it would be of no advantage in the essential business of subduing and conciliating them.'[16]

In portraying himself as having duped Sir Henry Pottinger, given Chinese accusations that he was far too cosy with the British and had conceded too much, poor Qiying may have been trying to save his face with the emperor. But whatever the truth, it was a similar divide in fundamental ways of seeing and being which may have given rise to the difficulties the *Keying*'s crew faced, as they prosecuted their long and arduous voyage. Charles Kellett and his colleagues thought they were heading to London to demonstrate the backwardness of China,[17] and the advent of a new dawn thanks to feats of British arms; they thought they sailed under the aegis of Qiying and with the willing support of their 'native' crew. The truth, as with comparative British and Chinese understandings of the outcome of the First Opium War, was rather different. There is much in a name.

Chapter 3
The Crew and the Voyage to New York

All Things Are Ready, If Our Mind Be So[1]

The *Keying* was sailed by a motley crew. Looked at from a 'top-down' European perspective, there were three European officers (Captain Kellett; G. Burton, mate; Edward Revett, second mate), possibly twelve other Europeans, fourteen if we include Douglas Lapraik and T. A. Lane, and possibly thirty, more probably forty, Chinese crewmen.[2] The latter were under their Chinese captain, So Yin Sang Hsi, from the point of view of the day-to-day operation of the ship, which is where an alternative 'bottom-up' way of seeing the ship's organization comes in, although one to which Western maritime law was entirely blind.

It is this fundamental difference in how the sailors from the respective traditions saw their relationships and their roles that would seem to lie at the root of all that followed. We can catch a trace of this in both *Account* and *Description*, especially the former, where what must have been quite normal Chinese shipboard conduct is described in terms of shock:

> These Chinamen . . . will, however, occasionally skulk from duty. Oftentimes two or three would decline work, which would have to be performed by some one more industrious. The one so employed, however, would use no harsh language to his compatriots.

And again,

> One evening a noise was heard below by Capt. Kellett, and on inquiry, he found the tiller had been deserted in a severe blow, and some of the crew were endeavouring to persuade the delinquent to return to his duty, for fear the vessel might broach to . . .

Table 1 The Itinerary

Date	Event
1846	
19 October	Left Canton
6 December	Left Hong Kong
1847	
26 January	Exited Sunda Strait
30 March	Passed Cape of Good Hope
17 to 23 April	St. Helena
8 May	Crossed Equator (in $17°40'$W)
9 July	Arrived in New York
November	Departed New York
18 November	Arrived in Boston
1848	
17 February	Departed Boston
15 to 25 March	St. Aubin's Bay, Jersey
28 March	Gravesend
(*possible visit to Antwerp, Belgium*)	
1853	
May	Departed London River
14 May	Arrived River Mersey
29 September	End of Active Life
1855	
6 December	Hulk (Tranmere Ferry)

At sunset, the Ty Kong or Managing man, used quietly to lower three reefs to the fore mainsail, and entirely lower the mizzen. All the crew would then go to their cabin, leaving the helmsman alone on deck. At midnight a supper was prepared, when the sleepers were awakened. A long yarn would be spun while they were eating, and after the meal was despatched, the helm would be relieved, and the men would go to their berths again. This slack system was, however, finally reformed, after some slight objections.

There, in a nutshell, we have a fundamental clash of maritime cultures. On the one hand, the relaxed, collegial world of the traditional trading junk with practices that were probably fairly similar to those of European trading craft in times before the complexities of larger ships dictated a more regimented, hierarchical system. On the other is the Western system, to which any such generous, collegial, easy-driving ways appeared to be mere slackness. It also highlights a problematic issue of authority. Who was in charge of whom?

The puzzle here is the role of the Chinese 'captain', from the point of view of mid-nineteenth-century Western maritime law. The case that was brought against the *Keying* by some of its crew in New York revealed much about the incapacity of Western maritime law to see that this might have been a matter at issue. If we only consider as germane the *Keying*'s status as a Chinese ship with a Chinese crew, then So Yin Sang Hsi was, vis-à-vis Charles Kellett and the owners, a sub-contractor. Thus he was responsible for finding, signing on and directing the crew, in addition to whatever responsibilities he bore. But whatever the practices whereby Chinese crew were acquired in Hong Kong and their shipboard life on a junk ordered, insofar as the *Keying* was considered a British ship in practice, So Yin Sang Hsi could not have been legally responsible for signing on and paying the Chinese crew nor for the operation of the ship at sea. That was the sole and ultimate responsibility of the ship's captain.

We have the names of twenty-six of the crew from the New York court record, though exactly what those names would be in modern *jyutping*, leave alone in written Chinese, is impossible to determine. Given that the court record states they were signed on in Whampoa (黃埔區)—the area that foreign sailors frequented being known colloquially as Bambootown[3]—it is possible that Charles Kellett found himself dealing with, in effect, two Chinese crews. One would have been the crew that came with the vessel and had signed on in Whampoa. The other would have been any supplementary crew that So Yin Sang Hsi had signed on in Hong Kong.

Whatever the various modalities of recruitment, the crew were quite fairly paid. The court record of the plaint made in New York notes their actual average daily wage was $7.19. This is consonant with Asiatic Articles' rates of some two-thirds of what contemporary Western seamen were paid.[4]

That the crew was pretty diverse can be gathered from one news story that appeared in the Western press as the *Keying* was readying for its voyage. This reported that the crew included a 'regular *corps dramatique*, with their tailor, property man, &c'.[5] There is no clue as to whether these were Whampoa or Hong Kong-garnered, but, clearly, if there is any truth in this, the Chinese crew will have included quite a few whose nautical skills would have been close to zero, and of whom little could have been expected.

Where So Yin Sang Hsi stood as between these two crews, if two there were, is extremely difficult to determine. The only evidence we have describes the twenty-six disaffected crew in New York, so the different provenance of the other dozen or so is conjecture. However, they do seem to have been loyal to Kellett and So: by inference, allowing for the further departures we know took place in Boston, some at least stayed aboard to form the nucleus of the 'show' when the *Keying* was in London. We also know that at least one of these Chinese crewmen returned to China. That at least suggests that their sense of obligation was different to that of Hia Siang, Sim Agu, Ung Ti, Ling Chensi, Kho Sing Thiam, Lia Lai, Lei Na Kung, Khor Per Le, Lip Hap, Chin Ten Yeng, Tam Sam Seng, Ung Tian Yong, Chein A Tai, Yer A Chin, Lim A Lee, Go Bun Hap, Che Va A Sa, Chi Va A Chan, Lim Tai Chong, Tan A Lak, Chia A Soey, Ong A Hiong, Chien A Te, Kho Te Sun, Ung A Cong and Sio A Chiok—the twenty-six who sued and left in New York.

It is likely that So played the traditional role of *batou* (把頭, gang boss), though whether for all the crew from both Canton and Hong Kong is unclear.[6] As such, he could normally be expected to find a crew that spoke a common dialect and shared a common cuisine, thereby greatly simplifying life aboard.[7] It follows that if he had been faced with crew members he did not recruit, and who as a result did not share such common traits, then his position on board must have been awkward, in two possible senses.

If not all the crew was of a single provenance, So may not have wielded the same authority across the whole crew. That this is probable is indicated not only by the different ports where sailors may have been recruited, but also by the names of some of the twenty-six who sought the arrest of the *Keying* in New York. Two at least (Che Va A Sa, Chi Va A Chan) have names that suggest a Vietnamese-Chinese background, though given romanizations of Chinese in the mid-nineteenth century, this is not a very robust inference. Insofar as it holds water, it reinforces the thought that a key factor in establishing a coherent ship's company along traditional Chinese lines was absent.

Second, from So's point of view and that of the crew, he was almost certainly the master of the ship in any accepted nautical sense of the word. That is, he was the man who took charge of handling the ship at sea, agreed with the crew what to do and was looked to by the crew as the source of authority. From the European officers' point of view, however, and in the eyes of the law, So would have served and could only have served as the *ty cong* (probably 頭工, *tougong*)—crewmaster would be a fair translation.[8]

The traditional Anglo-Indian term for So's position would have been *tindal*, *serang* or boatswain.[9] It follows that there were, at the outset, implicit difficulties with crew harmony and a mutually accepted chain of command. Whatever the rights and wrongs of the formal documentation, it would obviously have required great social and cross-cultural skill on the part of the very young Charles Kellett—almost certainly monoglot and not, we can safely assume, intensely interested in Chinese culture and folkways—to weld his disparate crew into a whole united by a common purpose.

There is also the possibility that So in practice 'came with' Charles Kellett, not with the *Keying*. This line of thought makes intuitive sense, tallies with how Westerners ran 'native'-crewed vessels in Asian waters and explains So's fidelity while the *Keying* was in New York.

This kind of relationship and the system it served is clearly and beautifully expressed in the novels of Joseph Conrad, in particular those featuring Tom Lingard, the central character in *Almayer's Folly* (1895), *An Outcast of the Islands* (1896) and *The Rescue* (1920), with their narrative theme of Lingard's misplaced good intentions and his 'benevolent despotism'.[10] As we learn from the opening chapter of *The Rescue*, the last of the trilogy written but the first narrative in Lingard's story, there were two European officers on the brig *Lightning*, the master, Tom Lingard, and the chief mate, Shaw. But the ship was crewed by lascars who answered to their 'boss', the *tindal* or *serang*, Haji Wasub. The *serang* was Tom Lingard's man and spoke sufficient pidgin—the lingua franca of the Asian maritime world—to ensure clarity in the chain of command.

It is therefore possible, even probable, that Charles Kellett and So Yin Sang Hsi had sailed together before, and that they knew each other's ways, like Tom Lingard and Haji Wasub, the person who formed the vital interface between him and his non-English-speaking crew.

We get a sharp flavour of the European officers' probable attitudes in Conrad's brief but dazzlingly clear summary of the mate Shaw's attitude to the Malay crew:[11]

as the chief mate of the brig . . . He felt himself immeasurably superior to the Malay seamen whom he had to handle, and treated them with lofty toleration, notwithstanding his opinion that at a pinch those chaps would be found emphatically 'not there'.

We also catch a glimpse of reciprocal attitudes in an exchange between the Malay helmsman, Sali, and Haji Wasub, after Shaw has glanced round the horizon with a telescope and declared, as the sun set and he and Tom Lingard went below for dinner, that there was nothing in sight:

'I am Sali, and my eyes are better than the bewitched brass thing that pulls out to a great length,' said the pertinacious helmsman. 'There was a boat, just clear of the easternmost island. There was a boat, and they in her could see the ship on the light of the west—unless they are blind men lost on the sea. I have seen her. Have you seen her, too, O Haji Wasub?'

'Am I a fat white man?' snapped the serang. 'I was a man of the sea before you were born O Sali! The order is to keep silence and mind the rudder, lest evil befall the ship.'

... Thus, with a forced and tense watchfulness, Haji Wasub, serang of the brig Lightning, kept the captain's watch unwearied and wakeful, a slave to duty.[12]

The relationship between Lingard and his *serang*—and in a far wider sense that between European officers and their highly experienced and skilled but non-European, non-English-speaking crew throughout this period—is succinctly expressed in an exchange they have about the boat that Sali had seen and Lingard and Shaw had not:

'*Serang!*' he called, half aloud.

The spare old man ran up the ladder so smartly that his bony feet did not seem to touch the steps. He stood by his commander, his hands behind his back; a figure indistinct but straight as an arrow.

'Who was looking out?' asked Lingard.

'Badroon, the Bugis,' said Wasub, in his crisp, jerky manner.

'I can hear nothing. Badroon heard a noise in his mind.'

'The night hides the boat.'

'Have you seen it?'

'Yes, Tuan. Small boat. Before sunset. By the land. Now coming here— near. Badroon heard him.'

'Why didn't you report it, then?' asked Lingard, sharply.

'*Malim* spoke. He said: "Nothing there," while I could see. How could I know what was in his mind or yours, Tuan?'[13]

Indeed how could Haji Wasub admit he had such privileged access to Tom Lingard's mind without fatally undermining the authority relations on which the *Lightning*'s chain of command precariously rested—as did the chain of command of the whole colonial order?

In addition to the working crew under So Yin Sang Hsi, there were two super-numerary crew members. One—of whom we know no corroborated detail and of whom all subsequent trace seems to have been lost—was the ship's artist, Sam Shing. The other, in effect and possibly in fact a passenger, was someone claiming to be a fifth-rank mandarin. This was He Sing (also Hesing, or in modern *jyutping* He Xing) as to whose entitlement to his claimed rank there are some doubts.[14] Of He Sing we do hear further, but finally he too drops out of the record as if he had never been there. However, when considering the events in New York, it is worth noting that both of these persons stayed with the ship; it is wholly improbable that both were unaware of the ship's destination as it left Hong Kong. This in turn urges caution over any tendency to accept uncritically the story told by the disaffected crewmen in the New York court.

However, if He Sing was responsible for the Chinese in the London *Description*, he may have been over-egging the cake with respect to his background, not least with respect to his own name, as given in characters with his portrait in the *Description* and on the commemorative medal struck by Halliday. In modern pinyin, it is Xi Sheng; in written Chinese, 希生. That would be 'Hei Saang' in Cantonese. However, Xi (希) is almost unknown as a family name in China and 生 is also an unusual given name.[15] The characters may well have been chosen, as with Qiying's name, solely for their phonetic value. In the Cantonese world, it is probable that the gentleman's name was Ho Shing, 何勝. Sadly, we shall never know the answer.

If what the twenty-six hands affirmed at the New York court hearing is correct,[16] then the crew were misled as to the nature of the voyage, if not in every minute detail. A duration of eight months is what we learn Kellett signed them on for, with *The Chinese Repository* reporting Singapore or Batavia (Jakarta) as destinations. In addition, the crew were to be free to leave the ship once it reached its destination, as well as to have their passages back to Canton paid.[17] That, at least, is one interpretation. In fact, the pleading in New York was not so clear-cut:[18]

> That they were shipped as mariners at Whampoa, near Canton, in China,
> in a certain vessel called a Chinese junk, bearing the name Keying, now
> lying in the port of New York, by one Kellet [*sic*], who is assumed to be the
> master thereof, for a voyage to Batavia or Singapore, for sugar or opium,
> and then to Chusan, or any other port, but the voyage was to continue only
> eight months, after which they were to continue with the ship or not, as
> they pleased; and whatever port they went to, they were to be sent back
> to Canton or Whampoa by the said Kellet, as master of the said vessel,
> who was to pay all their expenses in such foreign ports. That they were so
> shipped on the fourteenth day of September last, by a written contract,
> which was retained by said Kellet.

It seems fairly clear from this that Kellett did not claim the voyage was *only*
headed to Batavia or Singapore. These ports and Chusan[19] were mentioned, but
so—perhaps with deliberate dissimulation, perhaps not—was 'any other port' to
which the *Keying* might go within eight months.

This phrasing is ambivalent: implying either any other port in China or the
China Seas or any other port at all that could be reached in eight months' voyaging from Hong Kong. Reading this in the second sense, the terms have all the
air of standard catch-all language, covering a couple of fairly standard voyages
plus the possibility that further and other passages to other destinations might be
possible within the time frame.

More to the point, it is stated—hardly surprisingly—that the articles signed
by the Chinese crew were in Chinese.[20] We can be absolutely sure that none of
the Europeans in the crew, or among the lead investors whose names we know,
wrote or read Chinese. In their relations with the Chinese crew, they are likely to
have got by with pidgin, for those who understood it—probably So, one or two
of his leading hands, Sam Shing and He Sing—and gesture, shouting, red faces,
shoves and kicks, for those who did not.

We can also be fairly sure that most of the Chinese crew were illiterate. It
seems therefore possible that the Chinese articles which the crew were asked
to sign were a 'standard' set of articles used in the regional trade, referring to
what later generations of seamen referred to as the 'little triangle' (that is, the
South China Sea), because no other standard-issue Chinese-language contracts
referred to anywhere else. In such contracts, 'or any other port' was put in as a
catch-all, in case for one reason or another it was necessary to stray out of the
'little triangle' because that's where the available cargos led.

No doubt something like this was perfectly normal, if from a strictly legal point of view regrettable. The old saw springs to mind, that it is no defence of a bad law that its executors have good intentions. But the probability is that no one thought twice about it because 90 percent of voyages went off with no problems, so no court ever got to have a close reading of the articles seamen had signed. These were days before the increasingly complex rules and regulations governing all aspects of shipping had taken a firm hold globally. It was especially the case in the fluid world of the China coast, where everyone was playing the system to maximize profits and advantages and minimize costs and restrictions.

There are two things worth pondering when trying to evaluate this rather confusing state of affairs. One is that eight months was a perfectly reasonable duration for a voyage intended to reach European waters from Hong Kong. Wise's account[21] gives the average of 100 Indiamen's voyages to 114 days—four months, give or take a day or so. Insofar as Charles Kellett was allowing twice that time for the *Keying* to make the voyage—for he is unlikely to have had any exact sense as to its probable performance vis-à-vis Western craft—he was being both fair and realistic. In any case, the Asiatic Articles, already legally established, were shortly to set a one-year limit on any voyage embarked on by Asian (Indian, Southeast Asian and Chinese) crew; an implicit time limit was already widely understood.

Even so, it is not exactly clear how far the letter of Asiatic Articles would have been applied in Hong Kong, especially on a junk for a junk's Chinese crew. But as a fairly typical British ship's master of the era, Charles Kellett would have been extremely unlikely to have signed his Chinese crew aboard on any other terms than those already in force for lascars. It was widely believed that non-European crew could not perform as did Europeans—paying the same for their services would have made no sense.

The 1823 Merchant Shipping Act[22] put lascars, which category included Chinese seamen, in the lowest category of maritime labour, giving them less pay, worse accommodation and a different and usually less generous diet. It also meant that on a British ship headed for Britain, the sailors could *not* be signed or paid off on arrival in Britain. The terms of the act—precisely aimed at ensuring that lascar seamen did not remain in Britain—required that any lascars signed aboard were to be repatriated to their signing-on port, either aboard the ship that signed them on or by passage on another ship, to be paid for by the original ship's owners or charterers. In short, the articles the *Keying* sailors signed would appear to have been perfectly consonant with the provisions of extant British maritime law.[23] Whether the *Keying* also provided the Chinese sailors with two pairs of jackets and trousers, mittens, caps, shoes and bedding composed of three pairs of blankets sewn together—the regulation provision for East Indiamen—is more doubtful.[24] In short, all that the content of the articles revealed by the New York court indicates is that the *Keying*'s backers operated within existing British shipping law.

In addition, it was quite commonplace for a Western tramping voyage to wander from port to port, entirely as a function of the cargos the captain might find, and take anything up to four years to complete the voyage; it was thus impossible at the outset to list all the ports where the ship might call, bar, probably, the first. From what we know of articles as applied to Asian seamen, that sort of extended voyage was not possible, there being a clear time limit placed; in that, Kellett had clearly conformed to legal norms. Where ports of call were concerned, however, the record from New York makes it quite plain that a voyage beyond Asian waters was not necessarily ruled out, though a charge of deliberately misleading ambiguity would be hard to disprove.

At this remove, lacking detailed knowledge of how exactly the business of a ship's articles in Chinese for a Hong Kong-owned Chinese vessel was managed in Hong Kong in 1846, it is impossible to go further.

But there are clearly grounds for scepticism about innocents aboard being duped by an unscrupulous and colonialist British ship's master—grounds more extensive than comma-hunting in the crew's articles. For the *Keying* spent something like seven weeks in Hong Kong before setting out. Little of what happened during that time would support the idea, even in the dimmest crewman, that the ship was venturing forth on no more than a standard trading voyage from Hong Kong to the Archipelago and back, with sugar and opium for a cargo.

Both Kellett and So Yin Sang Hsi quite reasonably made this point in New York, claiming that the crewmen must have known that the destination was Europe because of Canton and Hong Kong waterfront gossip, as the project was public news. One can take a different view of course. Given European-Chinese relations in Hong Kong in the 1840s, perhaps the *Keying*'s crew was untouched by what others plainly knew. But the world of Hong Kong's waterfront in the 1840s was, like most contemporary waterfronts, polyglot. As already noted, the *Keying* had to be prepared and loaded. Moreover, the Chinese denizens of both the Hong Kong and Whampoa waterfronts would have been no innocent and gullible rubes. They are likely to have been pretty tough nuts who had been flouting Chinese regulations for many years; if not serving on Western-controlled ships, they were people at least aware of Western ways.[25]

Consider the general views as to the average quality of European and Chinese denizens of the Hong Kong waterfront in 1846. John M. Carroll cites a number of sources from the early days of Hong Kong, all of whom seemed unanimous in their views that both average European and Chinese members of the population were rogues unhung. The Canton authorities were thought to be exporting to Hong Kong 'every thief, pirate and idle or worthless vagabond'. Others comment that Hong Kong's Chinese population represented on average the 'lowest dregs of native society', 'of the lowest condition and character', 'thieves and robbers', while the European population were 'outlaws, deserters, reckless adventurers and speculators', 'scapegoats and scoundrels from the purlieus of London, creatures that only missed Botany Bay by good fortune'.[26] Allowing for hyperbole, it is difficult to swallow any claim that a crew drawn from such a waterfront—for even the crew signed on in Whampoa will have known Hong Kong's reputation and the extent to which they were both breaking Chinese law and, in consorting with the foreigners, being unscrupulous traitors—were poor, duped innocents taken advantage of by wicked British colonials.

More to the point, before the ship left, it was visited by Hong Kong governor, His Excellency Sir John Francis Davis, Bt., and Rear Admiral Sir Thomas John Cochrane, Kt., CB, the commander-in-chief of the China Station and 'all the Officers of the Fleet'. It seems unlikely that even the rawest Chinese deckhand in 1840s Hong Kong would not have asked why such great *fan kwae* dignitaries would visit a ship bound merely on a regular trading voyage to the Malay Archipelago and maybe afterwards to China. And a trading voyage, furthermore, which entailed the loading of no cargo in Whampoa or Hong Kong of the sort that might be carried to either Batavia or Singapore. For their ship was carrying only a fairly small collection of Chinese artefacts for which, if as is possible they were old hands in the *nanyang* trade, they would have been perfectly well aware there could be no demand, the items clearly being used rather than new and of a kind that could be found aplenty in the Chinese communities in the places they were purportedly going.

The First Leg

Smooth Sailing at First

The opening run down the South China Sea was a fair performance, but one on which—from a chance remark at a lecture two years later in London by T. A. Lane[27]—the first glimmerings of the larger crewing problem came to the surface. Charles Kellett and the mates, Messrs. Burton and Revett, had probably been in Hong Kong in connection with the opium trade and were therefore creatures of the hard-driven, disciplined opium ships.[28] It was a maritime world in stark contrast to that of Chinese junks, where a concern for conservative sailing and a remarkably democratic, indeed almost anarchic, approach to shipboard organization prevailed.

Given Kellett and Lane's descriptions of the first days out of Hong Kong, when the Chinese crew presumed *their* rules would operate and the *Keying* was sailed by one man under reduced canvas at night, the attempted imposition of hard driving ways must have been a shock. The South China Sea at the height of the northeast monsoon can be a tough stretch of water; given that the Chinese crew will have been more familiar with handling a junk than the Europeans, it seems likely that the more conservative approach prevailed, since the average speed made to Selat Gelasa was quite slow.

We know the *Keying* left Hong Kong on 6 December 1846, was in or near Selat Gelasa on 25 December and cleared the Sunda Strait on 26 January the next year. That gives a total elapsed time from leaving Hong Kong to clearing the strait of 50–51 days. The main part of the voyage—Hong Kong to Selat Gelasa— thus took 19 days; the *Keying* spent the next four and a half weeks (31–32 days) working through light airs, sailing by day and anchoring at night. This is inaccurately described by contemporary newspapers as waiting at anchor for six weeks for a favourable wind.[29] Thus, the first 1,950 nautical miles were sailed at an average of only 4.2 knots.[30] This was fairly slow sailing on the back of the

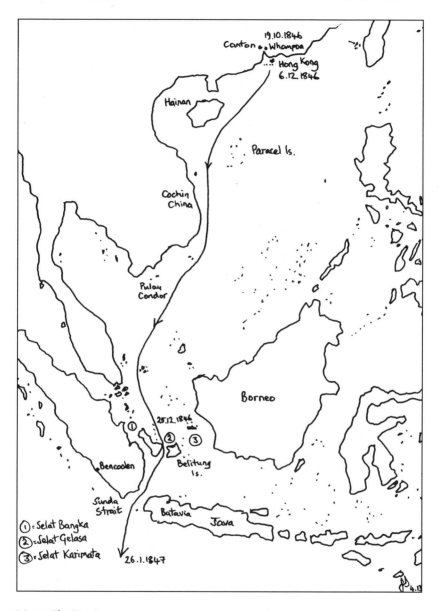

Map 2 The First Leg

northeast-turning-northwest monsoon[31] at its peak. The probability is that better speed was made over the first 1,200 to 1,400 nautical miles until near the latitude of Singapore and that the average was then hard hit by a slower passage thereafter.

A look at the pilot chart[32] for the month of January shows why this was a fairly modest initial performance. In the South China Sea north of about 10°N, for 75 to 85 percent of the time, winds blow steadily and freshly (force 4 to 5 and, in the northern part, often 6 to 7) from the east to northeast. Since the course was a long curve with the wind coming over the starboard quarter—almost every type of sailing rig's optimum point of sail—that means that any vessel, even one not very competently sailed, would have enough wind from the right direction to make close to its best speed. As the junk passed around 12°N latitude, the winds will have backed more northeast to northerly and begun easing, so that as the *Keying* got to the Equator the wind will have been mainly north around force 3, backing further and easing north to northwest, force 2–3 or, as she found to her distress, a lot less, when she closed the northern entrance to the Selat Gelasa or, as it was known at the time, the Gaspar Strait.

That is the simple view. Life aboard may have been rather less easy-going than this rapid description of a swift passage may suggest. The mid-twentieth-century narratives of Jose Maria Tey and Brian Clifford give a real taste of what making down the central part of the South China Sea, chased by the full-strength northeast monsoon, can be like.

> At three o'clock in the morning of January 18th the sea was rougher still, with waves twelve to fifteen feet high. The wind went on rising. The anemometer showed a speed of 31 knots, the equivalent of 7 on the Beaufort Scale. The waves kept washing over the deck. The water had to be pumped out of the hold continually. The tiller was too much for one man alone. It needed two ... We longed for daylight and thought of nothing else ... Dawn came ... Our tired eyes gazed with horror on the fury of the sea ... From the stern the waves looked like mountains ... They caught the junk and threw her around like a feather ... The day wore on. Wind and sea grew rougher and rougher. The waves were from twenty to thirty feet high and the wind was up to 10 on the Beaufort Scale (50 to 60 miles per hour) ... We could not move around at all without gripping very tightly to things ...[33]

Brian Clifford's account of a December voyage in 1961 in the *Golden Lotus* is even more dramatic. Steering just as the *Keying* did, with tackles to a tiller and in similarly boisterous weather as the *Rubia* experienced, the junk broke its tiller. Heavy swells rolling up from aft, typical of a fully developed northeast monsoon slewed the junk around; the strains on the Borneo teak (*yacal*)[34] tiller were too much. It broke. The replacement tiller, fitted with much difficulty, also came under great strain with the weather. When it broke and a hastily repaired first one was slotted back into its place, it was clear that continuing on course was not possible. Soon, the only recourse was to heave to and take the strain off the overworked steering system. The difficulties caused by the heavy weather continued until Clifford realized, from a sun sight he had snatched for his noon position, that the junk was in danger of drifting onto the Paracels (Xisha Liedao). After being nearly swept overboard by a rogue wave, Clifford decided to alter course towards Manila to seek refuge. He discovered, as we shall see Charles Kellett did, that junks do not work to weather, even when the wind is only just forward of the beam:

> At noon the next day—the sixth out from Hong Kong—my sight showed that . . . although we were sailing as close into the wind as we could we were still being swept so strongly by the current that our actual course was well to the south of the course we were steering. We were trying to make a course just east of south-east, but we were travelling south-south-east.

It got worse. By the next day, the best the *Golden Lotus* could manage was slightly west of south. The shallows and resulting chaotic seas of the Macclesfield Bank were directly under her lee. The *Golden Lotus* made it through the gap between the Paracels and the Macclesfield Bank and altered course again towards Singapore as they had at last made enough southing to have found easier winds and more benign seas. It was a fairly hellish seven days.[35]

It is not clear which route the *Keying* took from Hong Kong to its destination. Depending on Charles Kellett and his officers' confidence in their navigation—we do not know what chronometers or instruments they carried aboard—they had a choice. They could have gone direct and sailed the shortest route. However, that is not very likely. Much the most probable choice was the old sailing ship route.

The old route had been used for centuries in the *nanyang* trade as by East Indiamen since the seventeenth century. It ran generally southwest down the coast of Guangdong, passing close along the south coast of Hainan before, about the longitude of Yalong Bay (present-day Sanya), heading south-south-west towards the easternmost point of the coast of Vietnam near Da Nang, whence south to the ancient turning point of Pulau Condor (Dao Con Son). This route ensured a safe passage to leeward of the Paracels (Xisha), the graveyard of many, many ships over the centuries. From Pulau Condor, vessels aimed for Pulau Tioman or Pulau Aur off the east coast of present-day Malaysia, in order to pass clear north of the Anambas and Natuna islands. This also gave ships a reliable position check before they turned to head south towards the tricky approaches to the three straits—Selat Karimata (Karimata Straits), Selat Gelasa (Gaspar Straits) and Selat Bangka (Bangka Straits)—through one of which ships must pass to get to the offing of the Sunda Strait.

Each strait had its perils. Selat Karimata because it is longer and there are the dangers of having the low, coral-girt coast of Belitung under one's lee with its sprinkle of ill-charted islets spreading well to windward. Selat Gelasa because of the great dangers both of the northern approaches, of the strait itself and of the exit, which have been a graveyard no doubt since before the Batu Hitam wreck foundered in the tenth century. And, finally, Selat Bangka, an unlikely choice because of its length, strong tides, narrow, tortuous passage and ever-present danger of pirates. Charles Kellett chose the most direct, though navigationally most challenging route through Selat Gelasa.[36]

Charles Kellett is likely to have used as his 'bible' James Horsburgh's famous *India Directory*.[37] It would have been a very bold or foolhardy mariner who decided to disregard the sage's advice:

> SHIPS BOUND from CHINA to the Straits of Caspar, Banca, or Singapore, ought in March and April to adopt the Outer Passage by the Macclesfield Bank, which is the most expeditious route in these months, keeping to the Eastward at leaving China, and also in passing Pulo Sapata they ought to borrow towards the shoals, where the winds are more favourable in these months than farther to the westward. In April, the Vansittart, by keeping about 3 degrees more to the eastward than the Herefordshire, made as much progress in one day as the latter did in ten. At all other times, the Inner Passage by the coast of Cochin-China seems preferable. This is the shortest route, and the ease afforded to ships, by steering from the Grand Ladrone immediately before the wind, when blowing strong at N. Eastward, is a great advantage: whereas, by the Outer Passage, a S. S. E. course is steered for the Macclesfield Bank, often bringing the wind and sea before the beam, which strains a deeply laden ship.
>
> Many have strained so much, that, in order to gain upon the pumps, they were forced to bear away for the Inner Passage; others, by persevering

in the Outer Passage, have laboured excessively, and some of them at last foundered with their crews; some of the ships which, after leaving China, have been missing, have probably suffered from the same cause. Had those ships, at leaving Canton River, steered S. S.W. ½ W., or S. S.W. ¼ W., the direct course for the Inner Passage, they probably would not have strained in the least, but have reached their ports of destination in safety.

Horsburgh goes on to quote an endorsement of his recommendation, which adds that the opium clipper captains were of the same mind:

> Captain Blake, of H. M. S. *Larne*, adding to his own experience that of several commanders of the 'opium clippers', gives the following remarks.
>
> 'In beating against or running with the strength of the monsoon up or down the China Sea, ships should always pass to leeward of the Paracel Islands and shoals . . . on account of the invariable set of the current to leeward . . . In running down the China Sea with the North-east Monsoon, the direct line mostly adopted is nearly mid-channel between Hainan and the Paracels, holding rather to the latter, where a southerly current of 30, 40, and 50 miles a day is usual, and between 14° and 11° N, I have known it reach 60 miles in the twenty-four hours. Thence making the coast of Cochin-China about Varela, and shaping a course southward, so as to pass 30 or 40 miles outside of Pulo Sapata, from whence the course to Singapore is clear, giving the Anambas a berth of about 40 miles, and always, if possible, sighting Pulo Aor, to ensure the reckoning; more especially should the weather be thick, when the lead should be constantly attended to.'

More modern routes—trusting in compass, sextant, chronometer and the excellent British Admiralty and East India Company charts that by 1840 had been on sale to the public for a generation—are more direct and hence quicker. They are also more hazardous, and require a very good knowledge of one's position and a confidence in that knowledge. The nearly 100-nautical-mile passage between the Paracels and Macclesfield Bank that Horsburgh thought feasible for the quieter months of March and April looks rather wide on the chart. As Brian Clifford's experience shows, it was not if the northeast monsoon is boisterous, one has not had a position for a couple of days and the currents are unknown. The twentieth-century narratives of both the *Rubia* and the *Golden Lotus* are clear testimony to the risks. If one then continues direct without sighting Pulau Condor, supposing one has successfully threaded one's way through the Paracels/Macclesfield gap, to run on and pass successfully between the Anambas and the Natunas Islands requires supreme confidence—and, with an untried crew on a junk's steering gear and a mid-nineteenth-century steering compass, not a little luck.

Kellett may have had that confidence and belief in his luck, unambiguous though the advice of Horsburgh clearly was. If he had been so foolhardy—which given his seamanship is unlikely—his intention was not likely to have been shared by the Chinese captain on whose good will and help he and his fellow Europeans in the crew depended. So Yin Sang Hsi, like most experienced Chinese captains, will have been a traditional Chinese navigator. He may have used a Chinese junk skipper's route book, examples of which, compiled by their owners, we know existed and were widely used,[38] but he is likely, in addition, to have been a walking repository of orally transmitted knowledge, of courses and timings for a variety of traditional routes, that went back half a millennium and more. Any attempt by Charles Kellett to take a route which did not fit with this vast cumulation of traditional knowledge would have been a very difficult 'sell'. The probability is that the route taken to the Sunda Strait was a traditional one and hence rather longer than the direct route that fully equipped European steamships of the 1870s later took.[39] The longer traditional route would have been much the same distance as cited above—perhaps 100 miles or so longer—but nothing that would have added materially to the length of the passage.

Slow Progress and Problems

Now will have come the long and anxious working through Selat Gelasa and its many dangers, and on down the Bangka Island and Sumatra coasts in light airs. And then the equally slow work to transit Sunda Strait. There are two aspects of this stage of the voyage, neither fully documented, but at the very least probable, that are worth considering at some length.

The *Keying* evidently found light airs once it had passed the Riau and Lingga islands:

> While working towards the Sunda straits, after getting in with the coast of Sumatra, the vessel was occasionally brought to anchor. It being day and night work and different from what was usually customary, the men began to be a little refractory . . .[40]

On the following page, we read that it took the *Keying* at least five days to work through the Sunda Strait. In the meantime, we also learn that this was a moment when the gap between the world of the Western mariner and that of the Chinese crew was revealed to be as wide as it really was. For as soon as the *Keying* slowed down and the men waxed 'refractory', the Western crew closed ranks, presumed a plot to pirate the ship and armed themselves.

It is probably this instantaneous separation into two mutually suspicious camps, and the inevitable inefficiencies it must have brought in its train, that explains the four and a half weeks it took to work the ship just 400 miles or so. To move faster would have required the team-work needed to sail a ship through light airs, with its constant trimming and re-trimming of the sails. That sort of co-operation would have been an early victim of a rupture in already strained crew relations, especially since the skilled knowledge to trim a junk sail optimally to the wind would have been the preserve of the Chinese sailors.

However long it actually took to make the eastern entrance to the Sunda Strait proper, once there, Charles Kellett would have had his crew working hard during the five days of transit, to conform to the standard instructions for making through the strait along the north shore. Each time he realized they were making no headway at all, he would have decided to drop the anchor and wait until more favourable conditions came along.

This long and frustrating light-airs work, with all the hard graft of daily anchoring and lowering and hoisting of the massive sails with the crude gear of the *Keying*, will have been the first test of the coherence of the ship's company. In both *Account* and *Description*, we are told, for example, that the mainsail took forty crew half a day to hoist, with the latter text adding that the mainsail weighed 9 tonnes! The fact that the only suggestion of difficulty at this juncture is a concern the junk might be pirated by its own crew has to be read forward into the story that would be told in New York several months later.

Surely if it were true that the crew had been lured aboard by a contract promising them cessation at Batavia, they are unlikely to have been so terminally foolish and ignorant as to have waited on and off at anchor throughout nearly five long weeks, working up towards and through the Sunda Strait—with the obvious intent of passing through it—when Batavia was barely two days' sail further on? Without their work and co-operation, the *Keying* would have gone nowhere. All they had to do was refuse to work unless the ship went to Batavia. There seems to be no suggestion that mutiny on this scale was ever threatened.

One does not need to claim that the average Chinese junk sailor of the mid-nineteenth century was a navigational and geographical adept to find it inexplicable that this long hiatus seems to have passed successfully, if at the same time the crew were resisting sailing beyond Southeast Asian waters. The junk trade with the *nanyang* goes back to the Song dynasty and before. In an oral tradition—as most of traditional Chinese seamanship was—rough knowledge of the sailings[41] involved in getting from A to B to C will not have been exclusively confined to the ship's European navigator or its Chinese captain.

Early rumblings among the crew are, of course, the other explanation for the long delay. This would suppose Charles Kellett to have carefully edited his account of events; the reason for the long hiatus may have had less to do with fears of piracy, on the one hand and calms, adverse currents and adverse winds, on the other, than with a need to persuade a reluctant Chinese crew to sail onward. For if the story that emerged in the New York court hearing was true, then the mouth of the Sunda Strait was the obvious place at which matters to do with crew expectations will first have come to a head. As long as the strait had not been transited, the *Keying* was not committed to the long and always uncertain crossing of the Indian Ocean: a diversion to Batavia was, quite literally, a matter of just nipping round the corner.

That there was restiveness is attested in the *Account*, though not in the *Description*:

> . . . the men . . . were seen to be in knots talking together, and when any Europeans on board came near them, they would make gestures to each other to be silent.
>
> Captain Kellett deeming it to be prudent to watch their movements, which seemed to threaten the loss of the voyage, had twelve muskets loaded and a portion placed in the cabin. This had the desired effect. No further symptoms of disorder appeared, although the means of defence were invariably kept at hand.
>
> For five days in the straits, the *Keying* had a companion that appeared to be bound for Batavia. Her movements which in some measure resembled [the *Keying's*] during this time, led Captain Kellett to be particularly watchful.

Kellett's implication here, which given the reputation of the Chinese coast is hardly surprising, is that the crew may in part have signed on with piracy in mind, and could have had contacts in the other junk with whom, if circumstances allowed, a joint seizure could be effected. As with so many things about the *Keying*'s voyage, we shall never know the truth.

This episode of the long and wearisome work required to close and transit the Sunda Strait, the difficult passage through it and the worries about possible piracy also illustrate a key point with respect to voyaging under sail, whether in a junk or Western square-rigger: without favourable winds there can be no progress.

The Sunda Strait has always presented a significant obstacle westbound in the last months of the northwest monsoon, since the prevailing winds and currents are adverse.[42] These will have contributed largely to the *Keying*'s long wait,[43] though the uncertainties about crew morale would certainly not have helped. There is also the weak implication—as such, a foretaste of things to come—that when the wind fell light and contrary and the currents were not favourable, the *Keying* slowed to a halt.

Taking that thought aboard, it is just possible that shadowy crew memories of an older British archipelagic base, Bencoolen (present-day Bengkulu), just around the corner on the north side of the exit from the Sunda Strait, which the British had returned to the Dutch only twenty-two years previously, had lingered sufficiently to lull them into accepting the transit of the strait without fully appreciating what its completion would entail. After all, as the *Account* brusquely and dismissively put it:

> Instruction in China, is nothing more or less than a Government shackle, by which the young are kept in ignorance of other nations . . .[44]

So despite the Chinese crew's assumed knowledge of the *nanyang*, perhaps it was patchy and a mixture of out of and up to date. The absence of any significant record from the Chinese side of this voyage means we shall never know quite what it was that led thirty or forty Cantonese adults from Whampoa and Hong Kong to transit the Sunda Strait and set out on the long and arduous voyage towards Africa, if they truly believed they had only signed on for a short-seas voyage within the compass of the China seas.

Adding to that doubt, of course, is the simple fact that Chinese sailors from the Canton region had been signing aboard British Indiamen for some fifty years by the time the *Keying* set sail.[45] By the time the laden Indiamen prepared to sail back to Britain with their valuable cargos, disease, desertion and impressment had occasionally stripped a ship of a dozen and more of its crew. Working with the then-ruling assumption, echoes of which permeate both *Account* and *Description*, that to replace one lost British seaman one needed to sign aboard two or three Chinese sailors, Indiamen captains would arrange with local providers for a wholly illegal draft of willing—well, as far as the record goes—Chinese sailors to be brought out to their ships from Macao, which was beyond the effective jurisdiction of the Canton authorities, before they made their departure. Ships would sign aboard up to forty and more of these crewmen, provide them with clothing and inculcate them in the way of a British square-rigger, though as the *Account* notes,[46] the Chinese crew did not customarily work aloft.

The death toll was quite high, usually of cold, as the ship reached the North Atlantic, according to the record; initially, once the voyages had reached Britain, the poor crew were paid off and left to their own devices, with no guarantee of a return passage. This early caused complaint. By 1785–86, private measures were taken to relieve at least some of the destitution; in 1795, the first formal measures were taken to ensure that East Indian shipping interests were made responsible for repatriating lascar crew. Next, as of a British government enactment of 1815, the East India Company was made responsible for housing and feeding the seamen it had brought to Britain before it repatriated them. Then, finally, the 1823 'Lascar Act' formalized these obligations by ensuring they were complied with rather than dodged, as had up to that point been too often the case. In the 1823/24 log of the *Buckinghamshire*, for example, there is a record of eighty Chinese seamen—their names as impenetrable as those of the *Keying* crew in the New York court record—being carried back to China.[47]

It follows that a basic knowledge of the waters beyond the Sunda Strait may have been part of the common currency of Whampoa sailors, embroidered though it is likely to have been with the embellishments of travellers' tales. Some at least may have shipped aboard an Indiaman to venture into the wider world. So, although there is a circumstantial case to make that this first leg of the voyage was a monstrous deception of innocent Chinese seamen by British officers, the separation between their worlds was not so absolute as to make the claim entirely credible.

There is one final point: that the long, slow progress in the waters of the Sunda shelf would have been the last thing Charles Kellett and his crew wanted—not just because of the ennui of a long delay and the frustration of failed attempts to get through the strait, but because the long wait in a single set of water conditions was the perfect recipe for a maximum growth of marine life on a ship's bottom.

The waters of the Sunda shelf are some of the most fecund in the world. They are full of nutrient and of the minute forms of sea life—barnacles, tube worm, weeds and algae, small crustaceans—that depend on that nutrient to grow and prosper. In Singapore, when the author was voyaging, the links of the anchor chain could be completely closed up and locked together in a matter of two weeks by the accretion of marine growth.[48] In short, an unprotected ship's hull— chunam can protect against marine borers like teredo, but it has few if any powers to check marine growth—staying more or less immobile in these fecund waters for several weeks would very rapidly gather a thick layer of barnacles, tube worm and weed. Once that had started, it would foster more growth. Unless the ship was careened and burned off or, in the Western way when careening was not possible, it had a rope or length of chain dragged lengthwise along the bottom to wrench away the worst growth, the fouling could and would eventually get so bad as to make a ship all but immobile in any save a brisk wind. This may have been one further explanation of all the problems to come.

At last, on 26 January 1847, over seven weeks since leaving Hong Kong, the *Keying* won clear of the sail-shaped bluff of Java Head, or Tanjung Layar. A major waypoint had been passed; whatever may or may not have been in the air as to the junk's destination, there can have been no doubt in anyone's mind, as the mountains of Java and Sumatra fell astern, that a voyage within the confines of the China seas was no longer a possibility.

The Second Leg

Another Slow Passage

Once clear of the Sunda Strait, the *Keying's* course would have been for the tip of South Africa. In a steamship, this is an exercise in what is called Great Circle Sailing—a path for any voyage over around 500 nautical miles that minimizes the distance sailed. For sailing ships, however, the Great Circle route is not always the fastest course. For the aim is always to sail on whichever route promises the most constant winds and favourable currents, while avoiding the threat of severe weather. A typical example was named in 1759 after the Indiaman *Pitt*, when Captain William Wilson missed his monsoon, sailed via the Moluccas and then east of the Philippines to approach Macao from the east. The direct route from the Sunda Strait to Macao is around 1,800 nautical miles. Pitt's Passage, as Captain Wilson's route came to be called, is some 3,725 nautical miles—and quicker.

For this second leg of the *Keying's* voyage, it was recommended not to steer straight for South Africa on a roughly southwesterly course, but to head as directly to the trade winds as possible. In short, first to head south.

By Charles Kellett's day, the cumulation of experience recorded in ships' logbooks and distilled into the advice in Horsburgh's *India Directory*—probably the fifth edition—counselled that optimum conditions would be found by sailing south into the trades by passing through 16⁰S, 90⁰E. Once into the trades, Kellett will have headed directly to a position 200 miles south of Rodriguez Island at 23⁰S, 63⁰E, and then altered course southwestwards to pass 200 miles south of Madagascar. The rule, if calling at Cape Town, was then to close Great Fish Point about 200 miles south of Durban until in the strength of the Agulhas Current, which can run up to 5 knots at peak flow and averages 2–3 knots, then to ride that until abreast Mossel Bay before rounding Cape Agulhas 'a prudent distance' off, to follow the coast to Cape Town.

This 5,150 to 5,300-mile recommended route was the traditional East India Company passage from October until April; it would have taken the ship to Cape Town, the traditional stopover for rest and replenishment.[49] However, if the Cape could be passed on a favourable wind, and stores and other considerations

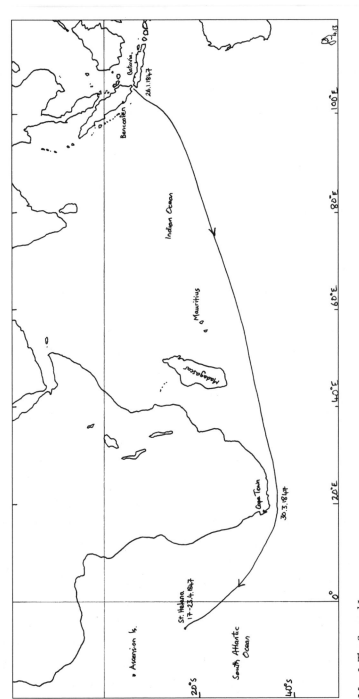

Map 3 The Second Leg

suggested such a decision—which would have been seldom in the days of Indiamen—a skipper would take his ship further south, heading on round the Cape of Good Hope and into the South Atlantic to the other Indiaman's stopping point of St. Helena. That is what happened with the *Keying*. Captain Kellett's narrative tells us he found a fair wind when in the offing of the Cape and took advantage of it to stand on for St. Helena.

The result was that an already long and slow passage was made longer.

Today, the exit from the Sunda Strait, even in the best season of late August and September, is still a notoriously uncomfortable and relatively slow-going exercise until one has made sufficient southing to get into the full flow of the trade winds. Even in this prime season, the first fifty miles or so are especially difficult, as a sailing vessel must contend with the heavy Indian Ocean swell rolling up on the port beam, shaking the often light winds out of the sails.[50] As the *Keying* made its passage four months after that recommended date, well after the optimal time recommended, life will have been harder.

Charles Kellett's account, extracted from his logbook and summarized in the *Description*, is puzzling:

> For the first seventeen days [the *Keying's*] rate varied from two to eight knots an hour; the greater part of the next three weeks were passed at anchor, and during the next week she scarcely averaged two knots. On 6th March, 1847, as the weather was calm, and the breeze so light that she scarcely moved more than a knot an hour, all hands were employed in getting in the rudder to examine the old, and fit new, rudder ropes: a necessary precaution against the heavy sea she would be sure to encounter in passing the Cape.[51]

In total then, we have something of the order of 45 days on passage, with light airs still plaguing the *Keying* 39 days after passing Java Head. The puzzle here comes in the second clause about the 'next three weeks' being passed at anchor. If the *Keying* had sailed at 2–8 knots for 17 days, she will have travelled something like 1,600 miles. By that time she would have been far out over the southern Indian Ocean's abyssal plain—far, far removed from the slightest chance of anchoring. It follows that the ghostwriter of the pamphlet has got something scrambled; what we have is an utter confusion with the first leg of the voyage, which actually took 51 days, but otherwise meets the above description pretty well. In short, what is presented as a description of the early part of the second leg is nothing of the sort. All we get is the intelligence that, after 39 days, the *Keying* had still not won into the southeast trade winds she was looking for.

Working out exact timings is therefore tricky. The leg from the Sunda Strait to the Cape of Good Hope took 63 days. For the *Keying*, that works out at an average of only 81 miles a day, a fairly low average speed over the whole passage of 3.4 knots. The probability is that the passage divided into two unequal parts. To begin with, a long, frustrating period that could have taken two or three weeks, perhaps longer, even the whole of the possible 39 days, to get the several hundred miles from the exit of the Sunda Strait to the belt where the southeast trades blow.

In January, what is known as the Intertropical Convergence Zone (ITCZ) lies in a wide band with its southern limit up to 10 degrees—400 to 600 nautical miles—south of Java. North of it, the winds are fitful and contrary, blowing lightly from anywhere from northwest through southwest, with frequent thunderstorms and torrential rain. For the *Keying*, the combination of a foul bottom, a poor performance in light airs and lively seas will have made for very slow progress—perhaps as little as 50 miles a day, with no progress at all on some days. Indeed, on the worst of days, the poor *Keying* may even have found itself going backwards, as the Equatorial Counter-current in the seas south of Java, flowing east-south-east to east at as much as half a knot in a broad swathe up to 250 miles across, took away the vestigial miles the crew's work may have gained hauling on sheets to keep the sails trimmed.

The author can remember a voyage between Fiji and the Carolines in the early 1990s in which the Pacific Ocean's stronger version of the same current at broadly the same time of year carried his and his partner's 11.8-metre yacht so steadily eastwards that a course of northwest, steered day after day at a boat speed of a bit over 5 knots, resulted in a course made good of due north at 2–3 knots. Instead of fetching Pohnpei as intended, we found the trade winds just in time to get into Majuro in the Marshall Islands, some 700 miles east of our hoped-for destination; otherwise, our only choice would have been to head for Hawaii and another three weeks at sea.

However, once into the trades and the South Equatorial Current, Charles Kellett's command should in theory have had a steadier, easier life as the ship ran its westing down towards Africa. But the season was late. It was early in the

Southern Hemisphere's summer, when the southeast trades are at their weakest. For in the northern winter months the southeast trades retreat to their furthest south,[52] blowing only force 3–4 on average (7–16 knots) with the occasional period of light airs and calms. So, in that season, even once the trades have been found, they often prove fitful; this seems to be what happened to the *Keying*.

The Indian Ocean leg was therefore slow-going until in the vicinity of the Cape, as borne out by a story from an April issue of the *St Helena Gazette*, reprinted in the *Glasgow Herald*,[53] where Captain Kellett is reported as saying that the whole voyage from the Sunda Strait had experienced very light winds. He also reported heavy weather south of Mauritius, perhaps a seeding tropical cyclone or just a thunderstorm 'super cell' common in the summer tropics and often a precursor to a cyclone, which would also fit the southern summer weather he was experiencing when the incidence of tropical cyclones is at its height. The narrative in the *Description* is terse but vivid:

> (Not long after the 6th March) . . . strong breezes with squally weather soon succeeded, and on the night of 22nd March, the wind veered all round the compass with vivid lighting and thunder, when, suddenly settling in the south-west, it blew a perfect hurricane; all sails were lowered, except half the fore-sail, till the wind, settling into a heavy gale, allowed a little more sail to be set. On this occasion twenty-five men were required to steer her.[54]

Once in the longitude of the Cape of Good Hope, and probably for the first time since the brisk voyage down the South China Sea to the Sunda Strait, Charles Kellett had his stroke of luck. In the original voyage plan, he may have imagined staging briefly in Cape Town to replenish and give his crew some respite from their long weeks at sea. It was what almost all sailing ships did, save those engaged on urgent business like carrying official despatches with vital news. Instead, perhaps because near the Cape the ship found a Cape Doctor—a fair, brisk, southeasterly wind—Charles Kellett chose to push on. Later, he wrote that it was specifically because of that fair wind that he chose to bypass Cape Town. He certainly had that reason, but two other factors probably played their part.

Charles Kellett will have wanted to try to pull back some of the lost time he had been accumulating since his ship had left Hong Kong. It was now late March. The northern hemisphere summer that would be his optimal season to gain the English Channel from the North Atlantic was fast approaching. Much more delay, especially since his ship was evidently no greyhound, and instead of summer he would be facing the autumn equinox which, in the nineteenth century at least, was believed to be a time of particularly adverse weather. After that would come the storms, cold and high seas of an advancing North Atlantic winter.

The *Keying* had left Hong Kong rather late in the season. Progress had been slow. Because of that, the *Keying*'s bottom will have been increasingly foul. What had anyway been proving a fairly slow passage on this Indian Ocean leg seems to have become very slow.

Although going southeast from the Java area, not southwest, the New Zealander Adrian Hayter's sail from the Bali Strait towards Fremantle, Western Australia, in his diminutive yawl *Sheila* in spring 1954 may be illustrative here. As a result of being jailed in Surabaya for some largely imaginary defect in his papers, Hayter—like the *Keying*—was late heading out into the Indian Ocean. After a tough four weeks at sea battling a leak and head winds, and with the boat's bottom getting more and more foul from growth, *Sheila* got slower and slower. Hayter began to run out of food and especially water, because his ship's tank had been contaminated. By the end, he was chopping up cabin furniture to fuel a primitive stove for distilling seawater in order to survive. A 1,600-mile voyage hard on the wind that should have taken perhaps three weeks ended up taking over eleven. A foul bottom can reduce speed to a crawl—in Hayter's case, an average speed of not quite one knot.[55]

The *Keying* was not hard on the wind, so not that slow. But given the fair trade winds, the 63 days the ship took to get from the exit of the Sunda Strait to the longitude of the Cape of Good Hope, passed on 30 March 1847, it had been far from fleet. Charles Kellett will have known he was lagging the 'normal' schedule and had to make back time when and where he could.

Of course, there is another reason why the siren call of Cape Town was so easily resisted. Recall that by the time the *Keying* quit the Sunda Strait not only had her crew been on board for 51 days, but there had been some early signs that all was not well. By the time the *Keying* was finally in the longitude of the Cape, they had been aboard 114 days, or something over sixteen weeks. That is well short of the maximum voyage time for which they had signed on, indeed only half of it, but it is not hard to imagine that there was an increasing sense of trouble in the air. Charles Kellett must therefore have known that, had he stopped at the

Cape, he was highly likely to lose a good number of his crew. Cape Town in 1846 was no metropolis. But it was, equally, no sleepy *dorp*. With a population of some 10,000,[56] it was a busy layover port for shipping; one where, to the determined, jumping ship was probably none too difficult. That would have applied to all the *Keying*'s crew. The Europeans could have jumped ship—either to sign aboard a whaler or join another vessel. The Chinese crew members could have looked to the small Chinese community to help them keep clear of the inevitable search.[57] So if the crew was fractious, and it almost certainly was, then bypassing the Cape and heading for St. Helena made sense. Jumping ship in St. Helena was impossible. The island was too small. With a population of around 6,000 or so and no hinterland into which someone could disappear until a hue and cry had died down, there was no place to hide.

The 1,700 miles from the longitude of the Cape to St. Helena, which took 17 days, must have helped rebuild morale. It was still leisurely progress, but compared to the passage from the Sunda Strait, the *Keying* had made a fair 100 miles a day, or 4.2 knots—a 20 percent improvement. Despite that relatively good performance over the first leg of the South Atlantic, by the time the *Keying* reached St. Helena it had been at sea, since leaving the Sunda Strait, for nearly twelve weeks. Even in the mid-nineteenth century, the 81 days that the voyage from the Sunda Strait had taken, with no prospect of some startling reward, such as went to ships with the first cargo of tea of the season to reach London, was a long time.[58] This was an average of only 3.5 knots—without question quite slow. A reliable sea boat the *Keying* quite certainly seems to have been, as Charles Kellett affirms:

> During the whole of her somewhat tedious passage, the '*Keying*' proved herself an admirable sea-boat; she encountered most violent storms, and behaved well in them all, as the extracts which are given from the log-book will prove.[59]

Fleetness in light to moderate winds was another matter. Independent of the junk's performance, by the time the *Keying* came to anchor off St. Helena, the crew had been aboard 135 days since leaving Hong Kong, or the best part of five months. Yet, of the intended voyage, the hardest 4,512 nautical miles were yet to come, something of which Charles Kellett would have been increasingly aware.

Light Winds and a Foul Bottom

There are two other possibilities for this relatively slow progress: light winds and a steadily more foul ship's bottom. The *Keying* was protected by *chunam*. But the efficacy of this compound against fouling has never been scientifically tested; its properties as an antifouling are at best anecdotal. There are two quite different, though equally important, properties of protective coatings for wooden hulls: protection against marine growth and protection against marine borers.

The tung oil in *chunam* appears not to be particularly poisonous. For humans regularly using it, contact dermatitis and ulceration have sometimes occurred. This may indicate properties that marine organisms may not much like, especially when compounded with lime (though given the role of lime in animal and plant nutrition, this seems unlikely).[60] Yet there is a fair amount of anecdotal evidence as to the relative *in*efficacy of the compound, certainly vis-à-vis either coppering or modern antifouling paints.[61] The properties of tung oil are highly unlikely to have been proof against six weeks moving very slowly and at anchor without careening and burning off—and there is no evidence that that was done, although, equally, no statement to the contrary, either. Certainly, the junk was not coppered, as almost all ocean-going Western sailing ships would have been at this date.

Equally relevant here is the rough finish of Chinese hulls. Marine life gets its lodgement in the slacker water created by the turbulence caused by irregularities on a ship's underwater surface. With a roughly finished hull, even treated with the far smoother surface of *chunam*, these irregularities are numerous. Once growth has started, the slack-water zones multiply and growth accelerates. The *Keying* would have been in double trouble.

But if deterring marine growth is important, preventing marine borers is vital for a wooden hull. It was the reliance on tung oil alone by the replica Han dynasty junk *Tai-ki*, in its attempt to cross the Pacific in 1974, that proved disastrous, because even a good tung oil treatment is simply not able to provide the protection against marine borers required over the long months of the voyage. The first part of the voyage seems to have gone well enough, but by 2 September 1974, after three months at sea, the invasion by marine borers rapidly escalated to the point of disaster, so riddling the hull planking that the junk was no longer viable and had to be abandoned.[62] For sea-going junks, therefore, the traditional practice for protection against marine borers was twofold. The 'failsafe' was a sacrificial layer (or layers) of additional planking, a practice that was also common in Western ships before coppering.[63] The first line of protection was *chunam*. Traditional Chinese maritime practices were orientated around relatively short-sea voyaging, with legs lasting at most three weeks to a month. If, during such a voyage, the vessel moves into or out of fresh water in rivers, where marine life cannot live, as would have been the case for most *nanyang* trade routes, any damage would not have resulted in disaster.

Virtually all pre-sixteenth-century Chinese voyaging—and probably most Western commercial voyaging too—was short-sea sailing. Not only were the legs short, but they were in relatively small ships that, working off beaches, could be dried out between tides and readily careened. So a fairly regular scrub or clean was part and parcel of every voyage; in consequence, marine growth very seldom managed to get to the point where it was a serious impediment to progress. Finally, just as working off beaches and having shoal draft made cleaning off the hull a simple, regular practice, so the regular visits to fresh or brackish water up river ports like Canton, Nanking, Ningpo or Tientsin were an aid in keeping growth down.[64]

Traditional craft like the *Keying* were largely protected against marine borers by traditional bottom treatments. If they were made of teak, which the *Keying* may have been, they were rather better protected because teak is itself resistant, if not strongly so, to *teredo navalis*, or the ship worm.[65] But that is not to say anything at all about the resistance of the hull's underwater surface coating to marine growth. In this respect, from all the evidence we have, the *Keying* had no protection at all.

A long period moving very slowly or stopped at anchor, followed by a long ocean voyage travelling slowly through warm, tropical and subtropical waters would have ensured a problem. Oceanic tropical waters are in fact surprisingly sterile,[66] so additional organisms acquired on passage will have been few and the food sources for the existing growth not plentiful. The only additional 'passengers' will have been goose barnacles, which are found offshore. But the heavy growth that likely followed six weeks in the Sunda Straits area would have a level of self-sustenance. Once the growth is thick enough, even if it grows only slowly, it not only slows a ship further but also provides the still-water areas that enable yet more algal and other growths to find a lodgement. The third problem for the *Keying* was that, as far as we can work out, she was sailing in ballast. That is, she was riding light or, as modern sailors say,[67] 'high on her marks'. The passage from the Sunda Strait to the Cape, once the *Keying* reached the trade winds, would have been largely downwind and down-sea. And the seas in question are characterized by long, ocean swells that have the vast distance between Australia and Africa to build, pushed along by the trade winds twelve months of the year. Of course, the strength of these winds comes and goes, but somewhere in the vast ocean the wind will be blowing, and the swells will roll from them.[68]

A light ship sailing downwind can be the devil to handle. That is because she will set up a steady roll as the waves pass obliquely beneath the hull. As she rolls, so the waterlines—the plane shape where the hull meets the water—will change. As the ship rolls to starboard, the shape of the waterline will encourage the ship to yaw to port, a tendency exacerbated by the sea coming up from behind, lifting the stern and dropping the bow. As the ship rolls to port, the reverse happens. Obviously, the faster the ship is running, the quicker things will happen and the bigger the 'wipe-out', if the helmsman loses control. This is called broaching and it can be catastrophic—as indeed it was to be for the *Keying* in the Atlantic crossing in 1848. It was a cause for apprehension as revealed in the first leg story of the helmsman who abandoned his post in strong weather. The fourth—additional, not alternative—explanation for a slow passage would be that the trip down the South China Sea may have rather frightened Charles Kellett.

A Junk's Steering System

We now need a short diversion into the steering system of Chinese junks. Put bluntly, they are brilliant exercises in rule-of-thumb development, but crude, vulnerable and the devil to work.

We know of the vulnerability and the fact that it worried Kellett from the *Description*:[69]

> On 6th March 1847, as the weather was calm, and the breeze so light that she scarcely moved more than a knot in an hour, all hands were employed in getting in the rudder to examine the old, and to fit new, rudder ropes: a

necessary precaution against the heavy sea she would be sure to encounter in passing the Cape.

The Chinese centreline rudder was developed several centuries before centreline rudders became common in the West.[70] However, there appears to be no evidence whatsoever that the Western sternpost-mounted rudder was copied from China. This is for two very good reasons. Its first appearance was in Scandinavia, the least likely endpoint of an intelligible transmission route for maritime technology transfer from China. And when the Western centreline, stern-hung rudder did appear, it was a quite different engineering solution.[71]

Basically, the Chinese rudder was a centreline-mounted steering oar that was pivoted until it was vertical and then gradually refined to make the rudder of the sort the *Keying* had. It was massive—Charles Kellett reported that the *Keying's*, made of ironwood and teak, weighed between 7.5 and 8 tonnes—and very weakly mounted.[72] Where the Western rudder was mounted on the sternpost (a constructional feature that junks do not have) by massive ironwork, the Chinese rudder rested in wooden guides or jaws, by the *Keying's* day usually closed but in many junks open, rather like rowlocks mounted on the transom. The rudder was hung by the top of the blade from one or more horizontal windlasses, high above in the poop. The stock rested in the guides and slid up and down in them, so that the rudder could be hoisted clear of damage in harbour or shoal water. In deep water, the rudder was lowered into clean water-flow sometimes several metres below the bottom of the hull. For example, as the *Description* notes, with her rudder hoisted the *Keying* drew 12 feet (3.66 metres), with it lowered she drew 24 (7.3 metres).[73] To hold the rudder in place once it was lowered, bowsing lines made of plaited grass and bamboo were led from the forward lower corner (the heel) forward along the ship's bottom either side of the keel and then up to a tensioning winch set between the high, forward-projecting 'wings' at the bow. The assemblage can be seen, if indistinctly, in some of the images we have.

From a hydrodynamic point of view, with lots of rudder blade down in clear water-flow towards the back of the ship, this made the Chinese rudder a wonderfully efficient steering device. It also had the advantage that it could act as a sort of centreboard to help counteract leeway—the tendency of sailing ships to be blown sideways by the wind they are using for propulsion.

From a mechanical point of view, however, the *Keying*'s rudder was desperately vulnerable, since only the bowsing line and fairly weak, wooden guide pieces on the transom served to hold it in place. It was also a poor solution to the problem of friction, since to hold the rudder in place the bowsing lines pulled it against the wooden guides, increasing rather than decreasing friction. There are few references to the guides being greased to reduce this problem, though there is evidence that the practice existed. The problem for the *Keying* spending so long at sea, with a following sea washing into the transom, is that any grease applied would regularly have been washed away.

For the *Keying*, these obvious problems would have been compounded for another constructional reason. All the images we have indicate that the *Keying*'s rudder, although fenestrated (which takes some of the strain off by relieving water pressure, without much diminishing turning moment), was unbalanced. This is a term of art, contrasting rudders like the *Keying*'s with what are called balanced rudders—a device Chinese watermen had discovered in the tenth or eleventh century, but which appear to have been used mainly by inshore and inland-waters craft.[74] The difference lies in the location of the axis of rotation of the rudder blade. If it is behind the leading edge by about one-third or more of the front-to-back dimension, then the rudder is described as balanced. If the axis of rotation is at the leading edge, it is unbalanced. To put it simply, balanced rudders do some of the work for the person or machinery steering, taking less effort to turn to begin a ship's alteration of course and to restore to the centreline when one again wants to steer straight. By contrast, unbalanced rudders, of the sort almost all Chinese sea-going junks had, require hard effort to operate.

Back to the ship. On deck, the head of the *Keying*'s rudder-post was attached to one of two tillers—an upper and a lower—turned from side to side to operate the rudder. Below decks on the weather deck was the long tiller aided by tackles. The short tiller for harbour- and shoal-water use, also worked with tackles, was shipped high up on the exposed poop deck when the rudder was raised. It is this aspect, allied to the unbalanced rudder and its delicate but far from friction-free mounting system, on that long, downwind voyage, which may have led Charles Kellett to take things easy.

There is an optimal length to a tiller for a given size of rudder and ship's waterline length.[75] For a ship the size of the *Keying*, this is some ten metres or more—in short, impracticable. So as in most junks, even the *Keying*'s longer tiller was shorter than was ideal. To make it possible to steer at all, multipart blocks and tackles were mounted to strongpoints on the deck or bulwarks at the ship's side, level with the end of the tiller. Steering was done by the helmsman, who hauled on the windward rope to move the tiller from side to side. There is some confusion in the descriptions here. Most of the newspaper coverage, repeating the *Description*, refers to at minimum two helmsmen in light weather; in one description we read:

> When let down to its greatest depth, (the rudder) requires occasionally the aid of fifteen men to move the large tiller, and even then with the aid of a luff tackle purchase, and the best patent blocks. Without this aid, it would require thirty men.[76]

Steering like this is enormously hard work. In stronger weather, as we know from the *Description*, each tackle would have the full complement of fifteen a side to heave and haul. This requires great co-ordination. In light weather or strong, the system is very slow to react. Think about how much rope has to be hauled in on a four-part tackle to move the tiller across the deck for the rudder to be moved over 10 degrees.

Now let us recall that the *Keying* was 'in ballast', or riding high. Any sailing ship running down-sea will tend to yaw either side of its course, to heave—that is, be moved vertically up and down by the sea—and also, as a result, to roll rhythmically as the seas pass beneath it and impart their changing dynamic forces to the ship's asymmetrical underwater shape. The higher a ship is riding, the higher in the hull will be the centres of gravity and buoyancy, the relationship between these two centres being a critical influence on stability. There are even more technicalities involved, to do with things like the metacentric height, but we can safely say that, with her very heavy rig and her hull riding light, the *Keying* will have been the devil to sail down-sea with the wind aft.[77]

Put all that together and you have some very good reasons why Charles Kellett would not have wished to give the *Keying* its head and have it rush down the trade wind-driven seas, where a broach could spell disaster. A ship riding high and running down-sea with a less-than-efficient steering system was hard to control—hence the prudence.

Traditional Chinese crewing practices, as revealed in the news coverage of the voyage, must also be factored in. The Chinese crew were accustomed to sailing very conservatively at night—as good seamen aware of the perils of darkness often are[78]—it is unlikely that Charles Kellett would have disregarded this entirely. So Yin Sang Hsi would have known the ship better than Kellett; Kellett would have known this. So there would likely have been a compromise between what traditional practice held to be safe and how the crew expected things to be and the possibly more thrusting expectations of someone who had spent time in the fast, hard-driven ships of the opium trade.[79]

It may be the experiences of this stretch, including the difficulties in the Sunda Strait, that began sowing seeds of doubt about the performance envelope of a traditional, *nanyang* trade junk out of her home waters and voyaging in a most uncharacteristic mode. The prospect of the onward voyage, at this point still intended to be the long, 4,512-nautical-mile leg to London, cannot have been alluring. The European sailors, at least, will have known that the next leg would be tough. It entailed crossing the doldrums at the height of the transition season, when winter/summer turns to spring/autumn, which for a ship that had already proved slow in light airs would be long and frustrating. Once that barrier had been franchised, the sail up the North Atlantic would follow, with the need to get round the Azores high-pressure area, into the prevailing westerlies. At the time of year they would be sailing this leg, there would likely be northeast headwinds, often light, for some 15 to 20 degrees of latitude. That is the best part of 900 to 1,200 miles, a bit under one-third of the 4,512-nautical-mile distance of the next leg. On the junk's performance to date, that section alone promised at least two or three weeks. The whole remaining passage on the optimal course would have taken over 60 days, on a prudent calculation to ensure sufficient water and stores. Allow for delays caused by calms and the indirect course forced on the ship by headwinds and currents and a further 70 to 80 days at sea was in prospect.

The Performance of a Sailing Junk

Some brief remarks now on the *Keying's* rig and its potential performance. She was a traditionally masted junk, with a large foremast stepped well forward and a mainmast stepped slightly forward of amidships. Aft and offset to port was the small mizzen. As in most junks, this was not really a driving sail but served primarily to help balance the rig, thus taking the strain off the chronically weak rudder fittings. It thus follows that the major power sources for the *Keying* were the fore and main sails. These were both made of woven bamboo matting, a traditional sailcloth with many fine attributes, though aerodynamic efficiency would not be high on the list.

The *Keying* was no greyhound, just the solid and reliable short-seas working craft she was designed to be. While the junk could not match the remarkable performances of the fastest square-rig western ships of her day, she was in no way worse than her strict equivalent, one of the many working brigs and ships of the late eighteenth century, which formed the majority of working craft in the heyday of sail. Even for the fabulous extreme clippers just coming onto the scene,[80] there were times when the wind did not serve and they struggled to make the 15,000-mile voyage from China in less than 140 days, or only around one knot faster than the *Keying*'s average. We need to bear that in mind.

For the onward journey from St. Helena, however, especially for the legs north of the Equator, a second issue will have been exercising Charles Kellett's mind. That of the point of sail—the direction a sailing ship is headed in relation to the direction of the wind. At their most sophisticated, square-rigged sailing ships of the mid-nineteenth century could sail at about 68 degrees to the true wind.[81] They were unable to point higher because the standing rigging holding up their masts got in the way of trimming the yards from which the sails hung closer to the fore-and-aft line of the ship. It follows that, in principle, the junk rig, given its unstayed, fore-and-aft, fully battened, balanced lug rig unimpeded by standing rigging, should have been able to outperform that. Certainly, it is often argued that the junk rig was and is aerodynamically vastly superior to Western square-rig. But there is a very large gap between principle and practice.[82]

With several thousand miles of experience and the prospect of headwinds in the North Atlantic, Charles Kellett's mind would have been focused on the possible windward performance of his vessel. And his judgements would have been quite independent of what an armchair theorist might contend to be true about some imagined, generic junk rig. If the *Keying* had had difficulty working to windward in light airs in the Sunda Strait area, then Kellett's apprehensions as to what lay ahead would have rested on some real experience. Why should he suppose she would fare any better in the brisker winds and livelier seas of the North Atlantic?

It is bold to claim—as, for example, Joseph Needham does[83]—that the sort of sail with which the *Keying* was rigged, *especially when allied with a traditional junk hull in ballast,* was in any way a rig that could power the *Keying* to weather off-shore, whether in light or strong airs. The aerodynamic properties of the junk, or fully battened balanced lug sail, that Needham celebrates are aerodynamic properties *in principle.* The rig is wondrously handy and, without question, because of the subtle, multi-part sheeting arrangements, well fitted for trimming to accommodate the natural sheer of the wind up the wind column.[84] But it is something else entirely to look at such a sail actually set and hard on the wind as a motive force to work a junk to windward in a seaway.

The long, fairly heavy and inflexible battens do not appear to have been designed to give the sail any sort of aerofoil section—that is, a curve when looked at in cross-section from above. Even had they been, woven bamboo sailcloth in separate panels is not the most malleable of fabrics, lacking many of the properties of canvas. Nor is there any evidence that it was woven or cut with any theory of aerodynamic shape in mind. Worcester comments, vis-à-vis the making of sails for junks (which, one notes, were in canvas):

> In China . . . the making of sails is very much a family affair and does not depend on any sail plans. The rough dimensions of the sail having been determined, the yard boom and battens are laid out on the ground and con-nected up to the bolt ropes so as to form a frame. The sail cloths are then laid over this framework; and various friends, wives and other relatives, indeed anyone who can handle a needle, are persuaded and pressed into service . . .[85]

The traditional junk sail was low-tech and almost always used, especially when offshore, to sail with the wind.[86] Had it been a conspicuous property of junks to make to windward offshore in a seaway, the junk trade would surely not have stuck for long centuries to the seasonal sailings on the monsoons that we know characterized China's oceanic passage-making. The extent to which the yards of a square-rigger could be braced forward set a clear limit on how closely the ships could get to the wind. It was not a limit faced by junks that could trim their sails to within perhaps 45 or even 40 degrees to the true wind.

So why did they not beat? The answer is simple. A sailing ship is not merely a solution to an aerodynamic problem; it is a solution to an aerodynamic *and* a hydrodynamic problem.[87] The problem with many junks—some of the Ningpo designs and the hybrid, Western-influenced designs of Guangdong partially excepted—is that, whatever the intrinsic aerodynamic genius of the junk rig, hydrodynamically the junk hull exhibited nothing that truly complemented it. It was a bluff-bowed load carrier, not designed with either speed or weatherliness in mind. The object was to build a low-cost, low-tech hull with good internal cargo volume that could successfully and economically ply traditional routes in traditional seasons. The object was, in general, brilliantly achieved.

Junks do not sail well to weather. This was the experience of Zheng Chenggong (Coxinga). The experience of the *Taiping Gongzhu* in 2008—the first Chinese junk to complete a circumnavigation of the North Pacific—was the same. Though obviously very much smaller, the sixteen-metre-long replica of a Ming dynasty *gangzeng*, or small warship, was in general conformity much as the *Keying* likely was.[88] In their west-to-east transpacific leg from Japan, the intended destination was Vancouver. Set south by the Alaska Current, the ship was steadily pushed away not only from Vancouver but from any chance of making either Vancouver or Seattle, both hoped-for ports of call. The junk's captain, Nelson Liu, did his best to haul his wind to make some northing. It was to no avail; the best that could be managed, after several days making very slow progress upwind and up current, was to make it into Eureka, California (40^0 50'N), some 445 nautical miles south of the Juan de Fuca Strait (48^0 15'N).[89] The *Taiping Gongzhu* had modern sailcloth and antifouling paint, so although she would not have had the *Keying's* advantages of displacement and length, and would have been hard put to punch her way to weather, her experience is indicative of why the *Keying* does not appear to have performed at all well on the wind. And if junks in general do not sail well to weather in a seaway, junks in ballast with dirty bottoms in the same conditions sail like a duck with no feet.

At St. Helena

It may have been a sense of what was to come over the last leg of the voyage that fomented the rot among the crew in St. Helena, where the *Keying* arrived on 17 April 1847. For during the junk's stay of one week—when it was apparently visited, rather improbably, by 3,000 people[90]—it became evident that the European crew were mutinous and the Chinese crew anxious to quit the ship. In fact, the voyage nearly came to an early end.

The number of visitors does not make much sense, for simple reasons. Any vessel at St. Helena must either heave to or anchor off the northwest side; all business with the shore has to be conducted by boat. If 3,000 people visited in a week, then, allowing a lost half-day at each end for formalities, and so on, in six days 500 people a day were ferried between the ship and shore. A longboat, which must be rowed, can carry no more than ten to a dozen passengers, if that; the round trip would be a minimum of 20–30 minutes, allowing time for loading and offloading. Forty to fifty trips a day, each taking half an hour, would require 20–25 boat hours. To ferry 3,000 visitors to the junk, at least three boats will have been working backwards and forwards almost non-stop during daylight hours for the duration of the visit. In the meantime, much of the normal life of the island must have ground to a halt! Much of the data about the *Keying* shows a similarly cavalier indifference to—or perhaps ignorance of—simple arithmetic.

Meanwhile, Charles Kellett had other problems to worry about. In his letter to Queen Victoria, written from Boston almost a year later, he refers to three of his European crew, 'my partners', quitting the ship; to the regaling of some of his Chinese crew with opium and 'ardent spirits' by an expatriate Chinese resident of the island;[91] and to his discontent with the balance of his European sailors. Evidently, Kellett and his brother deck officers were unable to resolve things. It took an appeal to the police magistrate of St. Helena, a Major Barnes, and to the captain of a British steam frigate, the *Penelope*,[92] to return the crew to their duties.

This will have exacerbated the problem. Strictly, Charles Kellett was acting entirely within his legal powers. In British maritime law, a crewman,[93] once signed on, was subject to the regulatory and disciplinary regimes in force. In consequence, he more or less lost his common law rights as a free man. So the law and its officers had to back Charles Kellett. But his resort to that recourse indicates how far the Western officers and their Chinese counterparts had by this stage lost any personal sway.

For it is personal sway that in the end must hold a ship's company together—especially a mixed company like the *Keying*'s. Under Western maritime law, 'the seaman, who fails to render himself on board according to his contract, can be pursued and arrested wherever he is found, and constrained to complete his engagement.'[94] As much to the point, 'It is the only form of service stipulated to be rendered by a free man of full age, known to the common law, in which the employer, by his own act, can directly inflict a punishment on the employed, for neglect of duty or breach of obligation.'[95] It is extremely unlikely that this legalistic, Western approach to shipboard relations would have been known to the Chinese crew or been thought in the smallest way acceptable if it was.

Once a seaman did sign on under British articles, there were restrictions on the master or owner's power to take the ship where he liked. Curtis observes:

> It is also an implied obligation that the voyage shall be definite and certain, and shall not be deviated from. The ancient maritime laws contained different provisions with respect to the obligations of the seamen, when the master, having arrived at the outward port of destination, should, of his own act, determine to go further. Under some codes, the seamen were discharged from their contract, and were not bound to go further without a new agreement. By the laws of some of the other codes, the master was obliged to give them an additional compensation, which they, however, were bound to accept, without the right to elect a discharge. But the modern rule is uniformly in favor of a strict compliance with the terms of the contract describing the voyage, and also that it shall be fairly and sufficiently described.[96]

Kellett had been reduced to holding his crew together by law and the threat of force. It was not a good omen. As the New York court case suggests, life aboard the *Keying* rested on a state of disciplinary affairs about as far removed from Chinese customary practice as is possible to imagine.

The Third Leg

Slower and Slower

Once it had departed St. Helena on 23 April 1847, the ship again made fairly slow time to the Equator. The distance from St. Helena to the Equator is some 1,180 nautical miles. The passage took 15 days, so over this leg, even pushed along by the southeast trades for part of the voyage, the *Keying* again averaged only 3.3 knots.

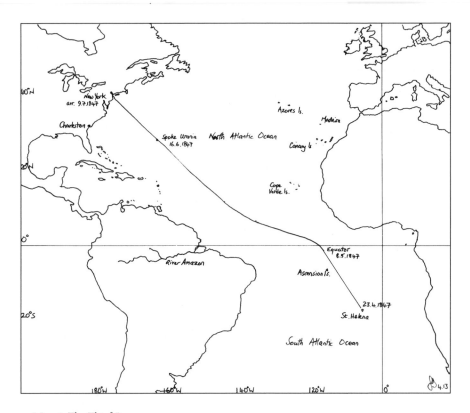

Map 4 The Third Leg

The Line was crossed, according to reports and Kellett's log as summarized in the *Description*, on 8 May in 17°40'W—well to the east and some 570 miles southwest from the nearest point of the bulge of Africa. It was a crossing point considerably at variance to what was recommended for sailing ships in this season; the difference was between 440 and 740 miles.

Kellett had thought to consult people more experienced than he with junk sailing performance; he had been told not to expect much by way of windward ability. So he explained his choice of crossing-point in terms of his apprehensions about the *Keying*'s probable performance when it met the northeast trades.

> We crossed . . . in order to be well to windward in making the north-east trade winds (imagined by mariners to be the worst part of the voyage for vessels of this class).[97]

No doubt, in addition, there would also have been the drift caused by the Equatorial Counter-Current during a prolonged transit of the doldrums.[98] Put both together and, when the *Keying* crossed the Line, it was well to the east, if Kellett was right, fairly placed to make a successful entry into the North Atlantic.

Kellett had at one stage also intended to follow the old Indiaman's practice and call at Ascension Island, in 8^0S, 14^0 15'W, at most no more than 150 to 180 miles to the east of the *Keying*'s track between St. Helena and where it crossed the Equator. Given that the only inhabitants were a British naval garrison, there should have been no fear of the ship losing its crew. And a good reason to stop there is that the island's turtles were staple additions to ships' provisions, an issue that must have exercised Kellett's mind.

We know that an Ascension call was at least possible. But, obviously, the aftermath of events at St. Helena was rumbling on:

> yet the mutinous condition of the crew was such that I could not safely venture to touch at Ascension. I therefore kept considerably out of the track: but in consequence of variable winds, we were driven towards thence, but not so near as to be observable to any but the officers; the crew still refusing to do more than they could possibly help; and this being a speculation which would not admit of more than the most requisite severity, we endeavoured to soothe their feelings; but on one occasion a number of them, under the excitement of opium, positively refused duty. It became necessary to make an example; I therefore punished one of the most turbulent with a few cuts of a rope's end. He jumped overboard; and when picked up I deemed it advisable to put him in irons. This had the desired effect and for a time all seemed to go on well.[99]

Early on in the voyage, the contrasts between Chinese voyaging and crewing practices and those on Western ships had become apparent. With this 'mutinous condition' and Kellett's reaction to it, combined with the Western attitude towards Chinese 'slackness', the difficulties are highlighted again of marrying the collegial, even democratic Chinese approach to crewing, on the one hand, with the regimental British approach, on the other.

It is not just a question of dramatically different ways of exercising authority. The Chinese crew worked as a group and dealt internally with any of their number who had problems. Organization for work on a junk seems to have been largely informal, task-driven and ad hoc; the leader for any non-routine task emerged

from the effort to deal with it rather than being pre-established in a formal hierarchy. Similarly, T. A. Lane's report of the crew's approach to night watchkeeping
reveals that that too was a minimally formalized, clock-driven matter.

Contrasted Crewing Systems

It is worth pausing a moment to contrast as clearly as possible the very different
ways of being at sea that were in play aboard the *Keying*. Let us take the British
system as it had evolved by the mid-1840s.

The crew was divided fairly strictly into four groups. At the top were the officers headed by the master, supported by his chief mate and second mate (in large
ships all the way down to sixth mate). They, in turn, were supported by the petty
officers—in the *Keying* the very existence of these is in doubt—each in charge of
both functional and watchkeeping groupings of the crew. Finally came the crew
who were ordered by watch and station. That is, each crewman belonged to a
'part of ship'—in large ships the four of the forecastle, foretop, maintop and quarterdeck; in middle-sized ships the three of forecastle, topmen and quarterdeck;
and in small ships, just forecastle and quarterdeck. Given her size, Kellett had
probably divided the *Keying* into three, allocating the European, and possibly the
Chinese, crew accordingly. All will also have been allocated their 'watch', either
'port' or 'starboard'. The fourth group, rather to one side, were the 'idlers' like the
sailmaker, carpenter, cook and bosun—and of course the passengers—who were
not required to stand watches.

It was in terms of these divisions that the Western ship's daily life was ordered.

Work was allocated by part of ship and would be carried out during daylight
hours (the working day) by hands who were not on watch. For example, pointing at the forecastle hands, the second mate might order, 'You, you and you'
from those off watch to go and grease the anchor windlass, shift stores from the
forward hold to the galley ready-use store, refresh the deck caulking around the
forehatch, paint the forecastle bulwarks, and so on.

But, when on passage, the ship also had to be steered and sailed. This was
done through a system of watchkeeping. Twenty-four hours a day, the duty
watch would attend to the steering, keep an all-round lookout, trim the sails and
refresh the nips on the running rigging.[100] Within the watch, its most competent

members[101] would stand their 'trick' at the helm—usually about two hours—or as a lookout—seldom longer than an hour—and otherwise stand by to perform any task as ordered by the officer of the watch or the petty officer or leading hand. This system worked to a rhythm dictated by the clock, marked aboard ship by the ringing of the ship's bell in a precise system.

Each day was divided into four-hour periods[102]—the first watch (2000–2359), the middle watch (0001–0400), the morning watch (0400–0800), the forenoon watch (0800–1200), the afternoon watch (1200–1600), the first dog (1600–1800) and last dog (1800–2000). Every half-hour of every watch was marked by the ringing of the ship's bell in a long established pattern and rhythm. The change of watch was 'eight bells' rung as four double rings, *ding-ding, ding-ding, ding-ding, ding-ding*. Half an hour later came one bell, and so on through the four-hour watch until eight bells again, the odd-numbered times being rung in a pattern of *ding-ding, ding* for three bells, *ding-ding, ding-ding, ding* for five bells, and so on. Time was counted in a time-honoured system, such-and-such happened at 'three bells in the forenoon watch'—or 0930, landsmen's time.

In a merchantman, which was usually crewed only with as many sailors as was absolutely necessary, the additional formalities and systematic world of precise commands shouted, or sounded with boatswain's calls or whistles characteristic of warships, were unknown. Crew were supposed to know their jobs and to spring to and perform them swiftly and correctly with the minimum of elaboration. The shout of 'Ready about!'—get ready everything required for the ship to change tack so that the wind blows onto the sails from the other side—was enough to ensure the duty watch (or, in rough weather, everyone) completed all the various tasks—readying sheets and braces, releasing bowlines, and so on—to ensure that all lines ran free and nothing jammed when the order came, 'Stand-by to tack ship!'

Organized on Western lines, each crewman's life was structured by his watch and part of ship; his day was structured into a clear and repeating 24-hour timetable.

As far as we know, it was not anything like that on Chinese ships. As we have seen, Chinese ships may have required a lot of muscle-power to work, but their subtle sailing rig required no such orchestrated ballet to control as did the complex, multi-sail, multiple-control-line world of Western ships. In like manner, their shipboard organization was far less formal and hierarchical. Less a matter of ordering this and commanding that than one of agreeing what next needed to be done and working together to do it.

Much the same seems to have been true of working part of ship. The extreme economy with which junks appear to have been operated—not an unnecessary cent expended—seems to have meant more breakdown than routine maintenance. Work 'part of ship' was most likely more spasmodic, occasioned by the sudden parting of a rope or breaking of a batten, than a matter of routine overhauling, inspecting, repairing and replacing. Spares are expensive; apart from a spare rudder, which many junks carried for reasons already considered, the spares inventory would appear to have been small. But to this we need to add that, because junks are 'low-stress' designs, the forces being exerted by the wind and the resulting stresses on the hull and the rigging will have been far lower, size for size, than on a Western vessel; thus the need for replacement and repair was far less. It is also worth noting that precisely because of the basic design and construction of a junk sail, it worked almost as well when full of holes as when intact, so the urgency of repair that faced a Western ship with a ripped sail was just not present.

For an example that points up the contrast, many a Western ship will have had two or three suits of sails. There would have been an old, patched suit—possibly with several spares as well—used for the gentler airs of the tropics and the steady, seldom rambunctious winds of the trades. And there would have been the newest set, ready for use in the stronger winds and rougher seas of higher latitudes.[103] Immediately, a world of work opens up that could have no place on a Chinese junk. Ripped sails have to be recovered, unbent, sent down to the deck and a replacement swayed up and bent on—imagine the skill, organization and co-ordination needed to do that with a topgallant sail attached by several lashings to a yard 35 metres from the deck. As a ship works out of the trades and into temperate latitudes, and vice versa, so the whole ship's company is set to work, to send down one suit and send up another. That meant lowering some 5 or 6 tonnes of canvas down to deck level and swaying the same weight of sail cloth up in heavy and ungainly 'sausages' of frapped sailcloth. On a Western ship of the *Keying*'s size, a topgallant sail, for example, would have weighed at least 350 to 400 kilogrammes.

So bells, commands, tasks to be done and the speed and regularity with which their completion will have been expected took specific form on a Western vessel and shaped the mindsets of those who had to do them. That established how one 'ought' to do things.

On a Chinese vessel, it was a different world. Not only no bells to mark the passing hours, but a completely different rhythm, punctuated by utterly different tasks.

The Chinese sailor used an extremely ancient way of measuring time quite different from the twelve double-hours, or 'watches' of the terrestrial Chinese day (時辰, *shíchen*). The Chinese sailor's day was decimal, split into 100 equal periods called *kè* (刻, roughly 14.4 minutes), each of which had 60 *fēn* (分, roughly 14.4 seconds).[104] One 'decimal' day was 6,000 *fēn*; the resulting shipboard 'watch' was 600 *fēn*—2.4 hours—confusingly, with the same name, *gēng* (更), as the 500-*fēn* landsman's 'watch'. There were ten *gēng* in a day for a Chinese sailor, so it is an interesting comment on crew relationships on the *Keying* that nowhere does Charles Kellett seem to explain whose system prevailed for whom . . . or even to show that he was aware there was a Chinese watch system and that it differed from, and did not map onto, the Western one.

Did the European crew keep European watches while So Yin Sang Hsi and his hands kept Chinese *gēng* (更), with neither being much aware of or interested in the other? We do not know. But we can surmise that sailors who had probably been working on junks for years, using traditional crewing structures and systems for ordering daily life on board, will have found bells and their ill-understood dictates to be a new, unfamiliar language, the necessity for learning which—they were on a junk, were they not?—would have seemed hard to grasp.

It is as likely that, in fact, the Europeans simply ignored the Chinese crew, save as brute and obviously reluctant labour that could be called on to heavie-hauly on the tiller tackles and halyards, but who were otherwise left to So Yin Sang Hsi to organize as he wished. Meanwhile, perhaps, the Europeans ran the daily routine of the *Keying* as if they were on a Western brig, the ship's bell telling the time, half the European deck hands handing over to the half, rubbing sleep from their eyes, the mates handing over the watch—while sullen and baffled Chinese crewmen were yelled at, 'Lee sheets there! Hey, johnny, haul on that **!!#* rope when I tell you. Haul away!', and otherwise left to stew.

Instead of wondering whether trying to run a Chinese junk as if it were a Western ship might not be the smartest way ahead, the Europeans found easier answers. The Chinese crew were 'slackers'. They were 'excited by opium'. They were 'refusing duty'. They needed to be punished; examples were set. Recalcitrant troublemakers were 'put in irons'. No wonder that, as the ship struggled towards the North Atlantic and provisions began to run out, it was only 'for a time [that] all seemed to go on well'.

Crawling Northwestwards

It is not known whether the junk's continued slow progress was from the Keying's protracted problems with the doldrums, although the likelihood is that they were. But the by-now usual suspects will have contributed too. There must have been an increasingly foul bottom. Ships have been known to become so foul as to be almost unable to make progress save in a strong wind. From a chance newspaper report, this seems to have been the case with the Keying. Once the ship got to New York, a story (reported to have originally been in the New York Express) reached England, that 'the bottom is very foul, which has prevented somewhat her sailing. She will have to be placed on the Sectional Dock to be cleaned.'[105]

There is also the fact that the Keying was effectively in ballast; that is, sailing 'light' and drawing very little water. Since we know that her mast, sails and rig were heavy—particularly if the accepted weight of the mainsail at something like 9 tonnes is correct,[106]—perhaps Charles Kellett continued to keep the ship under reduced sail, either to restrict what may have been an exaggerated and possibly dangerous roll, or to avoid the risk of being knocked flat by a gust of wind coinciding with a larger-than-usual wave—the two being aspects of the same problem. Whatever the reasons and causes, on her way north to the Equator and then on northwards to where she would meet the brisk but, for her, unfavourable northeast winds, the Keying made slow progress.

By late May, water and provisions had to be rationed; something that may have been started as the ship approached St. Helena. The Account notes that rationing in some guise was an early necessity:[107]

> (Once clear of the Sunda Strait) it became necessary to make some changes
> in the police of the ship and the distribution of stores and water. The

Chinamen were put on an allowance of four quarts of water per day, and the Europeans three quarts. It became absolutely necessary to do this, as the former has actually consumed up to this time, four gallons daily per each man. They had also burned up 1330 pounds of wood.

The *Keying* does not seem to have been part of a lavishly appointed expedition; short commons were probably normal.

A Bold Decision

As May drew on, Charles Kellett knew his ship was in trouble; his plans had to be revised. He accordingly abandoned Britain as a destination and headed for America.[108] His original stated intention was to head for Charleston, South Carolina, that being the nearest port when, in 12°N, 42°W, it had become clear they were running out of water and food. Putting that position together with a later one, when the *Keying* was closer to America, reveals the nature of the problem Charles Kellett would have faced had he tried to stick with his original plan.

Various sources give data from reports to Lloyd's from sightings of the junk during the voyage.[109] The first had been by the *Flora Kier* on 9 April, when the *Keying* was in 26°S 11°E and still on her way to St. Helena. The second was by the *Urania* on 16 June, when the *Keying* reported she was 'short of everything and likely to make for America'. The *Urania* reported the encounter to have been in 29° 12'N, 61° 59'W, well up the Atlantic and more or less where a sailing vessel would expect to begin to find the northeast trades easing, and being forced to take the longer, westerly passage around the Azores high-pressure area, within which winds were light and variable.

Given Kellett's Western captain's prerogatives on the one hand and the Chinese manner of operating a ship on the other, it would be interesting to discover how the decision to alter course for America was made. We know why, but whether Kellett made the decision and kept it to himself, made it himself and told his crew, or made it with some level of consultation, we do not know. Given the limits on the prerogatives of ship's masters, Western ships at this date were generally bound to a given voyage plan. However, especially with respect to tramping voyages, the ship's master seems to have had considerable discretion in practice. In any case, a plea of necessity would always be supported where there was any deviation from a previously intended route.

Chinese ships were not run on similar lines; from what is understood, any changes would have to be with the consent of the crew. If Charles Kellett acted within his Western skipper's prerogatives without getting his Chinese crew on side, it may be that this difference was yet another cause of the tensions and resentments that surfaced in New York.

This contrasts with an early Qing dynasty voyage recorded by one of the passengers, the monk Dashan. Dashan describes the ship's arrival off the coast of Vietnam and how the decision was made as to which port of call to head for:

> The captain-ship's owner and the merchants wanted to enter Hoi An harbor, the better to barter and sell. The group of monks wanted to go to Thuan Hoa harbor, the better to visit the king and his ministers. Confronting to each other, they asked for my arbitration. I said: 'Aren't we all anxious to go to shore?' They said they were simply anxious. I called for the *Fair winds escort thee* flag to be set up and spoke, saying:
>
> 'Now, let's see what will be the message of the wind. If it favors Hoi An, then Hoi An it is. If it favors Thuan Hoa then Thuan Hoa.' Thus it will be settled, we have no choice. The crowd said that this was for the best. However, the helmsman continued to steer toward Hoi An. At the time, the wind righted and filled the sails, the better to reach Hoi An. In a short while, the wind gradually [shifted favouring] Thuan Hoa. The sailors handed sail so that the ship lay to. Looking at the tips of the mountains, [we saw] they were still an immeasurable [distance away] . . .
>
> At the end of breakfast, I asked, saying: 'Go to Hoi An? Or go to Thuan Hoa?' They all said: 'Hoi An is favorable, Thuan Hoa is contrary.' I laughed and said: 'If so, then now we simply go to Thuan Hoa.' [110]

It is worth plotting the track of the *Keying* during this difficult stage. The track from St. Helena north to the Equator had been slow; the *Keying* had been steered by Charles Kellett well to the east. Yet the position given by Kellett when he first made a decision to head for Charleston, 1,880 nautical miles west-north-west by north of the position in which the junk crossed the Equator, shows that they had been carried or driven some 24^0 20', or about 1,450 nautical miles of westing for only 12 degrees, or some 720 nautical miles of northing during their crossing of the remainder of the doldrums and the sail northwards to the reliable winds of the northeast trades. The position Kellett found himself in at that point was 760 miles north-north-east of the mouth of the Amazon.

Here is the recommended track from St. Helena in *Ocean Passages for the World*:[111]

> steer a direct course for Ascension Island, passing it on either side, and crossing the Equator between 25°W and 30°W (in July between 20°W and 25°W, to ensure better winds). Then make a course to the N to reach the North-east Trade Wind as soon as possible (in July and August crossing the parallel of 10°N to the W of 30°W), and run through it. The North-east Trade Wind will probably be lost in about 26°N to 28°N, and 38°W to 40°W, when W winds may be expected, and on reaching these shape course for the English Channel.

From the position where we can infer the *Keying* found the northeast trades, somewhere around 7°N 37°W, Charles Kellett would have found it impossible to reach the westerlies he needed for the run to the Channel in anything like the longitude recommended. The furthest westing given in the recommended route for losing the trades and finding westerlies for the Channel was not far from where the *Keying* had found the trades in the first place. By inference, we can work out that the average Western vessel, crossing the Equator where recommended, would be expected to lose 10 to 15 degrees of westing as it gained 26 to 28 degrees of northing. By contrast, by the time the *Keying* reached the northern edge of the trades, it had lost nearly *eighty* degrees of westing—four to five times as much—and spent 54 days doing so—not far off half the lowest of the average Indiaman's voyage times for the entire trip from Hong Kong to the Channel. As Charles Kellett graphically put it,

> the wind though mostly NE, the vessel never making a better than a west by a north course, and sometimes worse ... disheartened us so much that we almost despaired of ever getting across the north-east trade winds. On reaching twelve degrees north latitude forty-two degrees west longitude, on examination we found that our provisions would not last the time our voyage seemed likely to endure ...

But supposing brisk westerlies had quickly been encountered and the *Keying* had altered for the Channel? The inevitable result, because of the slow speeds and the delays, would have meant the *Keying* was not heading up the North Atlantic at the optimal time of year. A vastly lengthy voyage would have transpired; given the state of the provisions, it was obviously out of the question. Given that any salvation in terms of the wind was extremely unlikely, Charles Kellett's decision was the only one he could make. In this, as in so much of the seamanship and navigation of the *Keying*, Kellett proved an astute and extremely capable skipper, whatever his shortcomings as the cross-cultural ambassador it probably never occurred to him either to want or to pretend to be.

The track of the *Keying*, between when we can infer it picked up the northeast trades and when it met the *Urania*, around 1,525 miles on, is pretty much steady northwest. The ship's course shows no sign of sailing more closely to the prevailing wind, because, as Kellett reported, she had no capacity to do so. Instead, the *Keying* made a course, given the variability in direction of the northeast trade and its tendency in June to be more east than northeast,[112] that will have been mostly a broad reach, with the wind occasionally hauling forward to a beam reach as the wind swung northeast—a soldier's wind.[113] The *Keying* spoke to the *Urania* on 16 June, 54 days after she had left St. Helena and 39 days after she had crossed the Equator. From St. Helena, she had thus made 3,060 miles in 54 days and, since the Equator, 1,880 miles in 39. These are averages of 2.4 and 2 knots, respectively. The *Keying* was crawling, even with 'a soldier's breeze'.

What followed sounds grim, with the crew refusing duty, the winds not co-operating and rations having to be eked out with the 'plentiful' fish they were able to catch. Kellett resorted to the 'mildest means' of inducing crew co-operation— by inference, the further occasional use of the rope's end when other means of persuasion failed. Fortunately, they fell in with an American brig, were able to get some supplies and equip themselves with 'a chart and coast pilot',[114] though we do not know exactly where this lucky meeting took place. The captain of the brig advised Kellett to head for New York, although on the way they ran into a gale that occasioned damage, including springing two masts and splitting the sails.[115]

Again, we can plot this stage of the voyage, supposing the *Keying* to be heading to Charleston until some few hundred miles from it—perhaps when still east of the outer edge of the Gulf Stream—then altering for New York. The result would have been a dogleg—or zigzag route steering first one way, then another. The *Keying* had been slightly east-south-east of Charleston when it met the *Urania*, so the question is what the wind was doing over this last stretch. Looking again at the recommended route, it is interesting that, when the *Keying* and the *Urania* met, the junk was in an excellent position for heading for New York—'For New York, try to reach 30°N, 70°W, and thence steer as directly as possible for New

York".[116] The *Keying* had easting in hand. Was it necessary? At this season of the year, the prevailing winds in a broad band from the American East Coast to the eastern side of the Gulf Stream tend to be southwesterly, so the *Keying* would have had a favourable wind, broad-reaching on the port gybe with the steady push of the Gulf Stream helping her on her way.

The final leg of this long passage was around 1,080 miles; as they eventually reached the approaches to the port of New York on 7 July,[117] it had taken a further 21 days at an average speed of about 2.1 knots. Since St. Helena, therefore, the *Keying* had sailed about 5,535 nautical miles over 75 days, at an average speed of 3.1 knots.

The passage is a stark illustration of the vicissitudes of the world of sail and of the difficult and demanding burdens that fell on the shoulders of its captains. London had been 4,512 miles from St. Helena—perhaps some 70 to 80 days distant, other things being equal. But it seems clear from the evidence of the voyage to New York that other things were very far from equal. Whatever may have been the potential performance envelope of a traditional junk as theorized by armchair sailors, in practice, the evidence shows that the *Keying* was not well suited to very long voyages or those requiring work against adverse winds. This should not, in fact, surprise. The traditional Chinese sea-going ship was designed over centuries for quite a different sort of voyaging. Namely, for relatively short passages—perhaps a maximum of 1,500 to 2,000 miles[118]—in benign waters, sailing with the following winds and currents of the favourable monsoon.

Indeed, herein lies another of the curious silences of the narrative record. Seventy-five days at sea is two and a half months. Standard reference books on the topic observe that the symptoms of scurvy, a debilitating and eventually fatal disease caused by the absence of vitamin C in the diet, make themselves manifest after one to three months at sea.[119] Chinese mariners seem early to have mastered this problem, though exactly what they understood it to be or what the cure was is not clear.[120]

The Western understanding is generally ascribed to the publishing of *A Treatise on the Scurvy* in 1753 by the British naval surgeon James Lind, though in fact the empirical correlation Lind had observed had also been noted by others, including the Dutch physician Johan Bachstrom, twenty years previously. Lind's book was not widely influential; scurvy continued to be a problem for the British into the late nineteenth century. The commanders of some of Britain's ill-fated quests for the Northwest Passage in the mid-nineteenth century, for example, believed the disease could be combatted by good hygiene, regular exercise and good morale.

One very common symptom of scurvy is lassitude, shortness of breath, especially in the case of any exertion, and feeling significantly under the weather. Given that this 75-day voyage had been preceded by an 81-day voyage, with only a brief respite in St. Helena, it is possible that some symptoms of dietary deficiency may have been evident. That Kellett may have understood the potential problem comes from the reference to 'plentiful fresh fish'. Fresh fish, while not as good a source as certain fruits and vegetables, is known to contain enough vitamin C to prevent scurvy's onset.

What Kellett and his partners had asked of their ship was far, far more than it had been designed for. Had Kellett stuck to the plan to reach London from St. Helena, the result would have been an agonizingly long passage in which very little forward progress was made. His decision to alter course for America, when he found himself in 12^{0}N 42^{0}W, was the decision of a fine and prudent seaman. He not only saved his crew from what may have been an even longer voyage than the one they actually completed. He very possibly saved them from death.

It seems unlikely anyone aboard appreciated this, bar perhaps the Keying's two mates, Mr. Burton and Mr. Revett, and maybe the Chinese captain, So Yin Sang Hsi. On the long, slow voyage from the Sunda Strait, the crew had been at sea and on ship's rations—there is no suggestion that anyone moved ashore during the stay in St. Helena—for 156 days. Allowing for the long wait and hard work in the area of the Sunda Strait, since the ship left Hong Kong they had been aboard for 210 days, or nearly seven months. The Keying was not a happy ship. It was to have a long and troubled stay, now that it had reached a haven.

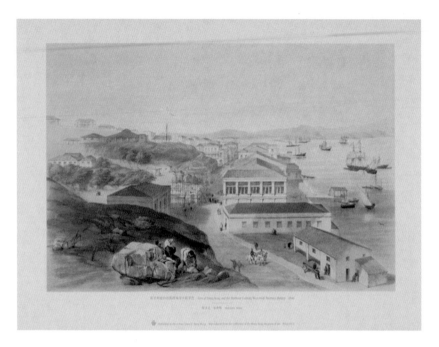

Plate 1 Murdoch Bruce, *View of Hong Kong and the Harbour Looking West from Murray's Battery, Hong Kong, 1846,* Hong Kong Museum of Art Collection

Plate 2 Murdoch Bruce, *View of Spring Gardens, 24th June 1846,* Hong Kong Museum of Art Collection

Plate 3 Murdoch Bruce, *View of Victoria: Looking West from the Garden of the Honorable John Walter Hulme, Chief Justice, Hong Kong, 20th August 1846*, Hong Kong Museum of Art Collection

Plate 4 Murdoch Bruce, *View of Jardine Matheson's Looking North-West from Causeway Bay, 28th September 1846*, Hong Kong Museum of Art Collection

Plate 5 *The Keying*, unknown China-trade artist, c.1847, gouache on paper, Hong Kong Maritime Museum Collection

Plate 6 *The Keying*, unknown China-trade artist, c.1847, gouache on paper, courtesy of Martyn Gregory Gallery

Plate 7 *The Chinese Junk "Keying"*, Nathaniel Currier, New York, 1847, coloured lithograph, Hong Kong Maritime Museum Collection

Plate 8 *The Great Chinese Junk Now on Her Voyage to England*, Edmund Evans, wood engraving, *The Pictorial Times*, Volume X, Issue No. 231, Saturday 14th August, 1847, London (UK), Courtesy of PictorialGems, United Kingdom

Plate 9 *Chinese Junk Keying*, unknown artist, Rock & Co., London, copper engraving, author's collection

Plate 10 *The Chinese Junk, Keying, Captain Kellett*, Rock Bros. & Payne, London, 1848, coloured aquatint, Hong Kong Museum of Art Collection

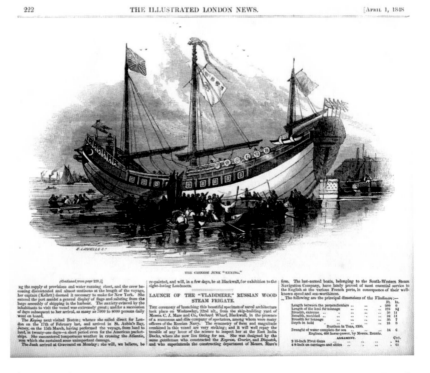

Plate 11 *The Chinese Junk "Keying"*, Birket Foster, engraver Ebenezer Landells, *The Illustrated London News*, 1 April 1848, p. 220, Hong Kong Maritime Museum Collection

Plate 12 *The Keying,* unknown artist, *A Description of the Royal Chinese Junk, "Keying",* 5th edition (London: J. Such, 1848), Hong Kong Maritime Museum Collection

Plate 13 *The Junk Keying Approaching England,* unknown artist, unknown (probably London), c.1848, National Maritime Museum, London

Plate 14 *Keying*, illegible, printed by Vickers, Holeywell [*sic*] Street, National Maritime Museum, London

Plate 15 *The Bay and Harbour of New York from* Italia, Samuel Waugh, c.1853, courtesy of the Museum of the City of New York

THE CHINESE JUNK.

Plate 16 *The Chinese Junk*, John Greenaway, in Walter Thornbury and Edward Walford, *Old and New London, A Narrative of Its History, Its People and Its Places. Illustrated with Numerous Engravings from the Most Authentic Sources*, vol. 3 (London: Cassell Petter & Galpin, n.d.), p. 289, Digital Collections and Archives, Tufts University

PORTRAIT OF HESING.

希生廣東老爺

Plate 17 *Portrait of Hesing*, in *A Description of the Royal Chinese Junk, "Keying"*, 5th edition (London: J. Such, 1848), Hong Kong Maritime Museum Collection

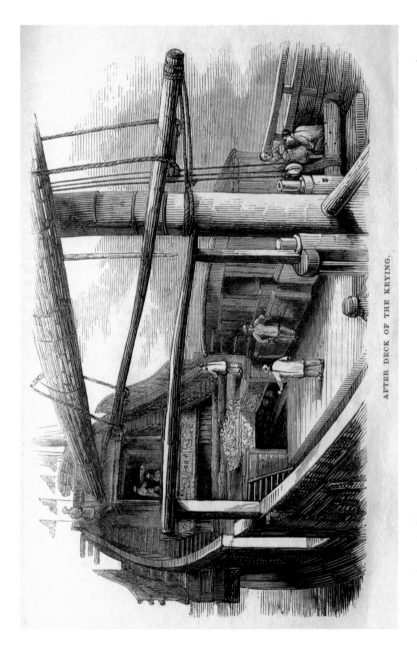

AFTER DECK OF THE KEYING.

Plate 18 *After Deck of the Keying*, in *A Description of the Royal Chinese Junk, "Keying"*, 5th edition (London: J. Such, 1848), Hong Kong Maritime Museum Collection

The decorated stern of the junk *Keying*

Plate 19 *Stern of the Keying,* in *A Description of the Royal Chinese Junk, "Keying",* 5th edition (London: J. Such, 1848), Hong Kong Maritime Museum Collection

SALOON OF THE KEYING.

LANDELLS.

Plate 20 *Saloon of the Keying*, in *A Description of the Royal Chinese Junk, "Keying"*, 5th edition (London: J. Such, 1848), Hong Kong Maritime Museum Collection

Plate 21 *A Passage of Arms*, in *A Description of the Royal Chinese Junk, "Keying"*, 5th edition (London: J. Such, 1848), Hong Kong Maritime Museum Collection

Plate 22 *The Opening of the Great Exhibition by Queen Victoria on 1st May, 1851*, Henry Courtney Selous, oil on canvas, courtesy of the Victoria and Albert Museum

Plate 23 *The Chinese Junk Keying*, medal in white metal by Thomas Halliday, Birmingham, England, Hong Kong Maritime Museum Collection

Plate 24 *The Chinese Junk Keying*, medal in white metal by J. Davis, Birmingham, England, 1848, National Maritime Museum, London

Plate 25 *The Mandarin Hesing*, medal in white metal by Thomas Halliday, England, 1848, National Maritime Museum, London

Plate 26 "During a General Salute the Elders performed the Cow Tow under the Union Jack according to Chinese Custom", Capt. Robert Jenkins RN, courtesy of Lok Man Rare Books, Hong Kong

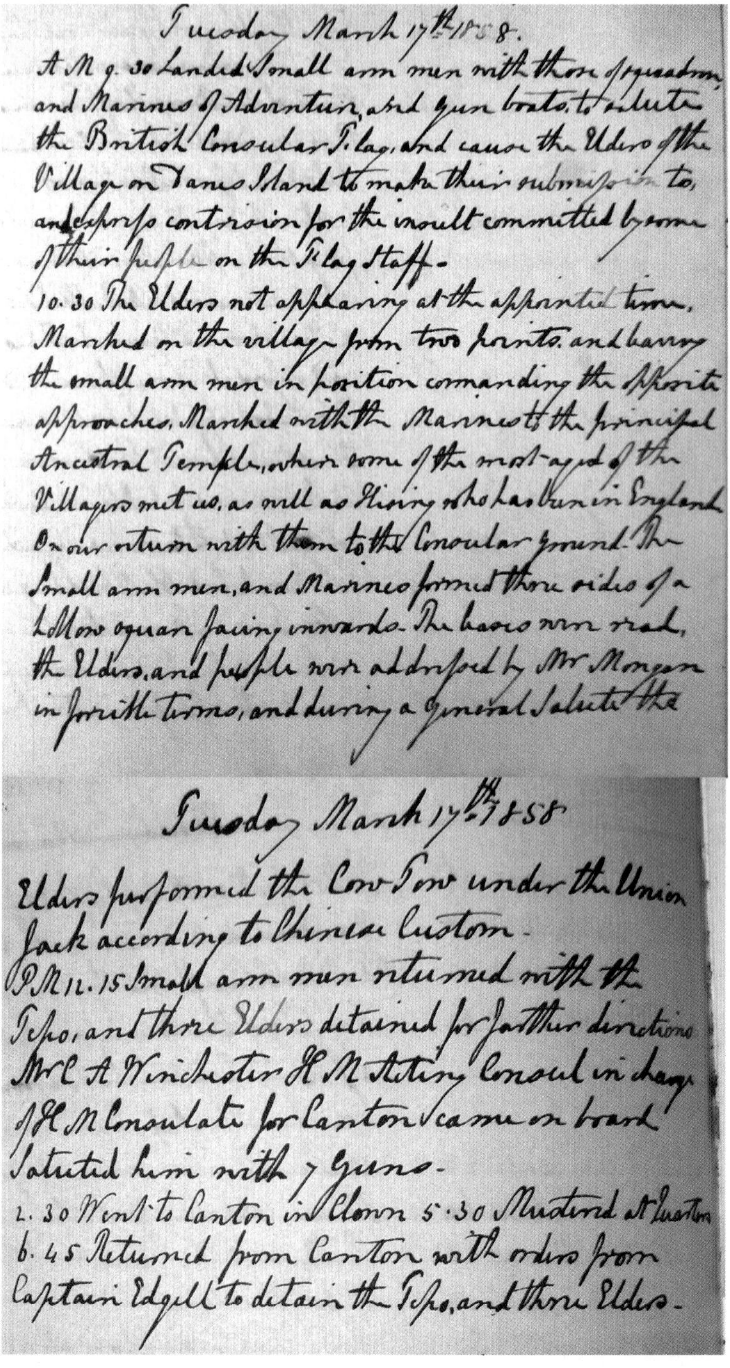

Tuesday March 17th 1858.

At AM 9.30 Landed Small arm men with those of squadron, and Marines of Adventure, and gun boats, to salute the British Consular Flag, and cause the Elders of the Village on Danes Island to make their submission to, and express contrision for the insult committed by some of their people on the Flag Staff.

10.30 The Elders not appearing at the appointed time, Marched on the village from two points, and having the small arm men in position commanding the opposite approaches. Marched with the Marines to the principal Ancestral Temple, where some of the most aged of the Villagers met us, as well as Hixing who has been in England On our return with them to the Consular ground. The Small arm men, and Marines formed three sides of a hollow square facing inwards. The bases were read, the Elders, and people were addressed by Mr Morgan in forcible terms, and during a General Salute the

Tuesday March 17th 1858

Elders performed the Cow Tow under the Union Jack according to Chinese Custom.

PM 12.15 Small arm men returned with the Tspo, and three Elders detained for farther directions Mr C A Winchester H M Acting Consul in charge of H M Consulate for Canton came on board Saluted him with 7 Guns.

2.30 Went to Canton in Clown 5.30 Mustered at Quarters 6.45 Returned from Canton with orders from Captain Edgell to detain the Tspo, and three Elders.

Plate 27 Extract from the Captain's logbook, HMS *Actaeon*, 17th March 1858, Capt. Robert Jenkins RN, courtesy of Lok Man Rare Books, Hong Kong

Chapter 4
The Troubled Stay in New York

The Arrival

Closing a coast after weeks at sea is always an emotional moment. It is when a mental switch is thrown. For weeks, one has been inwardly focused on the microcosm that has carried one across the ocean's vastness. One's small, shipboard world has been *the* world. Its sounds, smells, patterns and rhythms have been all that there is, the intensely familiar accompaniment of one's days and nights. Any change has one's senses alert and questing. There is an unfamiliar creak or other sound. The ship's movement alters slightly. An unaccustomed smell wafts in. A change in the weather? The helmsman nodding off? A sheet carried away? One's sensitivities are wholly locked into the way of one's ship. It has become an extension of the self—and the self of it.

One's fellow crew are one's whole society, the comforts and irritations they give exaggerated by an unavoidable proximity. The results of this 'total society', to use Erving Goffman's useful phrase, can be for good or ill.[1] A happy ship is a closely integrated organism, each crew person the support of the others, his or her personality completely absorbed in and woven into the single fabric that is the ship's company. Life aboard is life itself, which is why so many seafarers, when ashore, were out of their element, adrift and unable to cope until their feet were again treading the planking, and the familiar world of a ship had once more embraced them.

If happy ships are all alike, to misquote Tolstoy,[2] every unhappy ship is unhappy in its own way. As it approached the Ambrose Channel, the southern side of which had been marked by the 75-metre twin light towers of Navesink in

1828, a 26-metre-high lighthouse on Sandy Hook since 1764 and, since 1838, also by a lightship,[3] the *Keying* was a desperately unhappy ship. Its unique unhappiness was a product of the theme of this entire book: the vast gulf in understanding and sympathy that had opened up and was widening between the world of the industrializing and assertive West and that of the Earth's other peoples.

We know almost nothing of the detail, since Charles Kellett's log seems no longer to exist and the *Description* and the *Account* are silent. In St. Helena, the Europeans in the crew had been as much on Kellett's mind as had his fractious Chinese sailors. Had the vicissitudes of the Atlantic passage and the increasing tensions with the Chinese crew brought them back into line, in a display of cultural solidarity?

We do not know.

There is no mention in the press or in Kellett's accounts of wholesale disaffection in the *Keying*'s crew. From the record of the remainder of the voyage, and by inference from the article written by Charles Dickens in London, the European crew stuck with the ship. The real unhappiness will have been both with and within the Chinese crew, especially the original crew who had been signed aboard in Whampoa nearly nine months previously—a period of the length of which, in relation to the articles they had signed, these unhappy men will have been sharply aware.

Charles Kellett must have been eternally thankful for the chance meeting he had had with the unnamed American brig which had not only advised him to head for New York, not Charleston,[4] but had provided him with 'a chart and coast pilot'. To approach New York's harbour from the southeast, as the *Keying* did, without any sort of navigational aid would have been an extremely demanding, very high-risk option. For when one closes the east coast of the United States from almost any point between Florida and the Ambrose Channel, one sees almost nothing until within a few miles of the shore.

The New Jersey shore is low-lying: a long beach frontage with no land much higher than 15 to 20 metres above sea level until the 75-metre eminence of the Navesink twin light towers at Highlands, NJ, comes into view. It paints a clear picture of this coast when one realizes that the Navesink twin light towers are the highest point on the entire Atlantic coast of the United States, between the southern entrance to the Ambrose Channel and Florida.[5]

This stretch of coast between Cape May and Long Island is one of the grave-yard coasts of the sailing world. Somewhere between 4,000 and 7,000 wrecks are estimated to lie sunken between the entrances to the Delaware and Hudson rivers.[6] The records show that 338 ships were wrecked along the Long Island and New Jersey shores in the decade before 1848. That is almost three a month, every month.[7] Approaching this unknown coast with only a single chart and a coast pilot of unknown provenance will have been a huge test of Charles Kellet's navi-gation and seamanship.

The most probable pilot will have been the twelfth or fourteenth edition of Edmund M. Blunt's wondrously titled *The American Coast Pilot: containing direc-tions for the principal harbors, capes and headlands, of the coasts of North and South America: describing the soundings, bearings of the lighthouses and beacons from the rocks, shoals and ledges, &c. with the prevailing winds, setting of the currents, &c. and the latitudes and longitudes of the principal harbors and capes, together with a tide table*,[8] first compiled by Captain Lawrence Furlong in 1796 and published by Blunt, who subsequently took on the task of updating it.

Blunt's description of the approaches from the south, which takes up five densely packed pages, is simultaneously daunting and extraordinarily helpful. In the fashion of the day, the navigator is expected to find his way more by sound-ings and the nature of the seabed as sampled by the lead, than by care with compass courses and visual fixes. The reasons for that Blunt makes obvious. On the one hand, there is the very low-lying coast, barely visible until one is commit-ted to making in for one's destination. On the other, is the remarkable regularity of the seabed and the well-recorded differences in its composition from place to place. From Barnegat to Sandy Hook, we read of fine white and black sand in one place; mud, shells and gravel in another; and fine white and black sand on a very hard bottom in a third.

Supposing Charles Kellett to have been standing on the poop some 12 metres above sea level, the low-lying coast would not have hove into view until he was less than 15 nautical miles away. Only when he was 25 miles away—about 7–8 hours' sailing at *Keying*'s speed—would he have seen the Navesink light,[9] with its Fresnel lens from France installed only six years previously. With the low-lying coast under his lee and the 15-metre (50-foot) depth contour line 2.5 to 3 miles offshore, he will have had a leadsman busy, out on the *Keying*'s catwalk.

Like most experienced navigators, Kellett would have planned to make his landfall on the US coast by closing it so that as soon as it was in sight he would know which way to turn to find Sandy Hook lightship. In short, you come in on the coast either well north—and turn left—or well south and turn right. The second approach, which made sense for Kellett given his line of approach, is exactly what Blunt counsels:

> Coast Southward of Sandy Hook—If you come in near Cape Hatteras, be careful of its shoals and make your way to the N.N.E., which will carry you on the soundings of the Jersey shore. When you get 20 fathoms [36.6 metres], in lat. 40°N., then haul in to make the land, by which you will avoid the difficulties of the coast, and the shoals nearer in shore . . . taking care, as remarked before, not to run into less than 10 fathoms water, if night.[10]

He will have made sure he came in to the coast north of Barnegat Light at the northern end of Long Beach Island, though if he was being prudent he would not have been close enough to see its weak light.[11] The soundest plan would have been to close the coast between Barnegat Light and Sandy Hook, perhaps hoping to find Navesink light in the final hours of darkness, to give him confidence in his final approach. If Blunt was his guide—and probably anyway—he will also have made sure, as he made in towards the coast slowly during the night, that he stayed in water deeper than 30 metres, heaving to if necessary, thereby keeping the *Keying* at least 5 miles offshore. He would have made his final approach with the coming of daylight.

As the low-lying coast slowly hove over the horizon and they identified the exiguous landmarks, verifying that Charles Kellett had brought them safely to port, a welter of emotions must have played in the minds and hearts of the *Keying*'s riven and unhappy crew. For Charles Kellett and his officers, perhaps, a vindication of their decision to divert from their original plans. For the Chinese crew, maybe, an end to their miseries. For everyone, at last landfall and the end of a long, fraught and wearying passage.

But, first, the *Keying* hove-to off the Sandy Hook lightship, 'made her number' and got a message ashore to summon the help she would need to get her across the shifting shoals of the harbour entrance and up the last 12 to 13 nautical miles through the Narrows, to the quarantine anchorage off the Battery at the southwest end of Manhattan Island.

Blunt makes no bones about the possibility of a shipmaster taking his ship in on a making tide with a fair wind. But, given Kellett's unfamiliarity with the waters, the sprung mast and ripped sail, the fractious crew and the foul bottom, prudence would have suggested using all the help he could get.

No sources mention how long the *Keying* had to wait. The record says she was towed into New York, but one can be sure that she would first have taken a pilot, who would have been embarked when the *Keying* was nearing the Sandy Hook lightship.[12] This approach was a perilous business. Only a decade previously, over 400 lives had been lost:[13]

> The winter of 1835–1836 had been a particularly disastrous one for ship-ping along the coast. One winter's afternoon during that period two immi-grant ships—sailers, of course—had worked in close to the Sandy Hook lightship. The wind was east-southeast, blowing very heavy and approach-ing a gale. The two packets hove to off the lightship with signals flying for a pilot, firing guns to further attract the port scouts, whose boats were anchored well inside Sandy Hook bay. As has been stated, it was an off year for pilot efficiency in New York Harbor and the two immigrant packets were unable to get a pilot to bring them into the Narrows. The captains of the two immigrant ships had hove to with heads offshore and, not being able to beat to windward, were finally forced upon the Long Island shore. One of the ships went aground to the eastward of Rockaway and the other to the eastward of what is now known as Jones's Inlet. Each ship had from 150 to 300 passengers and by the break of the next day nearly every soul on board had perished.

When the *Keying* made in, the pilotage services of the states of New York and New Jersey at Sandy Hook would have had some forty pilots working in four pilot boats, three cruising in the offing and one on station near the Sandy Hook lightship. In 1845, the authorities had declared that the pilots, rather than waiting in Sandy Hook bay or close thereto, had to cruise out as far as 15 miles in the offing of Sandy Hook lightship, the better to intercept ships and provide them with a pilot when still safely offshore.[14] If a pilot was embarked, it is possible that the *Keying* came upon one when still several miles from Sandy Hook. With a pilot aboard, she would perhaps have kept going under her own sails as far as the southern entrance to the Narrows, where a tug would have been met to tow the junk to her anchorage off Castle Garden, The Battery, in New York harbour, where she arrived on 9 July 1847.[15] As 'she entered the port (she did so) amidst a general display of flags and saluting from the large assembly of shipping in the harbour.'[16]

There is a watercolour of her in this position, 'The Bay and Harbour of New York' by Samuel Waugh, painted some years later in 1853. She is wholly incidental to the painting's theme of Waugh's return from a 'grand tour' of Italy. The foreground has an Irish immigrant ship unloading at what was then the immigration station at the Battery; the *Keying* is anchored off in the middle distance. The painting, which is massive, concluded a large panorama, 'Italia', displayed as a public entertainment.[17] It is said that, at the same time that the *Keying* was in New York, some sort of copy was built and exhibited by P. T. Barnum, ostensibly starring the disaffected members of the *Keying*'s crew.[18] However, scholars who give any credence at all to the tale conclude that it is highly improbable the Barnum vessel featured Chinese crewmen, since contemporary reports indicate that Barnum's crew, of whatever vessel he was exhibiting, was composed mostly of Europeans and coloured Americans. Others deny there ever was a Barnum vessel, though how the two stories can in any way be reconciled is unclear. All that is evident is that contemporary sources are contradictory. An observation by Kellett suggests one solution. He claimed that the rumour *Keying* was not Chinese at all, but British and built in the state of Maine, was nothing more than a deliberately smearing canard.[19]

Entertaining the Public

The *Keying*'s four-month or so stay in New York must certainly have earned money, since some reports have 4,000 people a day visiting at US$0.25 a head. Among the visitors were the poet Walt Whitman, though his views of the vessel are not reported, and Orson Squire Fowler, America's most distinguished phrenologist (today of less *réclame* than in 1847!), who came to sadly predictable conclusions about the comparison between Western and Chinese human types.[20]

The visitor numbers are markedly discrepant. If we take the largest figure, 4,000 a day, it represents earnings of US$1,000 a day or some US$30,000 a month. Converted into 2007 money that is an absolutely enormous sum.[21] It is so enormous, indeed, as to indicate that the figure must be greatly exaggerated. That it almost certainly was exaggerated can be come at from another direction.

In a letter from Samuel Wells Williams,[22] who looms large in the *Keying* New York story, the whole stay netted a total of US$20,000, for a visitor total of 100,000. Clearly, the larger visitor numbers were inflated; indeed, from Williams' figures there must also have been some discounting of ticket prices. That said, in 1847, US$20,000 was a large sum, equivalent in today's terms to up to US$500,000. However, it also appears that whatever profits there may have been, Charles Kellett and his partners may not have seen much of them. In order to operate out of Castle Gardens, where visitors foregathered and were ferried to and from the ship, the owners of the facilities at there, Charles Heiser and Philip French, may have charged the *Keying* as much as 80 percent of the gross, or, if that is as improbable as it seems, evidently a hefty proportion. Given that a typical day's takings are reported as having been US$274.24 (for 7 August), that means visitor traffic of 977 people a day. The junk was open to the public from about 16 July until early September, roughly 40 days. If 7 August was average, we get a figure for gross receipts of about US$11,000 and for visitors of 39,000.[23]

So perhaps the visit was not a financial success. Such a conclusion would fit with the air of penury that hovered over the project. It would also, in the end, appear to have been a major reason for the tragic fate of this pioneering ship. The financial problems might also explain the problems with crew payment that surfaced during August. Finally, there is also evidence that the string of almost daily stories about the *Keying* in the *New York Herald*, written with what would have been at the time a typical racist slant, in some views written by Kellett himself, were a needed source of additional income and free publicity. The truth, either of the finances or the authorship of the letters, we shall probably never know.

The *Keying* Arrested by Her Own Crew

In August, a month or so after the ship's arrival—and therefore close to eleven months exactly since the crew had signed their articles, during which period they had been 'exhibited' by Kellett as part of the curiosities[24]—twenty-six of them tried to get their captain to respect what they felt was the letter of their contract. Their claim was that the Chinese captain, or perhaps Kellett, had not paid them (sources differ as to which, though the report in *The Globe* of 8 July 1847 is unequivocal that the action named So Yin Sang Hsi, as is the report in the *Caledonian Mercury* of 21 October 1847),[25] that they had been engaged only for eight months, and that they now wished to quit the ship and have their return passages paid as per their agreements. It would seem from some reports that the British officers constantly evaded any meeting; when, finally, the crew bearded Revett and tried to force him to listen to them by barring all egress, he called the police and had seven of them arrested for assault.[26]

At the time, one newspaper story argued that Kellett had boarded the *Keying* with money to pay the crew some of their wages—perhaps the US$12 each later mentioned in the court hearing—but that they were under the influence of opium and waxed fractious. Kellett called the police and had the seven ringleaders of the aggression arrested; the rest backed off. Given the narcoleptic effects of opium, this is an improbable tale. But, given the general tenor of the New York newspaper reports, with their mocking and contemptuous attitudes and peddling of racist stereotypes, the accusation of drug-induced violence was probably more a descriptive trope than an attempt at accurate reportage.

In the subsequent court case, the seven crewmen were represented *pro bono* by W. Daniel Lord,[27] a prominent New York attorney. Lord, a man closely connected with a growing sense that the lot of the contemporary seaman was a poor one and in need of remedy, found Samuel Wells Williams, who as a missionary had spent twelve years in China and knew enough Chinese. Williams, with the help of his New York-resident, Chinese Christian friend Lin King-chew, helped ensure the crewmen were able to tell their side of the story. They translated the crew's oral testimony and the written contract that had been signed in Hong Kong.[28]

It appears that Samuel Wells Williams was very soon convinced that Charles Kellett was the villain and the Chinese crewmen the victims. To what extent this was a cut-and-dried conclusion to be drawn from unequivocal evidence, or the product of a combination of the evidence and a personal reaction to Charles Kellett, it is obviously impossible to say. Wells Williams was a missionary, and extremely hostile to the opium trade.[29] If, as we have conjectured, Kellett and his officers had all been involved in the opium trade, it is more than probable that Wells Williams would have known it. This would not have inclined him to view them in a kindly light. There is also the possibility that Wells Williams, like many Americans who had spent time in China, was not a great fan of the British, which would have made two strikes against the officers of the *Keying*.[30]

In fairness to Wells Williams, he was certainly ahead of his time in his attitudes; it is not surprising that he should have taken so strongly against everything Charles Kellett, the *Keying*'s officers and the entire *Keying* project was about. Theirs was the philistine, populist, Sinophobic, run-of-the-mill, everyday-Joe's set of attitudes, probably not just to China but to anything different or non-European. This does not mean that Kellett and his officers were unable to like, get on with or help and support anyone at all who was foreign. No doubt they found individuals they liked and who liked them—So Yin Sang Hsi springs to mind. But their attitudes to China and the Chinese would have been conventional—as had become increasingly the case as the nineteenth century wore on, *de haut en bas*. The fundamental message and tone of the exhibition they mounted were denigratory in a distinctly condescending and belittling way. For someone with a genuine love of and real learning in the history of China—Wells Williams had been writing for *The Chinese Repository* from 1833 until his departure for America, was a recognized Sinologist in both the United States and Europe, and in 1846 had just begun working on his *The Middle Kingdom*—the *Keying* project and its organizers must have been an affront. In him, poor Charles Kellett, a Tom Lingard out of place and out of his depth, had met his come-uppance.

The case went forward on 3 September 1847, by which time, it is worth noting with an eye to the outcome of the case, the crew had been on the ship for at least 271 days—nearly nine months, or a good month longer than contracted. Indeed, if the time was counted from when they signed aboard in Whampoa— 14 September 1846—and if there was no shore leave between Whampoa and the departure from Hong Kong, they had been aboard just 11 days short of a full year, almost 50 percent more than their contracts had stipulated. So whatever the niceties of the actual articles, when viewed through the lens of standard operating practice on the British-dominated China seas, in a New York court there was a cut-and-dried case. In what follows, the various proceedings have had to be put together from newspaper reports and secondary accounts, the court record itself no longer being available.[31]

Daniel Lord very swiftly revealed—perhaps thanks as much to the arts of the advocate against the less polished court manner of seamen, especially when he was probably master of the translated contents of the sailors' articles and Kellett and Revett most likely were not—that Kellett and Revett should not be treated as credible witnesses. A key witness statement, which does not seem to have been successfully rebutted, argued that, when the crewmen who wanted to quit and be paid off were trying to talk to Charles Kellett, he began to leave the cabin while Edward Revett tried to force them to sign a receipt for money they had never received. They resisted, still trying to talk to Kellett and in the process holding him back; thus the struggle began that occasioned the summoning of the police.[32]

In successfully calling into question the basis of the arrest of the seven crew members, Daniel Lord made possible a fuller hearing of the grievances claimed by the disaffected majority of the *Keying*'s Chinese crew. Given the period, and the general public attitude as manifested in the tenor of the newspaper stories, it is to the credit of the New York city magistrate who heard the case that he dismissed the case of assault against the crewmen, reprimanded Kellett and agreed to hear the crewmen's case justifying the arrest of the ship.

This is a nice point in maritime law requiring a brief explanation. Once Kellett and Revett's case of assault had been thrown out, the crewmen would have been free to have their grievance heard by having the *Keying* arrested. Complaints in maritime law are against the ship, which is in effect held as surety against claims, thus requiring the ship's representative to argue against that arrest.

In this second hearing, Charles Kellett and his ship's officers failed again to convince. The magistrate ordered the *Keying*—that is, Charles Kellett, the responsible officer—to stand by the ship's articles, including the crewmen's right to have a return passage paid for them. This cannot have been a common outcome.[33] However, although we may applaud such an apparent meting out of justice, it is worth sparing a thought for Kellett and the possibility that a simple clash of cultures, both in general and in terms of the conduct of shipboard life, had resulted in Kellett losing his good name, more or less as the young wife from whom he had long been separated sailed into port. It must have been extremely hard to bear. Kellett was probably a typical mid-nineteenth-century bucko skipper, ready with his fists as in the habits of the day he would have had to be, and very much of the opinions typical of his background and times. Today we may deprecate this. But Charles Kellett was not living today; this should be remembered.

Kellett contested the ruling and refused to pay the fares or arrears of wages of the disaffected crew, offering instead just US$20 a head, his claim in his letter to Queen Victoria being that 'the men had four months' wages advanced prior to our departure from China, and on our arrival at New York, they were offered the full amount of wages due, but preferred only a small portion.' It is quite unclear why the court chose to disbelieve Kellett. Given the trust placed in him by his partners, it seems more than merely strange that he should have chosen to lie blatantly both on oath in court and in a published letter to his sovereign. If we have reason to suppose that Charles Kellett, like many a bucko young skipper, might be prone to hyperbole, we have no reason to conclude that he was a barefaced liar. Painting the lily is one thing; outright lying is another.

It is worth remarking that the 1840s were not a time in the history of maritime law in the United States (or indeed Britain) when it is likely that the court's bias would have been in any way in favour of a ship's captain. In 1840, Richard Henry Dana—who by 1849 and probably beforehand was acquainted with W. Daniel Lord—had published that classic of the sea, *Two Years before the Mast*, the account of his experiences working his passage on the brig *Pilgrim* from New York to San Francisco via Cape Horn in 1836, returning on the *Alert* in 1837. The book had, above much else, highlighted in stark terms the brutality of the life of the average American seaman. By 1840, Dana had qualified as a lawyer, specializing in maritime law with the avowed intent of improving the lot of the American seaman. In 1841, six years before the arrival of the *Keying* in New York, he published *The Seaman's Friend*, a book which remained for many years the standard handbook telling sailors of their rights, in defence of which Dana represented many seamen in court.[34]

As much to the point, on 21 July 1840, a bill had been passed by Congress, 'In addition to the several acts regulating the shipment and discharge of seamen, and the duties of Consuls',[35] which forms yet another element in what was clearly a 'sea change' in attitudes towards the lives and lots of ordinary seamen, no matter what their provenance. In short, the world of Western maritime law—there was no Chinese equivalent—which for centuries had favoured shipowner and ship's master, was beginning half a century of rapid change. Young Charles Kellett was caught in the transition.

So what would have been the key issues? These are not that simple to spell out, not least because of the following facts. First, the *Keying's* crew was Chinese and had been signed on in a quasi-customary fashion in Whampoa and Hong Kong with, at best, a post hoc nod at the strict requirements of British ship's articles. Second, they would have been signed on using either a standard form, or some variant thereby, of what had already become known as Asiatic Articles, geared, one suspects, to the specifics of short-seas voyaging within the China seas. As of 1846, Asiatic Articles had not become fully formalized, but they already differed in important respects from standard British articles, the full legal purport of which may not have been as apparent to Charles Kellett and Mr. Mate Revett as, with the advantage of hindsight, it is to us. In any case, as we noted in describing the beginning of the voyage, the probability that any of the ship's officers had a clue as to the exact wording of the articles, which were in Chinese, is vanishingly small. This opens a significant gap between what Charles Kellett might have thought the crew believed they were signing on for, what *he* thought they were signing on for, what *the crew* thought they were signing on for—it being possible that at best only a few were actually able to read the articles they were signing— and what they actually *did* sign on for.

This stresses a point that emerges from Wells Williams's own studies. He knew that literacy among sea people was close to non-existent:

> In the district of Nanhai, which forms part of the city of Canton, an imperfect examination led to the belief that nearly all men are able to read, *except fishermen, agriculturalists, coolies, boat people, and fuelers* . . . From an examination of the hospital patients at Ningpo . . . the readers . . . formed not more than five per cent of the men . . . [36]

So there is some question as to whether the disaffected crew members themselves were masters of the detail, or of what that might mean under the scrutinizing lens of late 1840s American maritime law. For finally, the matter was reviewed in an American court in which there was no concept of Asiatic Articles or the world that had begotten them. More power to the New York court indeed, though it is unlikely that Charles Kellett and his ship's officers could or would have seen things thus.

There is also the question of exactly who was responsible for what. This does not come out clearly in most accounts of the New York court case, but it is strongly implied in a story about the case in a contemporary British newspaper. Supposing the story is true, and we have no reason to doubt it since it is copied in at least one other paper, it seems clear that *both* Charles Kellett and So Yin Sang Hsi were witnesses for the defence.[37] It is worth quoting the story as it appeared in full:

> The New York Papers state that the Chinese sailors, to the number of twenty-six, who navigated the Chinese junk to New York, not having been paid their wages, had arrested the vessel, and Mr. Lord, their advocate, had pleaded for them before the civil court of the district. The crew claimed in the first place, their arrears of wages from the month of September, 1846; and in the second, to be sent back to Canton at the expense of the captain. According to the sailors' account, they were only engaged for eight months, and were not to go beyond Batavia and Singapore. The advocate of So-Yu-Sang-Hi [*sic*], the Chinese captain, replied that the sailors who had worked the ship could not pretend that they had been made to cross the Indian sea and the Atlantic, without their knowledge. With regard to the question of wages, the captain had promised to pay them on their return to Canton with the produce of the American goods which he was to take on his return. He added that he did not think the sailors had any right to complain; the large recompenses they had received fully compensated for what was owed to them.

We do not have the *Keying*'s articles. However, if we consider a typical example of nineteenth-century articles, those of the American brig *Union*, Captain Edmond Nason, of May 1831, we get a strong flavour of what the *Keying*'s crew probably signed. It is worth quoting at length:[38]

> It is agreed between the Master, Seamen or Mariners of the *Brig Union, Edmond Nason Master,* now in the Port of *Boston* and bound for *Pensacola and any other port in the United States or elsewhere for a period of Six Months.* That in consideration of the monthly or other wages against each respective seaman or mariner's name hereunder set, they severally shall, and will, perform the abovementioned voyage; and the said master doth hereby agree with, and hire the said seamen and mariners for the said voyage, at such monthly wages or price, to be paid pursuant to this agreement, and the laws of the Congress of the United States of America, and the custom and usage of the Port of *Boston.* And they, the said seamen or mariners, do hereby promise and oblige themselves to do their duty, and obey the lawful commands of the officers on board the said vessel, or the boats belonging, as become good, faithful seamen or mariners; and at all places where the

said vessel should put in, or anchor at, during the said voyage to do their best endeavours for the preservation of the said vessel and cargo, and not to neglect and refuse doing their duty by day or by night; nor go out of the vessel on board any other vessel, or be on shore under any pretence whatever, until the above said voyage be ended, and the vessel discharged of her loading, without leave first obtained of the captain, or commanding officer on board; that in default thereof, they will be liable to all the penalties and forfeitures mentioned in the marine law, enacted for the government and regulation of seamen in the merchants' service, in which it is enacted, 'that if any seaman or mariner shall absent himself from on board the ship or vessel, without leave of the master, or officer commanding on board; and the mate or other officer having charge of the log-book, shall make an entry therein of the name of such seaman or mariner, on the day on which he shall so absent himself; and if such seaman or mariner shall return to his duty within forty-eight hours, such seaman or mariner shall forfeit three days' pay for every day which he shall so absent himself, to be deducted out of his wages; but if any seaman or mariner shall absent himself for more than forty-eight hours at one time, he shall forfeit all the wages due to him, and all his goods and chattels which were on board the ship or said vessel, or in any store where they may have been lodged at the time of his desertion, to the use of the owners of the ship or vessel; and moreover, shall be liable to pay to him or them, all damages which he or they may sustain by being obliged to hire other seamen or mariners, in his or her place.' And it is further agreed by both parties, that each and every lawful command which the said master shall think necessary hereafter to issue for the effectual government of the said vessel, suppressing immorality and vice of all kinds, be strictly complied with, under the penalty of the person or persons disobeying forfeiting his or their whole wages or hire, together with everything together belonging to him or them aboard the said vessel.

And it is hereby understood, and mutually agreed by and between the parties aforesaid, that they will render themselves aboard the said *Brig* on or before the [left blank] day of *January 1831*.

And it is further agreed on, that no Officer or Seaman belonging to the said vessel, shall demand, or be entitled to his wages, or any part thereof until the arrival of the said vessel at the above mentioned port of discharge, and her cargo delivered. And it is hereby further agreed between the Master and Officers of the said vessel, that whatever apparel, furniture and stores each of them may receive into their charge belonging to the said vessel, shall be accounted for on her return; and in case any thing shall be lost or damaged, through their carelessness or insufficiency, it shall be made good by such officer or seaman, by whose means it may happen, to the master and owners of said vessel . . . That each seaman or mariner who shall well and truly perform the abovementioned voyage, provided always that there be no plunderage, embezzlement or unlawful acts committed on the said vessel's cargo or stores, shall be entitled to the payment of the wages, or hire, that may be due to him, pursuant to this agreement as to their names are severally affixed and set forth. That for the due performance of each and every one of the abovementioned articles and agreements, and acknowledgement of their being voluntary, and without compulsion, or any other clandestine means being used, agreed to, and signed by us; in testimony whereof, we have each and every one of us under affixed our hands, the month and day against our name as here underwritten.

This particular set of articles, signed by nine American sailors, is then endorsed beside the lower part of the articles where the crew severally signed their names,

We who have subscribed our names in this column do promise that the man who has engaged for this present voyage, and signed his name in the first columns of the same line, shall proceed to the said voyage agreeable to the shipping paper, or refund the advance money to *Daniel W Lord or order* on demand.

It will have been one of the earlier sets of articles that the young Daniel Lord witnessed as fairly and properly signed by the crew.

A thoughtful reading of those articles should make clear what the articles the *Keying*'s crew signed looked like and how they would have read. We can be almost entirely sure that the wording would have been a close variant adapted to Asiatic articles and to the relative vagaries of the planned voyage. These were quite standard formats as can be seen by the fact that all bar a few words appear as a pre-printed document. Where the specific description of the voyage is to be penned in, for example, the phrase 'Pensacola and any other port in the United States or elsewhere for a period of Six Months' could quite easily have been written by Charles Kellett to read 'Singapore or any other port in the Archipelago or elsewhere for a period of eight months'.

Something of that order will have been the burden of the Chinese text the *Keying*'s Chinese crew signed. Reading it and thinking about its implications vis-à-vis relations between officers and crew in a standard merchantman of the period under the Western shipboard system will reveal much about the mindset within which Charles Kellett will have been working, though almost certainly not his Chinese crew. Tucked into that long and elaborate wording was much that might have led young Charles Kellett to suppose that the right was on his side vis-à-vis what he perceived to be his skulking, non-cooperative, untrustworthy Chinese crew.

The story ended by confirming that the judgement had gone against the *Keying*, as already discussed. But, interestingly, the spokesman for the defendant, which as we have seen in admiralty law was the vessel and not any of its officers, was claimed to be the Chinese captain, *not* any of the English officers. Here, we can see that in So's view, as argued above, the claim that the crewmen were innocents aboard being imposed upon by unscrupulous *fan kwae* just does not stand up to scrutiny ... except in New York where, perhaps, anything might be believed of perfidious Albion.

Whatever the reasons for its finding, the court promptly had the junk arrested by the US marshal of the New York district. Meanwhile, the twenty-six crew members who wanted to leave the ship were accommodated in the New York Sailor's Home, at the *Keying*'s expense, and looked after by Lin and Williams. Finally, the court ordered Kellett to pay the fares and arrears of wages, obviously with the alternative of losing his ship, which could have been sold to defray all liabilities; he was obliged to comply. That So and Kellett may have assumed some sort of verbal agreement—in the Chinese junk trade system, more often than not the norm—that the crew would stick with the ship until it got back did not wash in a Western court. What may have been acceptable in the China seas was not so in a New York court in 1847.

A careful reading of the pleadings, however, reveals that the blanket 'these poor Chinese seafarers were unscrupulously duped' condemnation scarcely stands up. It is admitted in the pleadings themselves that all twenty-six crewmen had received at least three months' advance wages and one, at least four. All had received between one and two months' additional wages after arrival in New York, in the form of a flat payment of US$12 per head.[39] So the plaint really comes down to the matter of time elapsed. They had signed on for eight months. Eight months had passed. They were due the balance of their wages—between three and four months, so a gross of between US$585 and US$780—and a fare home (around US$150).[40] That makes a total levy on whatever money the *Keying* had made in New York of up to US$4,680, or between 25 and 50 percent of what it seems probable the junk grossed from ticket sales. After the payment that had to be made to the landing-place owners, the ship probably cleared very little, if anything, by way of profit from its New York stay.

The crewmen were repatriated to Hong Kong on 6 October 1847, aboard the *Candace*.[41] Sadly, at this point, Kellett is revealed to have been unable to admit that the court had made its finding, that he must pay up and accept that he, So Yin Sang Hsi and their advocate—a Mr. Barr[42]—had not convinced the magistrate otherwise. It also seems that he would not accept that those who had helped the seamen could not personally be held to blame. Kellett had Lin King-chew arrested on what is thought to have been a wholly trumped-up charge of theft. Since he then appears to have left New York without pressing the charges and Lin was released, whatever rancour there may have been was either short-lived— or New York had become too hot a town for Charles Kellett and the *Keying* to remain in.

An Appeal to Congress over Light Dues

Against that is the evidence that Charles Kellett's quest to have tonnage and light dues, charged on the ship's arrival in America, refunded by an act of Congress went ahead without check. In the first session of the Thirtieth Congress, a bill to that end was presented in the House of Representatives; Kellett had obviously garnered sufficient congressional support. Evidently, despite the New York court case, not all took him to have been proven a rogue.

The bill passed successfully through the House of Representatives on 22 December 1847.[43] After two readings in the Senate, it was sent to the reporting stage of the Committee of Commerce of the Senate on 26 December. The Senate record for three days later reads:

> Mr Dix, from the Committee on Commerce, to whom was referred the bill (H.R. 368) to refund to Charles A. Kellett the tonnage dues and light money paid on the Chinese junk 'Keying', reported it without amendment.[44]

At this point the bill would normally have been engrossed and read a third time and then returned to the House of Representatives for its concurrence. Curiously, the record is silent or, given its occasional lapidary conciseness, obscure; there is no other reference until 28 March 1848, when the record reads that Rep. Grinnell, speaking for the House of Representative's Committee on Commerce, sought that, the bill having been read twice and committed to the Committee of the Whole House on the State of the Union, the House:

> ... refund to Charles A. Kellett the tonnage duties and light money paid on the junk 'Keying':

> Be it enacted by the Senate and House of Representatives in Congress assembled, That the Secretary of the Treasury be authorized to refund to Charles A. Kellett, or his legal representative, five hundred dollars or such sum as may have been paid, to the collector of the Port of New York, for tonnage dues and light money collected on the entry of the junk 'Keying'; and the same is hereby appropriated out of any money in the Treasury not otherwise appropriated.[45]

Whether Charles Kellett, who was by this time in Boston, or whoever had been the *Keying*'s New York agent actually got the money back is unknown. But whatever the final outcome was, Kellett was obviously not *persona non grata* in official circles, as a result of his New York tribulations.

Understanding the Context

How much of the version of the affair in which Charles Kellett is the unalloyed villain is to be taken literally? To accept that version of the story is to place full and unquestioning credence in all that Samuel Wells Williams writes in his letters and elsewhere. What we do not know is how much Wells Williams may have been moved by an anti-British attitude, not at all uncommon among Americans in China, as well as by an antipathy, as a missionary and divine—he was to become president of the American Bible Society three years before his death—to the rather profane world of ships and the sea.

Wells Williams's motivations were unquestionably high-minded and the Chinese crew certainly in need of the humanitarian aid he was able to offer. But, as we have seen, the crew's claim that they were signed on only for a short-sea voyage to Batavia and were utterly ignorant of any other possibility is extremely hard to credit. In backing the crew's version of events as if there could be no other conceivable possibility, Lord, Williams and Lin—and the court—displayed a naïve credulousness with respect to the Chinese crew that was itself as patronizing as was Charles Kellett's bucko bullying. We have no more reason to suppose that Wells Williams's account is the only view of the relations between Kellett and his Chinese crew than we do to suppose the same of Kellett's version.

Charles Kellett was a young man—just 26 when he was given command of the *Keying*. We have no data on his command experience before the *Keying* voyage, but, given his age, it is not likely to have been great. He must have had qualities both as a man and a seaman that impressed his Hong Kong partners. And it must surely be the case—given that in court we can infer he had the support of So Yin Sang Hsi and that up to fourteen of his Chinese crew seemed happy enough to stay on, as would appear also to have been the case with He Sing, Sam Shing and the twelve or so European crew—that Kellett was able to get on sufficiently well with the other half of his crew.

Getting the *Keying* to New York was a great achievement. He must have been greatly reliant on the skills, seamanship and experience of his Chinese bosun or, more accurately, co-captain. If Kellett had been the person the court findings imply, it is hard to see why So Yin Sang Hsi should have been so loyal and, presumably, stood so well behind his captain during the trials of the voyage up and, later, across the North Atlantic. Even had Kellett in part have been the cause of the crew's disaffection, they were grown men and hardly the *crème de la crème*. As we have seen, their claims to have been duped as to the nature of the ship's intended voyage require us to take them for arrant simpletons. In considering Kellett's youth, his comparative inexperience, the tensions between British seamen's rights and those of seamen on Asiatic Articles, Kellett's almost certain ignorance of exactly what the Chinese articles actually said, plus the difficulties the ship had faced, we should not be surprised if in New York he felt a bit out of his depth and reacted accordingly.

To put the whole matter of Kellett's trouble with his crew into perspective, it is worth considering how Chinese junk crews were organized.[46] The initial and most important points to grasp are three. First, that there was *no* cross-mapping between the organizational structures of Chinese ship's crew and that of Western ships. Second, that the efficiency and effectiveness of a Chinese crew does *not* appear to have been a function of a clear shipboard chain of command, or of any system of regulations either within a ship or across anything resembling a merchant marine. Third, that China's seafaring people were strongly and sharply divided by locality, and relations between such coastal groups were often sufficiently acrimonious as to break out into wholesale violence. Fourth, that there was no clear system of Chinese maritime law of a kind that can be equated with the common law tradition of Admiralty Law.

Same Ship, Different Long Splices

The world of the *chuanzhu, huozhang, tougong, caifu, zongguan, hanggong,* of *yi-* and *erding, daliao, yi- er-* and *sanqian, yagong, jiku, xianggong* and *shuishou,*[47] as well as a host of other people ashore whose maritime roles fail to map onto their Western equivalents, is one that contrasted starkly with the structures, organization, expectations and hierarchy of Charles Kellett's maritime world.

The traditional junk crewing system had three or four *parallel,* but not necessarily hierarchically ordered, commanding elements. There was the *chuanzhu* or captain—or so translated in English—who was nearer to what in Western ships was called the supercargo. In effect, he was the owner or owner's representative; he supervised everything to do with the cargo and its management, including, presumably, the choice of destinations.

Beside the captain, but certainly not beneath him, came the *huozhang*—the pilot and navigator. The *huozhang* could advise the captain and the captain could advise the *huozhang.* What each decided to do was, however, up to him, respected as lying in his exclusive sphere of competence. That is why a pre-existing social relationship is likely to have been important in the operation of traditional junks.

Among the higher officers was also the *caifu,* who seems to have had a role intermediate between that of a purser and captain's secretary, combined with some junior mate's responsibilities.

Running in tandem with the captain, the *huozhang* and the *caifu,* but again formally independent of all of them, were the two men who actually sailed the ship—that is, made decisions on sail-handling, steering, maintenance and all the myriad elements of day-to-day ship management. These were the *songhan* and the *ty cong* or *tougong.* The first was a sort of loadmaster-cum-bosun; the second we have translated as 'bosun',[48] though his responsibilities would have combined some of a bosun's responsibilities with those of a coxswain and quartermaster, too. The *tougong* did have people who could be thought of as under his command, but in practice he was a *primus inter pares.*

The next people of importance in a junk crew were the 'skilled' crewmen—the nearest Western equivalent would be something of a cross between a petty officer and a topman (but even thinking this way is to miss the main point).

The skilled crewmen, part of the *chuanfu*, were the *toumou*, or head men. These were the *yi-* and *erding, daliao, yi- er-* and *sanqian, yagong, jiku, xianggong* and *shuishou*. They looked after parts of ship (though again not in the Western sense); for example, there was one man in charge of anchoring operations and another for sail-hoisting and -reefing. Below them, but again more collegially than hierarchically, came the *hoke*, the comrades, or rank and file of the ship's company, who did all the heavie-hauling and other manual work and were often quite unskilled.

Perhaps most significant of all, in a traditional Chinese vessel *all* of the crew, right down to the lowliest hand, were participants in the trade that was the purpose of the voyage, although, in fairness, by the end of the eighteenth century, the first changes towards a wage-based system are recorded, presumably making further headway during the first decades of the nineteenth. In the more traditionally run Chinese ships, the majority of the crew were unpaid, but were allotted at least some cargo space right down to the deck hands, who could load 933.33 pounds (7 *piculs*) out and back. It was space they could either sell or use to trade on their own account, to pay themselves for their work aboard.

Quite how Kellett and So Yin Sang Hsi bridged this vast gulf in expectations and arrangements is impossible to say. Obviously, by 1845, there will have been quite a few casual seamen on Hong Kong's waterfront who had perhaps had some experience of working on Western vessels or had worked as wage labour on those Chinese ships that had shifted to waged crews. But, even conceding that some of the *Keying's* crew may have fallen into this category, such experience would not have been ubiquitous or open to many. The perhaps one or two thousand men who had, over the period 1780–1830, served in Indiamen may have acted as a source of knowledge, but were not necessarily that widespread. More to the point, whatever may have been acceptable when the ship being sailed on was Western, even for those who had served time on Western ships, that would surely not have applied with the *Keying*, whatever its peculiarities as a junk?

In a normal Chinese crew, the entire ship's company would have been recruited by a *batou* (gang boss) from a single group. This was logistically efficient (in terms of a shared diet, and so on), operationally efficient (shared dialect and work practices) and organizationally efficient (an accepted social hierarchy). That there may have been two groupings aboard the *Keying* is suggested by the split between 'leavers' and 'stayers' in New York. None of this is surprising, if the *Keying*'s crew was not from a single clan, locality or group but from two or more found in the fluid world of Whampoa and the new, raw, polyglot waterfront of Hong Kong. Add the fact that the *Keying* was run by foreigners, recall exactly what the standard Western ship's articles quoted above reveal about the respective powers and duties of captain and crew and it is clear that the seeds of disaffection are likely to have been present from the outset.

The *Keying*'s situation was an accident waiting to happen. Traditionally, part of the social glue that ensured Chinese ships operated effectively was that the whole—from captain through bosun to ship's company—was from a single locality, bound by local, subgroup or even family loyalties, and sailing a familiar regional craft, constructed and rigged in a familiar style, on familiar routes to well-known destinations, with customary cargoes carried in customary ways. There was no question of a chain of command and an accepted law of the sea that enjoined obedience by junior to senior, as in Western ships, and which, as we saw in the chapter on St. Helena, could be imposed as the law by land-based legal officers. Indeed, from what Gützlaff observed, the crew obeyed the *tougong* and other officers only when they felt it was in their interests to do so. There was never any question of their obeying or not obeying the captain or pilot, since, within the Chinese traditional system, neither had anything to do with running the ship. Gützlaff describes the sailors as having 'full control over the vessel, and oppos[ing] every measure which they think may prove injurious to their own interest'; he goes on to observe that, as a result, captains and pilots often had to *beg* the crew to do things and ask them nicely to be in a better mood, if they were being obstreperous!

The vital question, though we shall probably never know the correct answer, is how the *Keying*'s crew was recruited in Whampoa and Hong Kong. For a Chinese crew of mixed provenance, serving on a Chinese vessel with what we can suppose was something like the normal complement of Chinese officers, but plus a supernumerary crew of Western officers and a handful of European seamen as well, is by itself a partial explanation of what happened in New York, independent of

Kellett's treatment of the crew or the legal niceties of a Western-style contract. And that is setting altogether to one side the inevitable consequences of the extraordinarily long, arduous and troubled voyage that had brought the ship thus far, and the fact that, by the time the case was brought, the contracted voyage time had long since passed.

Charles Kellett's position on the *Keying* was, within the Western way of seeing things, anomalous. He would have had two roles, neither of which mapped onto anything his Western experience had taught him. Worse, in the specific context of the *Keying*, neither role would have given him either the authority or the power those roles conferred in a Western ship. He was the captain and in some part the owner. But in Chinese junks those roles had *nothing* to do with running the ship. Equally, Kellett would probably have been acting as the *huozhang* (pilot or mate), a role that carried no authority over the bosun, who could take or leave any advice offered. If we map onto this the fact that the *Keying* had the usual panoply of European officers (captain, responsible for the entire ship and its operations; mate, responsible for ship operations and maintenance; second mate, responsible for navigation), then it is clear that the ship was an organizational nightmare.

The whole story of the New York court case shows that no allowance whatsoever had been made for this. It is equally probable that Wells was largely unaware of it—his monumental *The Middle Kingdom* in the 1882 edition has exactly ten pages on 'Various Kinds of Boats', two pages on 'Living on the water in China' and two pages on 'Chop-boats and junks'. There are significantly fewer pages on the subject in the 1848 edition. And in both editions there is no detail at all as to how the vessels were crewed, financed, regulated or operated.[49] If this is misleading as to the extent of his knowledge, then he appears to have made no allowances whatsoever for what any greater knowledge he may have had implied.

So one interpretation is that a socially and culturally inchoate ship's company held tenuously together by the ruthlessness of British shipboard organization, power structures and Kellett's personality (backed by his on-board European partners and their armoury), and with the Chinese crew held both together and in order by So Yin Sang Hsi, fell apart. One fragmentary bit of evidence that came out in the court hearing supports this idea of a fractured crew; indeed, the line of fracture split the Chinese crew among themselves. It was claimed that, in St. Helena, He Sing had sided with the Western officers, come aboard the ship from where he was ashore and told the Chinese crew that, unless they shut up and co-operated, they would be shot.[50]

It would thus seem that none of the usual structures, procedures and expectations on which Kellett would normally have been able to rely, to weld the ship's company back together and get them to work, and which are spelled out in the copy of standard Western articles above, will have been effective. All he could have recourse to was persuasion via his bosun, since there is no evidence that he spoke Cantonese, and when that failed, violence or its threat. That Heath Robinson lash-up had held the ship together as far as New York. There, it had finally fallen apart.

Basically the larger group in a bifurcated crew went on its way, leaving the other group—tied perhaps by clan or group loyalties to So Yin Sang Hsi, the bosun—to stay with the *Keying*. Captain/Bosun So will have been a very important figure; one wishes more was known about him. It seems possible that he had served with Charles Kellett or perhaps G. Burton, Edward Revett or even Douglas Lapraik before, and could act as *batou* recruiting the crew. Against this is the dual nature of the Chinese crew, with the major part, twenty-six in number, coming with the *Keying* when she was bought. That leaves the question of whether Captain/Bosun So was one of the first group—with the ship when she was bought—or was known to Kellett and the others as surmised and brought in to head up the Chinese side of the ship's operations and complete a full crew by recruiting up to a further fourteen Chinese sailors. The latter would presumably likely have had some sort of previous relationship with So Yin Sang Hsi, which would explain their loyalty in New York. However it actually was, one thing does seem clear: a fundamental prerequisite for an efficient and effective traditional Chinese crew was not met aboard the *Keying*. And that is leaving aside the fact that the traditional way of binding a Chinese ship's crew to its voyage—giving them a clear share in its outcome—was not used.[51]

Against the narrative that emerges from New York must be placed the alternative view from the admittedly self-serving letter Kellett wrote to Queen Victoria. To this must be allied the possibility that Samuel Wells Williams may have been just as constitutionally unable to see the 'other side' of the argument as Kellett seems to have been unable fully to have appreciated the disastrous collapse of his authority over his crew. Finally, Kellett and his officers, precisely because they were who they were, are likely to have been completely unable to grasp the extent to which their very project and all that it stood for could be read by someone better and more deeply informed about China than they were as a gross and culturalist travesty. To Samuel Wells Williams's evident disgust, the hordes of people who flocked to the *Keying* in New York, paid their money and mocked the Chinese crew supported Charles Kellett and his officers, whose views, however appalling to modern sensibilities, represented those of the contemporary mainstream.[52]

Chapter 5
The Final Leg—Towards Journey's End

Leaving New York

With the New York court case out of the way and perhaps with a need to get clear of the city, in November the *Keying* made its way to Boston with its remaining British sailors and up to fourteen remaining Chinese crewmen. Whether more Chinese or European crew were signed on before the ship left New York is unknown. It is equally obscure whether the visit to the Sectional Dock to have the bottom scrubbed actually took place, though some time must have been put aside for major maintenance before the next move. Not only was the bottom foul, but there were the sprung mast and the ripped sail to repair, and no doubt a host of minor problems with the running rigging, with individual timbers and with the deck gear that will have been building up during the long and arduous voyage. But repairs will have had to take second place to earning money through public admissions, and then to the major dislocation to schedules and finances that the court case will have caused.

Whether once it had quit New York the *Keying* sailed under its own power or was towed is unclear. We do not know when the *Keying* actually left New York other than sometime in early November. All we know is that she arrived in Boston on 18 November 1847, for a stay that was to last three months during the onset and early months of winter. Astonishingly, and as we shall see inexplicably, the junk then left what would have been a safe winter haven to complete its voyage to Britain in the worst conceivable month of the year.

The passage that Charles Kellett chose is likely to have been via the East River and then on up Long Island and Block Island sounds, round the notorious

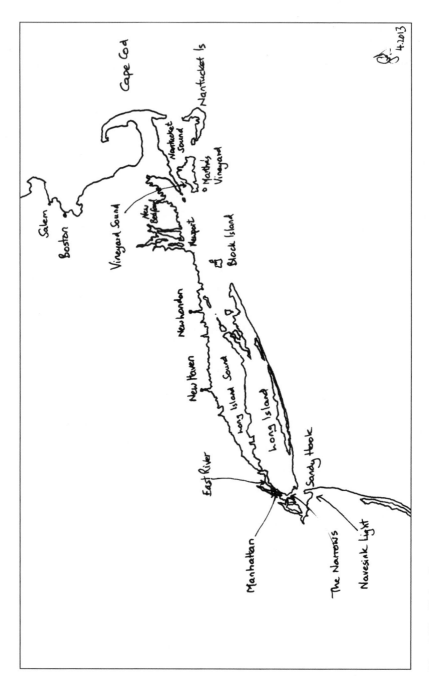

Map 5 New York to Boston

waters off Nantucket and Cape Cod to Boston. Most probably Charles Kellett had with him someone familiar with the passage to advise him, especially if he opted to take the demanding but more sheltered route through Vineyard Sound or Muskeget Channel and Nantucket Sound. It is a demanding passage, as one can work out by reading the forty-one pages of directions in Blunt's pilot backwards, editing out the irrelevant parts about havens and detours one does not intend to take.[1]

It would have been possible, bar the passage out round Cape Cod,[2] to day-sail the whole way, using either the bays of the north shore of Long Island or the many havens along the New York, Connecticut, Rhode Island and Massachusetts shores. Given the possibilities of calling in at the many ports along the way from Bridgeport to New Bedford, where one would assume there might have been some curiosity in the *Keying* worth slaking, one can only infer that Kellett had reason to get to Boston with some despatch. The rapid approach of winter is the most likely reason, though the long association of Boston interests in the China trade would argue another.

There is no evidence that the East River route was taken. All that can be said is that it is the most direct, and offers the relatively sheltered waters of Long Island and Block Island sounds for at least half of the passage. But it is, in any case, a nice conceit to entertain, largely because the *Keying* and its crew would have sailed past the shipyards of Brooklyn—principal among them those of Smith and Dimon—where the first of the fabulous tea-clippers were being built.

The first proto-clipper, Captain Nathaniel Palmer's revolutionary *Houqua*, built at Brown and Bell's yard, had been launched for the famous New York and Canton firm of A. A. Low and Brother on 3 May 1844. The following year, the John Willis Griffiths design *Rainbow* became the world's first 'true' or extreme clipper to be launched. New York and New York shipyards were abuzz with the continued excitement of the China trade. By early 1848—the year that gold was discovered in California—the clipper was *the* ship to build; many of the New York yards will have been busy with such orders. In the East River, there were over a dozen shipyards turning out 160 and more ships a year for the transatlantic routes alone.

At the same time, these were the early years of commercial steam. The SS *Great Britain* had been crossing the Atlantic since 1839, heralding the new world of shipping and helped by a government subsidy to the Cunard Line. In 1845, Edward K. Collins, head of the sailing packet Dramatic Line, convinced that the future was in steam, announced the sale of his sailing vessels. In 1838, he had failed to convince the US government to match British subsidies, but was undeterred; in early 1847, he announced the building at the William H. Brown shipyard of four large steamships.

Domestically, the battle between Cornelius 'Commodore' Vanderbilt and Daniel Drew over the Hudson River route to Albany, which begun when Drew founded The People's Line in 1834, resulted in Drew taking over North River Steamboat Association in 1845. By 1840, over 100 paddle-steamers were working on the Hudson, pushing forward the walking beam engine, side-wheeler vessels that within five years would provide the Pearl River and the Yangzi with their first steam-powered ferries. In parallel, New York companies like T. F. Secor & Co., taken over in 1850 to become the renowned Morgan Iron Works, were advancing the development of American-designed and -built steam engines.[3]

Equally, the bustling South Street—colloquially known as Packet Row— was where the hectic world of the transatlantic packets had its American focus. Surely, with the voyage across the Atlantic in prospect, Charles Kellett and his officers will have gone there to pick brains as to the best routes and timings? After all, with the scheduling revolution in the world of commercial shipping that the first transatlantic packet lines created as of 1818, when for the first time ships departed to a fixed schedule in every season of the year, a wealth of experience and knowledge of the North Atlantic in all moods and weathers had been accumulated. A call at the Tontine Coffee House at the intersection of Wall and Water streets, where brokers and underwriters, traders and owners gathered to exchange news and do business, would have been all but unavoidable.[4]

For the remaining Chinese crew, for whom we have no reason to suppose there was not shore leave, there was the small community of New Yorkers sympathetic to China, with whom the court case may have put them in contact via Samuel Wells Williams and Lin King-chew.[5] This was, after all, the year in which Yung Wing, Wong Shing and Wong Foon had arrived in New York in the Olyphant & Co. clipper *Huntress* to become the first Chinese students educated in America, landing on 12 April 1847 after a very swift 98-day passage from Whampoa. However, they had stayed only a few days; in Yung Wing's interesting account, no mention at all is made of meeting any other Chinese resident in the city.[6]

It seems impossible, for all the distractions of the court case and the showing of the junk to earn money, that the *Keying*'s crew, European and Chinese alike, could or would have held aloof from the world of New York shipbuilding and shipping, with the many innovations in design and technology that were in the air. New York was America's busiest port, indeed at the time one of the busiest in the world, much boosted by additional traffic from the Midwest, following the opening of the Erie Canal in 1825. As much to the point, in 1848, when word of the potential of 'Old Golden Mountain'—as the Chinese referred to California—reached China, emigrants from Guangdong Province would soon be flocking to Hong Kong to try their luck. Already, others had been lured—or conned—as more or less willing victims of the 'coolie trade', to work in the plantations and mines of Central and South America and the Caribbean.[7] In short, there will have been an atmosphere on the New York waterfront, with its commercial ties to China and its role in the design breakthroughs of the clipper era and nascent world of steam, that cannot but have drawn both parts of the *Keying*'s crew. For men like the young Charles Kellett and his friend Edward Revett, still at the beginning of careers as merchantmen's officers, then captains in the China trade, in one of these towering, wonderfully fleet epitomes of the world of Western sail, here was a brilliant chance to see how the ships were built and make connections with the people who designed, built, ordered and sailed them. And for the Chinese crew, for whom such potentially glittering paths were closed by Western prejudice and their own lack of relevant knowledge and skills, there will nonetheless have been a fascination in so much that was utterly new and strange.

In a passage down the East River, it will all have been laid before them.

The Stay in Boston

The voyage to Boston is around 270 miles. Given the cost, a tow was very unlikely, unless a benefactor made a tug available, as Robert Bennet Forbes was to do for the departure from Boston. So the probability is that the *Keying* made its own way along the sounds and out through the navigationally difficult waters around Nantucket and Cape Cod, the graveyards of so many, many ships. It is one of the most frustrating features of the narrative of the *Keying*, full as it is of hard to resolve puzzles, that this passage passes entirely without mention in any sources. Here was a fantastic test for the Chinese junk where a truly useful set of comparative data could have been generated for its performance vis-à-vis the working coastal craft of the Atlantic world. Scores—indeed hundreds—of working brigs, barques and ships, schooners, ketches and sloops worked these waters; from them, the data for their 'standard' New York-to-Boston passage can be derived. If we knew which route and how long the *Keying* took, there would be an immediate comparison. Instead, all is silence. No route. No timings. No comment at all. Even more remarkably—given that a junk sailing along in Long Island and Block Island sounds must have been an unrepeatable sight—there is no suggestion of a newspaper story. One can only conclude that the junk made a perfectly normal passage in pretty much the standard time without any attendant dramas or excitement, for all that she may also have been undermanned as a result of the loss of twenty-six crew in New York.

In that probability, however, there is a mute but possibly important point. Again, we have an example of a passage, albeit in temperate latitudes at the onset of winter, in which the *Keying* was doing what she was designed to do. Namely, the short-seas voyage in relatively shoal coastal waters with which the long voyage had begun. That nothing happened of note that Kellett made detailed reference to suggests that the *Keying* acquitted herself well. She broke no records that may have excited comment. She experienced nothing out of the ordinary. In her element doing what she was designed to do, the junk would seem to have given no reason for comment.

What we do not know that might add meat to the bones of these speculations is the time the passage actually took. If we knew the departure date from New York, speculation could cease. We do not. The best we can manage is to suppose that the *Keying* left New York sometime in the first week of November, reaching Boston on the 18th. That argues a voyage of somewhere between one or two weeks. For 270 miles, either would be slow, though not that unusual for a sailing vessel in the nineteenth century, if winds were adverse. In Long Island Sound in November they usually are, the historical average being a fairly regular swing between winds from the westerly sector (southwest through northwest) and those from the easterly sector (northeast through southeast) as frontal systems pass through, though speeds seem generally light and seldom above 15 knots unless there is a northeaster, bringer of the New England coast's worst gales.[8]

In Boston, after a mishap in which Kellett was unable to get the *Keying* to its chosen berth because the junk was 4 inches wider in beam to the limits of the side catwalks than the passage through a swing bridge on the Charles River, the ship again went on display. Once more, she was a popular attraction, according to the local newspapers, especially on Thanksgiving Day, traditionally the fourth Thursday in the month and in 1848 on 23 November. The *Keying* spent the next three months open to the public, trying to earn money and, presumably, held in port by an intention to get through the worst of the winter weather as well as preparing for what would be, in terms of the sea and weather conditions, the toughest passage of its long voyage.

Here, Captain Kellett obviously made contact with families long associated with the American trade with China, since the publicity booklet mentions his gratitude to Messrs. Forbes, Lamb[9] and Weekes. The first of these benefactors was Captain Robert Bennet Forbes, long associated, with his brother John Murray Forbes, with the American trading house in Canton of Russell & Co. Kellett notes that it was by the kind offices of Mr. Forbes that the *Keying* was towed by a steam tug 60 miles to seaward when it left Boston in February 1848. It is also interesting, and an indication of the financial state of the project, that the same encomium remarks that Mr. Forbes's gesture saved the ship an expenditure of £50—in today's terms some £4,000.

Beyond those bare facts, almost nothing can be said of the *Keying*'s winter in Boston. It seems that here, as almost everywhere the ship spent time in the Western world, such interest in it as there was turned out to be fleeting. It merits short paragraphs in newspapers. It gets, at best, one-liners in two standard annotations of Boston life by Edward H. Savage, a long-serving city policeman, in one of which its arrival is noted but its departure ignored—eclipsed, perhaps, by the illness and death on 23 February of the redoubtable John Quincy Adams, the sixth president of the United States (1825–29) and representative for Massachusetts from 1829 until his death.[10] The *Keying* never seems to have risen to headline news. If distinguished people visited, they seldom had much to say about the experience. Indeed, in Boston it would seem that, if such people did visit, it was not something they mentioned at all. Robert Bennet Forbes wrote a much-read biography in which he devotes some pages—though very few—to his life in Boston at around the time the *Keying* visited.[11] Given the assistance he gave to Captain Kellett and his vessel, one would have expected at least a passing mention. There is, in fact, not a single word nor any reference to the junk or Charles Kellett in Forbes's papers.[12]

The probable explanation for this is the *Jamestown* Expedition, in which Forbes took a leading part. This involved petitioning Congress in 1846 for the use of two US Navy ships—the *Jamestown* and the *Macedonian*—to carry aid to Ireland for the victims of the famine ravaging the population.[13] The actual expedition and the succour it brought occupied most of the first half of 1847; composing the narrative of the events must have taken up much of the balance of the year. And one must add that, during the same period, the stresses and problems of Forbes's business dealings, which ended with him returning to China in 1849 to rebuild his fortune, must also have taken their toll.

That said, something seems to have happened—perhaps increasing financial distress, perhaps some knock-on effect from the New York court case—to encourage Charles Kellett to take a considerable risk. There is one report that when the *Keying* was in Boston, presumably intending to winter over, a further ten of the Chinese crew jumped ship.[14] Whatever the cause, far from seeing the worst of the winter weather out in the safe confines of Boston, where he could have expected to find friends and supporters, Kellett decided to leave for his crossing of the Atlantic at the worst conceivable time of year. This is a decision that is very hard to reconcile with the very cautious way in which, we have concluded, the *Keying* had been sailed from Hong Kong to New York. This was a major risk not just to himself, his crew and his ship, but to the wife with whom he had only recently been reunited.

It had been at some unknown stage during the prolonged stay in America that Mrs. Jane Kellett joined the crew. Captain and Mrs. Kellett had been married since 1840, when they were wed in Liverpool. Beyond the bare facts—that Jane Kellett's maiden name was also Kellett and that she came from the small but busy nineteenth-century port of Ulverston, North Lancashire—we know little or nothing. There is no data about their early life together; none as to when exactly Charles Kellett had left for the Far East. However, allowing for the speed of mid-nineteenth-century sailing vessels and that, by 1846, Charles Kellett was evidently well enough known in Hong Kong to be able to find or be found as a business partner by those involved in the *Keying* venture, we can infer that the reunion in America followed a separation of at least three or four years.

The other possible hint to explain this daring departure—and this is more straw in the wind than well-grounded supposition—may lie in the impasse the *Keying* met when it tried to pass through the lifting bridge into the Charles River. This prevented the junk from reaching its preferred berth, which—we do not know—may have been on offer at some reduced charge and which, unlike the more open waters of the harbour, may have been a more feasible berth for wintering over than what was available elsewhere. Pushed back into the main commercial harbour—as busy as New York with the packet and general trades—the costs and risks, especially with the *Keying*'s Chinese anchors and ground tackle, may have been greater than the junk partnership's finances could bear.

It was in Boston that Kellett, no doubt smarting from what he will have felt to be the injustice of the judgement against him and his ship in New York, wrote his celebrated letter to the young Queen Victoria.[15] It is rather self-serving, but one should hardly expect otherwise. Kellett admits that, on at least one occasion, his treatment of a crewman was short and sharp, though, by the standards of the day, if the only occasion he started (a nautical euphemism for 'hit', as a punishment for slowness) a man with a rope's end is the one he reports, he was an officer of uncommon restraint. That the man chose to jump overboard—he was recovered—suggests that Kellett's account may paint the lily; the crew witness statements in New York and the further desertions in Boston further suggest that the typical violence of mid-nineteenth-century crew management on Western ships was ever-present on the *Keying* as well. What we cannot know, because sadly no one else has left any record, is whether his claim that his crew were opium-users and shirkers is true.

The Transatlantic Passage

The *Keying*'s subsequent voyage across the Atlantic, a first for a Chinese vessel if we discount flights of fancy as the evidence suggests we must, was full of drama; for Jane Kellett, it must have been an often frightening trial. The ship performed excellently as a sea boat, as she had since the outset of the voyage. However, the chronic weakness of the traditional design of junk steering systems, already apparent in the rambunctious final stages of the voyage across the Indian Ocean, struck again. On the Indian Ocean crossing, it had taken twenty to twenty-five

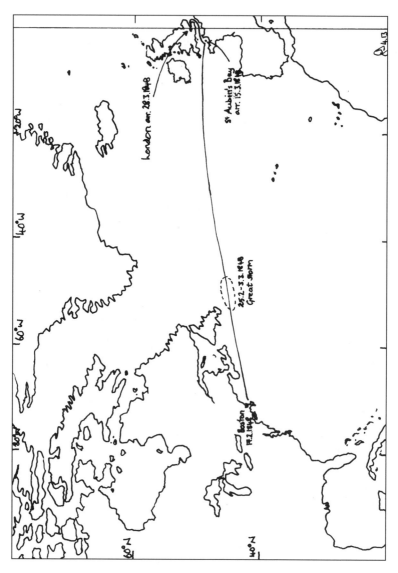

London arr. 28.3.1848

St Aubin's Bay
arr. 15.3.1848

25.2 - 3.3.1848
Great Storm

Boston
17.2.1848

120°W

100°W

80°W

60°W

40°N

60°N

60°N

40°N

Map 6 The Final Leg

crewmen to control the rudder—a massive piece of ironwood[16] joinery that was 23–24 feet in length, although it is not clear whether this is from the head of the stock to the foot of the blade. However, given the weight that is recorded of some 7 to 8 tonnes, the likelihood is that this was simply the lengthwise measurement of the blade, with an additional length of rudder stock above. This view is reinforced by the measurement of the height of the poop above the waterline, which is given as between 32 and 38 feet. Combine this with the statement that, fully lowered, the rudder gave the Keying a draft of 24 feet, and we have a clear implication that the ensemble of rudder stock and blade must have been near to 50 feet in length, certainly over 40 feet.

The *Keying* was towed down Boston Harbour on 16 February and had reached 60 miles to seaward by the 17th. Assuming she was towed on the first course of a composite Great Circle track to Europe, by the time the tow was dropped, the *Keying* will have been somewhere about 50 miles north-north-east of Cape Cod. To begin with, the *Keying* will have probably been carried slightly southward as it made its way across the thin finger of the residual, south-flowing cold tongue of the Labrador Current, before making it—after perhaps another hundred miles of sailing—into the westward flow of the warm Gulf Stream.

As we have remarked, there must have been a pressing reason for Charles Kellett to risk making this voyage, especially since he was carrying his wife with him. February is one of the worst months of the North Atlantic winter, when gales are 20 to 30 percent more frequent than in March or April. It is also arguably one of the coldest months of the year. And, if that is not enough to make the point, in February, the incidence of fog on the Grand Banks and off Boston is high, as is the chance of meeting an iceberg; the sea temperature would hover between five and ten degrees centigrade for the majority of the passage! The recommended earliest time for an Atlantic crossing for a sailing boat today is to start no earlier than mid-May. Of course, in the harder world of the mid-nineteenth century, when sail was still the main power source, waiting for gentler weather was not an option often considered. But the *Keying*'s voyage had by this time taken so long that waiting another month would have made little difference to any original plan, which must by this point have long since been abandoned.

The probability is that, after the New York débâcle, money was running short and the available crew to man her dwindling. If the *Keying* was to get to Europe at all, it would have to leave come wind or weather. If unpaid bills had started to accumulate, then Charles Kellett risked finding his ship arrested, at which point all hope of reaching London would have to be given up.

In short, February or not, the *Keying* had to sail and take what came. On this Atlantic crossing, worse was to happen to the ship than mere difficulty in controlling the rudder, as had been the case in stormy seas off Mauritius.

The Storm and Repairs at Sea

Eight days after the *Keying* had left Boston, the weather turned for the worse. The onset of stormy weather was very likely, as the ship approached the meteorologically ugly interface where the very cold winter air over the south-flowing Labrador Current met the warmer air over the Gulf Stream—a phenomenon known today as the Gulf Stream North Wall Effect. It is associated with vicious storms and tremendous seas.[17]

On 25 February 1847 a storm began—Kellett's sea-state descriptions and barometer reading (29.3 inches of mercury, or 992 millibars) suggest something between force 8 and 10—that lasted some twelve hours. During the storm, sometime on the morning of 26 February, one of the rudder ropes carried away. By implication, this was a bowsing rope, since when one of the tiller tackles had given way in the Indian Ocean this was explicitly stated: 'On one occasion when the Junk was running before a fresh gale, attended with hail squalls, a tiller rope of 9 inches [presumably the circumference] was snapped in two.'[18] It seems clear that the sea must still have been running too high for any repair to have been attempted, since no mention is made at this point of such a course of action being contemplated. No doubt it was intended to wait until things were less lively.

Three days later on 1 or 2 March, the weather again worsened to conditions rated by Kellett as the worst of the entire voyage from China. The weather was not only obviously awful. It was prolonged—very prolonged. It was on the third or fourth day of trying to control the *Keying* in the terrible seas that on 5 March the second bowsing rope carried away and the rudder ripped from its gudgeons, crashing the tiller down on the binnacle and destroying it.

It is not clear whether this disaster happened when the *Keying* was running before the storm or whether, as would have been the case had So Ying Sang Hsi been left to his own devices, it was when the ship had hove to in order to ride out the worst of things. A singular virtue of junks is the ease with which they heave to, their high poop decks aft leading them to weathercock and ride bow to wind. Whether Charles Kellett ever did this is not clear from the narrative, but one's inclination is to suspect not.

With the rudder out of action, the *Keying* will have had to do one of two things. It could lie a-hull—just drift without direction. With Western ships, this would usually be broadside to the seas, both extremely uncomfortable and extremely dangerous, the tendency being to 'shake the sticks out of her', that is, impose so much strain on masts and standing rigging that they carried away. But with a junk, the bow would probably weathercock up into the oncoming seas, thus helping the ship ride more comfortably. That tendency could be enhanced by opting for the second alternative, to heave to by deploying some sort of a sea anchor—in effect a drag—over the bow. Only that way is the ship likely to have become steady enough for a repair—by now absolutely essential—to be contemplated. Worth noting is that matters were made less desperate than they might have been by a feature of the junk rudder that is never found on Western ships. We noted earlier that the junk rudder can be slid up and down in its housing and even canted to keep it clear of the water and damage when in harbour. However, being such massive pieces of timber, junk rudders are permanently slung from a tackle. In the *Keying's* case, there were two tackles leading to simple barrel winches, one on each of the two uppermost poop decks. On the rudder blade, the ends were attached through a hole in the stout cross member at the top.

So when the second bowsing line parted and the *Keying's* rudder, unrestrained from ahead, swung up and smashed the tiller down on the binnacle, it did not then rip clear of the stern opening in which it hung and disappear into the raging seas. Instead, held by the hoisting tackles, it would have remained attached to the junk, if in an exceedingly perilous way, as its massive seven- to eight-tonne weight will have swung to and fro as the ship rolled, pitched, yawed and heaved, threatening to smash in the entire transom.

The repair could have been done in a couple of ways. Reeving a new rope from the bow-tensioning windlass back to the stern would have been very hard work, but relatively simple. Equally, a rope or maybe two might be passed beneath the hull from side to side so that, once the trickiest part of the exercise was over, the bowsing ropes could be dragged beneath the hull to their working positions. The truly difficult part, however, would have been linking the system up with the rudder.

The rudder, recall, was a massive entity. With the bowsing ropes parted, all that secured it to the *Keying* would have been the lifting tackles. With the ship plunging up and down and the rudder banging around and no longer vertical—though if the ship was hove to, then the quieter water in the lee of the huge transom would have made for less movement—hauling it up would have been both dangerous and viciously hard work. The risk of hypothermia in the frigid seas beneath which whoever was down at the rudder would be repeatedly plunged is obvious. Hard men. Hard days.

And yet, the trickiest part of the operation would require someone, or probably two or three people, to go over the back of the ship on a rope's end to try to secure the free end of the bowsing lines to the 'heel' (the forward, lower corner) of the rudder. It speaks volumes for his bravery and sense of duty that the volunteer for this nightmarish task was Kellett's friend and staunch companion the second mate, Edward Revett. It speaks greater volumes about the entire structure of the early Victorian, imperialist maritime world that we do not know whether Revett worked alone. The description—and the task—makes this extremely unlikely.

Repairing the damage took some six hours. It was completed successfully, but only at what may have been a terrible cost. On one—and only one—account, the second mate was drowned while he was over the side 'overseeing the work'.[19] The verb is interesting, since it leaves one wondering what Mr. Revett was up to. Obviously, he was not alone; by implication, there were other crewmen with him trying to secure bowsing ropes and rudder. Would they have been the remaining members of the Chinese crew, who could be expected to know what to do? Was it So Yin Sang Hsi? We do not know. It is yet another of the tantalizing unknowns which bedevil accounts of a voyage that could have been a remarkable insight into how the mixed crew learned to pull together—if they did. But then, it is almost certain that this one account is either wrong, or that whoever drowned was not Mr. Revett, since we learn from the later visit of Queen Victoria to the *Keying* in Blackwall, London, that Mr. Revett was presented to her.[20] Another unresolvable *Keying* puzzle.

Apart from strong winds, which we can assume continued to blow, there appear to have been no other breakages beyond, perhaps, the sort of run-of-the-mill stuff that any sailing man of those times would have taken as read. A ship's boat—charmingly described as a 'smuggling boat'—carried away. Parted ropes. Chafed gear. Broken blocks. Sails in need of patching. Nothing that was worth a special mention, just the normal hard work of life at sea.

Arrival in the English Channel

The British Channel Islands were reached ten days later on around 11 March. If we assume that the tow from Boston had been dropped late on 17 February, then the *Keying* had taken 20 to 21 days to reach the chops of the English Channel. The distance sailed would have been around 2,500 nautical miles, giving average day's runs of between 115 and 123 nautical miles, an average speed of around 5 knots. It was, again, not fast sailing. But against that, *Ocean Passages for the World* gives average times for the voyage, provided by the Glasgow firm of Messrs. Hardie & Co. for a sailing ship of some 2,000 tons 'which in good conditions could log speeds of 10–12 knots but generally averaged 100–150 miles a day' of 25 to 30 days. Compared to that set of averages, the *Keying* had clearly done well.

Sailing on a route with a following wind, as she was designed for, the *Keying's* transatlantic passage was thus more than merely average, as a look at contemporary transatlantic records shows. Of course, these were from New York to Liverpool, so the comparison is not exact, but they give a flavour of what could be managed by the hardest-driven Western ships of the time. By the mid-1820s, the packets were putting in average crossings—New York or Boston to Liverpool—of 24 days. To put that in perspective, the record west-to-east crossing, *against* wind and current, was set in 1840 by the redoubtable Captain Nat Palmer in the *Siddons*, when he made Liverpool to New York in 15 days! He had set a record for the eastbound crossing of 18 days in the 1830s, in the aptly named Dramatic Lines' *Garrick*. Closer to home for Charles Kellett, Robert Bennet Forbes's 1847 passage on the *Jamestown*, which no doubt Kellett will have heard about at first hand, was a flat 15 days.[21] So the *Keying's* 21 days, albeit from 60 miles to seaward of Boston only to the Channel Islands, was no poor performance but one close to the slower side of average for fleet packets and other hard-driven ships.[22]

According to a local report,[23] once into the Channel and making up towards Dover, the *Keying* found itself being pushed south of track by a northwesterly gale. The junk found itself too close to the menacing Roches Douvres west of Jersey, and accepted pilotage into St. Aubin's Bay, Jersey, where she anchored. The pilotage was given by the cutter *Pierson*, under the command of a Captain Chevalier, for which he was paid 60 pounds. The same local report says that, although many people went to the nearby shore to gaze at the apparition and some ventured out in boats for a closer look, no woman was allowed aboard because the right of being the first 'European woman to board was reserved for Queen Victoria'. We do not know whether that promise was kept; it seems unlikely, and in any case curiously excludes Jane Kellett.

The account continues:

> Two boatmen, John Stone and John Kimber, took a party of onlookers out. As they neared the junk the local packet from Plymouth the *Zebra* rounded Noirmont and steered a course close to the junk to also view the marvel. In doing so she swamped the boat of Stone and Kimber and the party were thrown into the water with Lieutenant Bassen of the Royal Navy, Boatman Kimber, and a boy George Hamon drowning, and those of the party that survived were as follows: Josue Brayn, George Ingouville Perchard, Jean De Gruchy, Thomas De Gruchy, M. Boisnet (of the Pomme D'Or), with his chef and commissionaire, Elias Tinckam, Samuel Tinckam, (George Hamon was their apprentice), James Murphy, and others.

At Jersey, the *Keying* waited for a tow up the Channel. This was given by the SS *Monarch*, Captain Priaulx; the *Keying* and her tug reached the River Thames at Gravesend on either 27 or 28 March.[24] The tug and its tow are not likely to have gone straight up to the *Keying*'s final berth at the Railway and Steamboat Pier, East India Docks, Blackwall, because there will have been formalities to complete and, most likely, a pilot to embark. But whatever the exact details of the arrival, by the last few days of March the *Keying* had finally made it to her intended destination.

An Assessment of the *Keying*'s Voyage Performance

In considering the *Keying*'s performance as a voyager under Charles Kellett's command and with the vital, skilled sailing master's input from So Yin Sang

Hsi, without whom the voyage would have been impossible, it is important that we compare like with like and do not make the mistake of contrasting the best Western ships of the era with the *Keying*. Later, we shall use the flying tea-clipper *Thermopylae* as a point of comparison, as it will show with great clarity the standard ways in which ships are compared with each other and, therefore, what would actually count as a fair comparator with the junk. Inevitably, the European equivalent for a late eighteenth- or early nineteenth-century short-seas trader is not easy to disinter from the records. Moreover, we need also to remember the *Keying* was sailing in ballast and that she was roughly built. The *Description* says, for example:[25]

> The whole of the work about her is of the roughest kind; the trees when found of a suitable size are cut down, stripped of their bark and sawed into convenient lengths, the sides are not squared, but left just as they grew . . . The Chinese . . . can see no reason for the employment of fine and elaborate workmanship, or delicate finish, where such is not necessary . . .

Her nearest equivalent would therefore have been a moderate-sized bark or large brig on the European short-seas trade or perhaps one of the 500- to 800-tonne late eighteenth-century Indiamen riding light. Such ships seldom averaged better than 3–5 knots over a long voyage, often a great deal worse.

The *Keying* reached New York 215 days out of Hong Kong—about 7 to 7.5 months, give or take a week.[26] This included four and a half weeks anchored or working the light winds and anchoring overnight in the Gaspar and Sunda Sea areas, and a week in St. Helena, so we are actually talking about 166 days, or just short of six months at sea. A typical Indiaman in the late nineteenth century would take four months from London to Canton. Henry Wise's *An Analysis of One Hundred Voyages to and from India, China &c.* shows that the average miles sailed were 13,398 and the voyage length 114.5 days.[27] That makes a voyage average of 4.9 knots—and Indiamen, if rather stately and bluff-bowed, were no-expense-spared ships.

Tables 2 and 3 show that, with 236 days on passage, mostly at between 3 and 3.5 knots, the *Keying* turned in a below-average set of voyage times when compared to the average Indiaman. As well as spending 122 days longer on passage, the junk, because it could not work to weather or make good speed in any wind, had to sail an additional 4,137 miles, as compared to the Indiaman.

Table 2 Voyage leg distances, durations and average speeds

Voyage leg	Rhumb-line distance	Time on passage (days)	Average leg speed (knots)
Hong Kong > Gaspar Strait	**1,930**	**19**	**4.2**
Gaspar Strait > Sunda Strait area	**> 410**	**< 32**	**> 0.53**
Sunda Strait > Cape of Good Hope	5,100	63	3.4
Cape of Good Hope > St. Helena	1,700	17	4.2
Sunda Strait > St. Helena	**6,800**	**81**	**3.4**
St. Helena > Equator	1,180	15	3.3
Equator > New York	4,355	60	3.0
St. Helena > New York	**5,535**	**75**	**3.1**
New York > Boston	**265**	**> 5**	**> 2.2**
Boston > St. Aubin's Bay	**2,500**	**21**	**5.0**
Hong Kong > Channel	**17,440**	**233**	**3.1**
St. Aubin's Bay > Gravesend	27	< 3	> 3.75
Hong Kong > Gravesend	**17,710**	**236**	**3.1**

Table 3 Total duration Hong Kong to London, and of each leg, including port calls

Voyage leg	Time on passage (days)
Hong Kong > dep. Sunda Strait	51
Hong Kong > dep. St. Helena	139
Hong Kong > New York	214
At New York	>127
At Boston	91
Hong Kong > dep. Boston	439
At St. Aubin's Bay	< 14
St. Aubin's Bay > Gravesend	< 5
Boston > Gravesend	50
Hong Kong > Gravesend	476

However, the occasional 144-day voyage was recorded by the tea-clippers when the winds did not favour them, damage was incurred or navigational mistakes were made. Against that, though allowing that the *Keying* needed to try to make money and therefore spent a long time in port, the total of 476 days from leaving Hong Kong to actually making it to London, the intended destination, is a very long time. Even the barque *Hospodar*, nearly forty years later, which held a record for one of the slowest voyages thanks to breakages and sickness, did not take any longer to get from Liverpool to San Francisco via Cape Horn.

However, although the results might disappoint the more fervent Gavin Menzies fan with an *idée fixe* that a junk could average 10 knots on a voyage round the world—a feat achieved by no sailing craft until the record-breaking, high-performance racing yachts and multi-hulls of the late twentieth century—one should not be quick to dismiss the *Keying*'s result as disappointing. We have records of Indiamen and clippers because of the sorts of vessels they were or the organizations they worked for. We do not have many published records of the thousands of working brigs and barques of the nineteenth century, but what we do have does not usually reflect average performances startlingly better than that of the *Keying*, which was *not* sailed by a crack and experienced crew driven by the lure of handsome monetary rewards for a record voyage. So if the *Keying*'s performance is not such as to make one sit up and take notice, it probably was not a great deal worse than that of many an equivalent, run-of-the-mill contemporary Western brig or bark that was a bit down on its luck. The final dash across the Atlantic—lost rudder, possibly shorthanded and all—was a sterling performance and shows exactly what a junk could manage when sailed as she was designed to be sailed, off the wind. She would not be dramatic, but she would reel off the miles; as Charles Kellett is reported as having said, she would do so without shipping a drop of water. He claimed she was the driest boat he ever sailed.

Chapter 6
Journey's End: The London Stay

The next two to three years of the story are clear enough. The ship was on display in two locations along the London River—first at the East India Docks at Blackwall and then briefly at the Strand. The move from Blackwall must have taken place sometime in early 1850, because there is a bill poster in the British Library announcing the 're-opening' of the *Keying* at the Strand on 10 June 1850 at Temple Bar Pier, Essex Street.[1] Fancifully, by this time the plain old *Keying* had become transmogrified into 'The Royal Chinese Junk *Keying*', presumably to try to pull the crowd which, in Britain at least, could be relied on to gawp at anything ostensibly royal. There is more to this move than that, as can be found out from the re-issue to coincide with the move, of a print by the popular London print makers and sellers, Rock Brothers & Payne that had been issued initially on 20 May 1848. The original title had read, 'The Chinese Junk, Keying, 其衣喊挨炯知, Captain Kellett. The first junk that ever rounded the Cape of Good Hope, or appeared in British waters. As she appeared off Gravesend 28th March, 1848, 477 days from Canton'. In the re-issue this is entirely replaced by the title, 'The Royal Chinese junk, Keying: the first vessel of Chinese construction which ever reached Europe, now on view at the temple-bar pier, Essex St. Strand London, manned by a Chinese crew, under the command of the Mandarin Hesing, of Canton, the preparer of the celebrated Hesing's mixture of royal Chinese junk teas'.[2] Had He Sing consented to have himself boosted up the hierarchy and begun claiming rather better connections than perhaps he had? What happened the following year at the Great Exhibition, as we shall see, rescues this conjecture from merely idle speculation. It is also possible to read in this a change in the role, and possibly fortunes, of the original investors. It is possible most had by

Map 7 The River Thames, London

this stage sold out of what was turning into a loss-making venture. Perhaps, if He Sing had been one of the original investors and the conduit through whom the junk had been bought, he was the only one left? We shall probably never know.

The major puzzle we are presented with as far as this move upriver is concerned is how it was done. A glance at a contemporary map of the Thames between Blackwall and Temple Bar Pier reveals a trio of obstacles for a vessel with a 90-foot mast (27.4 metres) and two other masts one of which would appear to have been at least 60 feet above the water (18.3 metres). These were the New London Bridge, Southwark Bridge and Blackfriars Bridge. The New London Bridge designed by John Rennie had opened in 1831, it was replaced in 1972, so data for the older bridge is hard to find now. However, the Port of London Authority gives the air draft of the new bridge at mean low water springs (MLWS), when the water level is lowest and the air draft greatest, as 15.4 metres.[3] Sadly, another of John Rennie's Thames bridges, the splendid cast iron arch of his 1819 Southwark Bridge, was also replaced, though rather earlier, in 1921. The air draft at MLWS of the replacement is 13.7 metres.

However, the obvious point here is that it is the lowest air draft that represents the obstacle, not the highest. And the lowest air draft is likely to have been Blackfriars Bridge. That's because although today's bridge is an 1869 replacement, it is extremely unlikely to have had less air draft than Robert Mylne's nine semi-elliptical arch, Portland stone bridge of 1769. Today's Blackfriars has an air draft of 13.5 metres at MLWS.

Since it is wildly improbable that any previous bridges were getting close to double the height of their replacements, there is obviously a major unknown with respect to the *Keying's* movement upriver and, later, back down again. However it was done, it must have been a remarkable feat and the silence of the newspapers of the day with respect to it is yet another example of the real level of public and learned interest in this singular visitor to London.

When the junk re-berthed upriver there was an accident, reported at the time in the newspapers in Jersey where, some two years after her brief visit, she was evidently still news:[4]

> The Chinese Junk—On Saturday last an accident of a very serious character, but unattended with any loss of life happened to a large wooden structure which had lately been in the course of erection at the Essex pier, at

the bottom of Essex Street, Strand, London, for the purpose of exhibiting the Chinese Junk. This building was erected on piles driven down into the river, and was 400 feet long, 60 feet high, and about 50 broad; and one side, the ends, and a portion of the roof had already been enclosed in boards. Throughout Friday night the whole shook and trembled under the influence of the wind, which was very high, and about ten on Saturday morning, while half a dozen workmen were engaged in securing the woodwork, the structure fell down with a large crash. A strong gust of wind was blowing at the time from the east, and the piles were not strong enough to resist the pressure occasioned by the wind acting on the whole length of the side. All the men escaped unhurt, except one, who was precipitated from a considerable height on the mud below, into which he sank several feet; and another who received such injuries on his arm as to render it necessary to remove him to the Hospital. Men had been employed on this building nearly a month, and the cost will be about £500.

The ship had certainly been a star attraction in her first year in London, being visited not only by Queen Victoria, the prince consort and other members of the royal family,[5] but also by the aged duke of Wellington and the famous novelist Charles Dickens, though for the *Keying* visit acting as a journalist. The lord mayor of London and several aldermen visited on Friday, 9 June 1848; no doubt these were just a few of the VIPs who felt they had to be seen at the latest thing in town.[6]

The ship was popular enough to survive for two years at Blackwall, though one suspects that the move to the Strand must have been motivated by waning visitor numbers and a desire to shift the attraction closer to where the likely audience would be found. Clearly, from the newspaper story about the accident, the move was thought worth the considerable expense—in 1850, £500 was a lot of money.[7] Further evidence of this need to drum up additional visitor income by 'rebranding' the junk as an attraction is the Rock Brothers and Payne print reissue (for a fuller discussion, see the Appendix). However, in the long run, even with He Sing and his celebrated tea, it seems the *Keying* could not compete as an attraction.

She was or had been sufficiently successful at some stage for Charles Kellett and his partners to take on additional staff. In any case, given the defections of the Chinese crew in New York and Boston, the Chinese 'tableaux' will have been significantly short of players; supplementary Chinese personnel would have been vital. If the total loss of crew in the two places is to be taken at face value, of the possibly forty originals who had left Hong Kong with the ship, by the departure from Boston thirty-six had left. It might be this drastic reduction in the Chinese component of the ship's company, down to So Yin Sang Hsi, He Sing, Sam Shing, four to six sailors and perhaps the tailor and acting troupe (if they had indeed been signed aboard), that prompted Dickens's comment, quoted in the introduction, that 'half-a-dozen English sailors . . . brought (the Chinese ship and sailors) over the ocean in safety'.

But additional personnel there certainly were. In July 1851, a lady of apparently easy virtue, Caroline Wilsted, is reported as having robbed the 'master of the band of the Chinese junk', a William King, of a pin worth five shillings. The learned judge issued an *obiter dictum*, observing that 'the Chinese Junk was now a great public nuisance; as they kept up music and dancing at all hours of the night, and the managers had better benefit by a warning, as they might be indicted'.[8] They nearly were. In August, indeed, the *Keying* was told it had to go:[9]

> The illuminations with music and dancing which have been for some time proceeded with on board the Chinese Junk, have been suddenly discontinued by the peremptory command of the City Navigation Committee, arising, it is said, from the complaints of some of the inhabitants of Essex-street and vicinity, tenants of the Duke of Norfolk, made through his Grace's solicitor.

But things were obviously beginning to slip. For once the *Keying* had been banished back downriver to Blackwall, it was too far from the public eye. And, in addition, the kiss of death may have been given a year after it had reached Temple Bar Pier, when Nathan Dunn's Chinese Museum, the very reason that things Chinese had been popular in London in the first place, returned to London in 1851 for the Great Exhibition in the new Crystal Palace.[10]

By that same year, 1851, Charles Kellett appears to have moved ashore and to have been living in Kent. He appears in the 1851 census as resident in the Sydenham subdistrict of Lewisham, giving his occupation as 'shipowner'.[11] Evidence that he had ceased having any day-to-day responsibility for the ship as its captain almost as soon as it reached London appears as an aside in an 1848 news story about Chinese Christian converts in Victorian Britain.[12] There we learn that Ating Ati (another hopelessly unhelpful rendering of a Cantonese name) from Macao had signed on as a steward on the *Eliza*, under Captain Pattison; on arrival in London and being signed off, he was employed as 'custodier or captain of the Chinese junk which lay for six months at Blackwall'. It was when that job finished, some time in 1848, that he was taken on as a 'shopman' at Labrey, Scholes, and Co., whose proprietor was an active member of the church. So we can conclude tentatively that, as soon as the *Keying* had reached London and the major visitations were over—say by the end of the summer in 1848— Charles Kellett's work as her captain was done, and he was merely a partner in a business operation earning sufficient, or in possession of sufficient, means to live ashore. We can also conclude He Sing's promotion to captain for the junk's move upriver. Modest financial success there evidently had been for Captain Kellett, leaving aside the accolades he merited for bringing a unique ship on a unique voyage to its distant destination.

There was also most certainly success for the mandarin-turned-captain He Sing. For the most singular moment in the *Keying*'s stay, given the doubts that have been expressed as his authenticity as a mandarin, must be the way he achieved prominence at the Great Exhibition as, in effect, an ambassador of China, or, as the story in the *Caledonian Mercury* put it, 'the worthy representative of China, at the opening of the Exhibition'. There is a large painting of the archbishop of Canterbury blessing the exhibition at its opening by the Victorian artist Henry Courtney Selous.[13] Queen Victoria and Prince Albert are centre rear, flanked on each side in the foreground by plenipotentiaries in glittering uniforms. The most striking figure in the right foreground, at the right of the line and nearest the queen, is the diminutive figure of a gentleman in a mandarin's robes. He Sing had achieved an extraordinary coup.

The year 1851 was just eight years after the signing of the Treaty of the Bogue, which wound up the First Opium War. If one of the intentions of that war had been to force the Chinese government to recognize other states as equal sovereign entities and thereby to enter the world of Western diplomacy, with embassies and ambassadors being exchanged, it had signally failed. The first Chinese representative in Britain, Guo Songdao, would not take up residence until 1877—and then as a commissioner.[14] What He Sing had managed to do, in a context where an actual representative of the government of China could in no way be expected to come to Britain, was convince someone, maybe the queen herself, that he could represent his country at an exhibition intended to show-case the arts and crafts of the world. It would not have been in Charles Kellett's imagined programme!

By the end of 1851, there were signs that not all was well. Brief columns appeared in the *Daily News* in September and October.[15] In the first month, the public is told that 'the Mandarin Hesing continues to receive vast additions to his visitors, both English and foreign'. But by the beginning of the second, the story changes, for the equally brief column indicates from the outset that the endgame was nigh: 'Last three weeks of exhibition previous to departure for foreign ports'. We cannot know whether this was a truthful report of a planned programme or a 'puff' intended to belay suspicion—and creditors.

That said, as early as 1849, there quite clearly had been a further itinerary planned, for in the newspaper report of T. A. Lane and Charles Kellett's talks on the relocation of the *Keying* from the Strand to Blackwall, an onward plan was described: 'From London she is to be moved to Paris, if water enough can be found to float her up the Seine, and if no other obstruction stands in the way between Havre and that capital.'[16]

The visit to Paris, it seems, never came off, for there would no doubt be French sources recalling the event, and there are none. However, it may be that, between October 1851 and the next piece of news we have, there was a final flourish to this first, action-filled volume of the *Keying* story. For there is a tantalizing hint in a catalogue of an exhibition of Chinese junk models, mounted in Antwerp in 1993, that there may have been a visit to Antwerp.[17] If it did happen, no defini-tive evidence has emerged. Winter is not a time for voyaging, even in Europe's narrow seas, so the junk's departure for foreign climes, even if only on the other side of the North Sea, is not that likely. Assuming the October *Daily News* report was accurate, then the planned onward voyaging was not scheduled to start until November. November's short days and the impending onset of the harsh winters of mid-nineteenth-century Britain[18] would not have been conducive to any sort of movement by sea that was not vital; the likelihood is that the *Keying* stayed in London to winter over.

Chapter 7
The Endgame

The Last Days of the *Keying*

The history of the *Keying*, after the first three years of her visit to London and before her departure for Liverpool some two years later, is largely obscure. We do not know whether all that time was spent in London after the shift from the upmarket berth on the Strand, or whether, having been moved on from Temple Bar Pier, the ship went visiting elsewhere. It is possible but, on balance, not probable. For there are indications that either the project's investors wanted to cash in and move on, or they were losing so much money they had to shut up shop. What we do know is that, when the next volume of the story opens, the ship was lying in the West India Import Dock, for sale.

Why she was moved from the East India Dock at Blackwall to the West India Import Dock—the more northerly of the two West India Docks that cross the northern part of the Isle of Dogs between Blackwall Reach and Limehouse Reach—is unknown. The initial welcome at the East India Dock was no doubt connected with the near-moribund East India Company's long involvement with the China trade. The Company would finally be wound up in 1874, after fighting a rearguard action under constant pressure since the first Government of India Act in 1773. In 1853, a further Government of India Act was passed that yet again sought to improve the dire finances and administrative shortcomings of the Company—again, it failed. In the incisive words of Karl Marx, one of the most acute contemporary commentators on the British administration of India:[1]

> That there is in India a permanent financial deficit, a regular over-supply of wars, and no supply at all of public works, an abominable system of

Map 8 British Waters

taxation, and a no less abominable state of justice and law, that these five
items constitute, as it were, the five points of the East Indian Charter, was
settled beyond all doubt in the debates of 1853, as it had been in the debates
of 1833, and in the debates of 1813, and in all former debates on India. The
only thing never found out, was the party responsible for all this.

The otherwise toothless 1853 act did address, by abolishing, the East India
Company's powers of patronage in appointments.[2] It may be that some moves
to try to outflank this very comfortable sinecure of the directors of the EIC had
the knock-on effect of forcing the *Keying* out of her berth at Blackwall. Perhaps,
to show that the EIC was a tightly run ship with no special deals for insiders,
a reduced berthing charge was suddenly raised to full commercial rates, so the
Keying had no option but to find a cheaper berth.

Thus, in 1852, the first volume of the *Keying*'s story was over. On 14 May 1852, the *Hull Packet and East Riding Times*, probably just one of a number of London and regional newspapers to do so,[3] carried a lengthy advertisement announcing the sale of the *Keying* and all its contents. The auctioneer was a Mr. Marsh of 2 Charlotte Row, Mansion House, London. The ship was offered as presenting 'an unequalled investment for the purpose of exhibition in the principal ports of Great Britain and Europe'.

What happened next shows that all with the *Keying* and its investors was far from well. For on 6 June, *The Era* of London carried an announcement, dated 3 June, that the auction had been held, but that the vessel and its contents 'did not find a purchaser'.[4]

Mr. Marsh was not deterred: according to the *Belfast News-Letter* on 7 June, the vessel was again being offered for auction and this time sold.[5] That the *Keying* came back on the block so quickly suggests that the need to sell was pretty urgent, an impression confirmed by the conclusion to the Belfast paper's story: 'It was knocked down for L2,900.'[6] When we recall how much the vessel is purported to have cost, according to the intelligence bruited around in New York noted above, it is clear that desperation was in the air. Another brief column in the *Caledonian Mercury* reported the sale 'for the sum of L2,900—about L6,000 below the original cost'.[7]

This raises again the problems concerning the real price of the *Keying* when she was bought in China. The auction data make the cost of the *Keying* in 1846 at about £8,900 pounds[8]—a far cry from the $75,000 (about £15,600) that was the highest estimate of the original price. If that price is right, Kellett and his partners must have lost their shirts. The source of the £8,900 figure, quoted in the *Caledonian Mercury*, is in question. Like so much in the *Keying*'s story, given its systematic neglect during the intervening 150 years or so, winnowing the chaff of disinformation from the grains of truth is at this stage impossible. At the exchange rate of the day, this amount was equivalent to $42,720—and the sale price $13,920. That is a fairly massive loss to the investors, unless the earnings in the intervening six years had compensated for so large a depreciation of the capital asset.

Against this putative $42,720, there is the much lower buying price quoted by the Hong Kong correspondent in the same discussion above. That price was

$19,000, which means the *Keying* cost the original investors some £3,950. As noted, this would seem on the face of it a much more realistic price for a venerable trading junk—the sort of price an astute man, as we have every reason to suppose Douglas Lapraik was, to pay. If the lower price is the correct one, then, given the vicissitudes the junk had been through and the fact that, after some four years on display, she must just about have exhausted the market, the price fetched at auction was remarkably good. If the partners had been depreciating their major asset at 5 percent a year, and it had cost them £3,950, then by 1854, eight years later, the value of the *Keying* will have been around £2,650 on the books. It is unlikely the contents cost the partners much more than £300 to £400, probably a very great deal less. In short, if showing the ship in New York, Boston and London had done better than pay its way, then the sale was no desperate last throw but a well-managed affair.

In the end, the evidence as to costs and income is so confusing and contradictory that no firm conclusions can be drawn. It is no more than a solid hunch, but taking on balance all the evidence we have seen and will see shortly, the probability is that the *Keying* had not been the success its investors and promoters expected when they embarked on the venture in 1846. Certainly, there is anecdotal evidence that in later life Douglas Lapraik claimed 'he received not a cent's return from his investment'.[9]

With the sale on 3 June 1852, the record again falls silent for eight months. It seems that whoever bought the vessel at auction had second thoughts. On 27 March 1853, according to *Lloyd's Weekly Newspaper*, the *Keying* and her contents were put up for sale again.[10] There is no indication whether the vessel was sold again or of the price paid. The best we can do, casting our eyes two years forwards, is to conclude that the purchasers in either 1852 or 1853 were speculative investors from Liverpool, possibly called Crippin and Forster—though this may be the name of the solicitors of the purchasers, since the two names appear in the context of the next sale.[11]

Within two months of the second sale, or attempt at sale, the *Keying* was on the move. No evidence has been found of the exact date of her departure, though we do know from the next story cited that she left from Blackwall. At some time in early May 1853, the junk left London, under tow from the steam tug *Shannon*, bound for Liverpool.

The next indication we have tells us that the tow had been southabout through the English Channel—a long and hazardous voyage out around Land's End and through the gale-prone Western Approaches. The *Freeman's Journal and Daily Commercial Advertiser* of Dublin on 13 May recorded the junk and her tug laying over in Holyhead, Anglesey, Wales, the cause for the layover being 'Heavy seas in the channel'.[12]

Owned by W. Pim (one of two brothers, Thomas & Wakefield Pim, iron-founders and makers of marine steam engines and boilers in Hull), the *Shannon* had been built at Hull in 1846. At 82 tons burthen, 70 feet long, 15 feet in beam and with a 9-foot draught, she was neither large nor powerful; the tow must have been long, arduous and very dependent on fair weather.[13] It is therefore not surprising that, when the seas built up, the tug and its tow took refuge.

One obvious inference is that the *Keying* could no longer be sailed on her own bottom, either because there were no longer any Chinese sailors available familiar with the rigging or, more likely, that after seven or so years of disuse, the sails and rigging were in a dilapidated state and could not have been used anyway. The condition of the ship aside, the tow itself must have been extremely difficult, both for the tugmaster and whoever was embarked on the *Keying*, to supervise. As we know, the *Keying* was in ballast, riding high in the water. We also know her steering system had both the virtues and the vices of the Chinese system. Keeping the junk steady behind the tug on the long, 660-nautical-mile voyage, in difficult waters with strong tides, must have placed high demands on both the tugmaster and the crew on the *Keying*. Any tendency to range from side to side of the direct line of tow, called sheering, which one imagines the shallow-drafted, high-freeboard *Keying* will have had, puts a huge strain on any tow. As the vessel reaches one end of her sheer—which can be so dramatic as actually to overtake its tug, far out to one side or the other—and is brought up, there is massive strain on the towline, as well as on the points on tug and tow where the towline is secured. There is a permanent risk of the tug being 'girted' or 'girded', that is, pulled over sideways so that it capsizes.[14]

The *Keying* arrived in the Mersey on 14 May 1853, anchoring off Rock Ferry on the Cheshire shore. On 18 May, her arrival was signalled in the *Manchester Times*, which seems also to suggest that the junk was an attraction, though whether she was already open to public visits is unclear: 'On Sunday, many thousand people visited the locality'.[15]

A relative silence falls for something over seventeen months. We have no idea whether she went on exhibition when she arrived. However, Rock Ferry, which still exists as a parish in Birkenhead, is right opposite the centre of Liverpool, so there are some grounds for supposing an exhibition may have been intended. The new purchasers are said in the *Manchester Times* story to have taken a lease on a pier at Rock Ferry for the purposes of public access, so we can assume that, at some time during this period, the *Keying* was open to the paying public.[16]

In 1853, Liverpool was without question Britain's second port, after London; with the rapid economic growth of the British northeast, it was a natural place for the *Keying* to try her luck. The growth of the ferry business and the establishment of the Royal Rock Hotel and bath house in 1836 had begun to put Rock Ferry on the map: 'Between then and 1870, the area received an influx of luxurious housing, the bath house of Rock Park and many other large houses around the Old Chester Road making Rock Ferry one of the most desirable addresses in the North West.' [17] But however the *Keying* was intended to pay her way, it can be concluded that she was not a sufficient success.

There is a suggestion, with what basis is unclear, that after her arrival at Liverpool she may have been renamed the *Royal Hesing* and in autumn that year made at least another promotional voyage.[18] One suspects the name change did not happen and is simply a misreading of London posters and advertisements announcing the move from Blackwall to the Strand. Although, of course, if He Sing had retained an interest as far back as 1850 and the move upriver in London to the Strand, perhaps he was still involved. However, the idea of a promotional voyage is more intriguing, though the only realistic possibility, in October on the Irish Sea, would be a visit to Dublin. At least one source claims there is evidence that, on 29 September 1853, the *Keying* was set to leave on a further promotional tour 'in three weeks', though no reference is given for the claim.[19]

That this second attempt to make the *Keying* a paying attraction failed is made evident by yet another sale by auction, as the lease on the pier at Rock Ferry came up for expiry. This was advertised in the *Liverpool Mercury* of 27 October 1854. A Mr. Jenkin had placed an announcement that 'the ENTIRE CONTENTS of the ROYAL CHINESE JUNK, moored at the Royal Rock Ferry, Cheshire' were for sale and that the auction would take place on 14, 15 and 16 November; he evidently expected that this time there would be no question of selling the ship lock, stock and barrel, but that things would be sold in individual lots.[20] The catalogue of the sale was available, at cost of sixpence, from either the auctioneer's offices in Liverpool or his home in Birkenhead. A further notice appeared in the *Liverpool Mercury* reminding people of the sale on 10 November. This notice reminded prospective purchasers, 'N.B. The junk is now on view daily until Monday next, at dusk, when it will be re-opened on Tuesday, at ten-o'clock. Steamers leave the landing stage every half hour for Rock Ferry, and parties from the country will find excellent accommodation at the Royal Rock and Star Hotels.'[21]

Again, the record falls silent. We do not know what the result of the auction was. By inference from an announcement of another auction some five months later, one of two things may have happened. The junk and contents may have been sold, or the junk may have been sold to one buyer and the contents to another.

The auction announced in the *Liverpool Mercury* on 9 March 1855 marks the penultimate chapter of the *Keying* saga. But what was for sale by the auctioneer, Henry Green of Hamilton Street, Birkenhead, were the junk's contents, not the junk.[22] That the junk and its contents had gone their separate ways at the 10 November auction is made clear by the advertisement of a separate auction, to be held in Liverpool by the auctioneers Howard, Fox & Co., for the *Keying* alone, that appeared some three weeks after Henry Green's contents' auction.[23]

Sometime during this rapid-fire sequence of sales, probably at the Birkenhead auction at Rock Ferry in November 1854, a small Cheshire shipyard, Redhead, Harling and Brown, acquired the vessel and began to dismantle it, reportedly 'for research'. Redhead, Harling and Brown are listed as 'shipbuilders, shipwrights, boat builders, block & mast makers, ship joiners and shipsmiths, Tranmere Graving Dock, Tranmere' in the 1857 *Cheshire Post Office Directory*.[24] But their intention to research the junk's construction is mentioned in only one report. Others make no mention of any purpose, merely that the *Keying* was broken up and 'her planking' used to make two ferries or tugs and some souvenirs,[25] though none of the latter seems to have survived to be actively traded today on the thriving auction market.

That the destruction of the vessel was not complete, which also puts in question the extent to which her timber was used to construct other vessels, may be inferred from a story that appeared two years later in a number of newspapers all over Britain:[26] 'The Chinese junk once a most popular attractive exhibition, is now rotting neglected and uncared for on the shore at Tranmere Ferry opposite Liverpool.'

That the story was run in Plymouth is probably just an indication of how early news syndication worked. However, Charles Alfred Kellett was born around 1820 in Plymouth, of which Devonport is the naval dockyard township. Perhaps there was a family connection, though another possible explanation lies in the story of the editor of the *Plymouth and Devonport Weekly Journal and Advertiser*. Mr. Isaac Latimer, editor and owner of that newspaper, had spent the earlier years of his journalistic life in London, as a contributor to the *Morning Chronicle*. It was he who had suggested to the proprietors, at the time they were publishing *Sketches by Boz*, that they give a job to Charles Dickens.[27] It seems that Dickens and Latimer kept in touch; perhaps Dickens's lively if dismissive interest in the *Keying* is what inspired Latimer to carry this last, sad piece on her fate.

The Fates of the Crew

Charles Kellett

Behind the end of this long story is what may be the equally sad tale of the crumbling of Charles Kellett's hopes. He had possibly hoped to found his fortune and future prosperity in the venture. It is not clear that he did or, if he did, that it was in the way that he had hoped. Certainly the probabilities are low, given Douglas Lapraik's claim to have made no money at all out of it.

In 1854, two years after the first sale of the *Keying*, Kellett and his family shipped out to New Zealand, presumably as emigrants. One can infer that the monies raised by the sale added to whatever profits had been made in over four complete years of exhibition to the public, once the whole had been distributed to the partners, were sufficient for Charles Kellett to imagine starting anew in a new land. But it was not a plan that immediately followed the break-up of the original partnership.

Was it a freely chosen decision to start again in the Antipodes or one that seemed the only recourse? On the side of the former, Susan Simmons, Charles Kellett's great-great-granddaughter, has found evidence that Kellett visited the

Australian immigrant ship *Coromandel* in August 1849.[28] So he may there have
heard something that told him Australia or New Zealand were places to put the
results of his venturesome voyage to work. On the other hand, as we shall see,
leaving Britain may have become partly unavoidable if Kellett wished to continue in his chosen profession. For the world had begun changing dramatically
for British merchant seaman officers.

The last half of the nineteenth century was a period of massive change in the
world of British merchant shipping marked, above all, by the epochal changes
inspired by Samuel Plimsoll and finally introduced by the Merchant Shipping
Act of 1876. Steamships were beginning their acceleration to dominance; the size
of ships was swiftly increasing. The science of navigation, thanks to better lighthouses, vastly improved charts and ships that moved almost independently of
wind and current, was shifting far beyond the more suck-it-and-see techniques of
the past; under the commercial pressure for faster, cheaper voyages, seamanship
learned in the days of sail had need of some significant revision. Industrialization
and specialization, along with increased sizes of ships, were transforming port
facilities. The standards required of ships' officers, in regard to their knowledge
of navigation, maritime law, ship construction, marine engineering and the arts
of lading, were undergoing rapid change. The result was increasing attention to
better regulation, beginning with the Mercantile Marine Act of 1850 dealing
with personnel, and the Merchant Shipping Act of 1854 consolidating decades
of legislation.

For Charles Kellett, the first significant change will have occurred in 1845,
the year before he left Hong Kong in the *Keying*. That year, the Board of Trade
Certificates of Competency for mates and masters on foreign-going service were
first introduced on a voluntary basis. By 1850, two years after the *Keying* arrived
in London and before the eventual endpoint of the project had been reached,
such certificates were compulsory for foreign-going masters and mates.[29] In
order to continue holding the jobs they had been doing, merchant seamen had
to satisfy the Board of Trade that they should be 'grandfathered' on the basis of
proven past experience, or they had to pass the new exams.

In an 1856 letter to the governor of New South Wales seeking assistance,
Kellett mentioned possessing a Certificate of Competence from the Board
of Trade.[30] Susan Simmons notes that, in the same letter, Kellett averred his

willingness to 'serve before the mast' (that is, not as a ship's officer), were his family circumstances not such that a master's berth was essential. He does not subsequently appear to have gained any master's employment in a foreign-going, British-flagged ship between 1852 and the date of his death, presumed to be in 1865 as a result of an unspecified accident in which both he and Jane Kellett died.

But Charles Kellett did not in fact have a Certificate of Competence. In 2013 his Master's Certificate of Service finally came to light from the British National Archives and the British National Maritime Museum, where it had languished unremarked for 162 years until modern, web-based genealogical databases made possible the sort of global searches that were previously a lifetime's work. It is a fascinating document that between the lines gives some hints about this period in Charles Kellett's life.

The key to understanding lies in the careful wording of Section 37 of the 1850 Act. It distinguishes sharply between two different forms of certification. The Certificate of Service and the Certificate of Competency:

> XXXVII. And be it enacted, That Persons who have before the First Day of January One thousand eight hundred and fifty-one served as Masters of Mates in the British Merchant Service, or who have attained or hereafter may attain the Rank of Lieutenant, Master, Passed Mate, or Second Master, or any higher Rank, in the Naval Service of Her Majesty or of the East India Company, shall be entitled, without Payment of any Fee, to Certificates as Masters or Mates (as the Case may be), differing in Form from 'Certificates of Competency,' and herein-after called 'Certificates of Service;' and each of such Certificates shall contain Particulars of the Name, Place, and Time of Birth, and of the Length and Nature of the previous Service of the Person to whom the same is delivered; and the 'Board of Trade' shall deliver to any Person who proves himself to have served as Master in such Manner and before such Time as aforesaid, or to have attained such Rank as aforesaid, and who also gives a full and satisfactory Account of the Particulars afore-said, a 'Certificate of Service' either as Master or Mate, as he may desire, and shall deliver to any Person who proves himself to have served as Mate in such Manner and before such Time as aforesaid, a 'Certificate of Service' as Mate; and the 'Board of Trade' may also, in Cases in which it thinks fit so to do, give Certificates of Competency in lieu of Certificates of Service to any deserving Persons who have attained such Rank as above mentioned, or who before his Act comes into operation have obtained Certificates from the 'Board of Trade,' without requiring them to be examined.

In short, Charles Kellett, despite his seventeen years at sea, had proved unable to satisfy the Board of Trade that it should give him a Certificate of Competency. By the time of the 1854 Act, exactly what was needed to satisfy the Board of Trade had been made clear. To qualify as a foreign-going master, Charles Kellett would have had to show evidence of having been six years at sea, at least one of them as first mate or only mate, another as second mate and one year in a square-rigger. There will also have been the need to satisfy all the formal requirements, in terms of specialist knowledge, that had been imposed. Charles Kellett was a thoroughly competent practical seaman, but he had clearly not been able to produce sufficient evidence that this entitled him to a Certificate of Competency. In the post-1850 world of British shipping, that would have been a handicap.

At least part of Charles Kellett's problem would have been that the logbook by means of which he would have hoped to prove his competence as master of a foreign-going ship was that of a highly unorthodox junk during a two-stage voyage lasting only some eight months, which, furthermore, was in neither the normal passenger nor cargo trade.

Indeed looking carefully at Charles Kellett's certificate two things stand out. He had been awarded it at the very last moment. The Mercantile Marine Act had given aspirants until 1 January 1851 to get their past service grandfathered and acquire their new certificates. After that the only route to certification would have been to take the relevant examinations. Charles Kellett's certificate is dated 1 January 1851. Recalling the evidence that Charles Kellett had moved ashore by 1851 and had recorded his occupation in that year's census as 'shipowner', one possibility is that already by 1850 things were sufficiently uncertain as far as the *Keying* venture was concerned for Charles Kellett to make sure he got his Certificate of Service 'just in case'.

The second interesting feature is that the official in the Registrar General of Seaman's office in London has carefully modified the description of Charles Kellett's service to indicate that none of it had been in the British home trade, not even his years as a boy. It states that Charles Kellett 'Has been employed in the Capacities of Boy, Mate & Master 17 years in the British Merchant Service principally in the Foreign Trade', implying by the deletion of 'principally' that as of 1834 Charles Kellett had only served on foreign-going ships. We can perhaps infer from this that the Certificate of Service was given on Charles Kellett's affidavit, perhaps endorsed by his fellow investors, but not supported by any solid evidence that would have shifted him up a category.

Despite his record-making voyage, Charles Kellett had fallen through the gaps of the new regulatory planking. The *Keying* was not manifestly a ship in the British Merchant service. Successfully skippering a Chinese junk was not something that the Registrar would apparently see as indicating Charles Kellett was a 'deserving person' meriting a Master's Certificate of Competency. Chinese shipping yet again didn't quite make the cut as both in and of the modern world.

There is no record of Charles Kellett skippering a ship in 1854, in any of British, New Zealand or Australian waters, by which he may have carried himself and his wife to a new life. Instead there is a record of a Mr. and Mrs. Kellett and a Mary (possibly Kellett) travelling as passengers in the *Northfleet* from London to Auckland in 1853–54,[31] which may be more than a mere coincidence in names. It follows that when Charles and Jane Kellett emigrated to New Zealand, it was as settlers of some sort. Sadly, in New Zealand, things evidently went swiftly and disastrously wrong: the Kelletts 'lost all', as we know from Kellett's 1856 letter to the governor of New South Wales. Within the year, again from evidence Simmons has unearthed, the Kelletts may once more have been passengers, this time bound from Auckland to Melbourne on the *Kestrel*. The next we hear of them is in the petition to the governor, following a further, unspecified domestic disaster in 1856.

Life must have been harrowing for the Kelletts after the slow demise of the *Keying* venture. According to Sydney Stanford Kellett's birth certificate, he had five siblings, two of whom, the twins Charles junior and Louisa, were born in 1855 and were still alive at his birth in 1857. All three of the others had died. Nothing is known of when or why, but one can infer the sort of family tragedy that suggests leaving the scene of it behind.

But, despite the misfortunes of his family, the likelihood remains that Charles Kellett was a victim of the rapid professionalization of the mid- to late nineteenth-century merchant marine. In the *Keying*, he had had his moment of maritime glory, perhaps hoping it would fund him into a 'better' way of life, possibly as the owner of his own vessel. But despite his failure to gain a formal qualification, according to family lore Charles Kellett does not seem to have abandoned the sea. There is certainly no evidence of him being captain of any ship after the

Keying, but it is wholly possible that he did find employment, perhaps even in his own vessel, in the flourishing coastal trade of rapidly growing Australia, where the punctilio of Board of Trade regulations took rather longer to make its impact felt.

The Chinese Crew and the Chinese Ship

There are, of course, two final, sad elements to this story: what happened to the Chinese 'stars', He Sing and Sam Shing, and the Chinese crew, including their gang boss and skipper, the evidently extremely competent So Yin Sang Hsi. There is also the question of the final fate of the scores of items on display in the *Keying*, which had gone under the auctioneer's hammer in Birkenhead on 23 March 1855.

Where the first are concerned, might one reason why the project began to come apart in London be that even the slender rump of the crew that was left when the *Keying* arrived in Britain had started drifting away? After all, the only advantage the *Keying* had over Nathan Dunn's Chinese Museum was that it had real, live Chinese people—not only the 'professionals' like He Sing and Sam Shing, but also the crewmen still remaining or subsequently recruited, everyday people from China whose presence could purport in some way to complement the paltry variety of objects on display and to give to the intended raree show for the gullible a dignity and authenticity that was probably accidental.

In the 1850s, immigration control was not an issue. The viciously racist turn that was to occur within a few years, in response to the gold rush period as well as a more generally exclusivist shift in social attitudes, had not at that point become as acute as soon they would. So, with the existing, if always small, Chinese community in the Limehouse area—a community that had begun life almost two centuries earlier—there was every likelihood that the sailors, tired of being exhibits whose habits and selves were objects of what was no doubt often derisive curiosity, and exploited for returns of which they would have seen a mere pittance, decided to disappear through London's porous waterfront.[32] What few remained when the ship got to Liverpool, if any, may then have done the same there.

One of the sorriest parts of the *Keying's* story is how little we know of the stories of the Chinese crew. Why did they sign up? Desperation? Curiosity? Loyalty to their *batou*? What did they think of the whole escapade? What did the majority who left in New York think of the minority who stayed, and vice versa? What happened to the majority when the *Candace* returned to China? What happened to the minority whose ship was sold from under them? They are classic victims of what E. P. Thompson once described as 'the enormous condescension of posterity'—the written tale of and for the few, from which the vast majority of those whose sweat and tears made possible what evanescent success and fame the few attained are utterly effaced.[33]

So far, only two traces have surfaced. One comes from a London newspaper of 1853, after the *Keying* had left London for Liverpool and before it was broken up.[34] It recounts the story of a bankruptcy case and has a quite startling dénouement.

An anonymous English grocer and tea-dealer was in debt to the tune of £1,600 and had been declared bankrupt. One of the claimants at the bankruptcy proceedings was his shopman, who identified himself as Chun Ahmen, and who appeared with an English-speaking Chinese friend to act as interpreter. Yet again there is that maddening impossibility of identifying a real Cantonese name, worsened in this case by the dark suspicion that the description 'Chinaman' has been tortured into the name 'Chun Ahmen'. But whatever his name, the claimant sought £38 as arrears of wages and in his deposition claimed he had been employed for two years, after having been 'one of the crew who came over in the Chinese junk'. Sadly, he was to discover that the laws of the *fan kwae* do not always seem fair to those who do not grasp its Pecksniffian, but legally vital niceties:

> The claim for £38 was for a year's service. He expected to be paid in full; but on its being explained to him that he could only receive three months' wages in full, and must prove and take a dividend for the remainder, he fell into a violent passion, and ultimately rushed out of court, threatening to hang himself if his claim were not at once discharged in full.

The hapless victim of this bankruptcy, unassuaged by the judicious even-handedness of bankruptcy law, reappeared before the court, spoke fiercely to the solicitor for the bankrupt, mimed his suicidal intentions and rushed out, followed by his anxious and solicitous friend. The report ends with a small bombshell:

It was stated that the Chinaman is the same who figured at the Exhibition as a Chinese mandarin and who, on the opening, was honoured with a place near her Majesty.

Poor He Sing.

Yet, thanks to another record, we do know that if the shopkeeper's assistant had been He Sing, he did not commit suicide. This record is an example of the *fan kwae* yet again letting the side down with their arrogant and dismissive certainties. It comes from China. The story surfaced half a century after the events of 1846–55, in the memoirs of a British naval hydrographer recalling his days in the Far East—as inhabitants of the Far North West think of everywhere east of India. William Blakeney's recollection implies that, whatever the recollections of the Europeans may have been, at least some of the Chinese crewmen, who stayed with the ship after New York and then made their way back to China, may have looked back with mixed feelings. Recalling events in 1858, he wrote:[35]

A few days after our arrival in Whampoa the Chinese cut away and walked off with the rigging of the newly-erected flagstaff marking the site of the future British Consulate. This was considered an insult to our flag, as it had been hoisted under a salute of seven guns from 'Noah's Ark.' So a proclamation was issued demanding the delinquent, and a small boy was produced who could not have lifted the stolen rope! Accordingly the Captain, as 'senior officer present,' sent an armed party after the four principal men and took them up to Canton before the English and French Commissioners. What became of them I have no record, but one of the four was in the crew of the junk *Keying* which, I remember, was brought to England about fifty-five years ago, when I was a schoolboy at Greenwich, and was for some time on exhibition in one of the London docks . . . This man—who could speak English fairly, had been made a sort of 'sea-lion' of in London society, and was careful to tell us that he had spoken with the Duke of Wellington, the 'Iron Duke'—and was very much aggrieved at being made to stand on our quarter-deck as a prisoner, held responsible for what he certainly had no part in and disapproved, but he was 'one of the elders' and our Captain always made for them.

Initially that was the totality of the story. It suggested at least one crewman had some positive memories of his time aboard the *Keying*. But then the logbook of Blakeney's ship, HMS *Actaeon*, missing from Captain (later Vice-Admiral) Robert Jenkins'[36] archive in Britain, turned up in Hong Kong in mid-2013.[37] It completes Blakeney's story by indicating 'what became of' the elders and the identity of the *Keying* crewman.

> Tuesday March 17th 1858.
>
> A.M. 9.30 Landed small arm men with those of squadron[38] and Marines of *Adventure*[39] and gun boats to salute the British Consular Flag and cause the Elders of the Village on Danes Island[40] to make their submission to and express contrision [*sic*] for the insult committed by some of their people on the Flag Staff.
>
> 10.30 The Elders not appearing at the appointed time. Marched on the village from two points and having the small arms men in position commanding the opposite approaches. Marched with the Marines to the principal Ancestral Temple, where some of the most aged of the Villagers met us, as well as Hising who has been in England. On our return with them to the Consular ground. The small arms men, and Marines formed three sides of a hollow square facing inwards. The (bases?) were read. The Elders, and people were addressed by Mr (Morgan?) in forcible terms, and during a General Salute the Elders performed the Cow Tow under the Union Jack according to Chinese Custom.

Just in case quite what this meant is unclear, Captain Jenkins appended to the entry the only pictorial image in the whole logbook. It is shocking. It shows a presumably aged Chinese village person having his forehead forcibly knocked on the ground by a British Royal Marine beneath the Union Jack on a short flag staff in front of a serried rank of British troops.

The nub of the entry is, however, that the *Keying* crewman is identified as He Sing and by inference that he was a native of Dane's Island. Whatever may have been He Sing's attitude towards his *Keying* experience before this incident is unlikely to have survived it unscathed.[41]

Lost Traces

And then there were the objects. They were an extraordinary collection—one later edition of the catalogue at which we have already glanced lists 129 identifiable items including parts of the ship's working deck—exhibiting nothing so much as the instincts of a magpie. They certainly exhibit no interest in or understanding of Chinese culture; indeed, rather the opposite. They ranged through gingals (hand cannon) and other weapons, via a coffin, household furniture and musical

instruments, to decorative items including paintings, ceramics, curiosities, lanterns and statues. There was the whole tray of opium pipes and opium-takers'
accoutrements and its pious condemnation of lax and improvident Chinese
ways. There were temple accoutrements, statuettes, a piece of the Canton city
walls (!), Chinese money and clothing, and parts of official uniforms. Various
maritime artefacts are listed, including model ships, a Chinese compass and
models of parts of the *Keying* as well as parts of the *Keying* itself. There was even,
at one stage, the stuffed ship's dog that had died in New York. Much of this would
of course have been worthless at the time, and perhaps even today. But all of it
would have been fascinating were it still together as a collection; it goes without
saying that it would be of great historical interest as a catalogue of what an exact
antithesis to Nathan Dunn's collection may have looked like.

Has anything survived? It would seem not. Bar many, many examples of the
two or three designs of commemorative medals and some copies of the various
editions of the visitor's guide, no artefact clearly traced to the *Keying* or her
collection has surfaced at auction in the last twenty to thirty years. Such items
may exist, but it seems likely that they have lost their provenance and are now
as untraceable to the *Keying* as any Benares brassware tray on its folding, multi-
legged stand is to a specific servant of the Raj. The one extant trace is somewhat
indicative of how late 1840s and early 1850s Britain, in the swollen hubris of its
imperial pride, saw the gewgaws that graced the *Keying's* saloon.

In a brief submission to *Notes and Queries* on 22 September 1906, a Mr. Aleck
Abrahams of 30 Hillmarton Road, London N. reported an entry in *The Daily
Graphic* of 16 July that year, to the effect that:

> Mr S.S. Mackrow presented to Prince Edward, a relic of the Chinese junk
> *Keying*, in the shape of a piece of her rattan cable. Mr Mackrow was present
> in May, 1848, when Queen Victoria and our present King (then aged seven)
> visited it.[42]

So, perhaps, lost in the depths of a royal collection, there is a relic of this singular
ship. Is it the only one?

The answer is that one almost as vestigial a relic does exist today. In the collection of the New York Historical Society Museum and Library at 170, Central Park
West in New York City—though apparently not on display—object INV.303 is
described as a 'Long, narrow fragment of wood with inscribed paper label, and

coil of twine'. The paper label in turn has the inscription, 'Wood and string from the / Chinese Junk Keying / New York Aug 1847 / [Lemuel W. Terell/]'. The Society's curators have added, with a faint note of dubiety, 'Due to ongoing research, information about this object is subject to change.'[43]

The provenance of these vagrant morsels offers a tantalizing hint of something far more interesting that further research might turn up, should the winds of fortune so blow. On 23 October 1849 patent number 6819 was granted to W. Lewis and W. H. Lewis of New York City. It was for 'an apparatus for holding daguerreotype'. The witnesses to this are cited as Wm. Terrell and Lemuel W. Terrell.[44]

Although it is surmised the Lewis' apparatus was never actually put into production, if the two Lemuel W. Terrells are the same person and were involved in the early years of the daguerreotype in America, the possibility exists that somewhere there may be an early daguerreotype, from the *Keying*'s New York days, of one of the ship's company—Charles Kellett? So Yin Sang Hsi? He Sing? Mrs. D. T. Davis' early account of the daguerreotype in America indicates that, 'By November, 1841, there were six studios in Boston, and a larger number in New York.'[45]

So the possibility exists that not only a fragment of wood and some light cordage have survived, but also a true likeness of one of the crew.

The story of the *Keying*, her captain and her crew is an important byway in maritime history, illustrating in bold colours and high relief the vexed situation that occurs when two widely disparate maritime traditions engage in a common endeavour, if not a common goal. The story testifies to the great seaworthiness and durability of the products of traditional Chinese naval architecture, and to the probable performance of Chinese junks both within and without their traditional working area. But the story is also evidence of the way in which, despite the scientific temper of mid-nineteenth-century Europe, when other traditions were seen as quaint relics of a disappearing past, prejudice prevented both a proper evaluation of its qualities, or even a proper record being made of them. Our knowledge of China's traditional naval architectural tradition is the poorer for it.[43] In Part II, when we turn to the other major character in the drama, the ship itself, we consider some further explanations as to why.

Part II

The Ship Itself: Type, Build, Performance

Chapter 8
What Kind of Vessel Was the *Keying*?

Identifying exactly what sort of junk the *Keying* was is as difficult, and important, as understanding this largely failed episode. The East sailed to the West, the ship got there physically, but that is about the *Keying*'s only achievement. East got to West on the West's terms and conditions, failed to impress, was generally misunderstood and thus forgotten. The crew fell apart. The main human actors were swallowed by the historical midden. The log of the voyage disappeared. And exactly what this singular example of Chinese naval architecture was in terms of its shape, its size and its provenance must be disinterred as broken shards from what little remains because no one was sufficiently interested to make a complete record.

Yes, the pictorial record is quite extensive. Yes, there are medals and bits of paper with this measurement and that. However, for anyone genuinely interested in marine ethnography, all this falls short on precisely observed technical detail and long on all the errors that can arise from a failure to understand what is being catalogued or depicted.

So what clues are there which might lead us towards a clearer idea of the kind of traditional Chinese sea-going vessel the *Keying* was? There are remarkably few, all from secondary sources.

Sadly, despite the fact that the first photograph had been taken (of a Flemish print) by the Frenchman Joseph Nicéphore Niépce as early as 1825 by the heliograph process, that Louis Daguerre had produced his eponymous daguerreotypes by the late 1830s and Fox Talbot shortly afterwards invented the calotype and the possibility of reproducing a positive from a glass negative, by 1846–55 progress had not been sufficiently rapid for photography to be widespread. Had the

Keying sailed just fourteen years later, by which time photographers like the Scot John Thomson and the remarkable Corfiot Felix (or Felice) Beato were making some of the first photographic images of Hong Kong and China, we might have less poorly interpreted and ambiguous sources to work with.[1]

As it is, the photographic revolution in seeing and recording was too much in its infancy. The result is records shot through from end to end with the assumptions and prejudices of jobbing artists and journalists made worse, in almost every case, by a relative unfamiliarity with ships and the sea. How much better off we should have been had a genuinely accomplished marine artist of the period—there were scores[2]—interested himself in the unprecedented arrival in American and British waters of this unique ship.

Just five years before the *Keying* arrived in London, the publication that, in effect, launched the modern discipline of marine ethnology had been published. The stunning *Essai sur la construction navale des peuples extra-européens, ou, Collection des navires et pirogues construits par les habitants de l'Asie, de la Malaisie du Grand Océan et de l'Amérique* was a pioneering work by François-Edmond Pâris (1806–93), an officer in the French navy, the Marine nationale, with 133 plates, of which 76 were tinted lithographs plus 57 line engravings. The drawings revealed in careful and exact detail the ethnic craft of places as far afield as Senegal, the Seychelles, India, Malaysia, the Strait of Malacca, Vietnam, China, Singapore, the Philippines, Indonesia, Australia, Chile, Brazil, Greenland and Oceania.[3] The data had been gathered by the young Lieutenant Pâris during the three French naval exploratory circumnavigations he took part in, under captains D'Urville and Laplace, on the ships *Astrolabe* (1826–29), *Favorite* (1829–32), and *Artémise* (1837–40). So important was this work that the French government, through the minister of the Navy, financed the lithographic reproduction of Pâris's drawings and their publication in a large and expensive folio volume. When Pâris retired from the French navy in 1871, after a long and extremely distinguished career, he became the fourth *conservateur* (director) of the French National Maritime Museum; using his own drawings, he had models made of the range of craft he had depicted, as a result of which the Musée national de la Marine today still has one of the finest collections of models of traditional ethnic craft that exists.

And yet when, just five years after Pâris had completed his formidable work, the *Keying* arrived in London and spent five years there, no one was interested. Pâris himself was perhaps not able to visit. Having been promoted to commander, from 1848 until 1854, he commanded a succession of ships—the *Gomer* in 1848, the *Orénoque* in 1850 and the *Fleurus* in 1854—which will have kept him fully occupied.

There would appear to have been no English Pâris. The collection of models gathered by the early nineteenth-century naval architect Sir Robert Seppings (1767–1840), which eventually found its way into Britain's National Maritime Museum in 1934 when that institution gained its official status, was narrowly parochial in scope, focused as it was on Seppings' own concern for improved design and construction—a field to which he made notable contributions in his fifty years of working for the British navy's dockyards.[4] Had Seppings still been alive in 1848, given that his key contribution to the advancement of naval architecture had been the strengthening and stiffening of wooden ships by diagonal bracing and trussing, turning Western-built hulls into strong, reinforced skeletons, he would surely have been intrigued to study how Chinese vernacular shipwrights had tried to solve the same problems of hogging, sagging and wracking, and come on a radically different solution.[5] For where Western vessels were built with a stiffened 'spine'—a stem, sternpost, keel and keelsons—and a frame of ribs, shelves, stringers, diagonals and beams, Chinese vessels rely for their longitudinal stiffness on heavy external wales down the ship's side, with solid internal frames against wracking.[6] The engineering principles involved are sufficiently different for direct comparison to be difficult. Had Seppings been alive when the *Keying* arrived in London, or had any other of the leading naval architects of the day like Scott Russell or Brunel been interested, perhaps we should know more of the *Keying* than we do.

That there was almost no interest, whether from artists or anyone else in Britain, could be argued as itself to be a statement of the fundamental problems of 'seeing' the vessels of a different culture. In that sense, to his eternal distinction, François-Edmond Pâris is a remarkable exception. The consequence of this almost deliberate 'blindness' among the British has been a bafflingly poor record of the *Keying*, despite the remarkable though evidently superficial 'visibility' of the junk as a potential subject for study or a painting, during its years on display in London.[7]

Only one painter recorded as a marine or maritime artist seems to have worked on the *Keying*, though the painting appears to have been lost. The painting was entitled 'The Chinese junk Keying in a gale' and was by Stephen Dadd Skillett (1816–88), whose first public exhibition had been in 1845, three years before the *Keying* reached London. The painting was exhibited at the British Institution in 1849 and must presumably have been based on descriptions Skillett gleaned from the ship's European crew. It may be that the painting was commissioned by one of the *Keying*'s partners or officers, perhaps in commemoration of the epic struggle with the rudder. Sadly, there is no modern record of the painting itself, so whether it succeeded in capturing the actuality of the *Keying* where most other images failed, we are unlikely to discover.[8]

It is possible that a Chinese voyage described in a scroll called the Fra Mauro Map of c. 1450 did pass the Cape of Good Hope blown before a gale, but if so, Fra Mauro's account, with its ambiguous reference to 'a ship or junk of the Indies', remains the only testament.[9] On that evidence, it is fair to argue that the *Keying* is the only traditional Chinese ship ever to sail from China via the Cape of Good Hope to New York and across the North Atlantic to Europe, and thus to make a major, temperate-latitudes oceanic crossing before the late nineteenth century.[10]

Three contemporary images of the vessel—two unique and little-known 'bird's eye views' by an unknown Chinese artist in gouache, the other a lithographic print by the famous New York printmaker Nathaniel Currier—are the best of the few guides we have to the conformity of the *Keying*. There are a handful of other images, all by jobbing engravers working for popular journals and printmakers. Most are evidently more the product of a lively imagination than of habits of close and careful observation.[11] There are, as well, medals to commemorate the ship's famous voyage, a variety of mementos in different metals, struck by companies including Halliday of Birmingham, the limned junks of which either directly copy one of the popular engravings or borrow heavily from them. All of these are in their various ways representative of the level of accuracy and detail of the only depictions of the vessel there are.

Despite the fleeting fame of the *Keying*, remarkably little technical detail is known about it. What there is, coming exclusively from contemporary measurements, descriptions and illustrations, is notoriously unreliable. As far as accurately reconstructing the *Keying* is concerned, such detail as we have, almost entirely from the promotional pamphlet prepared for publicity, lacks precision.[12]

Given that the *Keying* is the only Chinese ship ever to have visited the United States and Europe during the great mid-nineteenth-century efflorescence of Western interest in accurately measuring and quantifying almost everything, it is astonishing to note the complete indifference to the ship demonstrated by the many practising and accomplished marine artists of the day.

Notwithstanding the shortage of certainty as to how the *Keying* actually did measure up, there is an inevitable conflict between the features of the junk as these were portrayed in several contemporary images and what makes naval architectural sense. All images save one are exaggeratedly curved up at bow and stern—that is, the junk's sheerline, as the line of the deck is described, is too curved up at the ends. Exploring reasons for the error is a useful hook for considering the junk against the history of the calamitous meeting between the naval architectural traditions of China and the West. Calamitous, that is, for China's native naval architectural world, since the result has been the virtual eclipse of that millennial set of practices—mostly transmitted as an oral tradition—leaving present-day scholars and enthusiasts struggling to discover or recover and record, before it is too late, the designs, techniques and tools of China's maritime past.

Criticisms that focus on the artists' images approach the matter of the shape and structure of the *Keying* from the wrong perspective. On the one hand, they mistakenly privilege images made by Western artists who had never seen a junk before, hence had no visual frame of reference within which to interpret one and so very probably fell back on established 'exotic' stereotyping. On the other, they fail to take adequately into account what is known of the *Keying* and of the practices of traditional Chinese shipbuilding.

What did the *Keying* really look like? There is obviously no definitive answer. However, it is the purpose of this chapter to investigate this question via a detailed critique of the best known images of the ship, in terms of the measurements which we have. As we shall see, the measurements themselves are just sufficient to help us see that, although these images are greatly misleading and insufficient to develop a clear and detailed picture of the ship, they do offer a starting point.

We can start with the contrast between the most instructive of the images, referred to above, and the rest. The Chinese artist and Nathaniel Currier's images enable us to get somewhat 'behind' the other depictions produced in New York and London by artists little capable of 'seeing' Chinese hull forms and rigs. For it was and is the predominance of images of this second kind that have misled many commentators on the *Keying* for the last century and a half.

A key to understanding such images' potential to mislead is to recall that illustrated magazine and popular illustrated book engravers in the mid-nineteenth century were the news photographers of their day.[13] While unquestionably able draftsmen, they were working to tight deadlines, anxious to be the first into print with some new, sensational image that would be a 'hit' with the buying public. They would also usually, if perhaps not deliberately, be matching the expectations of their audiences by producing images that conformed to accepted prejudices about the 'strange' and 'exotic'.[14]

This was, after all, the period of a rapidly rising Western 'superiority' complex, in the context of which non-Western naval architecture could not be seen to be conforming to the product of 'scientific' Western shipbuilding.[15] In that sense, there would have been a natural tendency to exaggerate the non-conformity of a Chinese vessel with the more 'scientific' shape of Western ships. The tenor of the description of the *Keying* in the *Description* issued in London is typical:[16]

> Everything is different; the mode of construction, the absence of keel, bowsprit and shrouds; the materials employed, the mast, the sail the yard, the rudder, the compass, the anchor . . . Hundreds of European ships, with all their elegance of form and beauty and lightness of rigging, have been constantly before the eyes of the Chinese, without their appearing conscious of the superiority . . .

Equally, since the producers of such images were often jobbing artists, like graphic artists today they will have been working from an accepted canon of techniques, shortcuts, established stereotypes, and so on, as much as from any firsthand eyewitness sketches (this thought is more fully developed in the Appendix). A key to the 'mindset' within which the *Keying* was depicted may be found in the *Description*: 'The general appearance of the deck is very much like the make of the large early English men of war, such as the "Great Harry," with its lofty forecastle and aft-castle.'[17] Of course, looked at properly, the *Keying* was nothing like a galleon. But few who did draw or paint the junk would have been dedicated marine artists, familiar with ships and boats of all kinds and with the sea in all its moods. Indeed, a close inspection of the main engravings of the *Keying*, which purport to show her sailing, reveal an equally uninformed approach to the shape, form and run of the sea. What an artist cannot 'see', he or she cannot accurately depict.

The Western habit of exaggerating the curvature of junk sheerlines can be traced back to at least the seventeenth century and may reflect an earlier tradition of exaggerating almost all vessels' sheerlines, found in medieval imagery of nefs, carracks and galleons. It is instructive to compare the work of Pâris with typical mid-nineteenth-century illustrative material appearing in such publications as *The Illustrated London News, L'Illustration, Harper's Weekly, Harper's Monthly, Leslie's, Scientific American, La Nature, Engineering, The Sea, Merveilles de la Science* and *Meyers Konversations Lexikon*,[18] or with the paintings of any of the scores of marine artists whose work is depicted in Archibald's *Dictionary*, with their evident understanding of the form of hulls, set of sails and the run of the sea. Even with the most astute and informed observer, like the well-known marine artist William Huggins,[19] there is a difference between his depiction of Western vessels, which as an ex-seaman he knew intimately, and that of the junk.

One can detect a similar failing with respect to junk sheerlines—and a similar divide between the 'can sees' and 'can't sees'—among Chinese artists. In many Chinese depictions, among them a number of the best known images of junks,[20] the sheerlines are often grossly exaggerated. In a very small few, they are not. The reasons for this common and also cross-cultural 'failing' are not clear. One could speculate that the relative remoteness of the sea and even inland waters from everyday life engendered a concomitant unfamiliarity among average 'land-lubbers', including most jobbing artists, with what a 'fair' hull looked like and a consequent inability to 'see' the proportions of a fair hull and the absurdities of disproportion. As the eminent historian of marine art Sam Davidson puts it, 'Just as an artist's attendance at the "life classes" helps in the study and portrayal of the human figure, some sort of nautical equivalent is appropriate should the artist wish to concentrate on specific varieties of shipping.'[21]

An alternative and complementary analysis of this problem, looked at from an art history point of view, may be that when perspective was being discovered in

Europe in the fourteenth to fifteenth centuries, in respect of the realistic representation of three-dimensional objects on a plane surface, one of the most testing problems will have been the representation of curves foreshortened by oblique views, as with, for example, ships coming or going.

The tendency, when learning to draw ships and boats, is to bring the ends of curvature too close together, making a vessel look shorter than it is, hence exaggerating sheerlines. In general, one draws as one's guide to the sheerline a 'figure of eight' of the appropriate 'depth' and 'length' to draw a vessel in the required perspective. It takes a great deal of practice and an experienced eye sufficiently to elongate and narrow the two ends of the figure and then to draw the bow and stern accurately, in terms of 'depth below the sheerline', such that one achieves the form of a boat or ship one is trying to represent.[22] There is a fatal tendency to make the figure of eight too short and 'fat', and to draw the respective stem and 'out-of-sight' sternpost too long and in the wrong place on the figure's circumference, thus making bow and stern too 'deep'; then, to compound the error, the tendency is to exaggerate the curvature of the connecting line. The result is an over-beamy tub with an exaggerated sheer.

We have no images of the *Keying* from the China coast, save the gouaches with their unusual aerial view. Reviewing images by artists, both Western and Chinese, who did have experience of junks, while there was still often a tendency to exaggerate the curvature of the sheerline, there was at least a familiarity with the typical prows and poops of junks, which avoided the sort of distortions we see in the most common images of the *Keying*. It is this radical difference between Western and Chinese prows and poops that lies at the heart of the problem of the failure to 'see' the *Keying*; the way in which junks were 'seen' was still dominated by 'Western' ways of seeing ships and boats.

The gouaches are themselves fascinating, not least because there is a tendency to trust the depiction—after all by a Chinese artist—when there are some grounds to suppose that the opposite reaction would be more apposite. The reason is simple. There is an almost uncanny resemblance between what is portrayed in the gouaches and what is written in the *Description*, which is one of the reasons why Worcester, that signal expert in the traditional junk, observed:

> Contemporary drawings in the "Illustrated London News" of the 20th May 1848, together with the astonishing descriptions supplied by the pamphlets

and newspapers of the time, represent a type of junk which, if it ever really existed, is certainly extinct to-day, for the craft bears no resemblance to any class now to be seen in China.[23]

Worcester would have been more prudent to have written 'for the craft *as described* bears no resemblance'. The problem is not so much the *Keying* itself, but what we know of it from the skewed portrayals in word and image that have come down to us.

Let us revert to the gouaches and the *Description*. The latter claims that, aft, there was 'a raised quarter-deck; two poops, the first containing cabins; and a raised forecastle with a high veranda above that again.'[24] Almost all junks above a certain size had what can be described as a raised quarterdeck. Below it, accessed by a hatchway, was usually the main accommodation, when that existed. What of the 'two poops'?

If we look at the gouaches, the first poop with the cabins lies beneath the lower tiller—the steersmen are sitting on the deck that forms its roof. This is fairly normal in larger junks. The second poop is portrayed with two Westerners standing on it, engaged in what looks like an exercise in navigation. One is taking a noon-day sight with a sextant, the other presumably with a chronometer and a notebook for taking times and readings. Above them—a singular impediment to their astronomical observations—is a most elaborate quasi-deck, over which is mounted the horizontal windlass (*liao*, 繚) for raising and lowering the rudder. No late nineteenth-century photograph of a junk shows any such arrangement; one cannot help but conclude that the artist was working from the written description, not from life.

Forward, the gouaches show the 'high veranda', but without the essential element near it, the bow horizontal windlass, which was used to tension the rudder-toe bowsing lines—and fairly clearly depicted on the Currier print. Here again, there is an absence of evidence that the Chinese artist had been able to 'see' the subject of his painting.

In short, the Chinese painter of the gouache could reasonably be inferred to have constructed his painting from a general knowledge of what his junk looked like as well as from the *Description*'s most eccentric account, hamstrung by its use of English nautical vocabulary. But, even though possibly embarked, as with the blindnesses of Western painters, the Chinese artist's view of the *Keying* was wholly skewed by his lack of relevant maritime knowledge.

One might note in passing, that among the illustrations of the full hull of the *Keying* we have, only the gouaches and the J. Rock engraving offer any sort of view of the bow. That in the gouache is so oblique as to make very difficult any inference of much detail. The best one can suggest, going on what may be heavier members depicted in red, is that the bow suggests a Guangdong-built junk, since a similar feature is shown in the Japanese *Tosen no Zu* (in Chinese *Tangchuan zhitu*), considered further below. The Rock image, probably derived from the gouaches, shows more of the bow, but this is vitiated by the extent to which the artist probably did not really understand what he was seeing. The other images, perhaps because of the very strangeness of the shape of the junk and of its bow, avoid the issue altogether by offering views from astern, from a quarter, or from just aft of amidships, meaning that the actual shape of the bow does not appear.

Thus, the best known images of the *Keying* should be 'read' with caution.[25] In them, the vessel appears as an eccentric floating banana with a sheerline and lines of planking that appear arcs of a series of non-concentric circles. The result is scarcely different from a blunt-horned crescent moon. What the Western artists do not appear to have 'seen' in the *Keying* were the high, flaring-forward projecting 'wings' of a typical example of the Fujian 'family' of junks or the complex poop-and-rudder housing structure needed aft, or the bow platform and windlass forward entailed by the rudder bowsing ropes. Like so many marine artists, they would also appear not to have been seamen, so could not see the nautical impossibility of what they painted. If one imposes on any of the images a 'gauge' representing the known proportions of the *Keying* stated in the *Description* and various contemporary newspaper reports, all save perhaps the Currier fail to 'see' the junk, depicting the sheerline and planking in ways that make no sense.

The errors are many. The curvature of the sheer is grossly exaggerated; in so being, it also significantly exaggerates the relative heights of bow and stern. A pointer to this is the way in which the planking meets the bow. In junk topsides, it has only a moderate tapering and upward curvature to butt-join to the sides of the upper bow plate. That contrasts with the markedly tapered and upward curve required in Western, pointed-bow vessels to get the planking to converge into the stem rabbet. From what is known, none of the artists had ever been to China or seen a junk before. It is a credit to Nathaniel Currier that he tried to copy the proportions of what he saw rather than, with the exception of the run of the planking, conforming to any received ideas of a ship he may have had. Such representational fidelity may not always be seen as an artistic virtue. Historically, it is invaluable.

A vessel shaped as the *Keying* is most frequently shown would have such distorted waterlines that, when moderately heeled under way, she would be barely controllable. There is no way she would have been the comparatively well-behaved and fleet vessel described by her captain, capable of a 21-day passage across the North Atlantic. As much to the point, no traditional shipwright, building by eye and relying on rule-of-thumb proportions handed down through generations, would, or indeed could, have wrought such a monster.[26]

From the outset, there has been controversy with respect to exactly what sort of vessel the *Keying* was. One of the most thorough modern students of the *Keying*, the late Mr. Geoffrey Bonsall, noted that contemporary Hong Kong newspaper reports from December 1846 described her as a 'Thai' vessel.[27] There is also a suggestion in other documentation that she was of Vietnamese origin.[28] In short, quite where the *Keying* came from is uncertain. Against this, however, there is no question that she exhibits some remarkable similarities with both typical Fujian and Guangdong craft, chiefly in her highly decorated stern and the motifs on it.

Nonetheless, there are unquestionably significant variations from a standard Fujian ship, insofar as the descriptions we have are thought to be credible. For example, there is the form of the bow, which according to Worcester and van Tilburg, would be more typical of Zhejiang craft.[29]

In any case, citing a possible Thai or Vietnamese provenance does not really solve the problem. The typical Thai trader had its design roots in Fujian. The influence of Guangdong and Fujian on the design of eighteenth- and nineteenth-century trading junks from Vietnam was similarly strong.[30] Indeed, there is perhaps no better indicator of the ubiquitous influence of Fujian design throughout the China seas trading region than the stunning set of images in what are sometimes known as the Hirado Scrolls or, more properly, the *Tosen no Zu* (in Chinese, *Tangchuan zhitu*). These images were painted in the late eighteenth century by a local artist, at the behest of the ruler of the southern Japanese trading entrepôt of Hirado (a small island off the west coast of Kyushu, about 45 miles north-north-west of Nagasaki). The intention was for the ruler to have an effective 'ship recognition' guide. The result is a set of quite amazingly careful, annotated depictions, with very few of the traditional distortions that can make junks look so bizarre.[31]

Among the images—which include one of a Dutch *retourschip*—are ten of the typical sea-going junks in the *nanhai* trade.[32] These come from Amoy (Xiamen), Ningpo (Ningbo), Fujian, Guangdong, Taiwan, Siam (Thailand), Cochinchina (Vietnam) and Indonesia. What is amazing is how strikingly alike in general conformity all the junks are, bar one from northern Chinese waters. Given that the *Keying* may be at most half a century or so earlier than the period in which these images were made, and was just as probably contemporary with them, we may take it that they set certain parameters within which we should expect the *Keying*'s shape to fall.[33] The best known Western images of the *Keying* all fall *well* clear of any such bounds.

Typical to all the ten junk types shown, though larger in some than in others, are the forward wings on either side of the bow, which in a *fuchuan* soar above the sheerline, sometimes very high either side of the foredeck as well as projecting a considerable way forward of the bow plate. The wings help keep the deck sheltered and provide the locating points for the barrel ends of the essential windlass for tensioning the rudder bowsing lines—bowsing lines which are a feature of all the junks depicted, *except the Thailand junk*, which would appear to have a Western-style rudder. Aft, equally, are the various versions of the high bulwarks and taffrail that shelter the lifting rudder assembly and provide the secure location and essential height and clearance above the rudder, for the lifting windlass to raise the rudder and stock clear of danger when in harbour and for the tiller to have freedom of movement when under way.

In the majority of the *Keying* images, these high ends seem to have been treated as part of the hull planking. The result has been to 'read' the curvature of the hull planking as rising towards a stem- and sternpost. This necessarily means that the ship appears banana-like. Of course, precisely because the planks in the hull, wings and poop of a junk do *not* rise towards centreline stem- and sternposts[34]—the sides of transom and bow plate being well out from the centreline—the sharply rising angle is not present. The Western eye is deceived.

The best images avoid at least some of these errors. The Currier print is perhaps the only image made of the *Keying* in the West that, bar the planking, shows something that could just about be a credible Chinese traditional ship, built broadly on the lines of a vessel from Fujian Province and one that presents a reasonable 'fit' to the images we have from the Hirado Scrolls and from Chinese and China-based Western artists in the eighteenth and nineteenth centuries. Looking at it, a seaman can see that the sheerline makes reasonable sense and the junk has sweet, sea-going lines. There are still typical errors. The run of the planking is again somewhat misread. The massive wale running down the ship's side, close to where the bulwarks meet the weather deck, is hard to discern. The stern is presented as a curious, Western, stepped transom with a slot cut into it— there is no sense of the 'false stern' of traditional junks, the transom being inside the poop structure. The bow structure is out of proportion. But the gross exaggeration of the height of the bow and stern is avoided. And the bow quite clearly has the wings with a separated anchor windlass platform between the wing tips, although the wings are shown as a great deal smaller in height and forward projection, relative to the rest of the vessel, than is likely to have been the case.

The main value of the painting by the Chinese artist, despite not being painted from life and showing a conspicuously eccentric poop and exaggerated beam-to-length ratio,[35] is that it shows better than any other available the layout of the deck. It also shows the mixed crew, though here again evidently stereotyping rather than working from life. The image also shows a port-side cookhouse, interesting information that tallies, again, with the *Description*, though perhaps *not* part of the original vessel. To note all that is, of course, to mark again the significant problem that arises in discussing so many images of the vessel: we have no idea of the extent to which any painting was made 'from life'.

The Currier and Chinese gouache images, however, when placed in the larger context of what we know of Chinese vessels of the period from other contemporary images and descriptions, give us a reasonably clear idea of what the original is most likely to have been like, given the absence of any lines and a precise ethnographic description.

Chapter 9
A Re-appraisal of the *Keying*'s Likely Shape

Experts surmise the *Keying* was built largely on *fuchuan* lines, though Worcester, Audemard and others note the discrepancies between the written descriptions of the *Keying* and what is known of traditional Fujian vessels.[1] One probability is that at least some of these discrepancies are founded on errors in the popular descriptions, almost all by Western observers with little or no knowledge of traditional Chinese vessels and shipbuilding techniques. However, where some elements of the description—the cambered deck, the high bow wings, the transom decorations, and so on—fit a *fuchuan*, others like the fenestrated rudder and the teak build[2] are more apposite to a *guangchuan*, or Guangdong junk. Yet other features—the internal compartments divided by the structural bulkheads,[3] the heavy wales, the rudder bowsing lines, anchors, windlasses, and so on—are common to most of the sea-going vessels of the southern and southeastern Chinese seaboard.

A simple solution to these conundrums may be the vessel's age. In the course of a century, somewhat in the manner of 'my grandfather's axe', there will have been incessant repair work. According to almost all commentators,[4] the great majority of almost all junks were very roughly built, more often than not of soft woods. The repairs will have been done, a fortiori, where the vessel found itself, whenever the need arose. As we know from Worcester, Donnelly,[5] Audemard and others, the Chinese traditional shipbuilding world was extremely regional. Shipbuilding was an oral tradition, with knowledge and skills handed down the generations, much as is the case in all pre-industrial society.[6] Inevitably, even though there was a clear 'family resemblance' among sea-going Chinese junks, and one which does seem to exhibit some sort of Fujianese design hegemony, there were distinctive regional differences that would have been informed any repairs made. This may explain how a possible *fuchuan* came to have a Guangdong-style fenestrated rudder. The rudder is without question one of the weaker, if not the weakest, part of traditional junk design.[7] It would not be at all surprising that a *fuchuan* lost its rudder when in Guangdong waters and found itself with a replacement that incorporated Guangdong design features, especially such a useful one as fenestration, which relieves the rudder of some of the stresses likely to cause damage. With the *Keying*, even a fenestrated rudder was no guarantee against damage.

A further critical problem has always been the description of the vessel in terms of an 'absence of keel' and 'no kelson'.[8] This has been taken by many commentators to indicate that the *Keying* had no keel and was flat-bottomed. This is probably a false inference. All that may be implied is that the manner of construction could not be correlated with that customary in Western 'frame-first' construction, in which the floors and their futtocks are integral with keel and keelson. That in no way implies either that in the *Keying* there was no keel timber, since all junks have a centreline, larger scantlinged, usually scarfed, keel timber, though of widely varying moulding and siding; *fuchuan* have a quite evident, fairly massive scantling keel.[9] No more does it entail that the keel timber did not project below the garboards. As Worcester remarks, paraphrasing an article in the *Mariners Mirror*,[10] 'no scientific account of the vessel appears to have been written, and much of the contemporary information fails in technical clearness.' This is tragically true of almost all writing, Western or Chinese, about traditional Chinese vessels before the twentieth century—indeed, of far too much that has been written since.

The final, and apparently insuperable, problem is the reported heights of the bow and stern above the water. These are given in the *Description* as 'height of her poop from the water, thirty eight feet; height of her bow, thirty feet'.[11] These dimensions were apparently confirmed by British sailors who measured them from the China Squadron flagship, HMS *Agincourt*.[12] These numbers suggest the stern was 23 percent of the vessel's length above the water and the bow 18 percent, thus (the following drawings are all to scale):

As can be seen in that crude box diagram, there is no reason at all to see in the figures anything untoward for a junk, provided one does not 'read' the figures as implying a pair of measurements equivalent to establishing the stemhead and

Diagram 1 Simple *Keying* waterline profile, from dimensions measured by HMS *Agincourt*

taffrail of a vessel as if it were a Western-style ship, in which case, depending of course on draft, it would be rather top-heavy.

It thus becomes important to know whether the measurements were to the top of the bow 'wings' and stern taffrail-equivalent, or to the top of the respective sheerline ends. Sadly, we can never know for certain. However, the principles of charity and common sense, allied with some knowledge of Chinese traditional vessels, suggest to a very high degree of probability that we are considering the 'wings' and taffrail.

Consider the following two simple drawings (for ease of drawing, a Ningbo-style bow is shown):

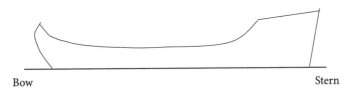

Diagram 2 Waterline profile of 'Westernized' junk to same scale

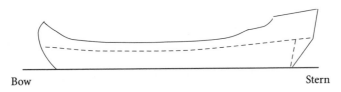

Diagram 3 Same profile adjusted to Chinese style, with deck and transom shown

Both the above drawings are proportionately in conformity with the measurements of heights of bow and stern and an overall length of 165 feet, being to scale with Diagram 1. Neither is quite as absurd as the drawings upon which most judgements of the form of the *Keying* are based. However, the upper, which assumes that the measurements are of a 'Western-style' hull, where the bulwarks are of a negligible height above the weather deck and the sheerline more or less parallel with the weatherdeck save for obvious forecastles and aftercastles, creates something at least related to the standard engravings and shows one possible source of their error. It also makes sense of the above quotation from the *Description*, likening the *Keying* to 'the make of the large early English men of war, such as the "Great Harry," with its lofty fore-castle and aft-castle'.

The lower drawing, where the typical sheerline of a Chinese junk is marked with a dotted line, as is the set-back transom beneath the poop overhang, shows a perfectly credible large *fuchuan*. The drawings also show how extraordinarily the Western artists exaggerated the *Keying*, a matter that can be shown more explicitly in graphic form, if one applies some sort of template gauge to any of the known images of the ship.

One can add a further element by recalling that most junk keel timbers had a rocker to them by virtue of being built in three parts: a fore keel timber, main keel timber and aft keel timber, the fore and aft timbers being rockered up from the line of the main keel timber by an amount traditionally a function of the purpose for which the junk had been built. A rough schematic, recalling that the *Keying* was an ex-sea-going cargo junk and thus with a long main keel timber and a slight rocker in order to maximize hold space, would thus be:

Diagram 4 A typical junk keel structure to same scale

If we add the second above-the-waterline diagram to this, with transom and bow plate meeting the keel timbers, we get:

Diagram 5 Full hull profile with keel to same measurements

The rough sketch above represents the *Keying*'s profile *as measured*,[13] and in consequence of her being 'in ballast'; that is, floating high on the natural marks to which she would float when laden. Note that her probable *actual* waterline is shown in Diagram 5 by the solid line. The critical dimension here, heretofore not mentioned, is what is called the moulded depth, or depth of hold. This is *not* the same as a vessel's draft. It is the distance between the top of the keel and the underside of the deck amidships; in the *Keying*, depending on source, this was between 12 and 19 feet. The diagram above assumes around 16 feet, or the average of the two. This brings us to the second, dashed line parallel to and above the actual waterline which represents a feasible laden draft—that is, where the sea surface would have been had the ship been carrying a full cargo.

Given what we know of the depth of hold and the height above the water-line of the *Keying*'s bow and stern, she had a very, very slight draft indeed on her voyaging. The probable actual waterline is shown as a solid line. Given the scale of the drawing, the vessel's draft may have been as little as between 6 and 7 feet, and certainly no more than the 12 feet we read in the *Description*. This is why the extreme depth of the rudder, 23 or 24 feet when fully lowered, was so very important to the weatherliness and sea-keeping qualities of Chinese junks in general, and the *Keying* in particular.

We know from the *Description*[14] that when the *Keying* left Canton after being purchased, she was in ballast. Little in the subsequent narrative leaves one to suppose she subsequently loaded any other cargo than that which she carried for exhibition, plus sufficient stores, water and spares for crew and maintenance—a quantum that even with the most generous estimates is unlikely to have exceeded 100 tonnes and was probably half that.[15] Indeed, that the *Keying* carried no other cargo is explicitly stated in two newspaper reports: 'The Chinese junk which is on her way to this country, does not bring any cargo of a merchantable description from China (for there would need to be) . . . official notification of report and entry, with the revenue authorities when such is the case'[16] and 'the *Keying*, from the British port of Hong Kong, which was come here for the sole purpose of exhibition and was not to bring merchandise of any description.'[17]

Much of the 'misreading' of the *Keying*'s form by Western artists is probably a function of the fact that she was not trimmed to her laden marks. Had she been, given that she was estimated to be able to load some 700 tonnes of cargo, she would probably have floated—as was characteristic of Chinese junks with their very high bulwarks—with her weather deck only a matter of one or two feet above the sea. That is, with a freeboard to the weather deck (though not to the top of the bulwarks) of as little as a foot. In Diagram 5 above, the dashed water-line and weather deck show a feasible laden freeboard; in Diagram 6, the junk is shown in side profile as she might have appeared laden.

Diagram 6 Waterline profile of a laden junk to same scale

This rough diagram of a laden junk, which conforms well with photographs of large, laden trading junks taken in the 1870s and 1880s, shows well how exaggerated the standard Western depictions of the *Keying*'s form are, perhaps in most part because the artists were simply unaware that they were looking at a vessel in ballast.

Here's what the *Keying* may have looked like afloat, using the preceding analysis as a guide. It is hardly surprising that Western artists, not knowing what they were seeing and with the distorting spectacles of prejudice, created an unseaman-like monster:

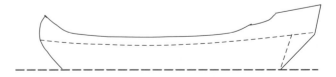

Diagram 7 Waterline profile of unladen junk to same scale

The rest of the detail in the *Description* Worcester rightly queries, though he draws from this what seems the mistaken conclusion that the vessel described is in some significant sense atypical. A closer scrutiny shows that the description *reads* as if it were written by someone who knew what he was writing about. Taken literally, the vessel described may seem extremely atypical. But if one realizes that all the terms used are Western terms, and that the writer is, as it were, shoehorning what he sees in the *Keying* into the conceptual framework dictated by his available technical vocabulary, a different picture emerges.

A glaring example is his description of how the *Keying* was built, contrasting it with the Western 'frame-first' method. How on earth would the author know this, given the age of the vessel and the strong likelihood that he was never anywhere near a Chinese shipyard? Worse, the writer's acquaintance with Western naval architecture seems slight. For example, it is almost impossible to work out what is meant by such impressive-sounding, but dubiously intelligible sentences as 'The next process is doubling and clamping above and below decks', 'Two immense beams of string pieces are then ranged below, fore and aft, which keep the beams in their places' and 'The deck frames are an arch, and a platform erected on it, protects it from the sun, and from other injuries otherwise inevitable.'[18] What?

Read with the thought that the writer actually had not much a clue of what he was seeing, such detail as the description does supply begins to seem very thin. So thin, indeed, that the only useable data, from the point of view at an attempt at reconstruction, are the dimensions of masts and yards, the overall dimensions of the hull, various comments on the weights of components like the anchors, sails and rudder, and some descriptions of the vessel's decoration and performance.

Even here, there is some of the skewed information and the credulity of ignorance. The mainsail, described as weighing 9 tonnes—though one would be interested to know who weighed it, how and why—and requiring the heft of all forty crew to hoist, is described as being 1,100 square yards in area and having 'eighteen reefs', each between two and four feet deep.[19] What the writer means, presumably, is that the woven bamboo sail material was in eighteen panels. That is, eighteen separate panels joined together at the battens, although this detail, like most others, is lacking.

This is, in fact, a useful number for evaluating the drawings in the light of the *Tosen no Zu/Tangchuan zhitu*. In the prints and medals, the *Keying* is shown with as many as sixteen and as few as seven panels in the mainsail. In the Japanese scroll, no junk has more than thirteen panels and none has less than ten. This suggests that either the *Keying*'s sail was unusually large or that the alleged number of panels was exaggerated. If there were eighteen panels, each separated by a batten, that might account for the extreme weight of the ensemble as reported.

There is a similar problem with the material of construction. For example, the term *ironwood* is used with remarkable promiscuity. We are told that the rudder was in part made of it—almost certainly true, since that was a traditional practice—and that the mast was, which is almost certainly false.[20] Again, the problem here is the technical ignorance, or perhaps indifference, which eschews care over detail. The mast is likely to have been made of Fujian pine or teak. Similarly, the wood used in the planking is likely to have been different from that used in the partial frames, wales and major transverse bulkheads—it would have been a very poor shipwright who built otherwise. So, to describe the ship, as the *Description* indicates Captain Kellett does, as 'built entirely of teak', which given the age of the vessel neither Kellett nor anyone else could possibly have known without laboratory analysis, should be taken, like timber used in boat-building, with a pinch of salt.[21]

To note these shortcomings is not wholly to devalue the *Description*. It was not intended as a technical analysis; it would be wrong to fault it for having failed in this regard. Some of the detail provided is unquestionably helpful, once one takes aboard the probability that it should be read with a carefully critical eye. More useful are the engravings in the *Description* giving views of the *Keying*'s deck. These suffer, as do most of the pictorial representations of the vessel, from the artist not being entirely sure what he is looking at. A typical example is the very eccentric depiction of the main boom and its attachments in the view aft.[22] However, a careful study, which accepts what one is seeing to be a 'publicity puff', so that the size of everything is hugely exaggerated by minimizing the size of the human figures, does help work out where the vessel has been 'mis-seen'.

For example, the stern can best be understood by looking at the more careful transom view and contrasting it with the highly impressionistic view aft, considered above. In the transom view, the side catwalks reach the transom along the sheerline, as one might expect, although the height of this above the water at the stern is exaggerated. And the aft overhang is shown, fairly exactly, as a decorated shelter for the rudder lifting tackle, with the rudder tucked away into its housing well. However, looking aft, the artist has evidently imposed on the *Keying* a way of seeing one suspects is loosely derived from sixteenth-century European galleons, with their piled aftercastles. The view aft fails to correlate with the transom view. The side catwalks sweep up towards the taffrail, whereas in the transom view they stick more closely to the probable sheerline. Finally, in the misleading view aft, the upper part of the poop is co-opted to form some sort of cabin, leaving no evident space for the rudder head and tiller, leave alone the lifting tackle, which are implicit in the normal conformation in the transom view.

In summary, the descriptive and graphical evidence we have of the *Keying* is significantly short of precision and detail. Not only is the vessel's age uncertain, so too are its construction and conformity. Because all the artists' renderings are much affected by a combination of ignorance and prejudice, and because no accurate measurements and drawings were ever made, evaluating the dimensions we do have needs care.

Chapter 10
The *Keying*'s Dimensions and Shape

The measurements we can glean from the *Description* more or less fit with all other sources, though since all of these probably came from Captain Kellett, any errors he made have merely been replicated. We know from the *Description*, for example, that an attempt to measure the *Keying* in New York caused so much trouble that those who made the attempt threw up their hands in despair and gave up.[1] However, even here there is confusion. Table 4 below gives the dimensions from various sources, from which it can be seen that we cannot even be confident of the measurements.

Table 4 The *Keying*'s dimensions from all known sources

Dimensions	*Description*	Other
Length overall	165'	160' (medal); 165' (Worcester, Wikipedia)
Beam	25' 6"	33' (Worcester); 35' (Wikipedia); 35' 4" (Haddad)
Depth of hold	12'	16' (Worcester); 19' (Wikipedia, medal)
Mainmast	95'	90' (Worcester); 85' from deck (medal)
Foremast	75'	75'
Mizzenmast	c. 50'	50'
Mainsail area	9,900 sq. ft. (1,100 sq. yd.)	11,000 sq. ft. (Worcester)
Tonnage	400 (measured)	700, 750 or 800 (Worcester, medals)
	700 (approx. deadweight)	800 tons (Wikipedia)
		800 Chinese measurement (medals)

The only additional piece of evidence from the *Description* is that the *Keying* was a Second- or B-class junk. There is no certain way of deciding what this actually means, since the bracket for B-class junks was quite wide and very hard to tie down in terms of actual size. Paul van Dyke's excellent *The Canton Trade*[2] gives the rough basis for calculating the length and breadth of an average B-class vessel as being from 15 to 20 measurement covids in beam and from 70 to 80 measurement covids in length. Milburn's *Oriental Commerce*[3] gives the range for a B-class junk as from 71 to 74 covids in length and from 22 to 23 covids in beam. The exact length of a covid is uncertain. It is given in Blunt's *The Shipmaster's Assistant and Commercial Digest* (1837) as 14.625 inches.[4] Against that, although in Milburn's extensive entry for China no value for the covid is given, his entries elsewhere value the covid or 'China cubit' as between 16 and 19 inches.[5] Using the full range implicit in these various values would make a B-class junk from 24.4 to 36.4 feet in beam and from 85.3 to 127 feet in measured length. Worcester also notes the variability of Chinese linear measure, depending on trade and purpose.[6]

This is obviously a far smaller value than we should expect for the *Keying*, but not necessarily a surprise, for two reasons. First, since the 'measurement covid' (or cubit) was a fiscal measure and does seem to have varied—though by how much, in which sense and in what years is unfathomable—turning a rough bracket of values into useable data is inevitably difficult. Second, the 'length on deck' measure was specified as the distance between the aft side of the foremast and the forward side of mizzen mast—or, according to William Hunter, the forward face of the rudder head[7]—so it is necessarily different from length overall.

Using the Currier print as a rough guide, the *Keying*'s foremast was about one-fifth of the length overall abaft the forward end of the 'wings'; the mizzen mast was about the same distance forward of the transom. However, although the measured length must therefore be adjusted by quite a bit, the beam would not change greatly. Allowing for plank thickness and the protrusion of the main longitudinal wales, but excluding catwalks, the actual beam to the ship's outside planking would probably be some two to six feet greater than what a B-class junk measured. Given the bracket of values above, that means a beam measurement of between 26.4 and 42.4 feet. This embraces all the beam measurements in Table 4. For the difference between measurement length and length overall, following the proportions shown in the Currier print, the length measurements above should range from 102.4 to 152.4 feet. Here, there is a marked difference to the values in Table 4, the junk seeming to measure as far too short.

This could simply be a mistake in the description of the *Keying*. She may have been an A-class junk, and therefore over 74 covids in measured length. Equally, it may be a product of the vagaries of a customary measurement system. Yet again, we find ourselves stymied by defects in the depictions of the vessel. Currier's proportions may be unhelpful.

The only remaining recourse for narrowing down the range of feasible values for the *Keying's* dimensions is to use the tonnage measurement that is often, if variably, cited in all the references in Table 4, supposing it to be an expression of the contemporary British system.

From 1720 to 1849, the regnant measurement tonnage calculation in Britain was the Builders Old Measurement (BOM) formula, where length on deck is reduced by a fraction of the beam to approximate the length of the keel[8] and beam is the maximum beam of the built hull (excluding side appendages).

$$\text{Tonnage} = \frac{(\text{Length on deck} - [\text{Beam} \times 3/5]) \times \text{Beam} \times \frac{1}{2}\text{Beam}}{94}$$

Diagram 8 Builders Old Measurement Formula

This 1773 formula was a development of older 'tons and tonnage' formulae, which more simply multiplied length of keel, beam and depth of hold to get an internal volume. Its intention (see note 8) was to be able to derive the length of the keel without having to have the ship in dry dock. This had the advantage that it was possible to assess tonnage from measurements on deck alone. It assumed the length of the keel was only 60 percent of the length on deck. It also assumed the depth of the hold was half the beam. Provided these assumptions were on average accurate, all was well.

The likelihood here, which explains one discrepancy in Table 4, is that the tonnage beam (25 feet 6 inches) was the breadth of the hull and the maximum beam (33 feet, 35 feet or 35 feet 4 inches) was the breadth including side cat-walks. This usefully explains the discrepancy in the table above between the

Description and the other sources, otherwise too great to disregard. This assumption also fits fairly well with the Guangdong shipwrights' rule of thumb (see Table 5), since with a keel length of around 140 feet, allowing for the aft and fore overhangs, a 25-foot 6-inch beam gives a 5.5 beam-to-length ratio.

The rules in question are simple to set out, based as they are—as similar rules in a great number of maritime traditions seem to have been—on a single base unit.

McGrail cites examples from Atlantic and Mediterranean Europe and, by derivation from medieval European practice, India.[9] In the earliest surviving European text on the matter, the manuscript of Michael of Rhodes dating from 1436, we learn that the key fundamental measure was the length of keel—all other measures derived from it.[10] In another early surviving treatise on shipbuilding, Fernando Oliveira's *Liura da fabrica das naos*, written around 1550, we read in the historical summary of ideas about shipbuilding from King Solomon's day

Table 5 Rules of thumb of traditional Guangdong shipbuilders

Dimension	Multiple of basic unit B
Beam at waterline = B	1
Length overall = L	3.5–4 (coastal vessels)
	5.5–6 (sea-going vessels)
Moulded depth	0.5
Height of stem	1
Height of stern	1.5
Breadth of transom	1.1
Breadth of bottom	0.6
Height of mainmast	3–3.3
Height of foremast	2.4–2.6
Leeboard length	1
Leeboard breadth	0.05L
Length of rudder post	1
Rudder area	(0.5B)
To which can be added:	
Fastening length + FL	2 x plank thickness
Fastening spacing	FL

to his own time: 'it is advisable to know that, in each ship, of any size or shape, a certain part of it is taken habitually to be the basis of the measurements of all the other parts of the same ship.' For cargo vessels, for example, Oliveira notes that the key component is the length of the keel, 'for once the length of the keel is known, the proper width is known, as well, and the height [i.e., moulded depth] to which the ship is to be built, and how great the bow and stern overhangs must be, and what the capacity will be, more or less.' His diagram summarizes this 'rule of thumb' with, interestingly, one of the units of measurement being the 'palm'.[11]

In the Guangdong case, as with several other traditions, the base unit is the beam at the waterline. From this single dimension and two general ratios, all other dimensions were derived, as shown in Table 5.[12] It is obviously difficult to claim that these rules of thumb will have persisted for over 200 years unchanged. That said, however, where a given shipbuilding tradition shows remarkable consistency through time, as I think can fairly be argued the Chinese tradition did between the Ming and Qing dynasties, then the rules of thumb used to construct ships are likely to have shown a similar consistency, as long as the fundamental designs and design envelopes were not changed. This is not to deny that changes may have happened, merely to assert that they are likely to have incremental in nature and small in overall effect.[13]

With the *Keying*, for tonnage purposes, the fore and aft projections of the anchor bowsing windlass platform and rudder hoist housing would not have counted, so the likely deck measurement length would not be more than 140 feet. If we assume the distance from the rudder post to the aft side of the bow plate would have been around 130 feet, then we get a measurement tonnage of 396.7 gross register tonnage (GRT). Note that this follows the *Description*, which presumably followed Kellett, in distinguishing between the measured tonnage and the actual load that could have been carried. To get a measured tonnage of 700 to 800 tons we have to assume the beam to be 35 feet—the largest mentioned. From knowledge of how measurement tonnage was (and is) calculated, and from the evidence that the problem with the Charles River Bridge at Boston was created by a maximum external beam, including catwalks, of 35 feet 4 inches, such a tonnage seems unlikely. Indeed, the most likely answer to this muddle is that those who struck the medals and all subsequent commentators failed to grasp the nice detail of the *Description*, which notes: 'from the best computation that can be made, it is supposed that she may measure about four hundred tons and carry seven hundred.'[14]

The final value to consider is that for 'depth'. We have noted that this does not mean 'draught', or the depth of water between the waterline and the bottom of the keel. However, the range of values given—12 feet for the *Description* and a maximum of 19 (from a medal) elsewhere—is puzzling. Two possible answers present themselves. One is that the higher values represent a measurement taken from the top of the bulwark to the keel. The other is that someone has mistakenly added the draught (6 to 12 feet) to the moulded depth. In the end we cannot know, but given the Cantonese shipwright's rule of thumb, the value in the *Description* is the most credible, since it tallies with the 1:2 ratio between beam and moulded depth given by the rule.

Reverting to the matter of dimensions in terms of measurement tonnage, there is one final measure worth pausing over, for what light it may cast on the general matter of the *Keying*'s dimensions and conformity. One of the medals gives the figure '800 tons Chinese measurement'. Depending on how we interpret the phrase, which appears on the 1848 Halliday commemorative medal, it may possibly confirm the measurements of the *Description*.

Exactly what the Chinese unit referred to is and how it was come upon is unclear. It is possible that it refers to the *liao* (料), a customary unit for measuring ship size, about which there is considerable discussion though not much agreement.[15] It is possible that the *Keying* was 800 *liao*, but if so, there is no agreed conversion factor or, indeed, agreement as to what exactly the *liao* measured, although it is most probably a capacity measure,[16] as is Western measurement tonnage.[17]

Traditionally, according to the *Kangxi Dictionary* (康熙字典, *Kāngxī zìdiǎn*) of 1716, the character 料 meant, among other things, 'a measure'. *Measure* is in English a word that can mean 'a unit of volume', as in the phrases 'a standard measure' or 'a single measure of rum'—which refers to something like the legally mandated standard measure in a British public house of a quarter gill.[18] Obviously, therefore, *measure* in this context describes an exact amount only if one can track down the regulation (or generally observed customary rule) which defines the contemporary value given to the measure in use. It does not yet appear that any scholars have definitively tracked down the relevant specifiers of the *liao*.[19]

Some clarification can be gained from a brief analysis of data in the *Longjiang Shipyard Treatise*. There, four ships and their dimensions are given in terms of length on deck, beam, moulded depth and *liao*. For example, a 400-*liao* warship is 91.3 feet overall; a 100-*liao* ship is 50.2 feet overall. In what follows, though the assumptions made are evidently large, we shall use these figures to see what light they cast on the *Keying*.

The relationship in terms of length on deck of the four ships with *liao* measurements (100, 150, 200 and 400) is not linear, but as Diagram 9 (showing only 200- to 800-*liao* variables) shows, seems rather to have a slight exponential

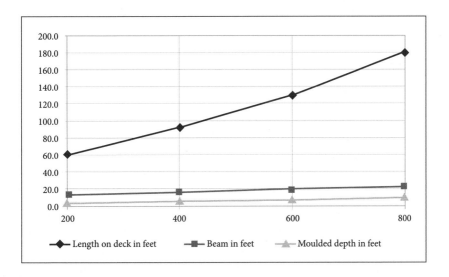

Diagram 9 Length, beam and moulded depth in feet per *liao*

Table 6 Length, beam and moulded depth in feet for vessels of specific *liao*

Junk size (*liao*)	Length on deck (feet)	Beam (feet)	Moulded depth (feet)
100	50.2	8.3	3.8
200	62.0	12.9	4.6
400	91.3	16.8	6.1
600	130.0	20.0	8.0
800	180.0	23.0	10.5

element. As the size of ship in *liao* increases, so the length increases in always slightly greater increments. At the same time, the beam seems to change in a more or less linear fashion, whereas moulded depth—which for various practical reasons, as with Western tonnage measurement, is not likely to have entered into the formula—is slightly exponential. The very crudely derived graph and associated table, based on data in the *Treatise* and extrapolated in a rather loose manner to give values for 800 *liao*, suggests (bearing in mind that the vessels in question were warships)[20] that an 800-*liao* vessel should be somewhere between 160 and 180 feet long, 25 feet in beam and have a moulded depth of around 10 to 12 feet.

These values are consistent with those given in the *Description* and therefore allow us to believe that, within reasonable margins of error, these dimensions can be trusted.

That said, the relationship between 800 tons Chinese measurement, supposing this to be some sort of reference to the *liao*, and the Western measurement tonnage should also give a further test of the reliability of the *Description*'s measurements, if it is possible to derive a relationship. This is evidently a very 'ballpark' approach, since we have no secure foundation for supposing that the figures from the *Longjiang Shipyard Treatise* are necessarily representative of the value of the *liao* with respect to vessel type, place or time. As noted above, and as with medieval European equivalents, many traditional Chinese measurements appear to have varied with respect to their application (for example, among different trades), their jurisdiction (as between cities and provinces) and the regnant dynasty.[21] However, the table of relative dimensions in the *Treatise* does give a value of the length of the keel, as well as values for beam and moulded depth, so at least allows us to calculate tonnage on the Western system. Even if the measurements in the *Treatise* are not necessarily measured exactly as they would be by a British marine surveyor, they will be close enough.[22] It follows, supposing that the unit remained fairly constant in shipbuilding through the Ming/Qing transition, that we can derive a loose tons burthen value for each of the vessels for which we have a measure in *liao*. Diagram 10 and its associated table should be approached with circumspection.

Here, we see that an 800-*liao* vessel, assuming the extrapolation of the curve from 400 *liao* is more or less indicative, would be around 468 tons burthen. While this tonnage is a bit larger than the measurement tonnage we have for

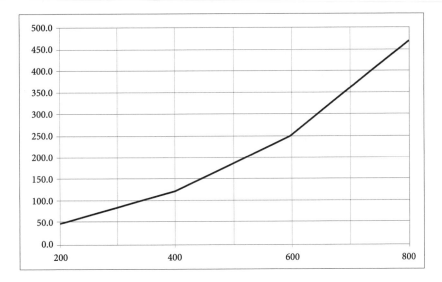

Diagram 10 Estimated relationship between *liao* (*x* axis) and tons burthen (*y* axis)

Table 7 Approximate equivalence between *liao* and tons burthen for selected values

Junk size (*liao*)	Tons burthen
200	47.7
400	122.3
600	251.1
800	467.7

the *Keying*, this was always only itself an estimate, the New York officials having thrown up their hands in despair and given up.[23] Table 8 gives the comparative values for BOM tonnage on a narrow range of lengths on deck, within which the *Keying* is likely to have fallen, assuming the two values for beam.

Interestingly, the British tonnage formula was beam-sensitive; the *Keying*, by the European standards that gave rise to the BOM formula, was a narrow vessel with a beam to length-on-deck ratio of something between 1:5.1 to 1:5.3, compared to a typical Indiaman's ratio of 1:3.1 or a working brig's ratio of 1:4. As Table 9 shows, had the *Keying* had more traditional European lines, with between a 1:3 and 1:4 beam-to-length ratio, she would have measured at over 1,000 tons

Table 8 BOM tonnage of the *Keying* on two values for beam

Length on deck (ft)	Beam (ft)	BOM tonnage	Length on deck (ft)	Beam (ft)	BOM tonnage
130	25.5	396.7217	130	35	710.2394
135	25.5	414.0156	135	35	742.8191
140	25.5	431.3094	140	35	775.3989

Table 9 BOM rule shown to be beam-sensitive

Length on deck (ft)	Beam-to-length ratio					
	1 to 3	1 to 4	1 to 6	BOM tonnage		
100	33.33	25.00	16.67	472.81	282.58	132.98
125	41.67	31.25	20.83	923.46	551.91	259.72
150	50.00	37.50	25.00	1595.74	953.71	448.80
175	58.33	43.75	29.17	2533.98	1514.45	712.68

burthen. As it is, her tonnage is roughly of the value one would expect. In short, we continue to have conditional support for taking the measurements in the *Description* as reliable.

Considering Table 9 in relation to the data presented in Diagrams 9 and 10 and Table 6, it seems fair to conclude that, whatever the formula for deriving *liao* measurements was—assuming of course that the measurement was derived from ship's dimensions—it seems to have been relatively beam-insensitive and, perhaps, length-sensitive. Diagram 10, for example, would appear to show that a steady rise in *liao* correlates with a slight, but nonetheless exponential, rise in tons burthen. It is interesting, therefore, to make the comparison the other way and see how *liao* measurements change with respect to a steady rise in tons burthen.

This comparison is shown in Diagrams 11 and 12, where the relationship— derived purely graphically by extending a smooth curve from the original, rather slender data and extracting from it rough values—is extended to 2,500 tons burthen.

Where, in Diagram 11, as the *liao* increase so tons burthen increase faster, in Diagram 12, as tons burthen increase, the rate of increase in *liao* stead-ily decreases. It is fair to infer from this that the beam-sensitivity of the BOM

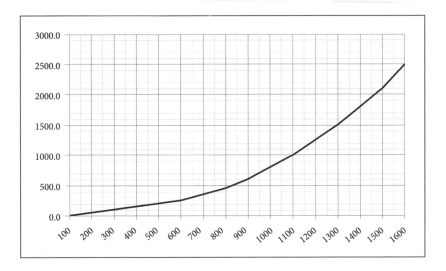

Diagram 11 Estimated relationship between *liao* (*x* axis) and tons burthen (*y* axis)

formula is not reflected in whatever was the basis of the measurement in *liao*. Indeed, one outcome of this difference, assuming the graphs reflect a strict mathematical relationship, is that, at a measurement of around 1,400 tons burthen/ *liao*, the comparative measures cross over. Thereafter, *liao* measurement increases at an ever-reduced increment, and BOM becomes close to asymptotic.

This suggests, assuming again that *liao* measurements were based on a formula, that *both* formulae operated meaningfully only within a relatively restricted size range, arguably from around 10 to around 1,200 tons burthen for BOM, and from something like 100 to possibly 2,000 *liao* for the system of measurement in China. Outside these ranges, both systems are likely to have delivered increasingly eccentric results.

Probably, both systems would also have operated successfully only within a fairly restrictive design envelope. Should there have been, for any reason, a significant change in the narrow range of beam-to-length ratios over which the formula was intended to operate—as we know to be true for the BOM formula, hence the introduction of the Moorsom System in 1854[24]—then the system's assessment of internal volume (the fundamental purpose of the measurement in the first place) would have become increasingly inaccurate, to the detriment either of the public exchequer or the shipowner.

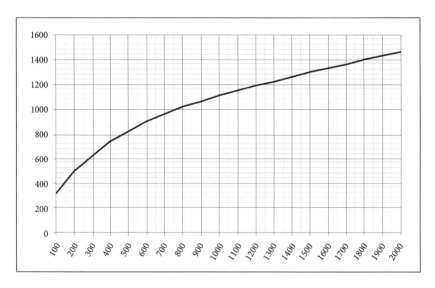

Diagram 12 Estimated relationship between tons burthen (*x* axis) and *liao* (*y* axis)

With the dimensions, as with the hull shape, the appendages and the rig of the *Keying*, we have to make the best informed guess that we can, given all the sources of information at our disposal. Our knowledge is a 'best fit', based on data which suggests that the *Description* gives us as accurate a set of values as is possible. In addition, it would be safe to assume from the exaggerations in the images of the junk, that the values for height of prow and poop above the water-line are to the tip of the 'wings' forward and the top of the taffrail aft. Only had lines been taken off the vessel before it was broken up, and accurate elevations made of profile, deck arrangements and rig, would a more precise set of dimensions have been available from which to derive a model or replica of the original. As with the images we have, however, the measurements given by other Western sources are more misleading than helpful.

In summary, it would seem as though the *Keying* was a junk built broadly on the lines of a vessel familiar in the *nanyang* and coastal trades of late eighteenth- and early nineteenth-century China. The exact design provenance is uncertain, but the vessel shows many of the broad lineaments of a *fuchuan*, albeit one which had acquired either from the outset or more probably as a result of post-build modifications and repairs, some Guangdong (*guangchuan*) characteristics.

Chapter 11
How Fast Could She Go?

If the sail area mentioned in the various descriptions is accurate, the *Keying* was quite generously canvassed. She was also a relatively slender vessel in comparison to contemporary Western equivalents before the clipper era, with a small beam in relation to her length. In theory, she should have sailed quickly. Taken together with other standard measures, however, we see that in most respects the *Keying* was a fairly typical working sailing ship, adequately canvassed for its expected working role, but no greyhound. In short, a perfectly sound seaboat and workhorse.

The best way to arrive at an assessment of the *Keying*'s performance envelope is to tabulate as much of the data with respect to her that can reasonably be worked out from the record. This is done in Table 10;[1] its results can be compared with Table 11, which looks at a clipper ship, the famous *Thermopylae*.

This might be thought an unfair comparison. It is not, for two reasons. The first is that the clippers represent a type of performance envelope with which, if he had worked in opium clippers, as we surmise to have been the case, Charles Kellett would have been relatively familiar. Second, as Jean Sutton points out,[2] the average clipper was not the same as the record-breaking flyers. Their actual average voyage duration from China to Europe was not vastly different from that of 114 days of the supposedly slower Indiamen. There are many records of clippers taking over 120 days to make the journey. Finally, *Ocean Passages for the World*, the standard reference for generations of sailors planning passages, notes that the bracket covering average voyages from Hong Kong to the English Channel was 110 to 120 days.[3] So using the *Thermopylae* is not wholly misleading.

Table 10 Dimensions and performance factors of the *Keying*

Hull built of teak or Fujian pine	
Length overall	160' (48.8 m)
Waterline length (LWL)	130' (39.62 m)
Length of keel	<120' (<36.6 m)
Beam	25' 6" (7.8 m)
Moulded depth	12'–16' (3.65–4.9 m)
Draught	12' (3.5 m)
Sail area	10,980 sq. ft. (1,020 sq. m.)
Tallest mast above waterline	90'–95' (27.5–29 m)
Displacement (est.)	683–700 lt (694–711 t)
BOM (burthen)	<812 tons
GT	495 tons
Max theoretical speed	15.3 kts
Best recorded speed	<8–9 kts
Best average speed	5–6 kts
Voyage average speed	3.5 kts
Beam-to-length ratio	4.8:1
Displacement-to-length ratio	626–935
Prismatic co-efficient	0.72–0.75
Sail area–to-displacement ratio	13.05

Traditionally, in this regard, the standard measures for comparing ships are those that gauge a ship's sleekness or bulkiness. That is, how easily the hull is driven through the water. This is measured by the block co-efficient and its variant, the prismatic co-efficient.

Simply put, you imagine either the area of a simple rectangular section into which the hull amidships will fit (block co-efficient) or the cross-section of the hull amidships (prismatic co-efficient). Now extend either cross-section forward and aft to the extremities of the ship. The results are a rectangular box as long as the ship and as wide and deep as it is wide and deep (the block), or a box-cum-hemi-cylinder, equivalent to the shape of the midships section (the prism).

The co-efficients are calculated as the ratio of the hull's actual volume to the volume of the boxes. Basically, the nearer to unity either coefficient is, the nearer

Table 11 Dimensions and performance factors of the *Thermopylae*

Composite build iron and wood	
Length overall	212' (64.6 m)
Waterline length (LWL)	207' (63.1 m)
Length of keel	<197' (<60 m)
Beam	36' (10.97 m)
Moulded depth	20' 11" (6.4 m)
Draught	18' 6" (5.64 m)
Sail area	17,520 sq. ft. (1,628 sq. m.)
Tallest mast above waterline	161' (49.1 m)
Displacement	1979 lt (2011 t)
BOM (burthen)	1,264 tons
Gross tonnage	947 tons
Max. theoretical speed	20.1 kts
Best recorded speed	17 kts
Best average speed	14.5 kts
Typical voyage average speed	6.9 kts
Beam-to-length ratio	5.5:1
Displacement-to-length ratio	223
Prismatic co-efficient	0.58–0.60
Sail area–to-displacement ratio	11

you have come to trying to push an unstreamlined box or hemi-cylinder through the water. As you can see from Table 10—though this is a 'guesstimate'—the *Keying*'s prismatic co-efficient was not that of a sleek ocean greyhound (somewhere around 0.5 to 0.6) but more that of an oil tanker (0.7 to 0.8).[4] Compared to a clipper like the *Thermopylae*, which like most clippers was quite a small ship with a co-efficient of around 0.58, and only about a quarter as long again as the *Keying*, the *Keying* was a blunt object. In short, to push its hull through the water, more power was needed (that is, more sail area) than would be necessary for a sleeker hull with a lower co-efficient.

The ability of a sailing vessel to make way is expressed by the naval architectural equivalent of a power-to-weight ratio. This is called the sail area–to-displacement ratio, or SDR. This ratio is more usually used for small vessels like pleasure yachts; it does not always work too well for larger vessels. However, it

Cross-section of block co-efficient   Cross-section of prismatic co-efficient

Diagram 13 Block and prismatic co-efficients compared

does offer a reasonable basis for comparison of like with like. Simply, the higher the value, the quicker and more easily-driven the ship because it has more sail area, that is power, available per unit of displacement or weight.

Almost no large sailing ships had high SDRs of the sort one would find with a modern racing maxi-yacht—up over 20. Simply put, they could not carry the press of sail that would give such figures, because the available materials for mast, stays, running rigging and sails could not have withstood the forces generated. For example, the extreme clipper ships, like the famous tea-clippers, would have SDRs of around 11 to 12; the beautiful and fleet *Thermopylae*'s was 11.0.[5]

A second reason for the comparatively 'low' SDR of the clippers is that the Western 'backbone, ribs and skin' design is very robust and hence quite 'heavy' per unit of length. By contrast, the 'box frame' construction of junks is a brilliant, relatively lightweight constructional system. For example, the *Thermopylae* was 9.4 tonnes displacement per unit of length. The *Keying*, by contrast, was only 4.4 tonnes per unit of length. Given that the 'plain sail' area of the *Thermopylae* was only 60 percent greater for a vessel 2.8 times the displacement, the higher SDR of the junk is explained.

We can see that the *Keying*—and by inference most traditional sailing junks— was amply powered. Yet where the *Thermopylae* and her cognates were known to have attained maximum speeds of the order of 17 to 18 knots, the *Keying* seems never to have logged better than around 12. Another way to see what that implies is to compare maximum actual speeds attained with the maximum theoretical speed for a hull of a given waterline length (LWL) as expressed by the formula

$$\text{Max. theoretical speed} = \sqrt{\text{LWL}} \times 1.34$$

Table 12 shows the comparison.

Table 12 Actual best speed against maximum theoretical speed of the *Keying* and *Thermopylae*

Ship	LWL	A √LWLx1.34	B (best speed)	% B of A
Thermopylae	207	19.28	17	88
Keying	130	15.28	12	78.5

With its towering masts, *Thermopylae* could be driven at very close to its maximum theoretical speed, even though its sail area was nothing like proportionate to its much greater displacement when compared to the sail area and displacement of the *Keying*. Some extreme clippers got even closer. They could also sustain speeds like this for hours at a time; clippers regularly averaged 11 or 12 knots for twenty-four hours. On the famous 1866 Tea Race from Fuzhou to London the best day's run of the *Fiery Cross* was 328 miles, or 13.7 knots average. And on the *Thermopylae*'s maiden voyage in 1869 she made one day's run of 348 miles, or 14.5 knots on average. By contrast, the relatively shorter *Keying*, with its mainmast only around half the height of that of the *Thermopylae*, even when performing at its best in strong weather, made only 78.5 percent of its theoretical maximum and that only once on the Atlantic crossing with a clean bottom. At other times the best seems to have been around 9 knots, or not quite 60 percent of what theory predicts. Equally, in light airs, where clippers were known to ghost along at 4 or 5 knots, evidently the *Keying* was dead in the water. The result was that the average speed of the *Keying* on the voyage from China to London was only half that of a flying clipper.

That, of course, brings us back to the co-efficients. Clippers would seem to have had prismatic co-efficients similar to those of modern warships like frigates, of around 0.6.[6] For example, the clipper *Lighting*, famous for its speed, has been calculated by Howard Chapelle as having had a prismatic co-efficient of 0.61; the *Thermopylae*'s is estimated by MacGregor to have been very similar—his proxy, the coefficient of under deck tonnage, is, as we have noted, 0.58.[7] It follows as night the day that, just as the engine horsepower that is required to shove a tanker through the water will propel a sleeker shape a great deal faster, so the same is true for sail power and different hull shapes.

We can accordingly reprise the *Keying*'s voyage and conclude that it demonstrates a number of things about a typical, working sailing junk designed for economical build and operation. The fundamental finding would be that, as the *Keying* illustrates, the design and performance envelopes of junks were fairly tightly focused on the requirements for seasonal trading voyages in specific waters.

The typical Chinese trading vessel was not designed to work to weather; it did not do so at all well. The *Keying* made no better than a beam reach in otherwise perfect sailing conditions, in which a contemporary Western square-rigger was expected to be able to keep sufficiently hard on the wind in the northeast trades to reach the westerly wind belt while still no further west than the midline of the North Atlantic or 38^0–40^0W. The *Keying*, we recall, was unable to hold to windward and by the same latitude was in 63^0W, or some 1,000 miles to leeward. But this is what we should expect, because junks were not designed to make to weather against a contrary monsoon; there was no operational or commercial reason for them to do so.

Junks were also not designed to go fast or be sailed flat out; their shipboard organization and operation did not aim to make them do so. That said, they turned in an absolutely solid performance, perhaps only a knot slower on average than a comparable Western vessel. The *Keying* was not ideally crewed. It strayed far from the waters for which it was designed. It was not loaded as it normally would have been. Yet over almost 300 days of sailing in a huge variety of conditions, from flat calm to a winter North Atlantic storm, it steadily averaged 3 knots, kept its crew dry and proved itself an excellent seaboat.

Given that junks of the *Keying*'s type were designed for and operated on relatively short-seas voyages, with the longest leg seldom over 1,500 miles and often only half that, their marginally slower average speed would not have made a vast difference in voyage times as compared to the slightly faster equivalent nineteenth-century Western sailing vessel—perhaps five days over the longest expected voyage. Finally, given their design, junks could carry more cargo than an equivalent Western vessel, because they had a lower displacement for an equivalent volume, though this was the one aspect of the comparison between a Western ship and a Chinese junk that was not tested on the otherwise epic and fascinating voyage of the *Keying*.

Part III

The Scrapyard of History

Chapter 12
Voyage Over

It remains a singular oddity, in the context of high Victorian imperial Britain, that the one example of a Chinese vessel that their scientists, shipwrights, artists and budding ethnographers had a chance to sketch accurately, measure with precision, make line drawings of, and a table of offsets for, they ignored. Equally, the one Chinese vessel the leading practitioners of the burgeoning field of marine art could have decided to paint with accuracy, they too, with the possible exception of Stephen Skillet, ignored.

This is the more astonishing, given that the *Keying* was in London during the Great Exhibition—more fully, the Great Exhibition of the Works of Industry of all Nations—at which one of its crew, the self-styled mandarin He Sing, managed to get himself accepted as a representative of the Chinese government, and in the organizing committee of which John Scott Russell, one of Britain's most innovative naval architects, had a part. For what better example of the work of the shipping industry of China could be found, literally on the doorstep, than the *Keying*?

Yet in the exhibition, as the catalogue reminds us, the exhibits devoted to China were all contributed by Western officials and merchants. By 1851, these Westerners were the default representatives of China in Western eyes, since China's recognition of a world of equal sovereign states was still several decades in the future; there was no formal Chinese government involvement. These Western residents in China are very unlikely to have a high estimation of China's maritime world. Even a China scholar like Samuel Wells Williams was not sufficiently impressed to devote more than a few pages of his lengthy description of Chinese life to its waterborne component—and that despite the enormous importance of water transport to China's economic system.

It is hardly surprising therefore, that the exhibition's catalogue contained just two mentions of China's naval architecture, both of them models of, respectively, a cargo boat and a mandarin boat (revenue). These were the ninth and tenth items of the sixteen objects contributed by the Shanghai and London business, Baring Bros. & Co., of London's Bishopgate Street.[1] The rest of the hundreds of items were indeed the works of China's industry, but primarily her retail craft and raw materials products.[2]

This is a puzzle, for whatever one may think about contemporary imperial arrogance and prejudiced Western attitudes of cultural superiority—and in the story of the *Keying* they predominate—they were never at the time inconsistent with a passionate interest in the acquisition of detailed empirical knowledge, by exact description, measurement and classification. This was the era in which the ideas for the great museums in London were germinating, and imperial expeditions of exploration and discovery were afoot. Why was the *Keying* so utterly ignored, save in terms of condescending disparagement?

Consider the maritime context. The famous voyage of the *Beagle* had ended in 1837; it would inspire a run of successors, with their embarked scientists. The voyage of HMS *Sulphur* (1836–42), under Sir Edward Belcher,[3] interrupted by the First Opium War, had been hotly followed by his voyage in HMS *Samarang* (1843–46), overlapping with the voyage of HMS *Herald* (1845–51), under Belcher's quondam deputy, Henry Kellett.[4] The voyage of HMS *Rattlesnake*, with Thomas Henry Huxley as its embarked scientist, was under way from 1846 to 1850. Both of the last were in progress at the very time the *Keying* was itself on voyage and in Britain.

Arctic fever was rife, with expedition after expedition being launched, only to fail to find the Northwest Passage with an incompetence only the best British explorers can manage with such consummate aplomb. Many were backed by Sir John Barrow, who had cut his China teeth on the ill-fated Macartney embassy to China in 1795, for which he served as Lord Macartney's household comptroller, and who, as secretary to the Admiralty, was the first to propose the equally unsuccessful Amherst embassy to China in 1816. Barrow had retired from public life only in 1845, after he had despatched the last, and most famous, Arctic failure, that of Sir John Franklin, whose disappearance with HMS *Erebus* and HMS *Terror* fired a series of attempts to find out what had happened that would last until the 1890s; as has often been remarked, these attempts lost more ships and men than had originally been involved.[5] The first left in the year the *Keying* arrived in London—bumbling Arctic high drama involving well-connected Westerners no doubt far eclipsed in scientific interest a successful voyage in a Chinese junk by a mixed nationality crew of undistinguished social background.

Equally, the institutions were being built on a large scale that were one way or another to house the achievements and the data from these explorations, the science and technology that made them possible and the cultural milieu that bred the turn of mind that saw such empirical enquiry as the correct path to intellectual, technical and, very much more arguably, moral progress. And more telling still, the committee that had the most significant hand in allocating the money to build them was masterminded by none other than John Scott Russell.

The Victoria and Albert Museum was founded in 1852 as the Museum of Ornamental Art and Manufactures. It was directly inspired by the Great Exhibition, from which several exhibits were purchased to form the nucleus of the collection. This was three years before the *Keying* was broken up; an alert Henry Cole, the museum's first director and among other things the inventor of a prize-winning teapot (under the pseudonym of Felix Summerly), could have acquired some or all of the junk in the interests of posterity.[6] He evidently was not interested, a junk being neither a piece of ornamental art nor, evidently, a product of manufacture and, above all, not a product of Western design. It is an index of the level of Cole's interest in the *Keying* that, in his two volumes of memoirs, he comments, anent He Sing's presence at the opening of the Great Exhibition, 'the Archbishop of Canterbury offered up a short and appropriate prayer, followed by the "Hallelujah Chorus", during which the Chinese mandarin came forward and made his obeisance,' footnoting with cavalier and inaccurate vagueness, 'He was a sea captain who brought his junk into the Thames for exhibition, and got a good deal of money.'[7]

The Science Museum was founded in 1857, two years after the ship's demolition; as its website notes, it was, as with the V&A, equipped 'with objects shown at the Great Exhibition held in the Crystal Palace'.[8] It did not acquire anything to do with the world of Chinese naval architecture until 1938, when a Chinese civil servant, Sir Frederick Maze, the inspector-general of the Chinese Maritime Customs Service (CMCS) who should have been directing such things to a

Chinese repository, gave it a collection of junk models he had had made under the supervision of G. R. G. Worcester by the Chinese employees of the CMCS. Adding insult to injury, as it were.

The omission of the *Keying* from this thirst for and cataloguing of knowledge—and, one might add, the all-but-complete omission of the entire world of the Chinese junk from it until the second decade of the twentieth century—is little short of astonishing, though perhaps revelatory of the extent to which China was seen by the Victorian British as in some way definitively 'other'. Simultaneously, indeed almost schizophrenically, China was looked upon as backward and primitive and, more accurately, as the home of the longest continuous advanced civilization known to humanity. Junks evidently belonged to the former aspect.

From the perspective of the Great Exhibition and its claims to look at the industry of all nations, Chinese naval architecture, once looked at carefully and its signal achievements in construction and propulsion fairly evaluated,[9] could not be subsumed as some primitive precursor to that on display in Class 8, West End Gallery and South West Gallery, exhibits 1–197, Naval Architecture.[10] Perhaps that is why, rather than looking closely at something like the *Keying*, or China's long traditions of and achievements in observational astronomy, cadastral surveying and sophisticated machinery, the Great Exhibition classified it all as part of the foreign and exotic, so by definition divorced from the forward march of triumphant science and technology. Thus the *Keying* remained, unworthy of close scrutiny, on display on the River Thames as a raree show. This, above all, explains why we have been left with so little by way of certain knowledge about this fascinating and singular ship, and its remarkable achievement. It is why all but a few, vestigial traces of its crew have disappeared. Racial and cultural—including class—prejudice always exacts a cost.

One result is a world in which any model or replica of the ship is deprived of the data on which alone a reliable, museum-quality model could and should be built. For example, neither the Hong Kong Museum of History nor the Hong Kong Maritime Museum models can be thought of as accurate. They err—in their very different ways—in manners typical of a failure to address the issues discussed above in sufficient detail. For example, the Hong Kong Maritime Museum model has favoured a hull form with no keel timber extending from the bottom, none of the characteristic *fuchuan* fineness of entry below the bow plate and a more extensive trapezoidal bow plate than may have been the case. The Hong Kong Museum of History has plumped—without much evidence—for a typical late-eighteenth-century *guangchuan* that, while it has a great deal more naval architectural plausibility, seems to have been built in absolute disregard of what visual and descriptive evidence there is. Given the gross uncertainties as to the exact conformity of the vessel, the resulting models in their different ways are probably as good as can be had if the result were to look at all like the familiar depictions, on the one hand, and actual known trading craft of the era, on the other.

The real mistake, therefore, has been too little careful analysis and a lapse into the error noted by McGrail with respect to ancient Chinese craft, but even more true for the *Keying*:[11]

> there is a strong temptation for historians to build theories based entirely and almost uncritically on literary and representational evidence, forgetting that early accounts of seafaring are not precise descriptions such as appear in twentieth-century manuals of seamanship and navigation, and that early illustrations and models are not craftsmen's drawings or scale models from which a ship could be built.

Bearing in mind McGrail's useful caution, an attempt has been made in the preceding pages to recover this fascinating voyage from the interstices of the historical record, and to relate it to the context in which it took place. The hope is to have explained why an event of such interest should have been so neglected for so long, why its protagonists were as they were and, insofar as is possible given the record, to try to understand better the ship that made it all possible and to recover as much as possible of its look, size, shape and performance.

The hope, of course, is that, with the voyage regaining a place in the limelight that is its due, and the lineaments of the ship, if not definitively recovered, at least confined a bit more tightly within a broad but reasonably well-known set of designs, the *Keying* too might stimulate the sort of interest with which we began. For the *Keying* and its voyage merit every bit as much the enthusiasm for a little-known, but not yet entirely lost, Chinese maritime past, and the world of experiences that it encompassed, as any other of the many historical replicas and re-enactments the world has seen brought to fruition over the last fifty and more years.

Few things would signal more clearly China's meteoric rise back to the maritime eminence it last enjoyed in the Ming dynasty, and Hong Kong's part in that achievement, than retracing the epic voyage of 1846–48. Few things would testify more effectively to the Western world's better appreciation in the present day of China's contributions to human progress, and of China's acceptance of a wider, more plural world than in Qing times, than a voyage from East to West in a Chinese vessel with a mixed crew—only this time, maybe, with a Chinese captain, officers and petty officers, a *fan kwae* crew . . . and a happier stay in New York!

Appendix: The Images of the *Keying*

There are thirteen images of the *Keying* at present known to the record. This count excludes the four limned images on the seven designs of white metal and brass commemorative medals, which would appear to borrow heavily from the images published as engravings in popular magazines, with only minor adjustments. It also excludes the interior and detailed views that appeared either in the *Description* or in popular illustrated magazines like *The Illustrated London News*, *The Pictorial Times* and the *Graphic*.

In the approximate order of creation, the thirteen images are:

- *The Chinese Junk "Keying"*, Nathaniel Currier, New York, 1847
- *The Great Chinese Junk Now on Her Voyage to England*, Edmund Evans, *The Pictorial Times*, 1847
- Two gouaches of the *Keying*, unknown Chinese artist, c. 1847
- *Chinese Junk Keying*, Rock & Co., London, c. 1848
- *The Chinese Junk Keying, Captain Kellett*, Rock Brothers & Payne, London, 1848
- *The Chinese Junk "Keying"*, B. Foster, *The Illustrated London News*, 1848
- *The Keying*, from the *Description*, unknown artist, J. Such, London, 1848
- *The Junk Keying Approaching England*, unknown artist, (probably London), c. 1848
- *Keying*, unknown artist, Vickers, London, c. 1848
- *Chinese Junk Keying in a Gale*, Stephen Dadd Skillett, London, 1848/49
- *Junk Keying in New York Harbour from* Italia, Samuel Waugh, New York, 1853
- *The Chinese Junk*, J. Greenaway, *Old & New London*, vol. 3, London, 1878

Ten of the images date from the ship's stay in London, one from between the New York stay and the arrival in London, and two from the stay in New York. One of the latter, by Nathaniel Currier (1813–88), is the earliest datable image and one which shows the least signs of any debts to any other of the images. It is for this reason, if no other, that the Currier image is one of the best guides we have of the *Keying*'s conformity.

In 1835 Nathaniel Currier started his own publishing company in New York and was soon publishing what at the time were innovative lithographs of current events. Whilst Currier was originally the artist of the images he published and appears to have drawn the *Keying*, in later years the firm used the work of many well-known contemporary American artists.[1]

It would appear that Nathaniel Currier had nothing to go on but what he could see with his own eyes. The result is therefore the nearest depiction we have of the *Keying* that seems to tally with the shapes shown in the earliest photographs of junks of the type the *Keying* is most likely to have been. Perhaps as indicative is the care with which Currier has shown the irregularities of the *Keying*'s mainmast—a matter specifically commented on in the *Description*. He is the only artist to do so.

The second of the New York images, dating from some six years later, was painted by the American artist Samuel Waugh around 1853. It appears entirely derivative. Interestingly, a comparison suggests that the derivation was not from Currier's image, but almost certainly from one of the London images—probably the most widely disseminated one. This appeared in *The Illustrated London News* on 1 April 1848. We shall return to Waugh below.

A New York period image, though actually done in London and much earlier than Waugh's, is the best example of what we may call 'informed fantasy', borrowing from known images of Chinese vessels and a verbal description, but connecting in no known way to the actual junk. This image appeared using a story filed in New York, in a popular British weekly magazine, *The Pictorial Times*.[2]

The image, the next in sequence and the first by a British artist, is a perfect example of the problem we are considering. It is evidently based upon existing western images of junks. There was probably some feed from America—notice the flag of the United States being flown as a courtesy flag at the foremast—though almost certainly this was not Currier's image. Otherwise the image is from the artist's imagination. Who he was we do not know, although we do know the engraving was done by the very young Edmund Evans, who was completing his apprenticeship to the great Ebenezer Landells—who we shall meet again—at the time. The sails are effectively European in form, since they are shown as gaff sails connected to the mast at the luff, or forward side, by parrels (or loops of rope). To compound the errors, each sail is shown as being controlled by a single sheet, as with western fore-and-aft sails. Since fully battened sails were at the time unknown outside China the result is a confabulation. Much the same is true for the hull—the bow has been copied from someone like William Alexander (1767–1816) or William Daniell (1769–1837). The stern is a travesty, muddling together a western transom and a Chinese rudder. The planking looks like nothing so much as that of a western clinker or lapstrake dinghy. And the deckhouse abaft the mainmast has come straight off a smart transatlantic packet ship. Finally, every mast is given a forestay—as with western ships—and the mainmast three shrouds supporting it at the side. The result is a nonsense. That in any case the artist was not very used to drawing ships can be seen by the western ship on the left. As it is shown, its masts lean drunkenly to starboard, quite out of the vertical in relation to the hull.

Of images with an unknown provenance, those painted by a Chinese artist are most puzzling.[3] All one can say of them is that there are two possibilities. Either they were the earliest known images done in Hong Kong by a shoreside artist and brought to London. Or they were done aboard the *Keying*, perhaps in Hong Kong, *en route*, in New York or in London, and may therefore be the only extant examples of the work of the ship's artist, Sam Shing. The use of brown paper in both cases makes it unlikely that work was done in Canton or Hong Kong, where white Chinese paper would have been more normal.[4] It is accordingly probable that the Chinese artist, or Sam Shing if it was he, also produced his images when the *Keying* was in Britain.

The most interesting features of the Chinese artist's work are the depiction of the junk's rig and the detail of the deck. There are clear differences that may point to the order in which the images were painted, since one image is very much more detailed than the other, almost as if a critical eye had been cast over the first effort, thereby ensuring that in the second the artist—who, as we have argued in the main text, was probably not a seafarer—got them right. Equally, of course, it may that the more accomplished and detailed painting is the original and the second a lazy copy.

From a nautical perspective in both, though in slightly different ways, what stands out is that the junk is shown as having shrouds supporting the masts. The less detailed picture shows shrouds only on the mainmast and the port side of the mizzen. The more detailed image shows shrouds on main and fore as well as the port side of the mizzen. There is also a triatic stay between foremast head and mainmast. These fascinating points of detail suggest the possibility that, for its long ocean voyage, Captain Kellett and the Western ship's officers may have been unhappy with the traditional, unstayed junk mast and insisted on fitting shrouds and the triatic. Certainly in the detailed image the shroud attachments—a mere gesture in the less-detailed example—are very un-Chinese ringbolts somehow clamped to the ship's sides.

The other difference is in the respective depictions of the deck, both in terms of its layout, which is again a matter of comparative technical detail, and also in terms of the crew. The technical differences in the deck need not deter us long, since they are mostly a matter of proportion and can be reconciled. It is important to note one shared feature, namely that these are the only images of the *Keying* that show the typical deck level bracing struts for foremast and main.

The one exception is the ship's boat. In the less detailed image this appears at first glance to be a stout, Western style gig with thwarts. But a closer look shows this 'top' part of the boat to be superimposed on a sampan hull. It would seem to be a curious conflation of the sampan the *Keying* carried, but which got carried away in the Atlantic storm, and whatever western dinghy was bought to replace it. By contrast, in the detailed image, the dinghy is clearly a double-ended, 'pea-pod'-type vessel.

In both cases, the deck has both Western and Chinese crew, but in the detailed painting the five people on deck become seventeen. The less detailed painting has just a hand on the foredeck, two helmsmen on the tiller tackles and two Europeans conferring on the poop deck. In the detailed painting, two Europeans are fishing off the bow; four Europeans are working on some shipwright work on the foredeck; a Chinese crewman is cleaning or lime washing the starboard rail water butt; to port of him a European is carrying a box forward and a Chinese crewman is leaning against a winch barrel; there is a cook in the galley on the port side abaft the mainmast; on the quarterdeck a Chinese crewman is sawing a timber lengthwise under the supervision of a Western officer wearing a peaked cap, and two hands are on the tiller tackles; on the poop deck one officer is taking a sight with a sextant, with another European either holding the chronometer or a notebook; and lounging off to starboard in a chair is a European in a white top hat.

I have placed the two Chinese paintings at this point in the sequence because of what comes next. These are two prints by the London stationer and print publisher Rock & Co., also trading as Rock Brothers and Payne, of 11 Walbrook, London.[5] The best known, *The Chinese Junk, Keying, Captain Kellett* is a coloured lithograph that views the junk from broad on the starboard quarter.[6] But there is a relatively unknown Rock & Co. print, which is quite possibly earlier.

The reason for that supposition is simple. The image is clearly based on the Chinese artist's view. The hull is more rolled away from the viewer, so that more of the ship's side and less of the deck are seen. But in almost every other detail of the ship, standfast the crew, the similarities are so striking that the source is manifest. All the standing rigging is there, as is the triatic between fore and main. And, as in the Chinese artist's images, the only flags shown are Europeanized swallow-tailed masthead pennant versions of the Chinese equivalents.

The main difference is in the bow, where quite clearly the artist did not understand what the Chinese artist had shown, namely the heavy framing timbers of the bow plate; instead he made the bow plate a simple trapezium of horizontally butted planks. In short, what may be the first British image of the *Keying* depended on an existing Chinese image.

The second, better known image then seems on inspection to be a derivation from the first. However, since it takes a stern rather than a bow view, the unknown artist had a greater licence to develop his ideas, possibly, we cannot know, with some input from Nathaniel Currier's image, which clearly could by this date have crossed the Atlantic, long in advance of the *Keying*. Certainly the *Keying*'s hull is planked far more as Currier shows it, with the addition of a pair of longitudinal wales like rubbing strakes in the centre part of the hull.

In this second Rock image the *Keying* is longer in proportion to her beam and the ends more exaggeratedly curved up. The sails show two variations, but they are slight: there is an additional panel in the main and the small main topsail has disappeared. More interestingly, the triatic has disappeared and the shrouds have been reduced to a single backstay set to weather on each of the three masts—something like a burton.

The interesting additional feature to this image is the 'dog' Chinese in its title as discussed in Chapter 2, where we noted that to an educated reader, the six characters are something of a nonsense, seeming to have been used solely for their phonetic value in Cantonese. For example, the first two characters sound like 'Keying' but are incorrect for Qiying's name.

This developed and evidently popular image seems to have contributed something to what are possibly the best known images—though with some possible input from the Currier, for example the furled, as opposed to spread sails. To most intents and purposes, these most broadcast images seem to be almost horizontally flipped copies of each other.

The two images are Birkett Foster's[7] from *The Illustrated London News*, engraved by Ebenezer Landells,[8] and the main print of the *Keying* in the *Description* by an unknown artist, which was produced, like the *Illustrated London News* image, shortly after the *Keying* berthed at Blackwall. This is possibly by Foster or an unknown artist to whom Foster owed his inspiration, or vice versa; it is unclear which image preceded which. Another of the illustrations in the *Description*—the 'Saloon of the *Keying*'—was engraved by Ebenezer Landells, so a connection is clear. The general compositions are very similar, most especially the angles of the furled sails, the running rigging, the exaggerated curvature and the ship's boat—again, something of a peapod. The bows are noticeably different, as is the freeboard amidships—the *Description* image having the *chunam*-ed hull below the bulwark almost touch the water. A further difference, one that becomes the norm in all subsequent images, is that these two images revert to Currier by eliminating all standing rigging.

An important feature of both these images, though curious in their differences, lies in the courtesy ensigns flown from the foremast. As we noted in more detail in Chapter 1, the choice of courtesy ensign is dictated by a ship's country of origin. That in both of these cases a British flag is flown as a courtesy ensign argues the *Keying* was not considered by its owners a British ship. The curious difference being that the *Illustrated London News* image has the *Keying* fly the

Union flag at the fore, where the *Description* has her flying the red ensign (or so one infers from the coloured Rock Brothers & Payne image). Whether this difference is a function of different choices made by the crew of the *Keying* or a muddle of some sort by the artists, we cannot know.

This detail is strong evidence that the *Keying* was being presented as a Chinese, not British, vessel. That this is a fair conclusion can be noted by returning to Nathaniel Currier's engraving of the *Keying* in New York, in which the American flag is being flown as the courtesy flag. The same corroborating evidence appears in Edward Evans' otherwise eccentric image in *The Pictorial Times* where the Stars and Stripes correctly appears, since the image title, *The Great Chinese Junk Now on Her Voyage to England*, implies a view taken whilst the junk was still in American waters.

Indeed a look at all of the images shows that the Western artists were all careful about this detail. Where the *Keying* is shown under sail in the approaches to London—the first Rock & Co. image and the 'Unknown artist' watercolour—there is no courtesy ensign. This makes sense because although at the date of the *Keying*'s arrival in western waters exactly when a courtesy ensign should be displayed was unsettled, the convention was becoming established that it should be hoisted as a ship arrived in the offing of its first port of call in a different country to that of its flag state. Accordingly in all the images in which the *Keying* has unquestionably arrived somewhere—the Currier, the Evans, the Rock Brothers & Payne, the Foster, the *Description*, the Vickers, the Waugh and the Greenaway—a courtesy flag is shown.

Whether the absence of a courtesy ensign in the two Chinese painted images can be taken as similar supporting evidence of the *Keying*'s Chinese identity is less certain. Since we do not know when or why they were painted or with what Western input, the flags they depict are a less clear guide. All we can remark is that whilst the masthead flags in the Chinese paintings match those in the images of the *Keying* at sea by Western artists rather than those of her either entering or in harbour, both Chinese images show the 'Treaty Port' ensigns on the taffrail. So whilst there are no courtesy ensigns in the Chinese gouaches, they clearly suggest that the *Keying* was not being shown as a British ship. The evidence being the curious, 'five-fold ensign' she is wearing at the taffrail, in the part of ship customarily reserved for the national flag of a ship's flag state.

In sum, all the artists concur in a negative. They are not showing a British ship. Though the Western artists can be argued to go one step further, in their use of the developing practices of maritime flag etiquette, to show their viewers a Chinese vessel 'home ported' in any or all of the newly established treaty ports.

The final point to note, with respect to the Rock Brothers and Payne print and the prints in *The Illustrated London News* and the *Description*, is that together they informed the images of the *Keying* in all but one of the limners who produced the souvenir medals. The exception drew its inspiration from the Vickers, Holywell Street, image I shall consider further below.

Of two further paintings of the *Keying*, the dating of one can be narrowed down to late 1848 or early 1849, but the date of the other is unclear. Sadly, there is no image of the first one. We know of Stephen Dadd Skillett's painting of *The Junk Keying in a Gale* only by report.[10] Since it was very probably done for one of the ship's officers or shareholders, it may have survived. However, it is lost to the public record. The other painting, a watercolour in the collection of the British National Maritime Museum in Greenwich, is by an unknown artist and seems to show the *Keying* passing the North Foreland on its way to the mouth of the Thames.

While charmingly coloured and well balanced, it is Sino-nautically—though in no way generally nautically—illiterate. The artist has the run of the sea well. His or her Western vessels are well depicted and are sailing correctly in relation to the true wind. Equally, the *Keying*'s running rigging is probably better observed than in most other images, especially the tackline from the foot of the mast to the forward end of the boom. But then the *Keying* is shown running before a wind from the starboard quarter—as shown by her mainmast pennant—with the sails all trimmed almost fore and aft, as if she were beating into a wind from ahead. It is hard to explain this oddity. The only candidate explanations are either mere convention, in that the artist was anxious to show the whole sail plan so the viewer grasped its nature or a complete inability to understand a fully battened junk sail as just a sail working on the same aerodynamic principles as any other sail.

It seems probable from the hull's conformity in this image that the painting post-dates those considered above, but not by much. The rig shows every sign of a connection with the Chinese artist's images, the coloured Rock Brothers

& Payne lithograph and the images of *The Illustrated London News* and the *Description*. Hence, the rough dating given above of 1848 or early 1849.

It is with the two Rock Brothers images, the Landells/Foster image and the *Description* image that the grotesque of the alien and the exotic becomes the image of the *Keying* that prevails and has endured. The curvature of the hull in all bar the watercolour is ludicrously exaggerated. The run of the planking is misread. The rig is not closely observed.

Nothing shows this general developmental—or perhaps regressive—trend so clearly as the print produced by Vickers of Holywell Street, London, also in the collection of the British National Maritime Museum.[11] Here the colouring of the *Keying*—a red hull with black and yellow bulwarks—is wholly unrelated to that in any other image. The hull in turn is more wildly exaggerated in curvature than even the *Illustrated London News* and *Description* images, to which it nonetheless evidently owes debts. More extraordinary still, the sails are rendered—most of all in the sheeting arrangements—as if they are the short-gaff rigs of a Dutch *botter*—though this is almost certainly an echo of *The Pictorial Times* image of a year previously. This is perhaps most clearly evidenced by the depiction of forestays on all three masts. For in this image too, there is an exaggerated version of the general tendency to torture the *Keying*'s rig into Western form with shrouds and stays. It is clear that with this print we have moved away from any drawing from life. This reliance on existing imagery then becomes the treatment of the *Keying* in the last two examples.

The first of these, Samuel Waugh's c. 1853 image of the *Keying* off the Battery, painted whilst the *Keying* was still afloat—though only just—is clearly directly derived from *The Illustrated London News*. The only difference is that the wind is coming from aft—an odd conceit since the ship is not shown moored bow and stern, so could be expected to lie head to wind. In all other respects there is no difference. Waugh was not specifically portraying the *Keying* but the scene off the immigration station at Castle Garden, near the Battery, which represented the end of his journey to Italy of which this was the last scene in his huge diorama presentation, *Italia*.[12] He evidently came to this exercise very late and it is perhaps not surprising that in seeking more accurately to contextualize the closing moments of his overseas excursion, but lacking the real vessel to paint, he resorted to adapting a popular image.

It is with the last image that fancy is finally let free of any restraints and, in doing so, echoes the earliest and similarly 'reality free' British image from *The Pictorial Times* of twenty years previously. It is placed as an illustration in the third volume of Walter Thornbury's *Old and New London*[13] by Edward Walford. This image by J. Greenaway is quite fantastical. The junk towers out of the water. There are still echoes of the dominant 1848 images—a tall tower to the right of the image and a stern obviously copied. But the bow becomes a massive, blunt, squared-off nonsense, possibly derived from the J. Davis commemorative medal. More peculiar still, the foresail is reversed and steeved up as if being used as a derrick. Both are wholly extraordinary. With this image, the exotic grotesque is complete and everyone's expectations of the primitive and absurd pandered to.

What we are seeing here is not merely a refusal to look at what is before the artists' eyes. Nor is it only the average jobbing artist's lack of familiarity with ships and the sea. It is as well a product of the working world that produced the images; a world of popular magazines for a newly emerging mass reading public[14] in which the goals of informing the public and entertaining them, of improving them and pandering to their prejudices became increasingly entangled. In a world of mass culture, what the public wishes to read trumps what someone with marked ideas of self-importance thinks they ought to read. If the broad public thinks that the moon is made of green cheese, it is a bold popular publisher who suggests they are all ignorant fools.

The world of popular weekly magazines in Victorian London was a viciously competitive one, as the fortunes of many of them—and those of their proprietors and contributors—show. A telling instance, involving several of those in whose magazines images of the *Keying* appeared, occurred in 1855, the year the *Keying* disappears from the record, when Ebenezer Landells, Thomas Roberts, John Maxwell and Herbert Ingram were named in the insolvency of the *Lady's Newspaper and Pictorial Times*. This conjoined publication had begun life as *The Lady's Newspaper* in 1847 founded by Landells. When *The Pictorial Times*, founded by Henry Vizetelly (1820–94) and others in 1843, folded in 1847, it was bought out by Herbert Ingram (1811–60), founder of *The Illustrated London News*, and merged with Landells' successful but underfinanced publication. In 1855 this publication was adjudged insolvent, though it struggled on to re-emerge eight years later, merged yet again, to become *The Queen, the Lady's*

Newspaper and Court Chronicle—which as *The Queen* is still being published.[15] A certain incestuous circularity of information and a common approach to news driven by the market is thus not surprising.

In addition, so small a world also ensured that few artists in the business worked independently. Edmund Evans was Ebenezer Landells' pupil and a close friend of Birket Foster and John Greenaway. So a recycling of material may have been as much a consequence of friendly cooperation as of competitive market pressures pushing all towards a common, publicly acceptable and expected imagery.

By the time the *Keying* had been more or less forgotten for twenty years, in case the reader of Walford's account of London, with its bizarre image of the junk missed the point, it is here that he repeats Charles Dickens's mocking description of a generation previously:

> Well, if there be any one thing in the world that this extraordinary craft is not at all like, that thing is a ship of any kind. So narrow, so long, so grotesque, so low in the middle, so high at each end, like a china pen-tray; with no rigging, with nowhere to go aloft ; with mats for sails, great warped cigars for masts, dragons and sea-monsters disporting themselves from stem to stern, and on the stern a gigantic cock of impossible aspect, defying the world (as well he may) to produce his equal—it would look more at home on the top of a public building, or at the top of a mountain, or in an avenue of trees, or down in a mine, than afloat on the water.

The great Sir Francis Beaufort once observed to the assembled worthies of the Royal Society, when again lamenting the paucity of the budget of the Surveying Service and the Hydrographic Department of which he was such a distinguished head, 'the tendency of all people is to undervalue what they do not understand'.[16]

Notes

Preface

1. Chinese bureaucrats—from a Portuguese root *mandar*, to command or order, influenced by a Sanskrit, via Hindi and Malay word *mantri* meaning 'counsel/councillor'—were called *mandarins* and were strictly ranked, though exactly how varied by dynasty. In the mid-nineteenth century Qing, there were nine civilian and nine military ranks, each distinguished by a badge (補子, *bŭzi*) on the chest and a differentially coloured button on the top of the official hat (清代官帽, *Qingdai guanmao*).

2. For the jugglers, see *The Leeds Mercury*, 8 May 1847.

3. The *Kon Tiki* (1947); the *Mayflower* (1956–57); the *Ra* (1969–70); the *Tai-ki* (1974); the *Golden Hind* (1973–80); the *Hokulea* (1976–present); the *Sohar* (1980–81); the *Argo* (1984); the trireme *Olympias* (1985–94); the *Batavia* (1985–2000); the First Fleet (1987–88); the *Santa Maria* (1990–91); the *Hsu Fu* (1993); the *Endeavour* (1994–97); the *Matthew* (1997); *L'Hermione* (1997–present); the *Duyfken* (2000); the *Samudra Raksa* (2003–04); the nao *Victoria* (2005–07); the *Götheborg III* (2005–07); the *Godspeed, Susan Constant* and *Discovery* (2007); the *Sea Stallion* (2007–08); and the galleon *Andalucia* (2008–10) cover the relevant date range comprehensively enough to make the point.

4. This issue is explored more fully in Stephen Davies, 'Maritime Museums: Who Needs Them?', Nalanda-Sriwajaya Working Papers No.11 (Singapore: Nalanda-Sriwajaya Centre, Institute of South East Asian Studies, 2012) at http://nsc.iseas.edu.sg/documents/working_papers/nscwps011.pdf; and Stephen Davies, 'Re-contextualizing the Prime Meridian: Interpreting Maritime Museum Collections for an Asian Audience', paper presented at the 2011 Conference of the International Congress of Maritime Museums, Smithsonian Museum, Washington DC, 10 October 2011.

5. For an excellently told story that exhibits exactly this historical interment of the world of the Western hewers of wood, see Robert Bickers, *Empire Made Me: An Englishman Adrift in Shanghai* (New York: Columbia University Press, 2004).

6. Richard Henry Dana, Jr., *Two Years before the Mast: A Personal Narrative of Life at Sea*, edited by Homer Eaton Keyes (New York: Macmillan, 1939), preface, referring to

James Fenimore Cooper's sea story *The Red Rover: A Tale* (London: Henry Colburn, 1827), e-book at http://www.authorama.com/ book/two-years-before-the-mast. html; accessed on 10 February 2013.

Introduction: Views from Different Seas

1. I shall use *junk* throughout this book to refer to the larger sea- and river-going Chinese vessels. It is a distinctly unsatisfactory term, either Javanese or Fujianese in origin, and as inadequately related to the Chinese vocabulary of ship and boat types as the equally unsatisfactory and etymologically errant *dhow* to the world of Arabic craft. Only its establishment in general English usage argues for it. It would be better to replace it with the generic English *ship*. See Pierre-Yves Manguin, 'The Southeast Asian Ship: An Historical Approach', *Journal of Southeast Asian Studies*, 11, no. 2 (1980): 266–76.

2. William Tarrant, *The Hongkong Almanack and Directory for 1846: With an Appendix* (Hong Kong: Office of the China Mail, 1846).

3. Remarkably little is known about Hong Kong's first Harbour Master: he has no entry in May Holdsworth and Christopher Munn (eds.), *Dictionary of Hong Kong Biography* (Hong Kong: Hong Kong University Press, 2011). Pedder was born in Ryde, Isle of Wight, in 1801 and joined the Royal Navy in 1814. His early service is not known, but in 1820 he joined HMS *Liffey* (50, 1813–1827; see Samantha Cavell, 'A Social History of Midshipmen and Quarterdeck Boys in the Royal Navy, 1761–1831', unpublished PhD thesis, University of Exeter, 2010, App. G7). He was made lieutenant in 1824 (see http://www.pbenyon1.plus.com/Nbd/exec/ OPQ/Index.html; accessed on 9 February 2013). He obviously lacked influence, since he is next recorded in HM Coastguard 1836–39—traditionally a parking place for officers unable to get a berth in a serving naval vessel. There is record of his having contemplated developing a site—perhaps to build a house—at Bell Mead, Whippingham, Isle of Wight, in 1831, though negotiations were evidently broken off (see http://www. nationalarchives.gov.uk/a2a/records.aspx?cat=189-jergps&cid=3-8&kw=Pedder,%20William#3-8; accessed on 9 February 2013). We know that before joining the *Nemesis* and subsequently coming to Hong Kong, he had been married and had a son (*The Naval Chronicle*, vol. 7, 1838, p. 503: 'At Fleet, near Weymouth, on Monday 21st of May, the lady of Lt. W. Pedder, R.N., of a son.'), but whether his family ever came to Hong Kong is not known. Endacott notes that 'he proved an efficient officer (in Hong Kong) until his death at Ryde in the Isle of Wight in March 1854, while on home leave' (see G. B. Endacott, *A Biographical Sketch-Book of Early Hong Kong*, edited by John Carroll [Hong Kong: Hong Kong University Press, 2005], p. 109). His will was proved on 26 May 1854 (see http:// discovery.nationalarchives.gov.uk/SearchUI/details?Uri=D62453; accessed on 9 February 2013).

4. The four images are *View of Hong Kong and the Harbour Looking West from Murray's Battery, 1846; View of Spring Gardens, 24th June 1846; View of Victoria: Looking West*

from the Garden of the Honorable John Walter Hulme, Chief Justice, Hong Kong and *View of Jardine Matheson's Looking North-West from Causeway Bay, 28th September 1846.* They were part of a set of twelve views of Hong Kong made by Bruce in 1846 and subsequently published in c.1847 as lithographs by Maclure, Macdonald & Macgregor, Lithographers, London, the actual lithography being done by A. Maclure.

5. Frank Walsh, *A History of Hong Kong*, revised ed. (London: Harper Collins, 1997), pp. 124–5. As Walsh points out, settling the treaty that ended the First Opium War and established Hong Kong was a long drawn out process, ending only in October 1843, with the Supplementary Treaty of the Bogue.

6. Walsh, *A History of Hong Kong*, p. 162.

7. W. H. Smyth, *The Sailor's Word-book: An alphabetical digest of nautical terms, including some more especially military and scientific, but useful to seamen; as well as archaisms of early voyagers, etc.* (London: Blackie and Son, 1867). Smyth's word book was edited for publication by an early denizen of the Victoria Harbour waterfront, Captain Sir Edward Belcher.

8. For the enduring look of traditional Chinese sail, see Stephen Davies, *Coasting Past: The Last South China Coastal Trading Junks Photographed by William Heering* (Hong Kong: Hong Kong Maritime Museum, 2013).

9. G. S. Graham, *The China Station: War and Diplomacy, 1830–1860* (Oxford: Oxford University Press, 1978) and William Laird Clowes, *The Royal Navy: A History from the Earliest Times to the Present*, 7 vols. (London: Sampson, Low, Marston, 1901), vol. 7, pp. 351–3.

10. 1,743-ton BM, two decks, 28×32 pdrs, 28×18 pdrs, 6×12 pdrs, 12×32 pdr carronades (short-range, brutal weapons), and 6×18 pdr carronades. See David Lyon and Rif Winfield, *The Sail & Steam Navy List: All the Ships of the Royal Navy, 1815–1889* (London: Chatham, 2004), Brian Lavery, *The Arming and Fitting of English Ships of War, 1600–1815* (Annapolis, MD: Naval Institute Press, 1989) and Brian Lavery, *The Ship of the Line: The Development of the Battlefleet 1650–1850* (London, Conway Maritime Press, 1984).

11. War junks in this fleet seem to have been armed with only twelve or so six- to twelve-pounder guns. It would have required fourteen junks armed with 12×12 pdrs to equal the *Agincourt's* 'weight of metal', but none could have come even close to the massive hammer blow of a thirty-two-pound ball from even one thirty-two pounder. Chinese war junks were aimed at defensive dissuasion, not massive and relentless aggression. Bruce A. Elleman, *Modern Chinese Warfare, 1795–1989* (London: Routledge, 2001), pp. 19–34, and Daniel R. Headrick, *The Tools of Empire: Technology and European Imperialism in the 19th Century* (Oxford: Oxford University Press, 1981), Ch. 2.

12. For a brilliant exposition on this huge complexity, see Trevor Kenchington, 'The Structures of English Wooden Ships: William Sutherland's Ship, c.1710', *The Northern Mariner/Le Marin du nord* 3, no.1 (1993): 1–43. Nothing significant had

changed by 1846 except in the direction of greater complexity, with such niceties as diagonal bracing to further strengthen hulls against stresses.

13. A made mast is one constructed from more than one tree, each part shaped and fitted to the others with the whole being held together by rope or iron bands called woolding. Smyth, *The Sailor's Word-book*, s.v.

14. Brian Tunstall and Nicholas Tracy (eds.), *Naval Warfare in the Age of Sail: The Evolution of Fighting Tactics, 1650–1815* (London: Wellfleet Press, 2001), Peter Padfield, *Guns at Sea* (London: St Martin's Press, 1974).

15. Cavell, *A Social History of Midshipmen and Quarterdeck Boys in the Royal Navy*, pp. 254–338 and 450. The *French Wars* is a shorthand term for the French Revolutionary Wars, 1792–1802 and the Napoleonic Wars, 1803–15.

16. It was claimed, for example, that it was a failure to understand Chinese signal flags that occasioned the fire from the British ships *Volage* and *Hyacinth* that began the First Opium War. E. H. Parker (ed.), *Chinese Account of the Opium War* (Shanghai: Kelley & Walsh, 1888), p. 11, '... the English mistook our red flags for a declaration of war, and opened fire;—for in Europe a red flag means war, and a white one peace' (this is a translation of the last two chapters of Wei Yuan [魏源, 1794–1857], *Sheng wu ji* [聖武記, Record of the military operations of the present dynasty]).

17. Michael A. Palmer, *Command at Sea: Naval Command and Control since the Sixteenth Century* (Cambridge, MA: Harvard University Press, 2007), p. 210.

18. Depending on when in 1846 we are looking out, this would either have been the *Minden*, an old third-rate or, when the *Minden* was sold for scrap, the hulked sixth-rate frigate *Alligator*.

19. That means sail closer to the wind and thus work upwind faster than those styled less 'weatherly' vessels.

20. The standard, if outdated, study, featuring an attitudes to things non-Western that has the power to shock, is Basil Lubbock's *The Opium Clippers* (Glasgow: Brown Son & Ferguson, 1933).

21. Tonio Andrade, 'Was the European Sailing Ship a Key Technology of European Expansion? Evidence from East Asia', *International Journal of Maritime History* 23, no. 2 (Dec. 2011): 17–40.

22. This was called Pitt's Passage, named after Captain Wilson's voyage on the Indiaman *Pitt* in 1759, though there is evidence the *Pitt* was not the first to try it. It involved a long detour via the Java Sea up through the Malukus and out through the straits north of New Guinea to the Pacific, whence east of the Philippines and to Macao via the Luzon Strait, enabling a vessel that arrived in the approaches to the China Seas too late in the southwest monsoon season to make Macao before the northeast monsoon swept in a chance not to lose a season.

23. John Fincham, *A History of Naval Architecture: To Which Is Prefixed an Introductory Dissertation on the Application of Mathematical Science to the Art of Naval Construction* (London: Whittaker, 1851).

24. John Fincham, *An Introductory Outline of the Practice of Shipbuilding, &c., &c*, 2nd ed. (Portsea: William Woodward, 1825).

25. These are almost self-explanatory. Skin-first build creates a structure of joined outer planking fastened to the keel, bow and stern, and then reinforces it with a light internal framework. Frame-first constructs a rigid frame on the keel, bow and stern and then covers it with planks.

26. There were at least two versions of this booklet, published as by an anonymous author, but probably either written by Charles Kellett or ghostwritten to his narrative. The first version, Anon., *The Chinese Junk "Keying," being a full account of that vessel, with extracts from the journal of Capt. Kellett* (New York: Israel Sackett No. 1 Nassau Street, 1847), accompanied the exhibition of the ship in New York. I shall abbreviate this as the *Account*. The second version, which went into at least five editions (although it would be more accurate to call them reprints, since the contents do not substantially vary), Anon., *A Description of the Chinese Junk, "Keying", printed for the proprietors of the junk and sold only on board* (London: J. Such, 1848), is the better known and more extensive, though less informative as to the details of the voyage, especially in the early phases in the offing of the Sunda Strait. As noted in the text, I shall abbreviate this to the *Description*. A third pamphlet, not seemingly written by or ghosted for Charles Kellett, though this is uncertain, is *The Chinese Junk, "Keying" Descriptive Particulars; with an account of her voyage from China* (London: W. Marshall News Agent, Blackwall Railway, Fenchurch Street, n.d) with a steel engraving by J. T. Wood, Holywell St., Strand, which appears to have been used by Halliday for one of the medals, with some of Wood's detail omitted and the junk's mainsail looking like a trysail; see H. H. Brindley, 'The Keying', *The Mariner's Mirror* 8, no. 4 (1922): 305–14 and 308.

27. *Description*, p. 12.

28. Technically, a design envelope is the set of requirements that enable a design to perform as it is intended to perform in its given environment. The performance envelope—the expected capabilities of the design in a normal operating environment—is usually *within* the design envelope. It follows that the claim here is that, by good fortune, the design envelope that had emerged from a congeries of traditional Western shipbuilding practices by, say, the mid- to late fifteenth century far exceeded the performance envelope that was initially expected, thus allowing for the significant developments in ship design that accelerated through the sixteenth and seventeenth centuries and slowed during the eighteenth century, as the performance envelope reached the limits of the design envelope, given wooden ships and sail propulsion. As the *Keying* set sail, of course, that coincidence of envelopes was in the process of being blown asunder by the twin revolutions in ship design of iron and steam.

29. For an excellent overview of this pattern of development, see Richard W. Unger (ed.), *Cogs, Caravels and Galleons* (London: Brassey Publications, 1999).

30. One can always scale up or down (miniaturize or enlarge) any built object, provided one has the materials and tools. Whether the result works is an importantly related issue, without which 'scalability' is in practice meaningless. A truly 'scalable' design creates a design envelope that allows the design to be scaled up not only

without loss of, but with enhanced functionality. See Stephen Davies, *Fathoming the Unfathomable: Even Leviathans Have Limits* (2005), an ebook available via www.1421exposed.com.

31. Consider Joel Mokyr, *The Gifts of Athena: Historical Origins of the Knowledge Economy* (Princeton, NJ: Princeton University Press, 2003). For a recent commentary on Mokyr's challenging thesis, see James Dowey, 'Mind over Matter: Empirical Evidence of the Industrial Enlightenment as the Origin of Modern Economic Growth', paper presented at London School of Economics Economic History PhD workshop, 25 January 2012, at http://www2.lse.ac.uk/economicHistory/seminars/EH590Workshop/LT2012papers/dowey.pdf; accessed on 11 March 2013.

32. Deng Gang, *The Premodern Chinese Economy—Structural Equilibrium and Capitalist Sterility* (London: Routledge, 1999).

33. I owe the idea of a vernacular architecture to Roger Scruton, *The Aesthetics of Architecture* (Princeton, NJ: Princeton University Press, 1980).

34. Davies, *Fathoming the Unfathomable*, passim.

35. This refers to a system of tonnage measurement prevailing in the Western world from the seventeenth to the mid-nineteenth century. The details are more fully explored in Part II. Tons burthen are a measure of internal capacity (volume), *not* of displacement (weight or mass). There is uncertainty as to the tonnage of the largest A-class junks of the *nanyang* trade.

36. This means the mast is made of a single length of wood shaped from a single tree. They are sometimes referred to as *pole masts*, but for reasons of fascination only to devotees, this is not strictly correct.

37. A gun or luff tackle is a four-part purchase rigged (rove) 'to advantage', which means, in this case of controlling a junk tiller, that there are five moving rope lengths at the tiller end of the tackle and four at the bulwark (ship's side) end. The gun/luff tackles in this use were also known in the West as relieving tackles, which was their purpose when conditions meant that the ship's wheel alone was insufficient to control the rudder.

38. A bowsing tackle is a set of ropes leading from something that needs to be tightened—here the rudder against its mountings—to what does the tightening—here a fixed winch in the bow. This is in fact an interesting example of the co-optation of a Western term of art to a use inconceivable in Western naval architecture for which, strictly, it is ill suited. Chinese-English maritime dictionaries, especially when dealing with traditional craft, run head on into these problems of non-translatability and the need to jury-rig existing terms.

39. The aerodynamic potential of the rig was never technically explored or fully realized while junks were a living maritime tradition in China. For a modern take on the rig and its virtues, see H. G. Hasler and J. K. Macleod, *Practical Junk Rig: Design, Aerodynamics and Handling* (London: Adlard Coles, 1988), and the wide range of information available from the Junk Rig Association, http://www.junkrigassociation.org.

40. Joseph Needham, et al., *Science and Civilization in China*, 7 vols. (Cambridge: Cambridge University Press, 1974–2004); the number of separate books is twenty-seven.

41. Care is needed because of the relative paucity of archaeological detail and the 'interpretability' of documentary evidence. This means that we do not know much concrete, factual detail about Ming and pre-Ming dynasty ships. We know they appeared relatively large vis-à-vis some unspecified idea of European craft, but not exactly how much larger or in comparison to exactly what—medieval and Renaissance descriptive travelogues were not given to precise quantification.

42. J. Scott Russell, 'On the Longitudinal System in the Structure of Iron Ships', E. J. Reed (ed.), *Transactions of the Institution of Naval Architects*, vol. 3 (London: Institution of Naval Architects, 1862), pp. 160–71, the quotations are from pp. 162–3.

43. For a description of the system, see Sir Joseph Isherwood, 'Economy in Modern Shipbuilding—II', *Shipping: A Weekly Journal of Marine Trades*, 22 June 1918.

44. Charles Dickens, 'The Chinese Junk', *Examiner*, June 24 1848, p. 403. See also Elizabeth Hope Chang, *Britain's Chinese Eye: Literature, Empire and Aesthetics in Nineteenth-Century Britain* (Stanford, CA: Stanford University Press, 2010), p. 115. For a very similar, though less technically based understanding of the differences here, see Catherine Pagani, 'Objects and the Press: Images of China in Nineteenth-century Britain', in *Imperial Co-Histories: National Identities and the British and Colonial Press*, edited by Julie F. Codell (Madison, NJ: Fairleigh Dickinson University Press, 2003), pp. 147–66, especially pp. 155–68, where the Dickens piece is also quoted.

45. Jerry Allen, *The Sea Years of Joseph Conrad* (London: Methuen, 1967).

46. See Nicholas Rodger's eminent *The Wooden World: An Anatomy of the Georgian Navy* (London: Collins, 1986) and the work of Michael Lewis for the Royal Navy. For the merchant service, see Peter Earle, *Sailors: English Merchant Seamen 1650–1775* (London: Methuen, 1998). These two works are the tip of a vast iceberg that has been growing for several generations now, to strain a metaphor, as the snowfall of centuries of documentation is sifted and its findings accumulated.

47. *Lascar*, derived from the Persian *laskari*, meaning 'soldier', via the Portuguese *lascari* was a generic European term for Asian crew from the seventeenth century through to the twentieth, though generally referring to those from South Asia more than Southeast Asia or China. For a good introduction, see http://www.lascars.co.uk/; accessed on 1 August 2010. See also Janet J. Ewald, 'Crossers of the Sea: Slaves, Freedmen, and Other Migrants in the Northwestern Indian Ocean, c.1750–1914', *American Historical Review* 105, no. 1 (Feb. 2000): 69–91. See also Douglas Jones, 'The Chinese in Britain: Origins and Development of a Community', *Journal of Ethnic and Migration Studies* 7, no. 3 (Winter 1979): 397–402; Marika Sherwood, 'Race, Nationality and Employment among Lascar Seamen, 1660 to 1945', *Journal of Ethnic and Migration Studies* 17, no. 2 (Jan. 1991): 229–44; and Diane Frost (ed.), *Ethnic Labour and British Imperial Trade (Immigrants & Minorities)* (London: Routledge, 1995).

48. Drawings collectively known as the *Tosen no Zu*, sometimes called the Hirado
    Scrolls, which were completed by a Japanese artist working for the daimyo of Hirado
    in around 1795. The drawings of some dozen different Chinese and Southeast Asian
    trading vessels and one Dutch *retourschip* are elegant and exact, though not obvi-
    ously to any scale, and all have careful measurements of key dimensions labelled. For
    a discussion of the dating and import of these drawings, see Oba Osamu, 'On the
    Scroll of Chinese Ships in the Possession of the Matsuura Museum—Materials for
    the Study of Chinese Trading Ships in Edo Period', *Bulletin of the Institute of Oriental
    and Occidental Studies of Kansai University* 5 (March 1972): 13–50.

49. G. R. G. Worcester, *The Junks and Sampans of the Yangtze* (Annapolis, MD: Naval
    Institute Press, 1971); the first edition was published in Shanghai by the Chinese
    Imperial Maritime Customs in 1940; G. R. G. Worcester, *Sail and Sweep in China:
    The History and Development of the Chinese Junk as Illustrated by the Collection of
    Models in the Science Museum* (London: HMSO, 1966).

50. A possible exception might be the *Longjiang Shipyard Treatise* (*Longjiang chuan-
    chang zhi* [龍江船廠志]) of 1553 by Li Zhaoxiang (李照祥), for my knowledge
    of which I am indebted to Sally K. Church, 'Nanjing's *Longjiang Shipyard Treatise*
    and Our Knowledge of Ming Ships', research in progress financed by the Golden
    Web Foundation and kindly made available to me by her, which looks *inter alia*
    at Hans Lothar Scheuring, *Die Drachenfluß-Werft von Nanking: Das Lung-chiang
    ch'uan-ch'ang chih, eine Ming-zeitliche Quelle zur Geschichte des chinesischen Schiffbaus*,
    Heidelberger Schriften zur Ostasienkunde, Band 9 (Frankfurt: Haag und Herchen,
    1987). This is a translation into German of the treatise.

51. Sean McGrail, *Boats of the World from the Stone Age to Medieval Times* (Oxford:
    Oxford University Press, 2001), p. 349, where McGrail quotes Yang Yu, 'On the
    Study of Ancient Sailing Ships', from S. Zhang (ed.), *Proceedings of the International
    Sailing Ship Conference* (Shanghai: Society of Naval Architecture and Marine
    Engineering, 1991), contending exactly this point.

52. The first Chinese maritime archaeology unit, under the auspices of the Underwater
    Archaeological Centre at the National History Museum of China, was established
    only in 1990 with the assistance of Australian specialists; see *China Heritage
    Newsletter*, No. 1 (March 2005), at http://www.chinaheritagequarterly.org/edito-
    rial. php? issue=001; accessed on 16 August 2010.

53. Ibid., p. 361.

54. J. Richard Steffy, *Wooden Shipbuilding and the Interpretation of Shipwrecks* (College
    Station: Texas A&M University Press, 1994), Ch. 3. See also Lionel Casson's ency-
    clopaedic *Ships and Seamanship in the Ancient World* (Baltimore: Johns Hopkins
    University Press, 1995).

55. 'Systemic' because there is evidence that few Chinese sailors and shipwrights were
    literate. This was a direct function of the lowly and excluded status of sea people—
    the core of the maritime world—in traditional Chinese society. This is not to say
    that all were illiterate. There is ample evidence that was not true. What appears to be
    missing in China's maritime tradition as a result is that stratum of literate observers

and theorizers that one finds emerging in the Western world around the fifteenth century and then growing in sophistication and importance through the following four centuries until, in the nineteenth century, a full-fledged and theorized naval architecture had come into being.

56. J. E. D. Williams, *From Sails to Satellites: The Origin and Development of Navigational Science* (Cambridge: Cambridge University Press, 1993); A. E. Fanning, *Steady as She Goes: A History of the Compass Department of the Admiralty* (London: HMSO, 1986); Alan Gurney, *Compass: A Story of Exploration and Innovation* (New York: W. W. Norton, 2004).

57. *Fan kwae* (番鬼, *fangui* in pinyin) or 'foreign ghost' was a mildly derogatory term for foreigners in the mid-nineteenth century, equivalent to the modern Cantonese *gweilo* (鬼佬).

Chapter 1 Origins, Purchase and Commissioning

1. Contemporary news stories state the *Keying* carried no cargo to avoid having to pay duty; see *inter alia Daily News*, 26 August 1847, and *The Morning Chronicle*, 11 March 1848.

2. See John Rogers Haddad, *The Romance of China: Excursions to China in U.S. Culture, 1776–1876* (New York: Columbia University Press, 2004), Ch. 4, and the same author's more recent essay, 'China of the American Imagination: The Influence of Trade on U.S. Portrayals of China, 1820–1850', in *Narratives of Free Trade: The Commercial Cultures of Early US-China Relations*, edited by Kendall Johnson (Hong Kong: Hong Kong University Press, 2011).

3. See, for a slightly different view, Catherine Pagani, 'Objects and the Press: Images of China in Nineteenth-Century Britain', in *Imperial Co-Histories: National Identities and the British and Colonial Press*, edited by Julie F. Codell (Madison, NJ: Fairleigh Dickinson University Press, 2003), p. 154.

4. William Langdon, *Ten Thousand Things Relating to China and the Chinese: An Epitome of the Genius, Government, History, Literature, Agriculture, Arts, Trade, Manners, Customs, and Social Life of the People of the Celestial Empire* (London: G M'Kewan, 1842). Langdon himself had spent time in China, where he and Nathan Dunn had been acquainted. Interestingly, there is considerable commonalty between Langdon's catalogue and a predecessor, see Enoch Cobb Wines, *A Peep at China in Mr. Dunn's Chinese Collection; with Miscellaneous Notes Relating to the Institutions and Customs of the Chinese and Our Commercial Intercourse with Them* (Philadelphia: Printed for Nathan Dunn, I Ashmead & Co, Printers, 1839).

5. Dunn had been assisted in amassing his collection by 'Howqua, Tingqua, and other Hong merchants of note' (*The Illustrated London News*, 3 December 1842, p. 469). On the close relationship between Dunn and Tingqua, and Tingqua's role in saving Dunn from ruin in the great fire in Canton in November 1822, see Haddad, *The Romance of China*, Ch. 4.

6. Langdon, ibid., pp. 269–73.

7. Ibid., pp. 272–73.

8. Another has 129 separate entries.

9. Anon., *A Description of the Chinese Junk, "Keying", printed for the proprietors of the junk and sold only on board* (London: J. Such, 1848), p. 29.

10. Or with any mention of the certainty that the investors in the *Keying* project were probably—and, in the case of Douglas Lapraik, certainly—heavily involved in the illegal smuggling of opium into China.

11. Zhaojin Ji, *A History of Modern Shanghai Banking: The Rise and Decline of China's Finance Capitalism* (New York: M. E. Sharpe, 2003), p. 45.

12. No one can read Robert Bickers's recent and excellent *The Scramble for China: Foreign Devils in the Qing Empire 1832–1914* (London: Penguin Books, 2011) without being struck by the levels of casual violence that often characterized life at sea at this time; one notes especially a voyage by a lorcha from Hong Kong to Shanghai in 1848, when 'during the whole passage the Master was constantly firing on every Native craft, without distinction' (pp. 106–7). See also Christopher Munn, *Anglo-China, Chinese People and British Rule in Hong Kong, 1841–1880* (Hong Kong: Hong Kong University Press, 2009), Chs. 3 and 7, and his discussion of the problem of piracy.

13. The data on Charles Kellett's birth and experience comes from his Master's Certificate of Service lodged in the National Maritime Museum, Greenwich and placed online by Ancestry.com (http://search.ancestry.co.uk/cgi-bin/sse.dll?db=GBMastersC ertificates&rank=1&new=1&so=3&MSAV=0&msT=1&gss=ms_db&gsfn=Cha rles+Alfred&gsln=Kellett&msbdy=1818&msbpn__ftp=Plymouth&dbOnly=_ F80062DE%7C_F80062DE_x&uidh=000, accessed on 1 May 2013). I owe this information to Charles Kellett's great-great-granddaughter Susan Simmons and her cousin Drummond Corrie.

14. No trace of Charles Kellett's sea service can be found until the Master's Certificate of Service of 1851 where it states that Kellett 'Has been employed in the Capacities of Boy, Mate & Master 17 years in the British Merchant Service in the Foreign Trade'. A system of voluntary examinations for masters and mates of foreign trade vessels had been introduced by the Board of Trade in 1845. Before that only relatively informal records exist and Charles Kellett's name does not appear in the 1.6 million record in the British National Archives, searchable online at http://www.findmy-past.co.uk/search/merchant-navy-seamen/results?event=S&locale=en&recordCo unt=-1&otherDataSet=2%3A41&forenames=CHARLES+Alfred&includeForena mesVariants=true&_includeForenamesVariants=on&surname=KELLETT&includ eSurnameVariants=true&_includeSurnameVariants=on&county=DEV&place=Ply mouth&birthYear=1818&birthYearTolerance=1&keyWord=# (accessed on 1 May 2013). We shall revisit this issue in Chapter 7.

15. For details on Lapraik, I am indebted to P. Hansell, 'The Colourful Douglas Lapraik (1818–1869)', *Antiquarian Horology* 27, no. 3 (2003): 331–2; a later note in the same journal by Mark Macalpine furnishes details of Lapraik's status as a freemason

in Hong Kong's Zetland Lodge, where Lapraik was treasurer in 1856 and 1857. See also Bernard North, 'Watch and clockmakers of Hong Kong', *Antiquarian Horology* 32, no. 2 (2010): 180–2.

16. William Tarrant (*The Hongkong Almanack and Directory for 1846: With an Appendix*, Hong Kong: Office of the China Mail, 1846, p. 40) has a different take, in that he has Leonard Just, Sr. running a watch and chronometer maker in Queen's Road, and Leonard Just, Jr. running the shop in D'Aguilar Street with Douglas Lapraik and George Saunders working for him.

17. North, 'Watch and Clockmakers of Hong Kong', pp. 179–80.

18. The company still trades today as one of Hong Kong's Admiralty chart agents (George Falconer [Nautical] Ltd.). The upmarket jeweller in the Peninsula Hotel, Falconer Jewellers, is now a separate concern, though it boasts a founding date of 1855, so is clearly connected (see http://www.falconer.com.hk/eng/profile.html).

19. May Holdsworth and Christopher Munn (eds.), *Dictionary of Hong Kong Biography* (Hong Kong: Hong Kong University Press, 2011), entry for Thomas Ash Lane and kin.

20. Tarrant, *The Hongkong Almanack and Directory*, p. 40.

21. Holdsworth and Munn, *Dictionary of Hong Kong Biography*.

22. There are only two Burtons in *The Mercantile Navy List* for 1850, Frederick John and Henry, so like his skipper, G. Burton rested his case for rank on time, not formal qualification. Sixty G. Burtons born between 1805 and 1825 appear in the pre-1845 British records of merchant seamen (http://www.findmypast.co.uk/search/merchant-navy-seamen/results?e=S&bY=1825&bYT=10&iSnV=true&sn=BURTON&fns=G&snNXF=true&oDS=2:41&rC=192&nOffset=50, accessed on 1 May 2013).

23. There is only one Revett in *The Mercantile Navy List*; Richard Revett. No Edward Revett appears in the pre-1845 records of merchant seamen. Only four Revetts are listed, two Benjamins, a George and a William (http://www.findmypast.co.uk/search/merchant-navy-seamen/results?event=S&locale=en&recordCount=-1&otherDataSet=2%3A41&forenames=&includeForenamesVariants=true&_includeForenamesVariants=on&surname=REVETT&includeSurnameVariants=true&_includeSurnameVariants=on&county=&place=&birthYear=1825&birthYearTolerance=5&keyWord=, accessed on 1 May 2013). The quarterdeck of the *Keying* was in no way reflective of the revolution in the standards of ship manning that had begun in 1845; see the notice setting out the formal position in ibid., pp. 13–9. Some sources give Revett's first name as one beginning with 'S', however, New York newspaper reports state Edward.

24. *Register of American and Foreign Shipping 1895*, p. 625, at http://library.mysticseaport.org/ initiative/ShipPageImage.cfm?PageNum=3&BibID=179721895&Series=Introduction&Chapter=; accessed on 5 August 2010.

25. E. J. Eitel, *Europe in China: The History of Hong Kong from the Beginning to the Year 1882* (Taipei: Cheng-Wen Publishing Co., 1968), Chs. 13 and 14.

26. This shift, roughly from admiration to denigration, and later to evident Sinophobia, is well canvassed by Haddad, 'China of the American Imagination'; see also Bickers, *The Scramble for China*, p. 37.

27. Bickers makes a similar point about Shanghai (*The Scramble for China*, pp. 131–2). See also John M. Carroll, *Edge of Empires: Chinese Elites and British Colonials in Hong Kong* (Hong Kong: Hong Kong University Press, 2007), pp. 41–2, citing Robert Montgomery Martin (colonial treasurer), Robert Fortune, Oswald Tiffany, the *Economist*, Rev. George Smith, Rev. Karl Gutzlaff and J. M. Tronson. Carroll gives a very clear picture of Hong Kong's rapscallion world.

28. Published by Rock Brothers and Payne, 11 Walbrook, London, on 20 May 1848. This shows the *Keying* as she appeared 'off Gravesend on 28th March, 1848, 477 days from Canton'.

29. Correctly and incorrectly, because etiquette requires the flying of the merchant ensign of one's host country, not its national flag. Things were somewhat more fluid in the 1840s; in any case, jobbing artists often paint what they think they ought to be seeing, not what is there—as we shall see when we come to consider more fully in Part II the popular images of the *Keying* published in her lifetime.

30. The nearest to be found on the standard vexillologist's website are what are described as Beijing 'drum and bell tower flags' (see http://www.crwflags.com/fotw/flags/cn_be.html).

31. For a very full discussion, see Mark C. Elliott, *The Manchu Way: The Eight Banners and Ethnic Identity in Late Imperial China* (Stanford, CA: Stanford University Press, 2001).

32. Haddad, 'China of the American Imagination', Ch. 5.

33. The trade dollar used in the China trade (basically the Mexican peso) and the US dollar were at this time more or less of the same value; see Maria Alejandra Irigoin, 'A Trojan Horse in 19th Century China? The Global Consequences of the Breakdown of the Spanish Silver Peso Standard', at http://www.lse.ac.uk/collections/economicHistory/seminars/Irigoin.pdfwww.lse.ac.uk/collections/economicHistory/seminars/Irigoin.pdf.

34. See K. C. Liu, *Anglo-American Steamship Rivalry in China, 1862–1874* (Taipei: Rainbow Bridge Book Co., 1962), p. 51. The Haekwan tael, a 'virtual' accounting value used by the Imperial Chinese Maritime Customs, was worth US$1.45 at that time; see Man-houng Lin, *China Upside Down: Currency, Society, and Ideologies, 1808–1856* at www.fas.harvard.edu/~asiactr/publications/pdfs/Lin%20Front%20Matter.pdf, so a small, 'old' steamer of 456 tons cost US$45,000 in 1861 and a fairly new steamer in 1865 cost US$108,000. This suggests the 'anonymous American' story was a canard, the price cited was false or that Kellett and Lapraik were unbelievably credulous.

35. See Melvin Maddocks, *The Atlantic Crossing* (Alexandra, VA: Time-Life Books, 1981), p. 88.

36. *The Northern Star and National Trades' Journal* (Leeds, England), 3 April 1847.

37. *Hampshire Telegraph and Sussex Chronicle*, 13 February 1847.

38. *Liverpool Mercury*, 26 February 1847.

39. *Manchester Times and Gazette*, 26 February 1847.

40. Anon., *The Chinese Junk "Keying", being a full account of that vessel, with extracts from the journal of Capt. Kellett* (New York: Israel Sackett No. 1 Nassau Street, 1847), p. 4.

41. *Caledonian Mercury*, 22 March 1847; *Preston Guardian*, 27 March 1847; *Aberdeen Journal*, 31 March 1847; *Derby Mercury*, 31 March 1847. The dating suggests one source copied on.

42. A fair inference from the *New York Tribune* story.

43. *Description*, pp. 23–31.

44. The only *Keying* in the contemporary register was an American brig, built in Newburyport in 1845 for J. N. & W Cushing and working out of Boston almost certainly in the China trade. The Cushings had been prominent in the American China trade from the earliest years, the well-known John Perkins Cushing having been a founder member of Perkins and Co., which in 1827 consolidated with Russell and Co., for which Robert Bennett Forbes worked and whom we shall meet later in the story. From the papers in the Library of Congress of Caleb Cushing, America's first envoy to China, it is clear that J. N. Cushing was a relative (see Special Correspondence, 1817–1899, n.d., Box 144). The *Keying* remained on the register until 1874, having been sold in 1865 to R. W. Cameron of Sydney, Australia, and in 1870 to an unknown owner in Hamburg, Germany.

45. Bickers, *The Scramble for China*, p. 157. At the time of the incident, the *Arrow*'s registration had in fact expired. Ill-timed, given the very recently ended Crimean War and the close-to-simultaneous outbreak of major civil disturbance in India. See also Samuel Wells Williams, *A Chinese Commercial Guide, consisting of a collection of details and regulations respecting foreign trade with China, sailing directions, tables, etc.*, 4th ed. (Canton: The Chinese Repository, 1856), p. 244, where the form of the new 'Certificate of British Registry' is shown and is revelatory of the fairly casual approach to such matters at this date.

46. *Account*, p. 8.

47. There is a well-known lithograph, based on an original painting by George Chinnery, of Charles Gützlaff, the Pomeranian missionary and linguist dressed in disguise as a Fujianese mariner. If the portrait is accurate (for the heavily mustachioed Gützlaff looks like nothing so much as a character in an opera about Levantine piracy), then it seems unlikely any disguises contrived by Europeans would have been very convincing. No doubt with their characteristic generosity towards the odder conceits of Westerners and their fidelity to the terms of a deal they had agreed, the Chinese people involved in this charade went along with the 'these aren't Westerners' game to save everyone's face.

48. Paul A. van Dyke, *The Canton Trade: Life and Enterprise on the China Coast, 1700–1845* (Hong Kong: Hong Kong University Press, 2005), especially Chs. 1 and 2.

49. *Account*, p. 4: 'She was purchased . . . after she had returned from Cochin China, to which country she had carried some Mandarins of high rank.'

50. Van Dyke, *The Canton Trade*, pp. 145–50.

51. That this was not mere racist fantasy but possibly a rational prudence is evident from the tales of such crew takeovers of European-officered vessels in Grace Fox, *British Admirals and Chinese Pirates, 1832–1869* (London: Kegan Paul, 1940), and the 1855 story of the fate of Captain Rees of the Ningbo barque *Psyche*: 'At Changzhou the Singapore-born mate was seized and thrown overboard by the Chinese crew. As he surfaced and before making his way to shore, he saw Rees stabbed on deck, and his body dumped into the river down which it floated, his blood leaking steadily out into Chinese waters.' Bickers, *The Scramble for China*, pp. 133–4.

52. *Chunam* is an Anglo-Indian word; see H. Yule and A. C. Burnell, *Hobson-Jobson: The Anglo-Indian Dictionary* (London: Wordsworth 1999 [1886]), s.v., where, interestingly, the noun refers solely to powdered lime. In China coast use, it tends to refer to two things: a coarse plaster used to render slopes and outside surfaces (in *Hobson-Jobson*, this only appears in verbal form as the substance used when one 'chunams') and a composition for marine use made of oil, fibre and lime. In the Chinese case— the Chinese term *yóushíhuī* (油石灰) means '(tung) oil lime'—the compound used crushed, burned seashells, tung (or, as often, colza) oil and bamboo fibre. When used as a bottom treatment, *chunam* was made from just the lime and tung oil and is what gives the characteristic bluish-grey white colour to the bottoms of junks in Chinese export paintings of the eighteenth and nineteenth centuries.

53. *The Belfast News-Letter*, 26 May 1848.

54. Reported in the British *The Northern Star and National Trades' Journal*, 3 April 1847.

55. For their un-Chineseness see Davies, *Coasting Past*, op. cit., pp. 55–6.

56. The available cargo volume in the *Keying* was roughly 650 to 700 cubic metres. The volume of around 100 tonnes of stores and household goods, which are not very dense, would be between 160 and 180 cubic metres. Calculations like these are run-of-the-mill for ship's officers, utilizing known tables of what are called 'stowage factors', expressed in cubic metres per metric tonne. See Maritime Cargo Transport Conference, *Inland and Maritime Transportation of Unitized Cargo: A Comparative Economic Analysis of Break-Bulk and Unit Load Systems for Maritime General Cargo from Shipper to Consignee*, Publication 1135 (Washington: National Academy of Sciences/National Research Council, 1963), p. 6, and Appendix B, pp. 57–8.

57. The modern term is 壓載 (*yāzài*).

58. *The Illustrated London News*, 1 April 1848, p. 222.

Chapter 2 The Ship's Name

1. Paul van Dyke, personal communication. See also Paul van Dyke, *Merchants of Canton and Macao: Politics and Strategies in Eighteenth-Century Chinese Trade* (Hong Kong: Hong Kong University Press, 2011), Ch. 4.

2. Probably Tian Hou (天后), queen of heaven, and her two acolytes Shùnfēng'ěr (順風耳), 'Favourable wind ears', and Qiānlǐyǎn (千里眼), 'Thousand league eyes'.

3. Anon., *The Chinese Junk "Keying," being a full account of that Vessel, with extracts from the journal of Capt. Kellett* (New York: Israel Sackett No. 1 Nassau Street, 1847), p. 10.

4. Fang Chaoying in A. W. Hummel (ed.), *Eminent Chinese of the Ch'ing Period (1644–1912)* (Washington: Library of Congress, 1943), pp. 130–4, gives a different ancestry, tracing Qiying back to Nurhaci's brother, not Nurhaci himself. The vexed matter of romanizing Chinese now seems to have settled with hanyu pinyin—though even the use or not of diacritical marks is a moving feast—but that is an achievement only of the last twenty years or so. Qiying's name accordingly appears in a number of forms, depending on whom one is quoting; thus, *Qíyīng, Ch'i-ying, Kiying,* and *Keying.* In this work, we shall stick with *Qiying* for the person and *Keying* for the ship.

5. *The Belfast News-Letter,* 26 May 1848; Anon., *A Description of the Chinese Junk, "Keying",* printed for the proprietors of the junk and sold only on board (London: J. Such, 1848), p. 10.

6. I owe my understanding of the Chinese characters that appear in the *Description* to my one time colleagues Ms. Catalina Chor, Ms. Moody Tang, Ms. Phoebe Tong and Ms. Jamie Mak.

7. *Account,* p. 12.

8. J. K. Fairbank, *Trade and Diplomacy on the China Coast: The Opening of the Treaty Ports 1842–1854* (Cambridge, MA: Harvard University Press, 1964), pp. 92–3.

9. Robert Bickers, *The Scramble for China: Foreign Devils in the Qing Empire, 1832–1914* (London: Penguin Books, 2011), p. 110.

10. The majority view—there were dissenters like *The Times* of London, which labelled the British fleet 'this engine of evil'—is admirably summarized in Bickers, *The Scramble for China,* pp. 109–12. *The Times* quotation is from Bickers, p. 83, citing p. 4 of the 22 November 1842 issue.

11. Bickers, *The Scramble for China,* p. 110. He remained plain Frederick Pottinger and came to a sad end as a dismissed New South Wales policeman who accidentally shot himself in the stomach while boarding a stage-coach on his way to plead the justified and widely supported case against his dismissal; 'The late Sir Frederick Pottinger, Bart.', *Sydney and Sporting Chronicle,* 15 April 1865, p. 2.

12. M. Levien (ed.), *The Cree Journals: The Voyages of Edward H. Cree, Surgeon R.N., as Related in His Private Journals, 1837–1856* (Exeter: Webb & Bower, 1981), p. 122.

13. Ibid., pp. 122 and 176–7.

14. Fairbank, *Trade and Diplomacy on the China Coast,* p. 270, fn c.

15. Frederic Wakeman, Jr., *Strangers at the Gate: Social Disorder in South China 1839–1861* (Berkeley: University of California Press, 1966) is an excellent guide on Cantonese attitudes to Westerners, particularly the British.

16. Ibid., p. 113.

17. The references to Chinese culture in both *Account* and *Description* are uniformly belittling. The *Account*'s terse summary of Chinese culture is representative: 'Their histories are fables, their romances silly and pointless, their poems unintelligibly imaginative, and their drama, though representing nature, are revolting' (p. 11).

Chapter 3 The Crew and the Voyage to New York

1. William Shakespeare, *King Henry V*, Act IV, scene 3. This is Henry's laconic one-liner between his brilliant set piece 'We band of brothers' and 'Dying like men' speeches in the English camp before the Battle of Agincourt. For the relevance of this, see Richard W. Schoch, *Shakespeare's Victorian Stage: Performing History in the Theatre of Charles Kean* (Cambridge: Cambridge University Press, 1998), esp. pp. 10 and 46.

2. The documentation is hopelessly confused. The *Account* notes only (p. 7) that to sail the *Keying* 'takes 40 men'. The *Description* (p. 6) claims '30 natives and 12 English seamen, with the officers', various newspaper reports have fifty Chinese crew. Given that twenty-six were repatriated from New York and another group left the ship in Boston, a number like forty solves the problem of the crewing of the junk across the Atlantic. Were there only to have been thirty, and twenty-six left the ship in New York and more in Boston, then the question of who took the ship across the Atlantic becomes a problem, as does the provenance of the 'performers' who were the core of the display when the ship reached London.

3. John Dickie, *The British Consul: Heir to a Great Tradition* (New York: Columbia University Press, 2007), p. 85, 'At Whampoa, an outpost 12 miles from Canton where the British community comprised three shipwrights, two surgeons, a master mariner, a ship's chandler and a clerk, the Vice-Consul had to make do with a floating consulate berthed near some shacks locally known as Bamboo Town where sailors spent their time ashore.' The vice-consul at this time, c. 1846, was Alec Bird. See also Mrs H. Dwight Williams, *A Year in China and a Narrative of Capture and Imprisonment When Homeward Bound, on Board the Rebel Pirate Florida* (New York: Hurd & Houghton, 1864), Ch. 7. Explanations of why it was called Bambootown vary.

4. See Erastus C. Benedict, *The American Admiralty Law: Its Jurisdictions and Practice with Practical Forms and Directions* (New York: Banks, Gould & Co, 1850), appendix, Practical Forms, 'No. 96 Libel in rem by the seamen of a Chinese junk for wages, expenses, and passage money home', pp. 496–8.

5. *Caledonian Mercury* (Edinburgh, Scotland), 22 March 1847.

6. For a discussion of the traditional system of junk operation, see Koizumi Teizo, 'The Operation of Chinese Junks', in *The Evolution of Traditional Shipping in China*, edited by Mark Elvin, translated by Andrew Watson (Ann Arbor: Centre for Chinese Studies, University of Michigan, 1972).

7. This was still the practice in Hong Kong-crewed ships until the 1950s. Thereafter, following an ILO resolution, the Hong Kong government insisted on a 'Westernized' crewing system; Stephanie Zarach, *Changing Places: The Remarkable Story of the Hong Kong Shipowners* (Hong Kong: Hong Kong Shipowners' Association, 2007), p. 162.

8. This, like so many such terms from an almost exclusively oral tradition, is hard to pin down in modern Chinese.

9. Pronounced (and sometimes spelled) 'bosun'. It is the oldest title of rank in English speaking navies and in the twelfth century meant the ship's captain.

10. Vernon Young, 'Lingard's Folly: The Lost Subject', *The Kenyon Review* 15, no. 4 (Autumn 1953): 522–39.

11. Joseph Conrad, *The Rescue* (London: Penguin Books, 1985 [1920]), p. 22.

12. Ibid., p. 25.

13. Ibid., p. 33. *Malim* is an honorific in Malay and here refers to the chief mate, Shaw.

14. The source of the doubt is an op-ed piece in the Edinburgh-published *Caledonian Mercury*, 25 September 1851, citing information from 'our Victoria (Hong Kong) contemporary' that He Sing, far from being a mandarin, 'is . . . or rather was, a ship-painter in Whampoa reach'.

15. For example, the name does not appear on the extensive list at http://freepages.family. rootsweb.ancestry.com/~chinesesurname/x.html#X (accessed on 10 February 2013), nor in most lists of the nine surnames romanized as Xi.

16. We shall be considering the court case more fully in Pt. I, 'The Troubled Stay in New York'.

17. John Rogers Haddad (*The Romance of China: Excursions to China in U.S. Culture, 1776–1876*, New York: Columbia University Press, 2008) gives this information, citing variously the *Boston Daily Advertiser* (2 November 1847) for the American originator, *Niles National Register* (7 August 1847) for the price Kellett paid and *The Chinese Repository* (December 1846) for the details of the crew contracts, although the relevant issue seems only to note that the vessel left Hong Kong with about sixty crew, half Chinese and half European. Kellett's version is quoted as appearing in the *London Morning Chronicle* (n.d.) and reprinted in Holden's *Dollar Magazine* (April 1848).

18. Benedict, *American Admiralty Law*, p. 497, first allegation.

19. Probably today's Zhoushan (舟山).

20. Haddad, *Romance of China*.

21. See Henry Wise, *An Analysis of One Hundred Voyages to and from India, China, &c. performed by ships in the honourable East India Company's service; with remarks on the advantages of steam-power applied as an auxiliary aid to shipping; and suggestions for improving thereby the communication with India, via the Cape of Good Hope* (London: J. W. Norie & Co and W. H. Allen, 1839).

22. The 'Lascar Act', as this law was known, further entrenched a radical difference between 'lascar' and all other crew that had first been made law in 1814. The law of 1814 and its 1823 successor distinguished between seamen who were British citizens and lascars who were not. It is instructive that this act was not repealed until 1963.

23. See Jonathan S. Kitchen, *The Employment of Merchant Seamen* (London: Croom Helm, 1980), pp. 179–81.

24. See Rosina Visram, *Asians in Britain: 400 Years of History* (London: Pluto Press, 2002), Ch. 2. Visram's book is primarily about lascars from the subcontinent, but

the same rules generally applied to Southeast Asian and Chinese crew, who from the point of view of the law were also lascars.

25. On Hong Kong's contemporary Chinese population, see, for example, J. K. Fairbank, *Trade and Diplomacy on the China Coast: The Opening of the Treaty Ports 1842–1854* (Cambridge, MA: Harvard University Press, 1964), pp. 219–23, and E. J. Eitel, *Europe in China: The History of Hong Kong from the Beginning to the Year 1882* (Taipei: Cheng-Wen Publishing Co., 1968), p. 221 passim.

26. John M. Carroll, *Edge of Empires: Chinese Elites and British Colonials in Hong Kong* (Hong Kong: Hong Kong University Press, 2007), pp. 41–2, citing Robert Montgomery Martin (the colonial treasurer), Robert Fortune, Oswald Tiffany, the *Economist*, Rev. George Smith, Rev. Karl Gutzlaff and J. M. Tronson. See also Christopher Munn, *Anglo-China: Chinese People and British Rule in Hong Kong, 1841–1880* (Hong Kong: Hong Kong University Press, 2009), Ch. 2.

27. *Daily News*, London, 9 April 1849.

28. Basil Lubbock, *The Opium Clippers* (Glasgow: Brown, Son & Ferguson, 1933).

29. *Glasgow Herald*, 16 July 1847; *Hampshire Telegraph & Sussex Chronicle, etc.*, 10 July 1847; *Bristol Mercury*, 17 July 1847.

30. A nautical mile is 1,852 metres and equals one minute of arc of a meridian (or one minute of latitude). It is also known as a knot, after the old method of measuring a ship's speed using a timed, knotted log line. The number of knots in the line counted in 28 seconds was the ship's speed. Hence speed at sea is known as knots, or knots per hour, though that locution is thought today to be rather unnautical.

31. Northeast/northwest because as the northeast monsoon winds near the Equator, they weaken and begin backing northerly, eventually backing some 90 degrees by around 5 to 10°S to blow northwest.

32. A pilot (US) or routeing (UK) chart is a special chart for each month for a large sea area like the Indian Ocean or South Atlantic, divided into large, roughly 10,000-square-mile squares, within which are plotted the average wind speeds and directions that can be expected in that area during that month of the year. In Charles Kellett's day, these boons to the passage planner were just emerging, the product of the energy and vision of Lt. Matthew Maury. USN, whose first 'Wind and Current Chart for the North Atlantic' was produced in 1847.

33. Jose Maria Tey, *Hong Kong to Barcelona in the Junk* Rubia (London: Harrap, 1962), pp. 18–25. The claim of force ten winds is almost certainly over-egging the cake, possibly at the publisher's suggestion. Infamously, it was the publisher who required the 'spicing up' of John Caldwell's *The Desperate Voyage* (New York: Little Brown, 1949).

34. A hardwood from the dipterocarp *Hopea* species found throughout Southeast Asia and known as *yakal* in the Philippines and Hong Kong; see H. G. Richter and M. J. Dallwitz, 'Commercial Timbers: Descriptions, Illustrations, Identification, and Information Retrieval', Version: 4 May 2000, http://biodiversity.uno.edu/delta/; accessed on 10 February 2013.

35. Brian Clifford and Neil Illingworth, *The Voyage of the* Golden Lotus (London: Herbert Jenkins, 1962), Ch. 6.

36. We know this from the shipping intelligence column of *The Morning Chronicle* (London, England), 10 April 1847, which noted a sighting report from 25 December in or close to Selat Gelasa.

37. The actual title is a wonderful example of nineteenth-century book titling: *The India Directory, Directions for sailing to and from the East Indies, China, Australia, and the Interjacent Ports of Africa and South America: Compiled chiefly from original journals of the Honourable Company's ships, and from observations and remarks, resulting from the experience of twenty-one years in the navigation of those seas* (London: W. H. Allen & Co., 1843). Kellett would have used the second volume of the fifth edition.

38. One extant example, which may or may not have been typical, are the Yale Maps removed from a Chinese trading junk taken as prize in 1841 by HMS *Herald*. The maps are a navigational guide to the sailing routes from Korea to the Gulf of Thailand, comprising written instructions for each leg accompanied by a series of some 120 coastal views, showing each main turning point or waypoint. See Stephen Davies, 'The Yale Maps and Western Hydrography: Influences and Contributions', *Proceeding of the International Workshop on Maritime East Asia, 1433–1840; The Chinese Navigational Map at Yale University and Its Significance*, 16–18 June 2010, National Chiao-tung University, Hsinchu, Taiwan.

39. The traditional route most likely to have been taken by the *Keying* can be inferred from the Yale Maps.

40. *Account*, p. 9.

41. Nathaniel Bowditch, *The New American Practical Navigator*, 2nd ed. (New York: E. & M. Blunt, 1826), Ch. 24. This deals with the seven modern mathematical sailings, but before that, in the days of oral pilotage that characterized traditional Arab, Chinese and pre-fifteenth-century European navigation, what one might call vernacular sailings—lists of the courses and durations necessary to get from A to B to C—were common currency and taught by way of long, chanted lists. See, for example, the discussion in G. R. Tibbetts, *Arab Navigation in the Indian Ocean before the Coming of the Portuguese* (London: Oriental Translation Fund/Royal Asiatic Society, 1981), Pt. 3.

42. Stephen Davies and Elaine Morgan, *Cruising Guide to Southeast Asia*, vol. 2 (St. Ives: Imray, Laurie, Norie & Wilson, 1999), p. 177.

43. Ibid., p. 25. One notes also in the *Indonesia Pilot*, vol. 2 (Taunton: Hydrographer of the Navy, 1975), para. 2.3, p. 22: 'WSW winds in December, W winds in January, and WNW winds in February . . .' which further mentions the possibilities of rough seas if the wind is brisk and, in para 2.4, the existence from October to March of an adverse northeast-to-north current of 0.75 knots. *Ocean Passages for the World*, 4th ed. (Taunton: Hydrographer of the Navy, 1987), makes the point that traversing the Sunda Strait in this season is a tough beat to weather (para. 9. 49. 9, pp. 218–9).

44. *Account*, p. 13.

45. C. Northcote Parkinson, *Trade in the Eastern Seas, 1793–1813* (Cambridge: Cambridge University Press, 1937), Ch. 7. Parkinson implies that the average Indiaman on the return trip of a China run had around fifteen to twenty Chinese crewmen.

46. *Account*, p. 8.

47. The Hong Kong Maritime Museum possesses the copy log of the fourth mate.

48. See Davies and Morgan, *Cruising Guide to Southeast Asia*, pp. 45–6.

49. See H. Whittingham and C. T. King, *Reed's Table of Distances between Ports and Places in All Parts of the World*, 11th ed. (Sunderland: Thomas Reed, 1929), p. 87.

50. Ibid., p. 177.

51. *Description*, p. 8.

52. See the relevant pilot chart for the Indian Ocean in March at http://www.nga.mil/ MSISiteContent/ StaticFiles/NAV_PUBS/APC/Pub109/109mar.pdf; accessed on 10 February 2013, which shows an average of force 4 winds east or southeast for 50–60 percent of the time. The same chart shows that very light and variable winds with 8 percent calms would have been likely from the exit of the Sunda Strait to the established trades, which were some 480 miles away, or ten days at 2 knots.

53. *Glasgow Herald*, 16 July 1847.

54. *Description*, p. 8.

55. Adrian Hayter, Sheila *in the Wind* (London: Hodder & Stoughton, 1959).

56. See http://www.rawlins.org/mormontrail/rbodily.html for the history of the Bodily family, which arrived in Cape Town in 1846. See also Nigel Worden, Elizabeth van Heyningen and Vivian Bickford-Smith, *Cape Town: The Making of a City* (Cape Town: David Philip, 1998), pp. 164–5, which notes that in 1839, 532 ships called— ten a week, not allowing for seasonal variations—and more were calling each year, to reach 600 by 1860. Thirty percent of these were replenishment calls by ships carrying emigrants and Indian and Chinese indentured labour, or coolies.

57. See Melanie Yap, Dianne Leong Man, *Colour, Confusion and Concessions: The History of the Chinese in South Africa* (Hong Kong: Hong Kong University Press, 1996), Ch. 1. Yap and Leong Man give no precise figures, but by inference the Chinese community in 1847 was probably two or three dozen.

58. Fifteen years later, tea clippers were making runs from China to London in record times of around 90 days, 88 days being the quickest. Most clippers averaged 100 to 110 days for the trip. The distance was around 15,000 miles, so the fastest clippers were averaging 7 knots and the middling performers a bit under 6.

59. *Description*, p. 8.

60. See http://www.mastergardenproducts.com/tungoil.htm for the properties of the oil. For the reference to the skin complaint, see C. H. S. Tupholme, 'Dermatitis from Tung Oil', *British Journal of Dermatology* 51, no. 3 (1939): 138–40, and more generally http://bodd.cf.ac.uk/BotDermFolder/BotDermE/EUPH-16.html. For the properties of lime, see Mel M. Schwartz, *Encyclopedia of Materials, Parts and Finishes*, 2nd ed. (Boca Raton, FL: CRC Press, 2002), at http://books.google.com/books ?id=aUJ5fVAVPfAC&pg=PA84&lpg=PA84&dq=is+lime+from+crushed+shells+

poisonous&source=web&ots=V3r3i93aPs&sig=QK0dJh_JgVE7kIShD4b3rDqEie
s&hl=en&sa=X&oi=book_result&resnum=3&ct=result; both sites accessed on 6
December 2011.

61. Whether covering the bottom of ships with copper to protect them is yet another
    Chinese technological first, leaving the late eighteenth-century European examples
    as johnny-come-latelies will probably never be decided. The evidence for Chinese
    precedence in the fourth century given by Needham (Joseph Needham et al.
    Science and Civilization in China, vol. 4: *Physics and Physical Technology* [Cambridge:
    Cambridge University Press: 1971], pp. 665 and 697) is at best extremely equivocal;
    if such was the case, it does not seem to have resulted in an established practice. The
    Keying was certainly not so protected.

62. See Kuno Knöbl, *Tai Ki: To the Point of No Return* (Boston: Little Brown, 1976), pp.
    202–4, for the description of the discovery of the problem and the traditional use of
    tung oil. Much the same point is made in G. R. G. Worcester, *Junks and Sampans of
    the Yangtze* (Annapolis, MD: Naval Institute Press, 1971), p. 36, though he is careful
    to add that this is a practice of river (fresh and brackish water) craft, not sea-going
    junks.

63. See Needham, *Science and Civilization in China*, vol. 4: *Physics and Physical
    Technology*. Western ships generally had a third line of protection beneath the fail-
    safe—a backing of tar and horsehair onto which the outer layer of planking was
    nailed (for a description of a recovered wreck that was so constructed, see J. Richard
    Steffy, *Wooden Shipbuilding and the Interpretation of Shipwrecks* [College Station:
    Texas A&M University Press, 1994], p. 156, where he discusses the wreck of the
    British-built HMS *Dartmouth*, which was built in 1655 and sank in 1690).

64. In his fascinating study of traditional Arab craft, Clifford Hawkins well describes
    the regular cleaning of the ship's bottom and refreshing the *chunam* (in Swahili,
    shahamu). There is no question of antifouling. See Clifford Hawkins, *The Dhow:
    An Illustrated History of the Dhow and Its World* (Lymington: Nautical Publishing,
    1977), p. 87, and especially the illustrations on pp. 34 and 56.

65. See C. R. Southwell and J. D. Bultman, 'Marine Borer Resistance of Untreated
    Woods over Long Periods of Immersion in Tropical Waters', *Biotropica* 3, no. 1
    (June 1971): 81–107. This and many other sources make the point that the resist-
    ance of teak to marine borers is far less than popular anecdote would suggest, and
    that no reliance should be placed on a teak-built hull as itself able to resist attack
    without adequate protection. See also J. R McNeill, 'Woods and Warfare in World
    History', *Environmental History* 9, no. 3 (2004), where the superiority of the resist-
    ance of Cuban cedar is mentioned at http://www.historycooperative.org/ journals/
    eh/9.3/mcneill.html; accessed on 3 March 2011.

66. When the author left on a 50,000-mile odyssey at sea in a small yacht, his partner,
    who wore contact lenses, was advised by a biochemist friend that once well off-
    shore, seawater was sufficiently devoid of organic life to work, untreated, as a per-
    fectly healthy saline solution! She took the advice and never suffered any adverse
    consequences.

67. Load lines for ships—their 'marks'—date from the British Merchant Shipping Act of 1876, which created the famous Plimsoll Line after the name of the member of parliament who had fought hard for the law. Interestingly, the actual position of the line on the hull was not fixed by law until almost twenty years later in 1894; see http://www.imo.org/TCD/mainframe.asp?topic_id=1034.
68. A wave is an undulation in the water surface occasioned by winds locally and experienced locally. A swell, by contrast, is defined as an undulation in the water surface caused either by winds that are no longer blowing or by winds remote from where the swell is being felt.
69. *Description*, p. 8.
70. See Lawrence V. Mott, *The Development of the Rudder: A Technological Tale* (London: Chatham Publishing / College Station: Texas A&M University Press, 1997), p. 121, for evidence of what may have been a centerline rudder in ancient Egypt.
71. See Mott, *Development of the Rudder*, Ch. 7 and passim.
72. *Description*, p. 17.
73. *Description*, p. 16, and also *The Belfast News-Letter*, 26 May 1848.
74. It is often claimed that it took the best part of 800 years for the West to catch up, the first balanced sternpost rudders not appearing until HMS *Bellerophon* in 1865. As Mott (*Development of the Rudder*, Ch. 3) points out, Greek and Roman quarter-oars used both balanced and semi-balanced designs.
75. See Dave Gerr, *Boat Mechanical Systems Handbook: How to Design, Install, and Recognize Proper Systems in Boats* (Camden, ME: International Marine/Ragged Mountain Press, 2008), p. 200.
76. *The Belfast News-Letter*, 26 May 1848; *Description*, p. 17.
77. An excellent discussion of all of these issues, with a full technical analysis, can be found in C. A. Marchaj, *Seaworthiness: The Forgotten Factor* (London: Adlard Coles, 1986), especially Chs. 8 and 10.
78. This is particularly true in the tropics when, on moonless nights, a strong squall can overtake one in the darkness with frightening suddenness. With too much sail up, all hell breaks loose. Indiamen were notorious for the conservative way in which they were sailed, reputed always to reduce canvas at night, although Jean Sutton quite rightly argues that this was no iron-fast rule, many an Indiaman's captain being quite prepared to press on if there was money to be made from a swift passage; see Jean Sutton, *Lords of the East* (London: Conway Maritime, 1981), pp. 94–5.
79. This is obviously conjecture, but a review of the list of ships calling in the port of Hong Kong between August 1841 and January 1843, compiled by M. Forth-Rouen, the French consul in Canton, from the harbour-master's reports and appearing in his letter book, now in the Ministry of Foreign Affairs archives in Paris, reveals some 80 percent were carrying opium; see Stephen Davies, *French Ships, Friendship* (Hong Kong: Hong Kong Maritime Museum, 2008), p. 35. This remained the main cargo until the restrictions on interport trade in China imposed by the 1843 Treaty of the Bogue were lifted, following the Second Opium War in 1856–60. One does not know who Charles Kellett sailed with before he became a partner in the *Keying*

project and the ship's captain, but his career is highly unlikely not to have involved the carriage of opium. Frank Walsh quotes *The Economist* of 8 March 1851, noting, 'The island (Hong Kong) is a kind of bonded ware house . . . for the opium trade', in the context of a larger comment on the absence of any significant growth in trade in Hong Kong's first decade of existence; Frank Walsh, *A History of Hong Kong*, revised ed. (London: HarperCollins, 1997), p. 197.

80. The Howland and Aspinwall-owned, John Willis Griffiths-designed *Rainbow*, the first 'extreme clipper', had been built by Smith and Dimon of New York and launched in 1845. See D. R. MacGregor, *Fast Sailing Ships: Their Design and Construction, 1775–1875*, 2nd ed. (London: Conway Maritime Press, 1988), p. 124.

81. The basic text is John H. Harland's brilliant *Seamanship in the Age of Sail: An Account of Shiphandling of the Sailing Man-of-War, 1600–1860* (London: Brassey, 1982); for how close to the wind a square-rigger could sail, see pp. 62–6.

82. See Stephen Davies, *Coasting Past: The Last South China Coastal Trading Junks Photographed by William Heering* (Hong Kong: Hong Kong Maritime Museum, 2013), pp. 35–64.

83. Walsh, *A History of Hong Kong*, pp. 595–9.

84. This says that the direction of the apparent wind acting on a sail twists away from the direction of the wind at sea level progressively with height, as the true wind speed increases with the decrease in surface friction. It follows that a sail must twist away to leeward progressively from deck to masthead level, in order to have the same angle of incidence and thus work as an aerofoil.

85. G. R. G. Worcester, *Sail and Sweep in China: The History and Development of the Chinese Junk as Illustrated by the Collection of Models in the Science Museum* (London: HMSO, 1966), p. 20.

86. Worcester, *Junks and Sampans of the Yangtze*, p. 86.

87. See C. A. Marchaj, *The Aero-hydrodynamics of Sailing*, 3rd revised ed. (London: Adlard Coles Nautical, 2000).

88. *Account*, p. 4: '[The *Keying*] possesses the combined qualities of a Trader and a vessel of War.'

89. Captain Nelson Liu, personal communication.

90. This is a rather interesting figure. 'A census in 1851 showed a total of 6,914 inhabitants living on the island' (http://en.wikipedia.org/wiki/Saint_Helena).

91. Yap and Man Leung (*Colour, Confusion and Concessions*, p. 13) indicate that, by around 1830, there may have been up to 200 Chinese residents. As of 1834, with St. Helena becoming a British colony as opposed to an East India Company possession, it became official policy to send the Chinese residents to Cape Town. By 1847, only a handful appears to have been left. The last Chinese resident died in 1875.

92. The letter was reprinted in the *Caledonian Mercury*, 17 February 1848. The *Penelope* was originally a sailing frigate launched in 1829. She was converted to a paddler at Chatham in 1832, by lengthening with a 63' 4" new mid-section; Lyon & Winfield, op. cit., pp. 152–3. At this date, the *Penelope* was commanded by Captain Henry

Wells Giffard, RN, and was nominally the flagship of Commodore Charles Hotham, commander-in-chief of the west coast of Africa.

93. British and American maritime law were not at this point greatly different, so what can be found in George Ticknor Curtis, *A Treatise on the Rights and Duties of Merchant Seamen according to the General Maritime Law and the Statutes of the United States* (Boston: Little and Brown, 1841), is germane and informs what follows above.

94. Ibid., Ch. 2, p. 11.

95. Ibid., p. 12.

96. Ibid., pp. 24–5.

97. *Caledonian Mercury*, 17 February 1848.

98. *Description*, p. 7. A composite chart from the United Kingdom Hydrographic Office Archive, created by an enthusiast to show the gripping Great Tea Race of 1865, when five crack clippers raced to be the first to London from Foochow, shows all five ships crossing the line in around 22˚W, though this was in August, not May. A copy of the chart is part of the HKMM collection. *Ocean Passages for the World* (p. 191) recommends crossing the Line in 25˚W to 30˚W.

99. Letter from Kellett to Queen Victoria, Boston, 14.1.1848 in *Caledonian Mercury*, Edinburgh, 17.2.1848.

100. That means, for example, pulling a halyard in a bit or easing it out to change the location of chafe points and reduce topical wear. This distributes wear and tear, extends the life of cordage and mitigates the chaos and danger of ropes parting.

101. In the British system, these more competent sailors were known as 'able seamen', whose experience had shown them able to 'hand, reef and steer'—that is, handle at deck level the ropes vital for swiftly and safely trimming, furling or reefing sails, to go aloft and reef or shake the reefs out of sails, and to steer the ship. Other seamen were boys (in effect, apprentices, though in the British merchant marine only future officers did a formal apprenticeship) or ordinary seamen, who did routine maintenance, kept a lookout and performed other tasks, including going aloft, under supervision. See Peter Kemp, *The Oxford Companion to Ships and the Sea* (Oxford: Oxford University Press, 1976), pp. 1, 373, 695–6 and 831.

102. Strictly, into seven four-hour periods and two two-hour periods known as the 'dog watches', from 1600–1800 and 1800–2000, which were intended to avoid the monotony of always standing the same watch, and had been in use since the seventeenth century. It is not clear how far the more elaborate system was used aboard run-of-the-mill small vessels like the *Keying*.

103. See Derek Lundy, *The Way of a Ship: A Square-rigger Voyage in the Last Days of Sail* (London: Ecco Press, 2004). The basic text on crew work is Harland, *Seamanship in the Age of Sail*.

104. I am indebted to Endymion Wilkinson's *Chinese History: A Manual*, revised and enlarged edition (Cambridge, MA: Harvard University Asia Center, 2000), Ch. 6, pp. 198–219. He was a sure guide through the labyrinth.

105. *Glasgow Herald*, 9 August 1847. A 'sectional dock' is a form of floating dock; by 1847, New York had several. Two are specifically mentioned in H. Johnson and F. S. Lightfoot, *Maritime New York in Nineteenth-Century Photographs* (New York: Dover Publications, 1980), p. 80, one south of Pier 41 and the other at Pike Street. J. H. Morrison (*History of the New York Shipyards*, New York: Wm. F. Sametz, 1909, p. 61) notes, 'The New York Sectional Dock Company had built a sectional dock from the plans of Phineas Burgess and Daniel Dodge in 1839 . . . This dock was located in the vicinity of the other floating docks on the East River.'

106. *Description*, p. 19.

107. *Account*, p. 10.

108. Some of the newspaper reports of the junk's arrival in New York attributed its arrival there to navigational error (see *Glasgow Herald*, 9 August 1847; *Preston Guardian*, 14 August 1847). There is no clue why this conclusion should have been jumped to, so astonishing an error being impossible unless the navigator was not so much inexperienced as completely ignorant; nothing in the ship's voyage thus far suggests anything but solid competence on Captain Kellett's part.

109. *The Morning Chronicle*, 23 July 1847; *Caledonian Mercury*, 26 July 1847; *The Aberdeen Journal*, 28 July 1847. H. H. Brindley ('The Keying', *The Mariner's Mirror* 8, no. 4 [1922]: 305–14) summarizes some of these reports. The *Hampshire Telegraph and Sussex Chronicle etc.*, 24 July 1847, has a vague report of the *Keying* near Bermuda and a speculation that she may have harboured there—a telling example of the extreme uncertainties as to the whereabouts of shipping in the mid-nineteenth century.

110. Charles Wheeler, 'A Monk's Tale: A Chinese Memoir of a Sea Passage to Vietnam in the Seventeenth Century', unpublished, p. 44, made available by Dr. Wheeler and quoted with his permission.

111. Ibid., p. 191.

112. See http://www.nga.mil/MSISiteContent/StaticFiles/NAV_PUBS/APC/ Pub106/106jun.pdf for the June North Atlantic pilot chart showing this.

113. Admiral Smyth tersely defines this as a wind 'which serves either way; allowing a passage to be made without much nautical ability'. Admiral W. H. Smyth, *The Sailor's Word-book: An alphabetical digest of nautical terms, including some more especially military and scientific, but useful to seamen; as well as archaisms of early voyagers, etc.* (London: Blackie and Son, 1867).

114. What are called sailing directions, which had been published to cover more of the world's waters in ever-increasing detail since the first examples in the fifteenth century, the practice accelerating rapidly from the end of the eighteenth century on.

115. *Description*, p. 8, and Kellett's letter to Queen Victoria, 'To Her Most Excellent Majesty the Queen', reprinted in *Caledonian Mercury*, 17 February 1848 (but dated by Kellett 14 January 1848, Boston). The definition of this mishap is: 'SPRING, a crack or breach running transversely or obliquely through any part of a mast or yard, so as to render it unsafe to carry the usual quantity of sail thereon'; William Falconer, *An Universal Dictionary of the Marine* (London: Cadell, 1780).

116. *Ocean Passages for the World*, p. 192.

117. Details from Kellett's letter 'To Her Most Excellent Majesty the Queen'.
118. This is about the longest passage faced by any junk on the traditional seaways of the trades from China; it would have been from a port on the southern part of the west coast of India—Calicut or Cochin—to one of the ports on the south coast of the Yemen (about 1,700 nautical miles) or directly across the Arabian Sea to somewhere in modern Kenya (about 2,000 nautical miles) that we know from the record were seldom followed by Chinese vessels after the early fifteenth century. Most routes were a great deal shorter, being under 1,000 nautical miles and, even at the *Keying*'s speed, likely to involve less than two weeks at sea.
119. Kenneth J. Carpenter, *The History of Scurvy and Vitamin C* (Cambridge: Cambridge University Press, 1986).
120. M. Torck, 'The Issue of Food Provision and Scurvy in East and West: A Comparative Enquiry into Medieval Knowledge of Provisioning, Medicine and Seafaring History', in *East Asian Maritime History I: Trade and Transfer across the East Asian "Mediterranean"*, edited by A. Schottenhammer et al. (Wiesbaden: Harassowitz Verlag, 2005), pp. 275–88. That Chinese mariners may in fact have been more disposed to the dangers of scurvy genetically is the conclusion of J. R. Delanghe, M. R. Langlois, M. L. de Buyzhere and M. A. Torck, 'Vitamin C Deficiency and Scurvy Are Not Only a Dietary Problem but Are Codetermined by the Haptoglobin Polymorphism', *Clinical Chemistry* 53, no. 8 (2007): 1397–1400.

Chapter 4 The Troubled Stay in New York

1. Erving Goffman, *Asylums: Essays on the Social Situation of Mental Patients and Other Inmates* (Garden City, NY: Anchor Books, 1961) is the *locus classicus*, especially 'On the characteristics of total institutions' (pp. 3–124), including ships specifically on page 45. In the introduction, Goffman describes the 'total institution' as 'a place of residence and work, where a large number of like-situated individuals, cut off from the wider society for an appreciable period of time, together lead an enclosed, formally administered round of life'.
2. The original forms the opening sentence of *Anna Karenina*.
3. The first lightship had been stationed off Sandy Hook in 1823 but removed in 1829 because of the construction of the Navesink Twin Lights. In 1838, a new lightship was placed on station, still apparently called Sandy Hook, the name 'Ambrose lightship' not being used until a new lightship further north at the entrance to the Ambrose Channel was installed in 1852. It follows that, when the *Keying* arrived in New York, the navigational aids available to guide her in had yet to be perfected; see George R. Putnam, *Lighthouses and Lightships of the United States* (New York: Houghton-Mifflin, 1917).
4. One has to wonder whether a thoughtful American skipper was conscious of the different attitudes of the antebellum South and considered Charleston likely to be a less welcoming port of call to a largely Chinese-crewed junk than more cosmopolitan New York.

5. See http://www.nps.gov/history/NR/twhp/wwwlps/lessons/131lighthouse/131 facts1.htm.

6. See http://njscuba.net/sites/index.html. The site has many detailed charts showing the density of wrecks. These are even more striking when one realizes that, for every wreck charted, there are possibly fifteen or twenty more that are not charted or have not yet been identified.

7. See http://www.uscg.mil/history/articles/CGNorthAtlantic.pdf. The historical service of the US Coastguard is exemplary.

8. Edmund M. Blunt, *The American Coast Pilot: containing directions for the principal harbors, capes and headlands, of the coasts of North and South America: describing the soundings, bearing or the lighthouses and beacons from the rocks, shoals and ledges, &c. with the prevailing winds, setting of the currents, &c and the latitudes and longitudes of the principal harbors and capes, together with a tide table*, 14th ed. (New York: Edward and George Blunt, 1842). Sailors are wont to be superstitious, so there was no thirteenth edition.

9. Delightfully, Blunt calls it Neversink.

10. Blunt, *The American Coast Pilot*, p. 213.

11. See http://www.uscg.mil/history/weblighthouses/LHNJ.asp. The light was improved in 1857.

12. Edward L. Allen (ed.), *Pilot Lore: From Sail to Steam and Historical Sketches of the Various Interests Identified with the Development of the World's Greatest Port* (New York: National Service Bureau, Sandy Hook Pilots Benevolent Association, 1922). The book begins with a list of the fifty-one pilots who lost their lives on service, 1852–1922.

13. Ibid., p. 6.

14. Ibid., p. 9.

15. John Kuo Wei Tchen, *New York before Chinatown: Orientalism and the Shaping of American Culture, 1776–1882* (Baltimore: Johns Hopkins University Press, 2001), p. 63.

16. *The Illustrated London News*, 1 April 1848, p. 222.

17. See the Museum of the City of New York's website for a photographic reproduction.

18. One of P. T. Barnum's good friends was Nathaniel Currier, the maker of what is probably the most realistic print of the *Keying*; see www.oldprintshop.com/artists/currier-ives-nat.htm. If there is any truth to the claim that Barnum had a replica junk created in order to offer one of his raree shows, then Currier's careful draftsmanship may have served the role of a useful database.

19. Kellett's letter to Queen Victoria.

20. John Rogers Haddad, *The Romance of China: Excursions to China in U.S. Culture, 1776–1876* (New York: Columbia University Press, 2008).

21. The Economic History website (http://eh.net/hmit/) offers five different comparators. On the most indicative of these, if the claimed visitor numbers are correct, the showing made around US$700 million in today's dollars. Equally, given that the population of New York City in 1847 was between 371,223 and 515,547 (Ira

Rosenwaike, *Population History of New York City*, Syracuse NY: Syracuse University Press, 1972, p. 36, Table 6), to suppose 480,000 people visited the *Keying* over four months is to suppose nearly 100 percent of the city's inhabitants were rowed out to the anchored vessel. Both analyses suggest the visitor figures were exaggerated.

22. Samuel Wells Williams (1812–84) had a long relationship with China, with Western inroads there and in his early days—he first arrived in Canton in 1833—with mission activity. In 1845–47, he was back in the United States, during which time he married Sarah Walworth and played a leading role in the *Keying* affair. The following year, he returned to Hong Kong and became the editor of the then leading news source, *The Chinese Repository*. He was closely involved in attempts to open up trade with Japan, beginning with a trip on the ship *Morrison* in 1837. In 1853, two years after he left the editorship of *The Chinese Repository*, he became Commodore Perry's official interpreter. In 1855, he became the secretary of the American Legation in China, playing a key role in negotiating the 'unequal' Treaty of Tientsin, then spending fifteen years as America's chargé d'affaires in Beijing. Following his resignation in 1875, in 1877 he became the first professor of Chinese language and Chinese literature at Yale University.

23. Numbers from Tchen, *New York before Chinatown*, p. 64.

24. Hadded, *The Romance of China*.

25. *Caledonian Mercury*, 21 October 1847.

26. Haddad, *The Romance of China*, citing *New York Herald* (4 August 1847).

27. W. Daniel Lord (1794–1868), a graduate of Yale, was admitted to the New York bar in 1817 and established the firm of Lord, Day and Lord with his son Daniel de Forest Lord and his son-in-law Henry Day in 1845; *Obituary Record of Graduates of Yale College Deceased during the Academical Year Ending in July, 1868 including the record of a few who died a short time previous, hitherto unreported* (New Haven: Yale College Alumni, 1868), p. 267. On 26 September 1849, Richard Henry Dana called on W. Daniel Lord in New York, which, given Dana's championing of seamen's rights, suggests that Lord was broadly of the same views and explains the eagerness with which he took up the *Keying* case.

28. There is a single document, called the Ship's Articles, which is a pre-printed form with blanks for the captain to fill in as indicated in the text.

29. Michael C. Lazich, 'American Missionaries and the Opium Trade in Nineteenth-century China', *Journal of World History* 17, no. 2 (2006): 52. http://www.history cooperative.org/cgi-bin/justtp.chi?act=justtop&url=http://historycooperative. org/journals/jwh/17.2/lazich.html; accessed on 26 June 2012. See also Haddad, *The Romance of China*, Ch. 6.

30. 'There were plenty of Anglophobic American officials and traders in China . . .'; Robert Bickers, *The Scramble for China: Foreign Devils in the Qing Empire, 1832–1914* (London: Penguin Books, 2011), p. 173, citing Eldon Griffin, *Clippers and Consuls: American Consular and Commercial Relations with Eastern Asia, 1845–1860* (Ann Arbor: Edwards Bros., 1939), pp. 180–2. Haddad, *The Romance of China*, Ch. 6, which is *inter alia* an essay on Williams, can be read as showing that Williams had

no admiration for the British other than as contingent agents of essential change to China.

31. Tchen, *New York before Chinatown*, p. 67.

32. Ibid., pp. 67–8.

33. The crew were fortunate in having Samuel Wells Williams as their interpreter. He saw in Kellett a duplicitous and brutal captain, as he noted in his letters to his fiancé Sarah Walworth; Haddad, *The Romance of China*, Ch. 6.

34. Richard Henry Dana, *The Seaman's Friend* (New York: Scribner, 1841).

35. Library of Congress, http://memory.loc.gov/cgi-bin/ampage?collId=llsb&fileName=026/llsb026.db&recNum=1563; accessed on 13 May 2009.

36. Samuel Wells Williams, *The Middle Kingdom: A Survey of the Geography, Government, Education, Social Life, Arts, Religion &c. of the Chinese Empire and Its Inhabitants, with a new map of the Empire* (New York: Wiley & Putnam, 1848), vol. 1, pp. 544–5, author's emphasis.

37. *Hampshire Telegraph and Sussex Chronicle*, 16 October 1847; *The Era* (London), 17 October 1847; *The Globe*, 8 July 1847.

38. See http://library.mysticseaport.org/initiative/PageImage.cfm?PageNum=2&BibID=28969, accessed on 22 April 2013. Letters in italics written in manuscript, the rest printed.

39. Erastus C. Benedict, *The American Admiralty Law: Its Jurisdictions and Practice with Practical Forms and Directions* (New York: Banks, Gould & Co., 1850), seventh pleading. One crewman was paid US$11 a month, two US$9, eleven US$8, and thirteen US$6. This actually works out at US$7.50 each a month on average.

40. The US dollar to pound sterling exchange rate in 1848 was US$4.87 = £1; a steerage passage from Melbourne to New York was about £38, so a fare from New York to Hong Kong/Canton would have cost between US$110 and US$200, at the lower end if a practice like the later 'Asiatic steerage' applied.

41. *American Lloyd's Register of American and Foreign Shipping*, 1864, has a two-deck bark, *Candace*, 398 tons, 117' long, 27' beam, built in 1845 in Warren, RI, master A. Schau, home ported in Altona, Hamburg and owned by J. C. D. Dreyer, a company involved in the West Indies trade 1800–1850. Early Lloyd's lists, British or American, are not always reliable as to details of ownership, since the transmission of intelligence before the electric telegraph was patchy. Haddad cites 'Sailing of the Chinese Sailors, belonging to the Cochin China Junk', *The American Magazine*, 13 November 1847, for the details. That the article refers to a Cochinchina junk (i.e., a junk from Vietnam) is a curious detail, adding further mystery to the *Keying's* provenance.

42. *New York Tribune*, 8 September 1847, Law Courts, United States District Court, The Chinese Junk.

43. *Journal of the House of Representatives*, 22 December 1848, p. 144. http://memory/loc.gov/ammem/amlaw/lwcr.html and http://www.gpo.gov/fdays/browse/collection.action? collectionCode=CREC.

44. *Journal of the Senate*, 26 December 1848, pp. 83–4 and 91 from the same electronic source.

45. Ibid., 30th Congress, 4th Session, H.R. 368 [Report No. 416], 28 March 1848.

46. For what follows, I am severally indebted to Mark Elvin (ed.), *Transport in Transition: The Evolution of Traditional Shipping in China*, translated by Andrew Watson (Ann Arbor: Centre for Chinese Studies, University of Michigan, 1972); Hans van Tilburg, *Chinese Junks on the Pacific: Views from a Different Deck* (Gainesville: University Press of Florida, 2007); and K. F. Gützlaff, *Journal of Three Voyages along the Coast of China in 1831, 1832, and 1833* (New York: J. P. Haven, 1833), p. 95, and Jennifer Cushman, *Fields from the Sea, Chinese Junk Trade with Siam during the Late Eighteenth and Early Nineteenth Centuries* (Ithaca, NY: Cornell University SEAP, 1993), especially Ch. 3.

47. Roughly the first four were officers: owner-cum-administrative captain-cum-super-cargo, sailing master-cum-navigator-cum-mate, purser-cum-mate-cum-captain's secretary, loadmaster-cum-bosun, cox'n-cum-quartermaster; the second group were petty officers: first and second anchor boss, chief mainsail haul, Nos. 1, 2 and 3 halyard easers, ship's husband-cum-carpenter, the armourer-cum-blacksmith, the ship's chaplain-cum-chronometer tankie, as it were, and then came the customarily and, it seems, ubiquitously lumpen world of the deckhand. These roles—by no means common to every Chinese ship, though fairly normal to oceangoing ships in the *nanyang* trades—can be found well differentiated, though as we shall note without any clear grasp of how they worked together, in Cushman, *Fields from the Sea*, pp. 100–5, and, particularly for northern China, in the essays by Japanese researchers of the 1930s and 1940s in Elvin (ed.), *Transport in Transition*.

48. It is usually translated as 'helmsman', but this fails to grasp the larger sense of the role unless we recall Mao Zedong's sobriquet of Great Helmsman.

49. Wells Williams, *The Middle Kingdom*, vol. 2, Ch. 8.

50. Tchen, *New York before Chinatown*, p. 70.

51. It is interesting to note in this regard that in George Ticknor Curtis, *A Treatise on the Rights and Duties of Merchant Seamen according to the General Maritime Law and the Statutes of the United States* (Boston: Little and Brown, 1841), p. 13, any such arrangements in European law would have rendered the seamen partners in the entire voyage. While this appears not have been at all uncommon in medieval European maritime trade, by the nineteenth century, bar perhaps in coastal shipping, it was evidently very unusual; only in some European civil law jurisdictions did it confer on the seamen the full and normal rights of a partner.

52. Wells Williams's outrage is extremely well conveyed in Haddad, *The Romance of China*, Ch. 6.

Chapter 5 The Final Leg—Towards Journey's End

1. Edmund M. Blunt, *The American Coast Pilot*, 14th ed. (New York: Edward and George Blunt, 1842), pp. 166–207.

2. The useful shortcut of the Cape Cod Canal would not be possible until 1914, when the New York financier August Belmont had the first, narrow and shallow channel dug.

3. See K. C. Liu, *Anglo-American Steamship Rivalry in China, 1862–1874* (Taipei: Rainbow Bridge Book Co., 1962) and the excellent *Steamboats on the Hudson: An American Saga*, hosted by the New York State Libraries at http://www.nysl.nysed. gov/mssc/steamboats/toc.htm.

4. For an excellent evocation of the world of the 1840s New York waterfront, see Melvin Maddocks, *The Atlantic Crossing* (Alexandria, VA: Time-Life Books, 1981), Ch. 3 and Barbara La Rocco (ed.), *A Maritime History of New York* (New York: Going Coastal, 2004) in general, but especially Ch. 8.

5. John Rogers Haddad, *The Romance of China: Excursions to China in U.S. Culture, 1776–1876* (New York: Columbia University Press, 2008), Ch. 5, noting the comparative isolation of Afong Moy, New York's first resident Chinese woman. Jack Chen (*The Chinese of America*, New York: Harper Row, 1980, p. 5) mentions no significant Chinese presence in New York by 1847; the statistics in Susan B. Carter, 'Embracing Isolation: Chinese American Migration to Small-Town America, 1882–1943', draft paper proposed for the 36th Annual Meeting of the Population Association of America, San Francisco, CA, 3–5 May 2012 (http://paa2012.prince-ton.edu/papers/121668; accessed on 11 March 2013), esp. Table 3, shows that for all of the United States by 1850 there were but 671 Chinese males of average age 24.

6. Yung Wing, *My Life in China and America* (New York: Henry Holt & Co., 1909), pp. 21–4.

7. Arnold J. Meagher, *The Coolie Trade: The Traffic in Chinese Laborers to Latin America* (New York: XLibris, 2008).

8. At this stage in history, weather was very ill understood and data scarce. Matthew Fontaine Maury's path-breaking work compiling digests of ships' logs, which would result in the first pilot charts summarizing average wind and currents, had only just begun. In Blunt, *The American Coast Pilot*, for example, there is nothing helpful at all offered about average seasonal weather on the US coast. For the data given here, see http://www.ndbc.noaa.gov/station_history.php?station=44039.

9. Almost certainly Thomas Lamb (1796–1887): as a Boston shipping merchant, he was active in the China trade, he was also president of the Washington Marine and Fire Insurance Co. (1832–57), president of the Suffolk Savings Bank for Seamen (1844–85), treasurer of the Boston Marine Society (1830–84), president of the New England National Bank (1846–84), member of the Boston City Council under Mayor Josiah Quincy, president of the Boston Pier and Long Wharf Corp. (1851–85) and treasurer of the Boston Sugar Refinery. Married in 1828 Hannah Dawes Eliot. Their children were: Emily Goddard (b. 1829), Margaret Eliot (b. 1831), Thomas (1834–38), Hannah Eliot (1836–38), William Eliot (b. 1839), Charles Duncan (1841–71), Rosanna (b. 1843), Caroline (1845–49), and Horatio Appleton (1850–1926); see the Massachusetts Historical Society website at http://www.masshist.org/.

10. Edward H. Savage, *Boston Events: A brief mention and the date of more than 5,000 events that transpired in Boston from 1630 to 1880 . . .* (Boston: Tolman & White, 1884), p. 25; and *Police Record and Recollections, or Boston by daylight and gaslight for two hundred and forty years* (Boston: John P. Dale, 1873), p. 86.

11. Robert Bennet Forbes, *Personal Reminiscences*, 2nd ed. (Cambridge, MA: University Press, John Wilson & Son, 1882), chs. 9 and 10.

12. *Guide to the Collection, Robert Bennet Forbes Papers 1817–1889*, Massachusetts Historical Society, at http://www.masshist.org/findingaids/doc.cfm?fa=fa0039#top; accessed on 7 December 2011.

13. Forbes, *Personal Reminiscences*, Ch. 9 and Robert Bennet Forbes, *The Voyage of the Jamestown on Her Mission of Mercy* (Boston: Eastburn's Press, 1847).

14. Arthur Bonner, *Alas! What Brought Thee Hither?: The Chinese in New York 1800–1950* (Madison, NJ: Fairleigh Dickinson University Press, 1997), p. 3.

15. It was printed, *inter alia*, in the *Caledonian Mercury*, 17 February 1848.

16. In one of the more detailed newspaper accounts, the rudder is described as made of 'iron wood and teak, bound with iron, its weight is from seven and a-half to eight tons'; *The Belfast News-Letter*, 26 May 1848.

17. Sebastian Junger, *The Perfect Storm: A True Story of Men against the Sea* (New York: W. W. Norton, 1997) is a thrilling narrative. For the technicalities, see Wayne Sweet, Robert Fett, Jeffrey Kerling, Paul La Violette, 'Air-Sea Interaction Effects in the Lower Troposphere across the North Wall of the Gulf Stream', *Monthly Weather Review* 109, no. 5 (May 1981): 1042–52.

18. *Account*, p. 5.

19. H. H. Brindley, 'The Keying', *The Mariner's Mirror* 8, no. 4 (1922): 305–14, is the source for this story, which appears nowhere else and certainly not in the *Description* in any edition. Since Brindley cites as the source for some of his intelligence Kellett's son, Captain S. S. Kellett, it probably has the support of family lore and documentation that the younger Kellett, who served for many years in Calcutta (Kolkata), is reported as saying had long since perished.

20. *Lloyd's Weekly London Newspaper*, 21 May 1848.

21. Forbes, *Voyage of the Jamestown*, appendix, 17, Letter to Josiah Quincy, Esq., Chairman, pp. xi–xv. Forbes mentions that the ship tacked only once from the Boston Navy Yard to Old Head of Kinsale and that, making in on the final day, the *Jamestown* was doing 13 knots with the wind 4 points on the port quarter—what today's sailors would call a screaming reach!

22. Maddocks, *The Atlantic Crossing*, pp. 97, 98.

23. *Glasgow Herald*, 20 March 1848, which prints a letter dated 15 March from a James Franchard, Jersey, with this information. For a brief account of the stay, see http://jouault.wordpress.com/2013/03/10/the-first-chinese-junk-to-visit-europe-in-march-1848/.

24. Sources differ on the exact date. To compound the problem, *The Illustrated London News'* shipping page gives the arrival of the *Keying* at Gravesend as 1 April, see www.iln.org.uk/iln_years/ilnships1846_1848.htm.

25. *Description*, p. 8. All the references to the qualities of her build agree that it was very rough and ready.
26. Given the dates in Table 1; Kellett himself and the *Description* claim 212 days.
27. Wise, *An Analysis of One Hundred Voyages to and from India, China, &c.* (London: J. W. Norie & Co, 1839), also quoted in Jean Sutton, *Lords of the East* (London: Conway Maritime, 1981), p. 105.

Chapter 6 Journey's End: The London Stay

1. See http://www.bl.uk/catalogues/evanion/Record.aspx?EvanID=024-000001375 &ImageIndex=0. The press mark is Evan.1570.
2. The only copy of this image that the author has been able to find is in the G.E. Morrison Collection in the Toyo Bunko in Japan, catalogue number E-3-9 at http://61.197.194.13/gazou/Honkon_dohanga-e.html, accessed on 23 April 2013.
3. See http://www.pla.co.uk/display_fixedpage.cfm/id/174.
4. From *The Jersey Times*, 5 April 1850, see http://www.jerseysocietyinlondon.org/ FNews/news.php?id=14.
5. The young queen and Prince Albert, with princess royal, the prince of Wales and four courtiers visited the *Keying* on 16 May; court circular, *The Times*, 17 May 1848, No. 19865, p. 6. Charles Dickens visited some time in midsummer 1848, his piece in *The Examiner* being published on 24 June that year—in majoritarian fashion, he declared the *Keying* a 'ridiculous abortion'.
6. *Daily News*, 13 June 1848.
7. The sum of £45,000 to £50,000, using standard conversions.
8. *Daily News*, 17 July 1851
9. See *Daily News*, 7 August 1851.
10. The Dunn exhibition had left London the year the *Keying* left Hong Kong, when it was sent around the British provinces.
11. See Susan Simmons's information at http://www.oulton.com/cwa/newsships.nsf /45cc5cb7c20526ef85256529004f20f0/38fbe91be88080918525719400052f25! OpenDocument. In the same posting, Susan Simmons notes that Jane Kellett was the same age as Charles and still alive, and that they had a maid of all work called Charlotte Hall.
12. *Manchester Times*, 25 November 1848.
13. It is now in the Victoria and Albert Museum; see Henry Selous, 'The Opening of the Great Exhibition', 1851. Museum no. 329-1889. See also V. E. Graham, 'The Mandarin Hesing and the Chinese junk the *Keying*', *Arts of Asia* 30, no. 2 (2000): 96–102.
14. Guo Sungtao (1818–91) was a native of Hunan Province. He presented his credentials on 6 February 1877. In 1878, he was made concurrently the representative to France and chose to live in Paris. His tenure of both posts was short. He was relieved in late 1878 and died in 1891. A. W. Hummel (ed.), *Eminent Chinese of the Ch'ing*

Period (1644–1912) (Washington, DC: Library of Congress, 1943), pp. 438–9 and Kuo Sung-t'ao, Hsi-hung Liu and Te-i Chang, *The First Chinese Embassy to the West: The Journals of Kuo-Sung-T'ao, Liu Hsi-Hung and Chang Te-Yi*, trans. J. D. Frodsham (Oxford: Clarendon Press, 1974).

15. *Daily News*, 6 September 1851 and 2 October 1851.
16. *Daily News*, 9 April 1849.
17. See W. Johnson (ed.), *Shaky Ships: The Formal Richness of Chinese Shipbuilding*, exhibition catalogue, May–December 1993, National Maritime Museum Antwerp, p. 8, where the then mayor of Antwerp, H. B. Cools, comments on 'the *Keying* which, in 1848, under the command of the English captain Kellett was the first Chinese junk to call at our port on its way to London'. There is no evidence at all that the *Keying* paid its call on its way to London from Jersey, but there is certainly a window within which it might have, before finally leaving London for Liverpool.
18. The year 1850 saw the last temperature minimum of what is known as the Little Ice Age in Europe; see http://en.wikipedia.org/wiki/Little_Ice_Age.

Chapter 7 The Endgame

1. Written on Tuesday 5 July 1853 and published in the *New-York Daily Tribune*, 20 July 1853, see http://www.marxists.org/archive/marx/works/1853/07/20.htm; accessed on 12 February 2013.
2. J. M. Compton, 'Open Competition and the Indian Civil Service, 1854–1876', *English Historical Review* 83, no. 327 (1968): 265–84.
3. The Hull newspaper copy mentions simultaneous notices in Birmingham, Liverpool, Manchester, Newcastle, Hull, Derby, Bristol, Plymouth, Exeter, Portsmouth, Brighton, Dover, Edinburgh, Glasgow, Dublin, Cork, Paris, Brussels, Le Havre, Calais, Boulogne, Dunkirk, Frankfurt and Amsterdam!
4. *The Era*, 6 June 1852.
5. *Belfast News-Letter*, 7 June 1952.
6. The use of the crossed pound sign (£) was not ubiquitous in nineteenth-century newspapers, not all of which bothered to acquire the additional piece of type, satisfying themselves with an uncrossed L.
7. *Caledonian Mercury*, 7 June 1853.
8. On the standard conversions, £8,900 in 1852 would be worth today between £708,301.77 and £963,548.94, which compares fairly well with the price given in chapter 1 of $75,000; see http://www.measuringworth.com/calculators/exchange/result_exchange.php.
9. *University Hall 50th Anniversary* (Hong Kong: University Hall Alumni, 2007), excerpted at http://www.uhall.com.hk/portal/aboutUhall/TheCastle.php; accessed on 13 February 2013.
10. *Lloyd's Weekly Newspaper*, 27 March 1853.
11. From the *Liverpool Mercury*, 27 October 1854.

12. The St. George's Channel between North Wales and Ireland, a very rough stretch of water. The story reference is *Freeman's Journal and Daily Commercial Advertiser*, 14 May 1853.

13. See http://www.humberpacketboats.co.uk/hull.html; accessed on 13 February 2013.

14. For a graphic account of how a large, dead-towed vessel can girt and sink her tug, see https://www.coastguard.net.nz/sartr/modules/Towing%20Techniques.pdf (pp. 80–1); accessed on 13 February 2013.

15. *Manchester Times*, 18 May 1853.

16. Tony Edwards explicitly states that the ship did exhibit in Liverpool; see http://www.danbyrnes.com.au/blackheath/reaction.htm.

17. See http://en.wikipedia.org/wiki/Rock_Ferry.

18. This is an inference from a brief forum contribution by Tony Edwards (13 July 2005) to the South West Maritime History Society's web page (http://www.swmaritime.org.uk/forums/thread.php?threadid=519). Edwards wrote: 'Keying the "Royal Hesing" left the Mersey in October to visit other ports, returned to the Mersey (date unknown) where she was dismantled.'

19. See http://en.wikipedia.org/wiki/Junk_Keying. The coincidence of the phrase 'in three weeks' suggests that this is a misreport and that what is being recalled is the notice to that effect in the London papers in October 1851, noted on page 17 above.

20. *Liverpool Mercury*, 27 October 1854.

21. *Liverpool Mercury*, 10 November 1854.

22. *Liverpool Mercury*, 9 March 1855.

23. *Glasgow Herald*, 2 April 1855.

24. See http://archiver.rootsweb.ancestry.com/th/read/Mariners/2005-11/113250 9846.

25. 'A Chinese Junk in London River', *P.L.A. Monthly* (January 1939): 59–62, states, 'Her staunch teak planking was used in building two ferry boats, one of them the *Victory*, and many souvenirs of her timbers were sold.' No reference is given for this claim; there is no trace of a regular Mersey ferry of the 1850s or 1860s being called the *Victory*. PLA stands for Port of London Authority.

26. See *Aberdeen Journal*, 21 November 1855; *Bristol Mercury*, 1 December 1855; and *Plymouth and Devonport Weekly Journal and Advertiser*, 6 December 1855.

27. See http://www.plymouthdata.info/PP-Latimer.htm.

28. Susan Simmons, private communication.

29. See http://gazette.slv.vic.gov.au/images/1851/N/general/79-a.pdf for the text of the Mercantile Marine Act 1850, formally *An Act for Improving the Condition of Masters, Mates, and Seamen and Maintaining Discipline in the Merchant Service*, 13 & 14 Vict. Cap 93. The 1854 act made this examined certification compulsory to skippers and mates in the home trade, too. Under the 1850 legislation, masters and mates who had already been serving in that capacity on foreign-going vessels before 1 January 1851 were granted Certificates of Service.

30. Susan Simmons, private communication.

31. According to *American Lloyd's Register of American and Foreign Shipping* of 1861, the *Northfleet* was a ship of 951 tons, built in Northfleet in 1853 and owned by D. Dunbar. The ship left London on 17 September 1853, arrived Wellington on 14 December 1853, Lyttelton on 13 January 1854 and Auckland on 2 February 1854.

32. That this is a perfectly reasonable conclusion to draw can be noted from the terms used in the *Daily News* advertisement on 6 September 1851 of the *Keying's* attractions: 'Chinese war demonstration by Natives, Admission 1s.', or on 2 October in the same year, 'the crew of Chinese sailors to give a Grand Assault of Arms, in addition to a Chinese Concert—Admission 1s.'

33. E. P. Thompson. *The Making of the English Working Class* (Harmondsworth: Penguin, 1968), p. 13.

34. *The Era*, 8 May 1853.

35. William Blakeney, *On the Coasts of Cathay and Cipango Forty Years Ago: A Record of Surveying Service in the China, Yellow and Japan Seas and on the Seaboard of Korea and Manchuria* (London: Elliot Stock, 1902), pp. 54–7. Blakeney was the paymaster of HMS *Actaeon*, at the time under the command of Captain Robert Jenkins.

36. Robert Jenkins (1825–1894) entered the Royal Navy in 1838, was made Lieutenant in 1846 and Commander in 1853. He fought in both the First and Second Opium Wars. He got his first command, HMS *Talbot*, in 1854 when he was sent to assist Edward Belcher's Arctic Expedition. He took command of HMS *Comus* in China in 1855 moving to the *Actaeon*, on the death of William Bate, in 1857 shortly after which he was promoted Captain. He was placed on the retired list as Rear-Admiral in 1875, with promotion to Vice-Admiral in 1880. T. R. Roberts, *Eminent Welshmen: A Short Biographical Dictionary of Welshmen Who Have Gained Distinction from the Earliest Times to the Present* (Cardiff & Merthyr Tydfil: The Educational Publishing Co. Ltd., 1908), vol. 1, p. 212.

37. I am extremely grateful to Lorence Johnston of Lok Man Rare Books, Hong Kong, for bringing this logbook to my attention and allowing me to extract and reproduce the relevant details.

38. Every British naval ship of the era had a component of the ship's company trained in the use of small arms (cutlasses, boarding axes and the standard long arm, the 1853 Enfield pattern rifled percussion musket). They would form the nucleus of boarding parties and, when needed, armed shore parties.

39. Iron screw storeship and troopship, 1593 tons burthen launched 19 February 1855, Commander Edward Lacy R. N. Launched as HMS *Resolute* in 1855 and renamed in 1857, she spent 1858–1860 on the China Station, returning from 1864–1871. She was decommissioned in 1877.

40. 長洲島, *Chángzhōu Dǎo*, also Dane's, Dane and Danish Island. It is the site of the foreigners' cemetery and, in 1924, of the famous Whampoa Military Academy established by Sun Yat Sen.

41. Others may also have remembered the humiliation and Robert Jenkins' role in it. We learn from Robert Hart's diaries that a few months later Robert Jenkins was 'attacked near Whampoa by braves in ambush. He was severely wounded as were also 6 or 8 of

his men.' He notes a day later 'Village near Whampoa, where Jenkins was wounded, completely destroyed.' Katherine Bruner, John King Fairbank, Richard J. Smith (eds.), *Entering China's Service: Robert Hart's Journals* (Cambridge [Mass]: Harvard University Press Harvard East Asian Monographs, 1987), p. 193.

42. Alek Abrahams, 'The Chinese Junk Keying', *Notes and Queries* 6 (July–December 1906): 227. A naval architect called George Mackrow was apprenticed to Ditchburn & Mare, later the Thames Ironworks & Shipbuilding Co., in 1844 at their shipyard on the Blackwall side of Bow Creek. So the source of the piece of cable is more likely to have been via shipyard work on the *Keying* than service aboard; Archer Philip Crouch, *Silvertown and Neighbourhood (Including East and West Ham): A Retrospect* (London: Thomas Burleigh, 1900), p. 61.

43. See http://www.nyhistory.org/node/29514, accessed on 10 September 2013.

44. The spelling of surnames in the 1850s was still much in flux, so the additional 'r' may be of no significance.

45. See Mrs. D. T. Davis, 'The Daguerreotype in America', *McClure's Magazine*, Vol. 8, No. 1 (November 1896), no page numbers, accessed at http://daguerre.org/resource/texts/davis/davis.html on 10 September 2013.

46. That this prejudice continued to operate, to the great detriment of our knowledge of the world of Chinese nautical technology, can be noted from Hans van Tilburg's remarks (*Chinese Junks on the Pacific: Views from a Different Deck*. Gainesville: University Press of Florida, 2007, Ch. 1, especially pp. 1–2) about the traditional Chinese junks sailed across the Pacific to America in the early twentieth century: 'Early twentieth-century observers in America typically regarded Chinese sailing junks as quaint and unwieldy creations constructed in the fashion of sea monsters, general appraisals including a mixture of surprise and contempt.'

Chapter 8 What Kind of Vessel Was the *Keying*?

1. Régine Thiriez, 'Listing Early Photographers of China: Directories as Sources' at http://pnclink.org/annual/annual2000/2000pdf/5-13-1.pdf, accessed on 25 April 2010. For Thomson, see the National Library of Scotland's website on him: http://www.nls.uk/thomson/china.html. For Beato, see the beautifully produced catalogue, David Harris, *Of Battle and Beauty: Felice Beato's Photographs of China* (Santa Barbara, CA: Santa Barbara Museum of Art, 1999).

2. See E. H. H. Archibald, *The Dictionary of Sea Painters of Europe and America*, 3rd ed. (Woodbridge: Antique Collectors' Club, 2000). The inimitably precise E. W. Cooke, R.A., F.R.S. (1811–80) was active and at his peak during the years of the *Keying*'s visit to London. The accomplished Samuel Walters (1811–82) was likewise at his flourishing peak (Sam Davidson, *Samuel Walters, Marine Artist—Fifty Years of Sea, Sail, and Steam* [Coventry: Jones Sands, 1992]); he had moved to London in 1845 to work with the late W. J. Huggins's son-in-law, the equally well-known marine artist Edward Duncan (1803–82) but had moved back to Liverpool by the

time the *Keying* arrived in London in 1847, where, as we shall see, he would have had ample opportunity to capture this unique Chinese ship. It is curious that no marine artist of repute seems to have been interested.

3. F.-E. Pâris, *Essai sur la construction navale des peuples extra-européens, ou, Collection des navires et pirogues construits par les habitants de l'Asie, de la Malaisie du Grand Océan et de l'Amérique*, 2 volumes (Paris: Arthus Bertrand, 1841).

4. *Dictionary of National Biography 1885–1900*, vol. 51, biographical sketch by Edward Milligen Beloe, at http://en.wikisource.org/wiki/Seppings,_Robert_(DNB00); accessed on 4 August 2010.

5. 'Sagging' happens when a ship is supported by a wave at the bow and stern with the trough beneath her midships; 'hogging' is when the midships is supported but the ends not. 'Wracking' or 'racking' is when the hull is twisted along its longitudinal axis. René de Kerchove, *International Maritime Dictionary*, 2nd ed. (New York, Van Nostrand, 1961), s.vv.

6. Hans van Tilburg, *Chinese Junks on the Pacific: Views from a Different Deck* (Gainesville: University of Florida Press, 2007), p. 58.

7. As interesting is the fact that George Chinnery (1774–1852), still painting in the mid-1840s, was evidently wholly uninterested in the *Keying* and its progenitors. Chinnery spent only six months in Hong Kong at the end of 1845 and then went back to Macao, from which the *Keying* and its impending adventure were not such as to draw him back across the Pearl River estuary. See Patrick Conner, *George Chinnery 1774–1852* (London: Antique Collector's Club, 1999).

8. Martyn Gregory, *Paintings of the China Coast by Chinese and Western Artists, 1790–1890* (London: Martyn Gregory Gallery, 1990), p. 48.

9. See Joseph Needham's seminal *Science and Civilization in China*, vol. 4: *Physics and Physical Technology* (Cambridge: Cambridge University Press: 1971), p. 501. Given the etymology of the word *junk*, and its established use in the India Ocean area to describe a large ship from the Eastern Archipelago or China, we have no fundamental reason to pick a Chinese over an Arab or Indian vessel as the cited venture (see Pierre-Yves Manguin, 'The Southeast Asian Ship: An Historical Approach', *Journal of Southeast Asian Studies* 11, no. 2 [1980]: 266–76).

10. By the early twentieth century, transpacific voyages by contrast were quite numerous, see Hans van Tilburg, *Chinese Junks on the Pacific*, in which the stories of ten of these adventurous voyages are reviewed.

11. I have discovered a total of thirteen images of the *Keying*, with one—the Skillett painting—known only by title. They are itemized in the List of Illustrations. Three of the images—the Chinese artist's gouaches and the Joseph Rock engraving— owe debts to each other. The direction of influence is not clear, though one's sense is that the gouaches were the original and the engraving was based on them. The Rock Brothers and Payne lithograph would also appear to have some affinity to the gouaches. By contrast, the Currier lithograph was obviously taken from life and the Edmund Evans image entirely invented. The *Illustrated London News* image by Foster, that by the unknown artist in the *Description*, and the *Keying* in Samuel Waugh's painting have a very strong family resemblance, connected, one suspects,

by imitation. The image by Greenaway and that published by Vickers are quite different from all the others and from each other, and possibly not based on direct observation though probably derivative of the entirely fictional image of Edmund Evans.

12. *Description.*

13. David Bland, *A History of Book Illustration: The Illuminated Manuscript and the Printed Book* (Cleveland: World Publishing Company, 1985). Patricia J. Anderson, *The Printed Image and the Transformation of Popular Culture, 1790–1860* (Oxford: Clarendon Press, 1991). See also the useful catalogue from the British Library, *Aspects of the Victorian Book* at http://www.bl.uk/collections/early/victorian/intro. html and the quirky but helpful review of graphic art, from a largely American perspective, at http://graphicwitness.org/ ineye/index2.htm.

14. A parallel and familiar example is the exaggeration of verticality, ruggedness and wildness in mountainscapes of painters of the Romantic period, with their focus on the 'sublime' in order to evoke feelings of 'surprise, terror, superstition, melancholy, power, strength', as John Constable put the matter. The Romantic 'discovery' of nature and the sublimity of the wild required a manner of depiction that highlighted those features for the viewer. See Bruce MacEvoy's excellent discussion in 'The Poetic Landscape' at http://www.handprint.com/HP/WCL/artist03.html; accessed on 24 April 2010.

15. It is worth noting that, in the 1840s, to write of 'scientific' naval architecture is rather to anticipate matters. The practice of naval architecture as a scientifically based technology was extremely young in 1840s Britain. While the dawn of scientific naval architecture can be traced to the mid-eighteenth century in France (for example, Pierre Bouguer's *Traité du navire* of 1746), in Britain a more practical, apprenticeship-based approach prevailed until the early to mid-nineteenth century. When the change came, however, it came from outside. In the 1840s, the rising generation, like Froude and Brunel, were engineers, not naval architects. It was their railway- and bridge-engineering expertise, not their knowledge of the principles of hydrodynamics, that transformed ship design as iron cladding and steam engines transformed ships; see Sir Westcott Abell, *The Shipwright's Trade* (London: Conway Maritime Press, 1981), part 3, para. 9, 'The Sorrows of Science', pp. 149–57. It is perhaps symptomatic of the British prejudice that Sir Westcott Abell chose the title for his book that he did and does not get around to mentioning naval architecture as a profession until page 152. The Institution of Naval Architects, one might note, was not founded until 1860.

16. *Description*, p. 13.

17. *Description*, p. 14.

18. For representative images, see Jim Harter (ed.), *Nautical Illustrations: 681 Permission-Free Illustrations from Nineteenth-Century Sources* (New York: Dover Publications, 2003).

19. William John Huggins (1781–1845) is unknown to the records before he became a seafarer with the East India Company. He was signed on the *Perseverance* (under

Captain Thomas Buchanan) as an ordinary seaman, but served as the captain's steward on a voyage to China from 1812 to 1814. Where he learned to paint is obscure, but his first painting is recorded, possibly apocryphally, as dating from the year the *Perseverance* returned to London. He first exhibited at the Royal Academy in 1817 and exhibited at the British Institution regularly after 1825. He was appointed a marine-painter to both George IV and to William IV. While his paintings were favoured by sailors, artists and art critics were less impressed. Huggins died at his home and studio of twenty-two years, 105, Leadenhall Street, London, on 19 May 1845. Pieter van der Merwe, 'Huggins, William John (1781–1845)', *Oxford Dictionary of National Biography* (Oxford: Oxford University Press, 2004); online ed., January 2012, http://www.oxforddnb.com/view/article/14053; accessed on 9 February 2013.

20. One thinks particularly of the famous Qing dynasty depiction of an ocean-going junk, probably a *fuchuan*, in Zhou Huang's *Account of the Liu Chiu Islands*, reprinted in Needham, *Science and Civilization in China*, vol. 4, pt. 3, p. 405.

21. Sam Davidson, 'What Makes a Marine Artist?' in his *Marine Art and the Clyde: 100 Years of Sea, Sail and Steam* (Upton: Jones-Sands, 2001), p. 15.

22. See, for a vivid demonstration of the requisite technique, the short video on YouTube by Danish artist Alek Krylow at http://hk.youtube.com/watch?v=h0p_aFWDSok.

23. G. R. G. Worcester, *Junks and Sampans of the Yangtze* (Annapolis, MD: Naval Institute Press, 1971), p. 603.

24. Ibid.

25. These images are 1) the best known coloured print of 1849 by Beck Bros; 2) the engraving in *The Illustrated London News* of 1 April 1848; 3) Samuel Waugh's paint-ing of the *Keying* lying off the Battery, New York, in the collection of the Museum of the City of New York; 4) a German engraving of the *Keying* under what may be reduced sail; 5) an image by J. Greenaway in vol. 3 of Walter Thornbury's *Old and New London: A Narrative of Its History, Its People and Its Places. Illustrated with Numerous Engravings from the Most Authentic Sources* (London/New York: Cassell, Peter & Galpin, 1872–78); and 6) the images limned on the celebration medals by Halliday, Davis and others. Two of the four prints and the Currier can be found in the collection of prints and watercolours obtained by Iwasaki Hisao from G. E. Morison in 1917 and viewable at http://61.197.194.13/ gazou/Honkon_dohanga-e.html. The three images are catalogue numbers E-3-8, E-3-9 and E-3-10.

26. Sean McGrail (*Boats of the World from the Stone Age to Medieval Times*, Oxford: Oxford University Press, 2001, p. 381) gives the traditional Guangdong rule-of-thumb proportions, unquestionably very similar to those of Fujian, which he sum-marizes from L. Liu and C. Li, 'Characteristics of Guangdong Wooden Junks' in *Proceedings of the International Sailing Ship Conference*, edited by S. Zhang (Shanghai: Society of Naval Architecture and Marine Engineering, 1991), pp. 275–85.

27. In a private communication.

28. See above, Ch. 3. One possible source for this may be the *Account* (p. 4), where the author notes the junk had been bought 'after she had returned from Cochin China, to which country she had carried some Mandarins of high rank'.

29. This and many other aspects of Chinese regional design variations are well canvassed in van Tilburg, *Chinese Junks on the Pacific*, p. 56. Tilburg is citing Worcester's *Sail and Sweep in China*, p. 17. Against this must be placed the shape of the bow of the Foochow (Fuzhou) pole junk depicted in Worcester, *Junks and Sampans of the Yangtze*, pp. 188–9, and the plate of the Science Museum model of the 'Fukien seagoing junk', in *Sail and Sweep* (Plate 8), which clearly has the upswept 'wings'.

30. A consideration of the comprehensive reviews of typical early mid-twentieth-century traditional Vietnamese sailing craft given in Pierre Paris, *Esquisse d'une ethnographie navale des peuplespeoples Annamites*, 2nd ed. (Rotterdam: Museum voor Land- en Volkenkunde en het Maritiem Museum "Prins Hendrik" Rotterdam, 1955) and J. B. Piétri, *Voiliers d'Indochine*, new ed. (Saigon: S.I.L.I, 1949) reveals no commonality in conformation, rig or construction between any Vietnamese craft and any feature of the *Keying*.

31. These images were originally thought to originate from the early seventeenth century. Careful scholarly work by Professor Oba Osamu and a cross-correlation of Oba's findings with work done separately on a copy of the scroll in Australia by Captain Ian MacRobert, brokered by Joseph Needham, has resolved the dating question, concluding that Oba's late eighteenth century date of 1795 is correct. See http://janus.lib.cam.ac.uk/db/node.xsp?id=EAD%2FGBR%2F1928%2FNRI2%2FSCC6%2F36, where the Needham archive's holdings on this matter are excellently and clearly displayed. Oba published his work as 'On the Scroll of Chinese Ships in the Possession of the Matsuura Museum—Materials for the Study of Chinese Trading Ships in Edo Period', *Bulletin of the Institute of Oriental and Occidental Studies of Kansai University* 5 (March 1972): 13–50. The most important feature of the images are the careful annotations which give names and dimensions, making these images the closest known from the Asian tradition of the 'General Arrangements' sheets of Western-style lines drawings.

32. That is, the deep-sea as opposed to coasting (or *nanyang*) trade, although the vocabulary here does not seem to have been absolutely fixed, *nanyang* (see next note) referring as well to the Chinese diaspora in Southeast Asia.

33. The late Jennifer Wayne Cushman's fascinating *Fields from the Sea: Chinese Junk Trade with Siam during the Late Eighteenth and Early Nineteenth Centuries* (Ithaca, NY: Cornell Southeast Asia Publications Program, 1993), p. 53, marks the resemblance of the *Keying* to a *fuchuan*, as well as commenting in general (pp. 48–58) on the effective hegemony of *fuchuan* styles in the ocean-going trading junks of the *nanyang*.

34. This is a slightly abbreviated discussion. In fact, more or less at the waterline and below in a *fuchuan* the planking does converge on rising elements of the keel which act as stem- and sternpost; however, above that point one finds the triangular or trapezoidal bow plate and ovate transom characteristic of the *fuchuan* design, which have the effect of making the planking above the waterline less steeply inclined at the ends than in comparable carvel or clinker-built Western vessels.

35. The Hong Kong Maritime Museum has an antique model of a *fuchuan* dating from sometime around the mid-nineteenth century, which shares this tendency to exaggerate the beam-to-length ratio, resulting in a junk that looks shorter and fatter than we have reason to believe was the case, from traditional rules-of-thumb or such scrupulous portrayals of traditional craft as can be found in Pâris, *L'Essai sur la construction navale des peuples extra-européens*.

Chapter 9 A Re-appraisal of the *Keying*'s Likely Shape

1. G. R. G. Worcester, *The Junks and Sampans of the Yangtze* (Annapolis, MD: Naval Institute Press, 1971), pp. 603–5; L. Audemard, *Juncos Chineses* (Macao: Museo Maritimo de Macao, 1994), pp. 150–1.

2. This, of course, is typical of the entire problem. We read of the teak build, but there is no evidence that the *Keying* actually was built of teak. Fujian pine (松木, *song mu*, or *pinus massoniana*) is characterized as a hard wood, with age becoming extremely hard. Worcester (*Junks and Sampans of the Yangtze*, pp. 187–94) comments that, in a traditional Fuzhou pole junk, the transverse bulkheads, wales, timbers and many other critical timbers are all of this hardwood. Only the planking is made of softwood, the Fujian fir (杉木, *shan mu*, or *Cunninghamia lanceolata*). This too, when aged and long pickled in salt water, hardens and darkens, so with a junk between fifty and one hundred years old, a misidentification of the wood from which she was built, in default of any laboratory analysis, would not be surprising. Equally, on the 'grandfather's axe' theory, selective or even wholesale re-planking in the course of a very long life might have been in teak.

3. The fifteen compartments are exactly the number typical of a Fujian *huapigu* (花屁股, literally 'flowery arse', describing the highly decorated transom), of which the *Keying* has been said to be an example; see Worcester, *Junks and Sampans of the Yangtze*, p. 184, and for the *Keying* references, pp. 603–5.

4. Including the writer of the *Description*. See also Worcester, *Junks and Sampans of the Yangtze*, p. 34, and *Sail and Sweep in China: The History and Development of the Chinese Junk as Illustrated by the Collection of Models in the Science Museum* (London: HMSO, 1966), p. 8, where he remarks, 'The work of the Chinese shipwright, although ingeniously conceived and skilfully carried out, is of the crudest. This necessarily makes the caulkers' task a formidable one.' This is not to say that all Chinese shipwrights' work was crude and rough, but the workaday vessel is unlikely to have been exemplary of the finest work, any more than were workaday craft elsewhere.

5. I. A. Donnelly, *Chinese Junks and Other Native Craft* (Shanghai: Kelly & Walsh, 1930).

6. Joseph Needham et al., *Science and Civilization in China*, vol. 4: *Physics and Physical Technology* (Cambridge: Cambridge University Press: 1971), p. 413, though Needham, does note (p. 480) that in the high days of Ming maritime power, during the period of Zheng He's Treasure Fleets, there was a design office in Nanjing where

the chief designer and builder, Jin Bifeng, made 'many working drawings (*thu yang*)' (圖樣, *túyàng*), without, however, any further detail on exactly what sort of drawings these were. Certainly, the working drawings in the *Longjiang Shipyard Treatise* are crude 'lists of parts' more to act as visual *aides mémoires* than anything remotely resembling a working drawing in the accepted modern meaning of that term.

7. See the introduction. The full argument of this position is too long to recapitulate here, but will be presented in a later article discussing the history and development of Chinese axially mounted steering systems. Van Tilburg's discussion is a useful overview (though he appears not to have read very thoroughly L. V. Mott's *The Development of the Rudder: A Technological Tale* [London: Chatham Publishing / College Station: Texas A&M University Press, 1997]).

8. *Description*, p. 12.

9. See the analysis of known wrecks recovered by archaeologists in Sean McGrail, *Boats of the World from the Stone Age to Medieval Times* (Oxford: Oxford University Press, 2001), pp. 366–79, and the detailed cross-sectional line drawing of a Kiangsu (Jiangsu) trader, showing its keel timber, in Worcester, *Junks and Sampans of the Yangtze*, p. 164, or, more pertinently, the evident keel in the detailed drawings of a *huapigu* on pp. 188–9. There is a good discussion of this issue in Van Tilburg, *Chinese Junks on the Pacific*, pp. 60–3.

10. Worcester is citing H. H. Brindley, 'The Keying', *The Mariner's Mirror* 8, no. 4 (1922): 305–14. There was a subsequent article by L. G. Pritchard. 'Chinese Junks [Keying 1806–1912, incl compartments]', *The Mariner's Mirror* 9 (1923): 89–91.

11. *Description*, p. 8.

12. Information from the late Mr. Geoffrey Bonsall and also from the *Account*, p. 5.

13. Though it is worth noting that in the report on the *Keying* in the *Aberdeen Journal*, 18 August 1847, the height of the stern above the water is given as 32 feet, not 38, above the water. I am indebted to Susan Simmons for this newspaper clipping.

14. *Description*, p. 1.

15. The hint at a different interpretation, although had it been true it would not have argued for a massive increase in laden displacement, was an advertisement in *The Times*, 16 May 1848, p. 11. It reads: 'Arrival of the Chinese Junk Keying. Just landed, and for SALE, the following beautiful productions from CHINA: CHINESE LACKERED LOO TABLES, ladies work tables, tea-caddies, cigar-boxes, work-boxes with ivory fittings, mandarin jars from fice to 60 inches high, pagodas, junks, old bronzes, gongs, cups and saucers, paintings on rice paper, ivory fans, paper ditto, silk and ivory-faced hand screens, and a thousand other curious and beautiful articles from Canton and Shanghae, at extraordinarily low prices. W. Hewett and Co. Chinese warehouse, 18 Fenchurch-street'. It would have been intelligent for the *Keying* to have carried a cargo. However, this is almost certainly a London businessman capitalizing on a heaven-sent opportunity.

16. *Daily News*, 26 August 1847.

17. *The Morning Chronicle*, 11 March 1848. I owe both these references to Susan Simmons.

18. *Description*. It is fairly clear that the pamphlet is the work of a jobbing writer who has been given detail by Captain Kellett which he does not necessarily understand. As much to the point, it is not in fact likely that Kellett was either a competent naval architect or shipbuilder—he would merely have had a sound seaman's grasp of the basic structure of ship—nor that he had more than the slightest passing acquaintance with, and that through the eyes of deeply engrained prejudice, the techniques and practices of traditional Chinese shipbuilding. Captain Kellett was a fine seaman. He was not a marine ethnographer.

19. *Description*, p. 10.

20. It should be noted that Chinese ironwood is not always the same as what is normally meant by the English term. As Needham points out (*Science and Civilization in China*, vol. 4: *Physics and Physical Engineering*, p. 646, fn.b), 'there are a number of tropical woods known as ironwood: e.g. *Casuarina equisetfolia, Fagraea gigantean, Intsia bakeri, Maba buxifolia* and *Mensua ferrea*'; he adds (ibid. p. 416, fn.g), *Tsuga sinensis* as well. An online source lists twenty-one different tree species that are called ironwood (see http://encyclopedia.thefreedictionary.com/ironwood). Further confusion is added when one realizes that Cantonese shipwrights sometimes refer to Malaysian *chengal* (*Neobalanocarpus heimii*) as *either* ironwood *or* teak!

21. *Description*, p. 8.

22. *Description*, facing p. 14.

Chapter 10 The *Keying*'s Dimensions and Shape

1. *Description*, p. 12.

2. Paul van Dyke, *The Canton Trade: Life and Enterprise on the China Coast, 1700–1845* (Hong Kong: Hong Kong University Press, 2005), pp. 24–30.

3. William Milburn, *Oriental Commerce of the East India Trader's Complete Guide* (London: Kingsbury, Parbury & Allen, 1825), p. 468. See also J. Chalmers, 'The Chinese Ch'ih Measure', *China Review* 13 (1884): 332–6, where a value for the 'cubit' in Canton is given as 14.1 feet. Samuel Wells Williams (*A Chinese Commercial Guide*, 4th ed., Canton: The Chinese Repository, 1856, p. 300) offers a range between 12.1 and 14.81 feet, with 14 feet 1 inch as the tariff measure.

4. Joseph Blunt, *The Shipmaster's Assistant and Commercial Digest* (New York: E. & G. W. Blunt, 1837; reprinted London: Macdonald and Jane's, 1974), p. 426.

5. Milburn, *Oriental Commerce*, pp. 415, 445 and 527. In various Western sources, there is a curious hesitancy to give any value to linear measures used in Canton, for example J. H. Tuckey, *Maritime Geography and Statistics*, vol. 3 (London: Black, Parry & Co., 1815), p. 547.

6. G. R. G. Worcester, *Sail and Sweep in China: The History and Development of the Chinese Junk as Illustrated by the Collection of Models in the Science Museum* (London: HMSO, 1966), p. xi: 'the Chinese commercial guide gives 100 different values of the ch'ih (*chi* 尺) as actually in use'.

7. William C. Hunter, *An American in Canton (1825–1844): A Reprint of* The Fan Kwae at Canton before Treaty days (1825–1844) *and* Bits of Old China, edited by G. Bonsall (Hong Kong: Derwent, 1994), p. 60.

8. This is a common manner of reference; *The Oxford Encyclopaedia of Maritime History*, vol. 4, edited by John B. Hattendorf (Oxford: Oxford University Press, 2007) p. 143, for example, gives length on deck as the value for 'L'. In fact, the 1773 act, quoted by D. R. MacGregor, *Fast Sailing Ships: Their Design and Construction, 1775–1875*, 2nd ed. (London: Conway Maritime Press, 1988), p. 271, is unequivocal: 'The length shall be taken on a straight line along the rabbet of the keel of the ship, from the back of the main-post to a perpendicular line from the fore part of the main-stem under the bowsprit; from which subtracting three-fifths of the breadth, the remainder must be esteemed the just length of the keel to find the tonnage . . .'

9. Sean McGrail, *Boats of the World from the Stone Age to Medieval Times* (Oxford: Oxford University Press, 2001), pp. 245, 164, 276 and 381.

10. See http://brunelleschi.imss.fi.it/michaelofrhodes/ships_design.html; accessed on 2 August 2010.

11. Fernando Oliveira, *Liura da fabrica das naos* (Academia de Marinha/Museu Maritimo de Macao, 1995), pp. 165–6 (a beautifully produced trilingual edition). For an excellent summary of extant texts reflecting such practices in Europe, see Texas A&M University's outline at http://nautarch.tamu.edu/shiplab/index_03treatises.htm; accessed on 2 August 2010.

12. They are translated and adumbrated in McGrail, *Boats of the World*, p. 381, from L. Liu and C. Li, 'Characteristics of Guangdong Wooden Junks', in *Proceedings of the International Sailing Ships History Conference*, edited by S. Zhang (Shanghai: Society of Naval Architecture & Marine Engineering, 1991).

13. For the application of the rules of thumb to the last examples of South China coastal trading junks, see Stephen Davies, *Coasting Past: The Last South China Coastal Trading Junks Photographed by William Heering* (Hong Kong: Hong Kong Maritime Museum, 2013).

14. Ibid. Utter confusion as to the difference between displacement (roughly, all up weight) and measurement tonnage (measured internal volume) is remarkably common in writing about the sea.

15. See, for example, A. W. Sleeswyk, 'The *Liao* and the Displacement of Ships in the Ming Navy', *The Mariner's Mirror* 82 (1996): 3–13; Richard Barker, 'The *Liao* and the Displacement of Ships in the Ming Navy: Defoe's View of Chinese Claims, c. 1700', *The Mariner's Mirror* 82 (1996): 484; John F. Coates and David K. Brown, 'The *Liao* and the Displacement of Ships in the Ming Navy', *The Mariner's Mirror* 82 (1996): 484.

16. There is an alternative that on one reading might be implied by the *Longjiang Shipyard Treatise*. This is that the *liao* in question has nothing to do with the size of the completed vessel, whether carrying capacity or total capacity, but is instead a measure of the volume of all the timber, or possibly the main keel, wales, framing and planking timbers required to build a given vessel.

17. As a previous note indicates, it is extremely important to keep distinct in the mind the difference between a *tonne* as a measurement of mass (or weight, in popular parlance)—*displacement*, as the nautical term has it—and a *ton burthen* or *measurement ton*, which is a measure of carrying capacity, assuming, today, that 100 cubic feet of volume accommodates the mass of a notional average tonne of cargo. There is no strict relationship between measurement tonnage and displacement; one cannot be derived from the other.

18. One gill, or 142.0653125 millilitres, is a quarter of an imperial or customary British pint. A standard pub measure of a quarter gill is today 35 millilitres.

19. In Tang Zhiba, Xin Yuanou, Zheng Ming, 'The Initial Textual Researches and Restorations Studies on Zheng He's 2000 *Liao* Wooden Treasure Ships (the 5th version)', *Zhenghe's Voyage Studies* 2 (2005): 32–48, a formula for calculating *liao*, referenced to Chen Xiyu, *Chinese Junks and Overseas Trade* (Xiamen: Xiamen University Press, 1991) is given as (length of keel x beam x moulded depth) x 10, where measurements are in *zhàng* (丈). Using the data from the *Longjiang Shipyard Treatise*, this formula is wrong by an order of magnitude, and even when corrected becomes less and less accurate as the size of vessel increases, as Table 13 shows.

Table 13 The Tang/Xin/Zheng formula for *liao* corrected

Junk size (*liao*) in treatise	Length of keel in 尺	Beam in 尺	Moulded depth in 尺	*liao* by formula	*liao* by Tang/Xin/Zheng formula corrected
100	34.2	8.1	3.7	1025.0	102.5
200	42.5	12.6	4.5	2409.8	241.0
400	60.5	16.5	6.0	5989.5	598.9
600	86.7	19.6	7.8	13328.2	1332.8
800	120.0	22.5	10.3	27854.7	2785.5

20. Though in most instances in China, the designs of warships and merchant vessels were not greatly different.

21. A good general discussion of this issue can be found in Endymion Wilkinson, *Chinese History: A Manual*, revised and enlarged edition (Cambridge, MA: Harvard University Asia Center, 2000), pp. 234–40. Worcester, *Sail and Sweep in China*, p. xi, notes that, when he was gathering data in the 1930s, 'the Chinese commercial guide (gave) 100 different values of the *ch'ih* (Chinese foot) as actually in use.'

22. One possible source of difference might be the respective ratio of length-on-deck to length-of-keel in Chinese and European traditions. In the *Longjiang Shipyard Treatise*, length-of-keel and length-on-deck are given for twenty-one vessel types. With the exception of two barges for which, not surprisingly, ratios are close to 1:1, the majority have a ratio of between 1:0.65 and 1:0.75, with an average of 1:0.69. A quick comparison with typical European ships listed

in R. Gardiner (ed.), *The Heyday of Sail: The Merchant Sailing Ship 1650–1830* (London: Conway Maritime Press, 1995), pp. 33 and 54, using the ratio of keel = 3 x beam, given in W. Hutchinson, *A Treatise on Naval Architecture*, 4th ed. (Liverpool: T. Billinge, 1794; reprinted London: Conway Maritime Press, 1969), pp. 35–6, shows the European examples to favour a range of 1:0.8 to 1:0.9.

23. *Description*, p. 12.
24. The point is simple. All rules can be evaded by design which exploits the loopholes. The BOM, precisely because it penalized beam but, for calculation purposes, treated moulded depth as half the beam (a ratio that had been true for most European vessels until the early eighteenth century), led to designers producing ever relatively narrower, deeper vessels. The result was a change to tonnage measurement in 1854, following the recommendation of the Moorsom Committee of 1849, whose secretary was Admiral George Moorsom. Moorsom's committee devised the formula for tonnage measurement used throughout the steamship era that was superseded, though not significantly varied, only following the 1969 International Convention on Tonnage, that was in force from 1982 to 1994.

Chapter 11 How Fast Could She Go?

1. I owe the waterline length figure, a best estimate, to a combination of the *Illustrated London News* picture and a photograph in the collection of the Nimitz Library, U.S. Naval Academy, Annapolis, of a junk from Shantou (Swatow) that looks very like the *Keying*. It was taken in China by Lt. J. G. Moses Lindley Wood in 1884–85. Dimensionally, the vessel in the photograph fits reasonably, so is no bad guide; it is controlled by data from other sources. Length of keel is an estimated length of the keel plank. Displacement has been recalculated, to cross-check the figures we have, based on a simplified formula from http://boatdesign.net/forums/showthread.php?t=930, where wetted surface area = $(L \times [B + T]) \times 0.75$, added to the author's own rough formula for area above the waterline = $(2 \times L \times F) + (bB \times bF) + (tB \times tF)$ (where L = overall length, B = beam, T = draught, F = freeboard, bB = average beam across bow section, bF = average freeboard at bow, tB = beam across transom, tF = average freeboard at transom). To this is added $([0.87 \times L] \times D)$, $(7 \times B \times D)$ (where D = moulded depth) for the internal bulkheads (the *Keying* had fifteen athwartships bulkheads) and L x B for the deck. This is multiplied by 0.7 on the assumption of 8-inch-thick planking (a probable underestimate) for the gross volume of timber in the vessel. The cubic footage of timber is then multiplied by 43 pounds (the weight of teak per cubic foot) and divided by 2,240 to get long tons. The result is a displacement probably to within ±10 to 15 percent of actuality. Best average speed is based on the *Keying* having taken 26 days to cross the Atlantic, from Boston to the English Channel. The sail area-to-displacement ratio is based on the mid-value displacement, though given that the ship was in ballast, the performance potential may have been better.

2. Jean Sutton, *Lords of the East* (London: Conway Maritime, 1981), p. 94.

3. *Ocean Passages for the World*, 4th ed. (Taunton: Hydrographer to the Navy, 1987), p. 182.

4. See Klaas van Dokkum, *Ship Knowledge, Ship Design, Construction and Operation*, 5th ed. (Enkhuizen: DOKMAR, 2008), pp. 34–6.

5. D. R. MacGregor, *Fast Sailing Ships: Their Design and Construction, 1775–1875*, 2nd ed. (London: Conway Maritime Press, 1988), p. 247.

6. Van Dokkum, *Ship Knowledge, Ship Design*, p. 135.

7. MacGregor, Fast Sailing Ships, p. 20, citing Howard Chapelle's *The Search for Speed under Sail, 1700–1855* (New York: W. W. Norton, 1967), pp. 43–5 and 404–7.

Chapter 12 Voyage Over

1. The eminent British banking house acted for many of the best-known Western trading firms in China, including Russell & Co., Augustine Heard & Co., Nye Parkin & Co., etc.

2. See *Official Catalogue of the Great Exhibition of the Works of Industry of All Nations, 1851*, corrected edition (London: Spicer Bros., 1851), p. 216.

3. When the *Sulphur* and her tender the *Starling* had been in South America in 1839, prosecuting their researches, they were told to drop everything and make haste for the Pearl River Delta, where they formed the spearhead of an impressive Royal Navy concentration of hydrographic surveyors, whose work was to prove of signal importance in the British campaign.

4. It is frequently but mistakenly assumed, that Henry and Charles Kellett were related, if only on the wrong side of the blanket. They do not appear to have been. No connection has been found between the modest Plymouth and Ulverston Kellett families and the more distinguished Irish Kelletts from Clonacody House, Fethard, Co. Cork, Ireland, who settled in Ireland in the early 18th century. Much work by Charles Kellett's descendants has turned up no background information about Charles Kellett's childhood or parentage. See for Henry Kellett http://fethard.com/index.php?topic=115.0 and http://www.clonacodyhouse.com/History.html

5. Sir John died eight months after the *Keying* docked at Blackwall. That the Franklin expedition's ships may have foundered was discovered by a joint British-American effort in 1850. What actually happened to Franklin was discovered by the Scottish doctor and explorer Dr. John Rae in 1854, but because it went against the heroic image fostered by Lady Franklin and, worse, suggested that these paragons of heroism had resorted to cannibalism, Rae was ignored and ostracized. Victorian Britain preferred not to entertain heterodox ideas about itself; as with Chinese naval architecture, so with Arctic blundering. Interestingly, three of the British naval officers caught up in the Franklin farrago could well have crossed our story's path. Sir Edward Belcher, Henry Kellett and Richard Collinson had all been participants in the First Opium War and went on to join the select band of nineteenth-century

explorers and surveyors. Sir Edward was voyaging and surveying in China and Southeast Asia in the *Samarang* in 1841–47. Kellett and Collinson were surveying on the China coast in the *Plover* and *Young Hebe* in 1841–46. All got tangled up in the search for Franklin: Belcher in the *Resolute* 1852–54; Kellett in the *Herald* in 1848–52; Collinson in the *Enterprise* 1850–55. See Fergus Fleming, *Barrow's Boys: The Original Extreme Adventurers—A Stirring Story of Daring Fortitude and Outright Lunacy* (London: Granta, 2001).

6.   For the teapot, see Victoria and Albert Museum item C.262:1, 2-1993 at http://collections.vam.ac.uk/item/O8088/henry-cole-tea-service-oxford-teapot-cole-henry-sir/. The V&A's collection notes give a strong indication of why Cole and teapots were not a stimulus to Cole on China—the design inspiration was classical Greek.

7.   Henry Cole, *Fifty Years of Public Work of Sir Henry Cole, K.C.B., Accounted for in His Deeds, Speeches and Writings*, 2 vols. (London: George Bell & Sons, 1884), vol. 1, p. 279.

8.   See http://www.sciencemuseum.org.uk/about_us.aspx; accessed on 24 April 2010.

9.   An interesting exercise in exactly this approach, some 165 years after it could first have been essayed, was conducted by the naval architect Michael Trimming; see Michael S. K. Trimming, 'The Pechili Trader: A Hull Lines Plan', *The Mariner's Mirror* 97, no. 3 (2011). Trimming sees, for example, that the trader's cargo compartment design conformed remarkably well to modern self-trimming designs for bulk carriers; the Pechili trader's typical load was a bulk cargo.

10.   *Official Catalogue of the Great Exhibition*, pp. 50–4.

11.   Sean McGrail, *Boats of the World from the Stone Age to Medieval Times* (Oxford: Oxford University Press, 2001), p. 349.

Appendix: The Images of the *Keying*

1.   Currier was a pioneer lithographer in the United States having learned his craft from William and John Pendleton of Boston, who had introduced lithography to America and to whom Currier had been apprenticed. He was well-established by the time of the *Keying* visit. It was with the advent of James Merrit Ives (1824–1895) to the business in 1850, and his partnership to form Currier & Ives in 1857, that the firm became the premier popular image publisher in the United States, with some 7,500 images in their list between 1834 and 1907, when the firm was liquidated. Information on Nathaniel Currier comes principally from the Currier and Ives Foundation at http://www.currierandives.com/history.html, but also Morton Cronin, 'Currier and Ives: A Content Analysis', *American Quarterly*, Vol. 4, No. 4 (Winter 1952): 317–30.

2.   *The Pictorial Times*, Volume X, Issue No. 231, Saturday 14 August 1847, p. 100.

3.   A careful review of the two paintings suggests that they are the work of a single hand. I am indebted to Patrick Conner of the Martyn Gregory Gallery for providing a copy of the second image.

4. I owe this insight to Anthony Hardy, by whom I was introduced to the art and artists of the China Export School and from whom I have learned much.

5. The company was founded by William Frederick Rock (1802–90). After schooling in London, he became a partner with the playing card maker Thomas De La Rue in the 1820s before setting up business as a fancy stationer with his brother Henry in 1833 at 8, Queen Street 1833–38. Around that year they were joined by their younger brother Richard and moved premises to 11, Walbrook, where the business stayed until 1895. They traded as William and Henry Rock 1833–38; as Rock and Co. 1838–95. In 1845 John Payne became a partner at which point they also traded as Rock Brothers and Payne. Their business as fancy stationers included pictorial writing paper with steel line engraved vignettes. See Ralph Hyde, 'A year for celebrating W. F. Rock', *Print Quarterly* 19 (2002): 341–52 and http://www.devon.gov.uk/print/index/cultureheritage/libraries/localstudies/lsdatabase.htm?url=etched/etched/100127/1.html.

6. There were evidently at least two editions of this image, a later version replaced the original caption with details of the voyage with one that read, 'The Royal Chinese junk, Keying: the first vessel of Chinese construction which ever reached Europe, now on view at the Temple-Bar Pier, Essex St. Strand London, manned by a Chinese crew, under the command of the Mandarin Hesing, of Canton, the preparer of the celebrated Hesing's mixture of royal Chinese junk teas.'

7. Myles Birket Foster (1825–99) served his apprenticeship with the notable wood engraver, Ebenezer Landells, working on illustrations for *Punch* magazine and *The Illustrated London News*. He later left Landells employment, though continued working for *The Illustrated London News* and *The Illustrated London Almanack* and became a popular illustrator, watercolour artist and engraver.

8. Ebenezer Landells (1808–60) was a pupil of the eminent engraver Thomas Bewick (1753–1858). He moved to London in 1829 and began his own engraving workshop, becoming one of the founders of *Punch* in 1841, though financial difficulties meant his involvement was short-lived. When *The Illustrated London News* was founded in 1842, Landells became its first artist correspondent and worked for the magazine until his death. He was one of the most important of Victorian illustrators.

9. In *Shipbuilding & Shipping Record: A Journal of Shipbuilding, Marine Engineering, Dock, Harbours & Shipping* 78 (October 1951), Commander Hilary Poland Mead, RN, noted that there were no rules on what was or was not a courtesy flag where there were differences between the national flag and the merchant ensign. There still are none, just conventions.

10. See Martyn Gregory, *Paintings of the China Coast*, 1990.

11. A copy is also in the G. E. Morrison Collection of images in the Toyo Bunko archive in Tokyo, catalogue number E-3-10, see http://61.197.194.13/gazou/Honkon_dohanga-e.html.

12. See Kevin J. Avery, 'Movies for Manifest Destiny: The Moving Panorama Phenomenon in America', in Kevin J. Avery and Tom Hardiman, *The Grand Moving Panorama of "Pilgrim's Progress"*, Montclair, NJ: Montclair Art Museum, 1999. The

painting was not part of Waugh's original 1849, 2.4 m (8') high, fifty-scene panorama of the tour—the 'Mirror of Italy'—but was painted later when the panorama
was extended to 800' in length to create the later, longer 'Italia'.

13. Edward Walford, *Old and New London: A Narrative of Its History, Its People, and Its
Places. Illustrated with numerous engravings from the most authentic sources: Westminster
and the Western Suburbs*, vol. III, London: Cassell Petter & Galpin, 1878, Ch. xxxvii,
p. 289.

14. Richard D Altick, *The English Common Reader: A Social History of the Mass Reading
Public*, 2nd ed., Columbus: Ohio State University Press, 1998; Kay Boardman,
'"Charting the Golden Stream": Recent Work on Victorian Periodicals', *Victorian
Studies* 48 (2006): 505–17; Matthew Rubery, 'Journalism' in *The Cambridge
Companion to Victorian Culture*, ed. Francis O'Gorman, Cambridge, UK: Cambridge
University Press, 2010, pp. 177–94.

15. See *The London Gazette*, Court for Relief of Insolvent Debtors, 1855, p. 3346, at
http://www.london-gazette.co.uk/issues/21775/pages/3346/page.pdf, accessed
on 11 April 2013.

16. L. S. Dawson, *Memoirs of Hydrography, including brief biographies of the Principal
Officers who have served in H.M. Naval Surveying Service between the years 1750 and
1885*, Part 2: *1830–1885* (Eastbourne: Henry W. Keay [The Imperial Library],
1885), p. 3.

Bibliography

Primary Sources

Anon. *The Chinese Junk "Keying," being a full account of that vessel, with extracts from the journal of Capt. Kellett.* New York: Israel Sackett No. 1 Nassau Street, 1847.

Anon. *A Description of the Chinese Junk, "Keying", printed for the proprietors of the junk and sold only on board.* London: J. Such, 1848.

Newspaper stories from 1846 to 1855 in:
    Aberdeen Journal, The Belfast News-Letter, Bristol Mercury, Caledonian Mercury, Daily News, Derby Mercury, The Era, Glasgow Herald, Hampshire Telegraph & Sussex Chronicle, Hull Packet and East Riding Times, The Illustrated London News, Jersey Times, Liverpool Mercury, Lloyd's Weekly Newsletter, Manchester Times & Gazette, The Morning Chronicle, New-York Daily Tribune, New York Tribune, The Pictorial Times, Plymouth and Devonport Weekly Journal and Advertiser, Preston Guardian and *The Times.*

Library of Congress. *The Congressional Record.* 30th Congress. http://memory.loc.gov/ cgibin/ ampage?collId= llsb&fileName =026/llsb026.db&recNum=1563

Library of Congress. *Papers of Caleb Cushing. Special Correspondence, 1817–1899,* n.d., Box 144. http://lccn.loc.gov/mm78017509

The London Gazette, Court for Relief of Insolvent Debtors, 1855, http://www.london-gazette.co.uk/issues/21775/pages/3346/page.pdf

Unpublished Sources

Caplan, Aaron. 'Nathan Dunn's Chinese Museum'. BA thesis, University of Pennsylvania, 1986. http://www.amphilsoc.org/mole/view?docId=ead/Mss.069.C17n-ead.xml; query=;brand=default

Cavell, Samantha. 'A Social History of Midshipmen and Quarterdeck Boys in the Royal Navy, 1761–1831'. Unpublished PhD thesis, University of Exeter, 2010.

Church, Sally K. 'Nanjing's *Longjiang Shipyard Treatise* and Our Knowledge of Ming Ships' [On Li Zhaoxiang (李照祥), *Longjiang chuanchang zhi* (龍江船廠志), 1553]. Research in progress financed by the Golden Web Foundation made available to the author by Dr. Sally K. Church.

Secondary Sources

Abell, Sir Westcott. *The Shipwright's Trade*. London: Conway Maritime Press, 1981.

Abrahams, Alek. 'The Chinese Junk Keying'. *Notes and Queries* 6 (July–December 1906): 227.

Allen, Jerry. *The Sea Years of Joseph Conrad*. London: Methuen, 1967.

Altick, Richard D. *The English Common Reader: A Social History of the Mass Reading Public*. 2nd ed. Columbus: Ohio State University Press, 1998.

American Lloyd's Register of American and Foreign Shipping. New York: American Lloyd's, 1861.

Anderson, Patricia J. *The Printed Image and the Transformation of Popular Culture, 1790–1860*. Oxford: Clarendon Press, 1991.

Andrade, Tonio. 'Was the European Sailing Ship a Key Technology of European Expansion? Evidence from East Asia'. *International Journal of Maritime History* 23, no. 2 (December 2011): 17–40.

Archibald, E. H. H. *The Dictionary of Sea Painters of Europe and America*. 3rd ed. Woodbridge: Antique Collectors' Club, 2000.

Audemard, L. *Juncos Chineses*. Macao: Museo Maritimo de Macao, 1994.

Avery, Kevin J. 'Movies for Manifest Destiny: The Moving Panorama Phenomenon in America'. In *The Grand Moving Panorama of Pilgrim's Progress*, edited by Kevin J. Avery and Tom Hardiman. Montclair, NJ: Montclair Art Museum, 1999. http://www.tfaoi.com/aa/3aa/3aa66.htm

Barker, Richard. 'The *Liao* and the Displacement of Ships in the Ming Navy: Defoe's View of Chinese Claims, c. 1700'. *The Mariner's Mirror* 82 (1996): 484.

Benedict, Erastus C. *The American Admiralty Law: Its Jurisdictions and Practice with Practical Forms and Directions*. New York: Banks, Gould & Co., 1850.

Bickers, Robert. *Empire Made Me: An Englishman Adrift in Shanghai*. New York: Columbia University Press, 2004.

———. *The Scramble for China: Foreign Devils in the Qing Empire, 1832–1914*. London: Penguin Books, 2011.

Blakeney, William. *On the Coasts of Cathay and Cipango Forty Years Ago: A Record of Surveying Service in the China, Yellow and Japan Seas and on the Seaboard of Korea and Manchuria*. London: Elliot Stock, 1902.

Bland, David. *A History of Book Illustration: The Illuminated Manuscript and the Printed Book*. Cleveland: World Publishing Company, 1985.

Blunt, Edmund M. *The American Coast Pilot: containing directions for the principal harbors, capes and headlands, of the coasts of North and South America: describing the soundings, bearings of the lighthouses and beacons from the rocks, shoals and ledges, &c. with the prevailing winds, setting of the currents, &c. and the latitudes and longitudes of the principal harbors and capes, together with a tide table.* 14th ed. New York: Edward and George Blunt, 1842.

Blunt, Joseph. *The Shipmaster's Assistant and Commercial Digest.* New York: E. & G. W. Blunt, 1837. Reprinted in London: Macdonald and Jane's, 1974.

Boardman, Kay. '"Charting the Golden Stream": Recent Work on Victorian Periodicals.' *Victorian Studies* 48 (2006): 505–17.

Bonner, Arthur. *Alas! What Brought Thee Hither?: The Chinese in New York 1800–1950.* Madison, NJ: Fairleigh Dickinson University Press, 1997.

Bouguer, Pierre. *Traité du navire.* Jombert, 1746.

Bowditch, Nathaniel. *The New American Practical Navigator.* 2nd ed. New York: E. & M. Blunt, 1826.

Brindley, H. H. 'The Keying'. *The Mariner's Mirror* 8, no. 4 (1922): 305–14.

Carpenter, Kenneth J. *The History of Scurvy & Vitamin C.* Cambridge: Cambridge University Press, 1986.

Carroll, John M. *Edge of Empires: Chinese Elites and British Colonials in Hong Kong.* Hong Kong: Hong Kong University Press, 2007.

Carter, Susan B. 'Embracing Isolation: Chinese American Migration to Small-Town America, 1882–1943'. Draft paper proposed for the 36th Annual Meeting of the Population Association of America, San Francisco, CA, 3–5 May 2012. http:// paa2012.princeton. edu/papers/121668

Casson, Lionel. *Ships and Seamanship in the Ancient World.* Baltimore: Johns Hopkins University Press, 1995.

Chalmers, J. 'The Chinese Ch'ih Measure'. *China Review* 13 (1884): 332–6.

Chapelle, Howard I. *The Search for Speed under Sail, 1700–1855.* New York: W. W. Norton, 1967.

Chen, Jack. *The Chinese of America.* New York: Harper Row, 1980.

'A Chinese Junk in London River'. *P.L.A. Monthly* (January 1939): 59–62.

The Chinese Repository, Journal of Occurrences, Article IV, vol. 15. Hong Kong (December 1846): 624.

Clifford, Brian, and Neil Illingworth. *The Voyage of the* Golden Lotus. London: Herbert Jenkins, 1962.

Clowes, William Laird. *The Royal Navy: A History from the Earliest Times to the Present,* 7 vols. London: Sampson, Low, Marston, 1901.

Coates, John F. and David K. Brown. 'The *Liao* and the Displacement of Ships in the Ming Navy'. *The Mariner's Mirror* 82 (1996): 484.

Codell, Julie F., ed. *Imperial Co-Histories: National Identities and the British and Colonial Press.* Madison, NJ: Fairleigh Dickinson University Press, 2003.

Cole, Henry. *Fifty Years of Public Work of Sir Henry Cole, K.C.B., Accounted for in His Deeds, Speeches and Writings,* 2 vols. London: George Bell & Sons, 1884.

Conner, Patrick. *George Chinnery, 1774–1852.* London: Antique Collector's Club, 1999.

Conrad, Joseph. *The Rescue*. London: Penguin Books, 1985.

Corbin, Alain. *The Lure of the Sea: The Discovery of the Seaside in the Western World, 1750–1840*. Berkeley: University of California Press, 1994.

Cronin, Morton. 'Currier and Ives: A Content Analysis'. *American Quarterly* 4, no. 4 (Winter 1952): 317–30.

Crouch, Archer Philip. *Silvertown and Neighbourhood (Including East and West Ham): A Retrospect*. London: Thomas Burleigh, 1900.

Curtis, George Ticknor. *A Treatise on the Rights and Duties of Merchant Seamen according to the General Maritime Law and the Statutes of the United States*. Boston: Little and Brown, 1841. Online edition: http://www.archive.org/details/treatiseon rights00curt

Cushman, Jennifer Wayne. *Fields from the Sea: Chinese Junk Trade with Siam during the Late Eighteenth and Early Nineteenth Centuries*. Ithaca, NY: Cornell Southeast Asia Publications Program, 1993.

Dana, Richard Henry, Jr. *The Seaman's Friend*. New York: Scribner, 1841.

———. *Two Years before the Mast: A Personal Narrative of Life at Sea*, edited by Homer Eaton Keyes. New York: Macmillan, 1939.

Davidson, Sam. *Marine Art and the Clyde: 100 Years of Sea, Sail and Steam*. Upton: Jones-Sands, 2001.

———. *Samuel Walters—Marine Artist: Fifty Years of Sea, Sail and Steam*. Coventry: Jones Sands, 1992.

Davies, Stephen. 'Archaeology, History and Modeling the Past'. In *Proceedings of the International Symposium on the Penglai Ancient Ships*, edited by Xi Longfei and Cai Wei. Wuhan: Changjiang Press, 2009: 320–47.

———. *Coasting Past: The Last South China Coastal Trading Junks Photographed by William Heering*. Hong Kong: Hong Kong Maritime Museum, 2013.

———. *Fathoming the Unfathomable: Even Leviathans Have Limits*. E-book, 2005. http://www.1421exposed.com

———. *French Ships, Friendship*. Hong Kong: Hong Kong Maritime Museum, 2008.

———. 'Maritime Museums: Who Needs Them?' Nalanda-Sriwajaya Working Papers No. 11. Singapore: Nalanda-Sriwajaya Centre, Institute of South East Asian Studies, 2012. http://nsc.iseas.edu.sg/documents/working_papers/nscwps011.pdf

———. 'Re-contextualizing the Prime Meridian: Interpreting Maritime Museum Collections for an Asian Audience'. Paper presented at the 2011 Conference of the International Congress of Maritime Museums, Smithsonian Museum, Washington DC, 10 October 2011.

———. '"Same Ship, Different Cap Tallies": Conflicting Ideas of Ship Organization in the Junk *Keying*'. In *Of Ships and Men: New Comparative Approaches in Asian Maritime History and Archaeology*, edited by Calanca, Paola P-Y Manguin and Eric Rieth. Paris: École française d'Extrême-Orient, forthcoming.

———. 'Seeing the *Keying*'. In *The Position and Mission of China's Maritime Culture*, edited by China Maritime Museum. Shanghai: Shanghai Bookstore Publishing House, 2011: 134–83.

————. 'The Yale Maps and Western Hydrography: Influences and Contributions'. Paper presented at the *International Workshop on Maritime East Asia, 1433–1840; The Chinese Navigational Map at Yale University and Its Significance*, 16–18 June 2010. Hsinchu, Taiwan: National Chiao-tung University.

Davies, Stephen, and Elaine Morgan. *Cruising Guide to Southeast Asia*, vol. 2. St Ives: Imray, Laurie, Norie & Wilson, 1999.

Dawson, L. S. *Memoirs of Hydrography, including brief biographies of the Principal Officers who have served in H.M. Naval Surveying Service between the years 1750 and 1885, Part 2: 1830–1885.* Eastbourne: Henry W. Keay (The Imperial Library), 1885.

Delanghe, J. R., M. R. Langlois, M. L. de Buyzhere and M. A. Torck. 'Vitamin C Deficiency and Scurvy Are Not Only a Dietary Problem but Are Codetermined by the Haptoglobin Polymorphism'. *Clinical Chemistry* 53, no. 8 (2007): 1397–1400.

Deng, Gang. *The Premodern Chinese Economy—Structural Equilibrium and Capitalist Sterility.* London: Routledge, 1999.

Dickens, Charles. 'The Chinese Junk'. *Examiner*, 24 June 1848.

Dickie, John. *The British Consul: Heir to a Great Tradition.* New York: Columbia University Press, 2007.

Dictionary of National Biography 1885–1900, vol. 51, edited by Sidney Lee. London: Smith Elder & Co., 1897.

Dokkum, Klaas van. *Ship Knowledge, Ship Design, Construction and Operation*, 5th ed. Enkhuizen: DOKMAR, 2008.

Donnelly, I. A. *Chinese Junks and Other Native Craft.* Shanghai: Kelly & Walsh, 1930.

Dowey, James. 'Mind over Matter: Empirical Evidence of the Industrial Enlightenment as the Origin of Modern Economic Growth'. Paper presented at London School of Economics Economic History PhD workshop, 25 January 2012. http://www2.lse.ac.uk/economicHistory/seminars/ EH590Workshop/LT2012papers/dowey.pdf

Earle, Peter. *Sailors: English Merchant Seamen 1650–1775.* London: Methuen, 1998.

Eitel, E. J. *Europe in China: The History of Hong Kong from the Beginning to the Year 1882.* Taipei: Cheng-Wen Publishing Co, 1968.

Elliott, Mark C. *The Manchu Way: The Eight Banners and Ethnic Identity in Late Imperial China.* Stanford, CA: Stanford University Press, 2001.

Elvin, Mark. *The Retreat of the Elephants: An Environmental History of China.* New Haven, CT: Yale University Press, 2004.

———— (ed.). *Transport in Transition: The Evolution of Traditional Shipping in China*, translated by Andrew Watson. Ann Arbor: Centre for Chinese Studies, University of Michigan, 1972.

Ewald, Janet J. 'Crossers of the Sea: Slaves, Freedmen, and Other Migrants in the Northwestern Indian Ocean, c.1750–1914'. *American Historical Review* 105, no. 1 (February 2000): 69–91.

Fairbank, J. K. *Trade and Diplomacy on the China Coast: The Opening of the Treaty Ports 1842–1854.* Cambridge, MA: Harvard University Press, 1964.

Falconer, William. *An Universal Dictionary of the Marine.* London: Cadell, 1780. Online at National Library of Australia. http://southseas.nla.gov.au/refs/falc/title.html

Fanning, A. E. *Steady as She Goes: A History of the Compass Department of the Admiralty*. London: HMSO, 1986.

Fincham, John. *A History of Naval Architecture: To Which Is Prefixed an Introductory Dissertation on the Application of Mathematical Science to the Art of Naval Construction*. London: Whittaker, 1851.

——. *An Introductory Outline of the Practice of Shipbuilding, &c., &c*, 2nd ed. Portsea: William Woodward, 1825.

Fleming, Fergus. *Barrow's Boys: The Original Extreme Adventurers: A Stirring Story of Daring Fortitude and Outright Lunacy*. London: Granta, 2001.

Forbes, Robert Bennet. *Personal Reminiscences*. 2nd ed. Cambridge, MA: University Press, John Wilson & Son, 1882.

——. *The Voyage of the* Jamestown *on Her Mission of Mercy*. Boston: Eastburn's Press, 1847.

Fox, Grace. *British Admirals and Chinese Pirates, 1832–1869*. London: Kegan Paul, 1940.

Frost, Diane, ed. *Ethnic Labour and British Imperial Trade (Immigrants & Minorities)*. London: Routledge, 1995.

Gardiner, R., ed. *The Heyday of Sail: The Merchant Sailing Ship 1650–1830*. London: Conway Maritime Press, 1995.

Gerr, Dave. *Boat Mechanical Systems Handbook: How to Design, Install, and Recognize Proper Systems in Boats*. Camden, ME: International Marine/Ragged Mountain Press, 2008.

Graham, G. S. *The China Station: War and Diplomacy, 1830–1860*. Oxford: Oxford University Press, 1978.

Graham, V. E. 'The Mandarin Hesing and the Chinese Junk the *Keying*'. *Arts of Asia* 30, no. 2 (2000): 96–102.

Gregory, Martyn. *Paintings of the China Coast by Chinese and Western Artists, 1790–1890*. London: Martyn Gregory Gallery, 1990.

Griffin, Eldon. *Clippers and Consuls: American Consular and Commercial Relations with Eastern Asia, 1845–1860*. Ann Arbor, MI: Edwards Bros., 1939.

Gurney, Alan. *Compass: A Story of Exploration and Innovation*. New York: W. W. Norton, 2004.

Gützlaff, K. F. *Journal of Three Voyages along the Coast of China in 1831, 1832, and 1833*. New York: J. P. Haven, 1833.

Haddad, John Rogers. 'China of the American Imagination: The Influence of Trade on U.S. Portrayals of China, 1820–1850'. In Johnson, *Narratives of Free Trade*, 57–82.

——. *The Romance of China: Excursions to China in U.S. Culture, 1776–1876*. New York: Columbia University Press, 2008.

Hansell, P. 'The Colourful Douglas Lapraik (1818–1869)'. *Antiquarian Horology* 27, no. 3 (2003): 331–2.

Harland, John H. *Seamanship in the Age of Sail: An Account of Shiphandling of the Sailing Man-of-War, 1600–1860*. London: Brassey, 1982.

Harris, David. *Of Battle and Beauty: Felice Beato's Photographs of China.* Santa Barbara, CA: Santa Barbara Museum of Art, 1999.

Harter, Jim, ed. *Nautical Illustrations: 681 Permission-Free Illustrations from Nineteenth-Century Sources.* New York: Dover Publications, 2003.

Hasler, H. G., and J. K. Macleod. *Practical Junk Rig: Design, Aerodynamics and Handling.* London: Adlard Coles, 1988.

Hattendorf, John B., ed. *The Oxford Encyclopaedia of Maritime History.* Oxford: Oxford University Press, 2007.

Hawkins, Clifford. *The Dhow: An Illustrated History of the Dhow and Its World.* Lymington: Nautical Publishing, 1977.

Hayter, Adrian. Sheila *in the Wind*, London: Hodder & Stoughton, 1959.

Holdsworth, May, and Christopher Munn, eds. *Dictionary of Hong Kong Biography.* Hong Kong: Hong Kong University Press, 2011.

Hope Chang, Elizabeth. *Britain's Chinese Eye: Literature, Empire and Aesthetics in Nineteenth-Century Britain.* Stanford, CA: Stanford University Press, 2010.

Horsburgh, James. *The India Directory, Directions for sailing to and from the East Indies, China, Australia, and the Interjacent Ports of Africa and South America: Compiled chiefly from original journals of the Honourable Company's ships, and from observations and remarks, resulting from the experience of twenty-one years in the navigation of those seas.* 5th ed. London: W. H. Allen & Co., 1843.

Hummel, A. W., ed. *Eminent Chinese of the Ch'ing Period (1644–1912).* Washington, DC: Library of Congress, 1943.

Hunter, William C. *An American in Canton (1825–1844): A Reprint of* The Fan Kwae at Canton before Treaty Days (1825–1844) *and* Bits of Old China, edited by G. Bonsall. Hong Kong: Derwent, 1994.

Hutchinson, W. *A Treatise on Naval Architecture.* 4th ed. Liverpool: T. Billinge, 1794. Reprinted in London: Conway Maritime Press, 1969.

Hyde, Ralph. 'A Year for Celebrating W. F. Rock'. *Print Quarterly* 19 (2002): 341–52.

Hydrographer to the Navy. *Indonesia Pilot*, vol. 2, NP 36, 1st ed. Taunton: Hydrographer of the Navy, 1975.

———. *Ocean Passages for the World.* 4th ed. Taunton: Hydrographer to the Navy, 1987.

Irigoin, Maria Alejandra. 'A Trojan Horse in 19th Century China? The Global Consequences of the Breakdown of the Spanish Silver Peso Standard'. http://www.lse.ac.uk/collections/economicHistory/seminars/Irigoin.pdf

Isherwood, Sir Joseph. 'Economy in Modern Shipbuilding—II'. *Shipping: A Weekly Journal of Marine Trades*, 22 June 1918.

Ji, Zhaojin. *A History of Modern Shanghai Banking: The Rise and Decline of China's Finance Capitalism.* New York: M. E. Sharpe, 2003.

Johnson, H., and F. S. Lightfoot. *Maritime New York in Nineteenth-Century Photographs.* New York: Dover Publications, 1980.

Johnson, Kendall, ed. *Narratives of Free Trade: The Commercial Cultures of Early US-China Relations.* Hong Kong: Hong Kong University Press, 2011.

Johnson, W., ed. *Shaky Ships: The Formal Richness of Chinese Shipbuilding*. Exhibition Catalogue. Antwerp: National Maritime Museum, 1993.

Jones, Douglas. 'The Chinese in Britain: Origins and Development of a Community'. *Journal of Ethnic and Migration Studies* 7, no. 3 (Winter 1979): 397–402.

Junger, Sebastian. *The Perfect Storm: A True Story of Men against the Sea*. New York: W. W. Norton, 1997.

Kemp, Peter, ed. *The Oxford Companion to Ships and the Sea*. Oxford: Oxford University Press, 1976.

Kenchington, Trevor. 'The Structures of English Wooden Ships: William Sutherland's Ship, c. 1710'. *The Northern Mariner/Le Marin du nord* 3, no. 1 (1993): 1–43.

Kerchove, René de. *International Maritime Dictionary*. 2nd ed. New York: Van Nostrand, 1961.

Kitchen, Jonathan S. *The Employment of Merchant Seamen*. London: Croom Helm, 1980.

Knöbl, Kuno. *Tai Ki: To the Point of No Return*. Boston: Little, Brown, 1976.

Koizumi, Teizo. 'The Operation of Chinese Junks'. In Elvin, *The Evolution of Traditional Shipping in China*, 1–14.

Kuo Sung-t'ao, Hsi-hung Liu and Te-i Chang. *The First Chinese Embassy to the West: The Journals of Kuo-Sung-T'ao, Liu Hsi-Hung and Chang Te-Yi*, translated by J. D. Frodsham. Oxford: Clarendon Press, 1974.

Langdon, William. *Ten Thousand Things Relating to China and the Chinese: An Epitome of the Genius, Government, History, Literature, Agriculture, Arts, Trade, Manners, Customs, and Social Life of the People of the Celestial Empire*. London: G M'Kewan, 1842.

La Rocco, Barbara, ed. *A Maritime History of New York*. New York: Going Coastal, 2004.

Lavery, Brian. *The Arming and Fitting of English Ships of War, 1600–1815*. Annapolis, MD: Naval Institute Press, 1989.

———. *The Ship of the Line*, vol. 1: *The Development of the Battlefleet 1650–1850*. London: Conway Maritime Press, 1984.

Lazich, Michael C. 'American Missionaries and the Opium Trade in Nineteenth-century China'. *Journal of World History* 17, no. 2 (2006): 197–223. http://www.history cooperative.org/cgi-bin/justtp.chi?act=justtop&url=http://historycooperative. org/journals/jwh/17.2/lazich.html

Levien, M., ed. *The Cree Journals: The Voyages of Edward H. Cree, Surgeon R.N., as Related in His Private Journals, 1837–1856*. Exeter: Webb & Bower, 1981.

Lewis, Michael. *The Navy in Transition, 1814–1864: A Social History*. London: Hodder & Stoghton, 1965.

Li Zhaoxiang (李照祥). *Longjiang chuanchang zhi* (龍江船廠志) [Longjiang shipyard treatise], 1553.

Lin, Man-houng. *China Upside Down: Currency, Society, and Ideologies, 1808–1856*. http://www.fas.harvard.edu/~asiactr/publications/pdfs/Lin%20Front%20Matter. pdf

Liu, K. C. *Anglo-American Steamship Rivalry in China, 1862–1874*. Taipei: Rainbow Bridge Book Co., 1962.

Liu, L., and C. Li. 'Characteristics of Guangdong Wooden Junks'. In Zhang, *Proceedings of the International Sailing Ship Conference*, pp. 275–85.

Lubbock, Basil. *The Opium Clippers*. Glasgow: Brown, Son & Ferguson, 1933.

Lundy, Derek. *The Way of a Ship: A Square-Rigger Voyage in the Last Days of Sail*. London: Ecco Press, 2004.

Lyon, David and Winfield, Rif. *The Sail & Steam Navy List: All the Ships of the Royal Navy, 1815–1889*. London: Chatham, 2004

MacEvoy, Bruce. 'The Poetic Landscape'. http://www.handprint.com/HP/WCL/artist03.html

MacGregor, D. R. *Fast Sailing Ships: Their Design and Construction, 1775–1875*. 2nd ed. London: Conway Maritime Press, 1988.

Maddocks, Melvin. *The Atlantic Crossing*. Alexandra, VA: Time-Life Books, 1981.

Manguin, Pierre-Yves. 'The Southeast Asian Ship: An Historical Approach'. *Journal of Southeast Asian Studies* 11, no. 2 (1980): 266–76.

Marchaj, C. A. *The Aero-hydrodynamics of Sailing*, 3rd revised ed. London: Adlard Coles Nautical, 2000.

————. *Seaworthiness: The Forgotten Factor*. London: Adlard Coles Nautical, 1986.

Maritime Cargo Transport Conference. *Inland and Maritime Transportation of Unitized Cargo: A Comparative Economic Analysis of Break-Bulk and Unit Load Systems for Maritime General Cargo from Shipper to Consignee*. Washington: National Academy of Sciences / National Research Council, 1963.

McGrail, Sean. *Boats of the World from the Stone Age to Medieval Times*. Oxford: Oxford University Press, 2001.

McNeill, J. R. 'Woods and Warfare in World History'. *Environmental History* 9, no. 3 (2004): 388–410. http://www.historycooperative.org/journals/eh/9.3/mcneill.html

Mead, Hilary Poland. 'Courtesy Flags'. *Shipbuilding & Shipping Record: A Journal of Shipbuilding, Marine Engineering, Dock, Harbours & Shipping* 78 (October 1951): 426.

Meagher, Arnold J. *The Coolie Trade: The Traffic in Chinese Laborers to Latin America*. New York: XLibris, 2008.

Menzies, Gavin. *1421: The Year China Discovered America*. New York: Harper Perennial, 2004.

————. *1434: The Year a Chinese Fleet Sailed to Italy and Ignited the Renaissance*. New York: William Morrow, 2008.

The Mercantile Navy List, corrected to 20th December 1849. London: Bradbury & Evans, 1850.

Milburn, William. *Oriental Commerce of the East India Trader's Complete Guide*. London: Kingsbury, Parbury & Allen, 1825.

Mokyr, Joel. *The Gifts of Athena: Historical Origins of the Knowledge Economy*. Princeton, NJ: Princeton University Press, 2003.

Morrison, J. H. *History of the New York Shipyards*. New York: Wm. F. Sametz, 1909.

Mott, Lawrence V. *The Development of the Rudder: A Technological Tale*. London: Chatham Publishing / College Station: Texas A&M University Press, 1997.

Munn, Christopher. *Anglo-China: Chinese People and British Rule in Hong Kong, 1841–1880*. Hong Kong: Hong Kong University Press, 2009.

The Nautical Magazine and Naval Chronicle for 1838: A Journal of Papers on Subjects Connected with Maritime Affairs, vol. 7. London: Simpkin, Marshall & Co., 1838.

Needham, Joseph, et al. *Science and Civilization in China*, vol. 4: *Physics and Physical Technology*. Cambridge: Cambridge University Press, 1971.

North, Bernard. 'Watch and Clockmakers of Hong Kong'. *Antiquarian Horology* 32 (2) (June 2010): 180–2.

Oba, Osamu. 'On the Scroll of Chinese Ships in the Possession of the Matsuura Museum—Materials for the Study of Chinese Trading Ships in Edo Period'. *Bulletin of the Institute of Oriental and Occidental Studies of Kansai University* 5 (March 1972): 13–50.

Official Catalogue of the Great Exhibition of the Works of Industry of All Nations, 1851. Corrected ed. London: Spicer Bros., 1851.

Oliveira, Fernando. *Liura da fabrica das naos*. Macao: Academia de Marinha / Museu Maritimo de Macao, 1995.

Padfield, Peter. *Guns at Sea*. London: St Martin's Press, 1974.

Pagani, Catherine. 'Objects and the Press: Images of China in Nineteenth-Century Britain'. In Codell, *Imperial Co-Histories: National Identities and the British and Colonial Press*, pp. 147–66.

Palmer, Michael A. *Command at Sea: Naval Command and Control since the Sixteenth Century*. Cambridge, MA: Harvard University Press, 2007.

Pâris, François-Edmond. *L'Essai sur la construction navale des peuples extra-européens ou Collection des navires et pirogues construits par les habitants de l'Asie, de la Malaisie, du Grand Océan et de l'Amérique dessinés et mesurés pendant les voyages autour du monde de L'Astrolabe, La Favorite et L'Artémise*. Paris: Arthus Bertrand, 1841.

Paris, Pierre. *Esquisse d'une ethnographie navale des peuples Annamites*. 2nd ed. Rotterdam: Museum Voor Land en Volkenkunde en het Maritiem Museum 'Prins Hendrik' Rotterdam, 1955.

Parker, E. H., ed. *Chinese Account of the Opium War*. Shanghai: Kelley & Walsh, 1888.

Parkinson, C. Northcote. *Trade in the Eastern Seas, 1793–1813*. Cambridge: Cambridge University Press, 1937.

Pickford, Nigel, and Michael Hatcher. *The Legacy of the* Tek Sing: *China's Titanic—Its Tragedy and Its Treasure*. London: Granta, 2000.

Piétri, J. B. *Voiliers d'Indochine*. New ed. Saigon: S.I.L.I., 1949.

Pritchard, L. G. 'Chinese Junks [Keying 1806–1912, incl compartments]'. *The Mariner's Mirror* 9 (1923): 89–91.

Putnam, George R. *Lighthouses and Lightships of the United States*. New York: Houghton-Mifflin, 1917.

Richter, H. G., and M. J. Dallwitz. 'Commercial Timbers: Descriptions, Illustrations, Identification, and Information Retrieval'. 4 May 2000, at http://biodiversity.uno. edu/delta/, accessed on 10 February 2013.

Rodger, N. A. M. *The Wooden World: An Anatomy of the Georgian Navy*. London: Collins, 1986.

Rosenwaike, Ira. *Population History of New York City*. Syracuse NY: Syracuse University Press, 1972.

Rubery, Matthew. 'Journalism' in *The Cambridge Companion to Victorian Culture*. ed. Francis O'Gorman. Cambridge, UK: Cambridge University Press, 2010: 177–94.

Russell, J. Scott. 'On the Longitudinal System in the Structure of Iron Ships'. In *Transactions of the Institution of Naval Architects*, vol. 3, edited by E. J. Reed. London: Institution of Naval Architects, 1862: 160–71.

Savage, Edward H. *Boston Events: A brief mention and the date of more than 5,000 events that transpired in Boston from 1630 to 1880, covering a period of 250 years*. Boston: Tolman & White, 1884.

———. *Police Record and Recollections, or Boston by Daylight and Gaslight for Two Hundred and Forty Years*. Boston: John P. Dale, 1873.

Schoch, Richard W. *Shakespeare's Victorian Stage: Performing History in the Theatre of Charles Kean*. Cambridge: Cambridge University Press, 1998.

Schottenhammer, A., et al., eds. *East Asian Maritime History I: Trade and Transfer across the East Asian "Mediterranean"*. Wiesbaden: Harassowitz Verlag, 2005.

Schwartz, Mel M. *Encyclopedia of Materials, Parts and Finishes*. 2nd ed. Boca Raton, FL: CRC Press, 2002.

Scruton, Roger. *The Aesthetics of Architecture*. Princeton, NJ: Princeton University Press, 1980.

Sherwood, Marika. 'Race, Nationality and Employment among Lascar Seamen, 1660 to 1945'. *Journal of Ethnic and Migration Studies* 17, no. 2 (January 1991): 229–44.

Sleeswyk, A. W. 'The *Liao* and the Displacement of Ships in the Ming Navy'. *The Mariner's Mirror* 82 (1996): 3–13.

Smyth, W. H. *The Sailor's Word-book: An alphabetical digest of nautical terms, including some more especially military and scientific, but useful to seamen; as well as archaisms of early voyagers, etc.* London: Blackie and Son, 1867.

Southwell, C. R., and J. D. Bultman. 'Marine Borer Resistance of Untreated Woods Over Long Periods of Immersion in Tropical Waters'. *Biotropica* 3, no. 1 (June 1971): 81–107.

Steffy, J. Richard. *Wooden Shipbuilding and the Interpretation of Shipwrecks*. College Station: Texas A&M University Press, 1994.

Sutton, Jean. *Lords of the East*. London: Conway Maritime, 1981.

Sweet, Wayne, Robert Fett, Jeffrey Kerling and Paul La Violette. 'Air-Sea Interaction Effects in the Lower Troposphere Across the North Wall of the Gulf Stream'. *Monthly Weather Review* 109, no. 5 (May 1981): 1042–52.

Tang Zhiba, Xin Yuanou and Zheng Ming. 'The Initial Textual Researches and Restorations: Studies on Zheng He's 2000 Liao Wooden Treasure Ships (the 5th version)'. *Zhenghe's Voyage Studies* 2 (2005): 32–48.

Tarrant, William. *The Hongkong Almanack and Directory for 1846: With an Appendix.* Hong Kong: Office of the China Mail, 1846.

Tchen, John Kuo Wei. *New York before Chinatown: Orientalism and the Shaping of American Culture, 1776–1882.* Baltimore: Johns Hopkins University Press, 2001.

Tey, Jose Maria. *Hong Kong to Barcelona in the Junk Rubia.* London: Harrap, 1959.

Thiriez, Régine. 'Listing Early Photographers of China: Directories as Sources'. http://pnclink.org/ annual/annual2000/2000pdf/5-13-1.pdf

Thornbury, Walter, and Edward Walford. *Old and New London: A Narrative of Its History, Its People, and Its Places,* vol. 3: *Westminster and the Western Suburbs.* London: Cassell Petter & Galpin, 1878.

Tibbetts, G. R. *Arab Navigation in the Indian Ocean before the Coming of the Portuguese.* London: Oriental Translation Fund / Royal Asiatic Society, 1981.

Torck, M. 'The Issue of Food Provision and Scurvy in East and West: A Comparative Enquiry into Medieval Knowledge of Provisioning, Medicine and Seafaring History'. In Schottenhammer, *East Asian Maritime History I: Trade and Transfer across the East Asian 'Mediterranean'*, pp. 275–88.

Trimming, Michael S. K. 'The Pechili Trader: A Hull Lines Plan'. *The Mariner's Mirror* 97, no. 3 (2011): 121.

Tunstall, Brian, and Nicholas Tracy, eds. *Naval Warfare in the Age of Sail: The Evolution of Fighting Tactics, 1650–1815.* London: Wellfleet Press, 2001.

Tupholme, C. H. S. 'Dermatitis from Tung Oil'. *British Journal of Dermatology* 51, no. 3 (1939): 138–40.

Unger, Richard W., ed. *Cogs, Caravels and Galleons.* London: Brassey Publications, 1999.

University Hall 50th Anniversary. Hong Kong: University Hall Alumni, 2007.

Van Dyke, Paul A. *The Canton Trade: Life and Enterprise on the China Coast, 1700–1845.* Hong Kong: Hong Kong University Press, 2005.

———. *Merchants of Canton and Macao: Politics and Strategies in Eighteenth-Century Chinese Trade.* Hong Kong: Hong Kong University Press, 2011.

Van Tilburg, Hans. *Chinese Junks on the Pacific: Views from a Different Deck.* Gainesville: University Press of Florida, 2007.

Visram, Rosina. *Asians in Britain: 400 Years of History.* London: Pluto Press, 2002.

Wakeman, Frederic, Jr. *Strangers at the Gate: Social Disorder in South China 1839–1861.* Berkeley: University of California Press, 1966.

Walsh, Frank. *A History of Hong Kong.* Revised ed. London: HarperCollins, 1997.

Waters, Dan. 'Hong Kong Hongs with Long Histories and British Connections'. *Journal of the Hong Kong Branch of the Royal Asiatic Society* 30 (1990): 240–1.

Webb, Walter Prescott. *The Great Frontier.* Reno: University of Nevada Press, 2003.

Wei Yuan (魏源). *Sheng wu ji* (聖武記) [Record of the military operations of the present dynasty], vol. 3. Beijing: Zhonghua shuju, 1984.

Whittingham, H., and C. T. King. *Reed's Table of Distances between Ports and Places in All Parts of the World*. 11th ed. Sunderland: Thomas Reed, 1929.

Wilkinson, Endymion. *Chinese History: A Manual*. Revised and enlarged edition. Cambridge, MA: Harvard University Asia Center, 2000.

Williams, H. Dwight. *A Year in China and a Narrative of Capture and Imprisonment When Homeward Bound, on Board the Rebel Pirate Florida*. New York: Hurd & Houghton, 1864.

Williams, J. E. D. *From Sails to Satellites: The Origin and Development of Navigational Science*. Cambridge: Cambridge University Press, 1993.

Williams, Samuel Wells. *A Chinese Commercial Guide*. 4th ed. Canton: The Chinese Repository, 1856.

———. *The Middle Kingdom: A Survey of the Geography, Government, Education, Social Life, Arts, Religion &c. of the Chinese Empire and Its Inhabitants, with a new map of the Empire*, 2 vols. New York: Wiley & Putnam, 1848.

Wise, Henry. *An Analysis of One Hundred Voyages to and from India, China, &c. performed by ships of the honourable East India Company's service; with remarks on the advantages of steam-power applied as an auxiliary aid to shipping; and suggestions for improving thereby the communication with India, via the Cape of Good Hope*. London: J. W. Norie & Co, 1839.

Worcester, G. R. G. *The Junks and Sampans of the Yangtze*. Annapolis, MD: Naval Institute Press, 1971.

———. *Sail and Sweep in China: The History and Development of the Chinese Junk as Illustrated by the Collection of Models in the Science Museum*. London: HMSO, 1966.

Worden, Nigel, Elizabeth van Heyningen and Vivian Bickford-Smith. *Cape Town: The Making of a City*. Cape Town: David Philip, 1998.

Yale College Alumni. *Obituary Record of Graduates of Yale College Deceased during the Academical Year Ending in July, 1868 including the record of a few who died a short time previous, hitherto unreported*. New Haven, CT: Yale College Alumni, 1868.

Yap, Melanie, Dianne Leong Man. *Colour, Confusion and Concessions: The History of the Chinese in South Africa*. Hong Kong: Hong Kong University Press, 1996.

Young, Vernon. 'Lingard's Folly: The Lost Subject'. *The Kenyon Review* 15, no. 4 (Autumn 1953): 522–39.

Yule, H., and A. C. Burnell. *Hobson-Jobson: The Anglo-Indian Dictionary*. London: John Murray, 1886. Reprinted in London: Wordsworth, 1999.

Yung Wing. *My Life in China and America*. New York: Henry Holt & Co., 1909.

Zarach, Stephanie. *Changing Places: The Remarkable Story of the Hong Kong Shipowners*. Hong Kong: Hong Kong Shipowners' Association, 2007.

Zhang, S., ed. *Proceedings of the International Sailing Ship Conference*. Shanghai: Society of Naval Architecture and Marine Engineering, 1991.

Websites

Air draft of River Thames bridges. http://www.pla.co.uk/display_fixedpage.cfm/id/174

Boatdesign.net. Simple displacement calculation formulae. http://boatdesign.net/forums/showthread. php?t=930

Botanical Dermatology Database. Information on tung oil. http://www.botanical-dermatology-database.info/BotDermFolder/EUPH-16.html

British Library. Aspects of the Victorian Book. http://www.bl.uk/collections/early/victorian/intro.html

British Library. Catalogue of Posters. http://www.bl.uk/catalogues/evanion/Record.aspx?EvanID=024–000001375&ImageIndex=0

Byrnes, Dan. The Blackheath Connection—Feedback Files (for data on Blackheath and district during the *Keying*'s time in London). http://www.danbyrnes.com.au/blackheath/reaction.htm

Certificates of Service for Masters and Mates pre-1851. http://search.ancestry.com/search/db.aspx?dbid=2271

China Heritage Newsletter. March 2005 issue. http://www.chinaheritagequarterly.org/editorial.php? issue=001.

CRW Flags Online Catalogue. Beijing Drum and Bell Tower Flags. http://www.crwflags.com/fotw/flags/ cn_be.html

Currier and Ives. History of the Firm. http://www.currierandives.com/history.html

Devon County Council. Biographical Dictionary L–R. http://www.devon.gov.uk/print/index/ cultureheritage/ libraries/localstudies/lsdatabase.htm?url=etched/etched/100127/1.html

Free Dictionary. 'Ironwood'. http://encyclopedia.thefreedictionary.com/ironwood

Graphic Witness. Visual Arts and Social Commentary (for a quirky but helpful review of graphic art from a largely American perspective). http://graphicwitness.org/ineye/index2.htm

The Illustrated London News. Index. http://www.iln.org.uk/iln_years/ilnships1846_1848.htm

International Maritime Organization. http://www.imo.org.

Janus. Papers of Joseph Needham as a Historian of Chinese Science, Technology and Medicine. http://janus. lib.cam.ac.uk/db/node.xsp?id=EAD%2FGBR%2F1928%2FNRI2%2FSCC6%2F36

Jersey. http://jouault.wordpress.com/2013/03/10/the-first-chinese-junk-to-visit-europe-in-march-1848/

Junk Rig Association. http://www.junkrigassociation.org

Kellett family. http://fethard.com/index.php?topic=115.0 and http://www.clonacody-house.com/History.html

Krylow, Alek. Drawing Boats. http://hk.youtube.com/watch?v=h0p_aFWDSok

Map of London 1849: Cruchley's New Plan of London Showing all the New and Intended Improvements to the Present Time. http://commons.wikimedia.org/wiki/File:

1849_Cruchley_Pocket_Map_of_London,_England_-_Geographicus_-_ London-crutchley-1849.jpg

Mariners-L Archives. http://archiver.rootsweb.ancestry.com/th/read/Mariners/2005– 11/1132509846

Mariners-L. Details of 1854 certification requirements for ship's officers. http://www. mariners-l.co.uk/GenBosunMastersExam.html

Marxists.org. Karl Marx's article on the 1853 India Act of 12 February 2013. http://www. marxists.org/ archive/marx/works/1853/07/20.htm

Massachusetts Historical Society. http://www.masshist.org/

Master Garden Products. Tung Oil. http://www.mastergardenproducts.com/tungoil. htm

Measuring Worth. Online source for calculating the historical value of money. http:// www.measuringworth.com/calculators/exchange/result_exchange.php

Mercantile Marine Act, 1850. http://gazette.slv.vic.gov.au/images/1851/N/general/79-a.pdf

Merchant seamen in British service pre-1845. http://www.findmypast.co.uk/search/ merchant-navy-seamen/

Museo Galileo. Institute and Museum of the History of Science. Michael of Rhodes (the earliest known systematic treatise on naval architecture). http://brunelleschi.imss. fi.it/michaelofrhodes/ ships_design.html

Museum of the City of New York. http://www.mcny.org/collections/painting/pttcat32. htm

Mystic Seaport. Online access to shipping registers, 1850–1900. http://library.mystic-seaport.org/initiative/ ShipPageImage.cfm?PageNum=3&BibID=179721895&Ser ies=Introduction&Chapter=

National Data Buoy Center. For weather data in the centre of Long Island Sound. http:// www.ndbc.noaa. gov/station_history.php?station=44039

National Geospatial-Intelligence Agency. http://www.nga.mil/

National Library of Scotland. Photographs of John Thomson. 'China' Thomson. http:// www.nls.uk/ thomson/china.html

New York State Library. Steamboats on the Hudson: An American Saga. http://www. nysl.nysed.gov/ mssc/steamboats/toc.htm

Old Print Shop. Nathaniel Currier, 1813–1888. http://www.oldprintshop.com/artists/ currier-ives-nat.htm

Oriental Library. Hong Kong Copperplate Engravings and Water Color Paintings (Iwasaki Hirao's collection of G. E. Morrison prints and drawings). http://61.197.194.13/ gazou/Honkon_dohanga-e.html

Plymouth Data. Isaac Latimer, 1813–1898. http://www.plymouthdata.info/Who%20 Was%20Who-Latimer%20Isaac%201813%201898.htm

Rawlins.org. The Journey of the Robert Bodily Family. http://www.rawlins.org/mor-montrail/rbodily.html

TheShipsList-L. Thread on *Keying* and 1851 census records for Sydenham sub-district of Lewisham. http://www.oulton.com/cwa/newsships.nsf/45cc5cb7c20526ef85256 529004f20f0/38fbe91be88080918525719400052f25!OpenDocument

South West Maritime Historical Society. Thread on *Keying*. http://www.swmaritime.org. uk/forums/ thread.php?threadid=519

Steffy, J. Richard. Ship Reconstruction Laboratory. http://nautarch.tamu.edu/shiplab/ index_03treatises.htm

Wikipedia. *Keying* (ship). http://en.wikipedia.org/wiki/Keying_%28ship%29

Wikipedia. Little Ice Age. http://en.wikipedia.org/wiki/Little_Ice_Age

Wikipedia. Rock Ferry. http://en.wikipedia.org/wiki/Rock_Ferry

Wikipedia. Saint Helena. http://en.wikipedia.org/wiki/Saint_Helena

Index